Louis Richard Klemm

European Schools

or what I saw in the schools of Germany, France, Austria and Switzerland

Louis Richard Klemm

European Schools
or what I saw in the schools of Germany, France, Austria and Switzerland

ISBN/EAN: 9783337198305

Printed in Europe, USA, Canada, Australia, Japan

Cover: Foto ©Paul-Georg Meister /pixelio.de

More available books at **www.hansebooks.com**

International Education Series

EDITED BY

WILLIAM T. HARRIS, A. M., LL. D.

VOLUME XII.

INTERNATIONAL EDUCATION SERIES.

Edited by W. T. Harris.

It is proposed to publish, under the above title, a library for teachers and school managers, and text-books for normal classes. The aim will be to provide works of a useful practical character in the broadest sense. The following conspectus will show the ground to be covered by the series:

I.—History of Education. (A.) Original systems as expounded by their founders. (B.) Critical histories which set forth the customs of the past and point out their advantages and defects, explaining the grounds of their adoption, and also of their final disuse.

II.—Educational Criticism. (A.) The noteworthy arraignments which educational reformers have put forth against existing systems: these compose the classics of pedagogy. (B.) The critical histories above mentioned.

III.—Systematic Treatises on the Theory of Education. (A.) Works written from the historical standpoint; these, for the most part, show a tendency to justify the traditional course of study and to defend the prevailing methods of instruction. (B.) Works written from critical standpoints, and to a greater or less degree revolutionary in their tendency.

IV.—The Art of Education. (A.) Works on instruction and discipline, and the practical details of the school-room. (B.) Works on the organization and supervision of schools.

Practical insight into the educational methods in vogue can not be attained without a knowledge of the process by which they have come to be established. For this reason it is proposed to give special prominence to the history of the systems that have prevailed.

Again, since history is incompetent to furnish the ideal of the future, it is necessary to devote large space to works of educational criticism. Criticism is the purifying process by which ideals are rendered clear and potent, so that progress becomes possible.

History and criticism combined make possible a theory of the whole. For, with an ideal toward which the entire movement tends, and an account of the phases that have appeared in time, the connected development of the whole can be shown, and all united into one system.

Lastly, after the science, comes the practice. The art of education is treated in special works devoted to the devices and technical details useful in the school-room.

It is believed that the teacher does not need authority so much as insight in matters of education. When he understands the theory of education and the history of its growth, and has matured his own point of view by careful study of the critical literature of education, then he is competent to select or invent such practical devices as are best adapted to his own wants.

The series will contain works from European as well as American authors, and will be under the editorship of W. T. Harris, A. M., LL. D. The price for the volumes of the series will be $1.50 for the larger volumes, 75 cents for the smaller ones.

Vol. I. **The Philosophy of Education.** By Johann Karl Friedrich Rosenkranz. $1.50.

Vol. II. **A History of Education.** By Prof. F. V. N. Painter, of Roanoke, Virginia. $1.50.

Vol. III. **The Rise and Early Constitution of Universities.** With a Survey of Mediæval Education. By S. S. Laurie, LL. D., Professor of the Institutes and History of Education in the University of Edinburgh. $1.50.

Vol. IV. **The Ventilation and Warming of School Buildings.** By Gilbert B. Morrison, Teacher of Physics and Chemistry in Kansas City High-School. 75 cents.

Vol. V. **The Education of Man.** By Friedrich Froebel. Translated from the German and annotated by W. N. Hailmann, Superintendent of Public Schools at La Porte, Indiana. $1.50.

Vol. VI. **Elementary Psychology and Education.** By Joseph Baldwin, Principal of the Sam Houston State Normal School, Huntsville, Texas. $1.50.

Vol. VII. **The Senses and the Will.** Observations concerning the Mental Development of the Human Being in the First Years of Life. By W. Preyer, Professor of Physiology in Jena. Translated from the original German, by H. W. Brown, Teacher in the State Normal School at Worcester, Mass. Part I of THE MIND OF THE CHILD. $1.50.

Vol. VIII. **Memory.** What it is and how to improve it. By David Kay, F. R. G. S. $1.50.

Vol. IX. **The Development of the Intellect.** Observations concerning the Mental Development of the Human Being in the First Years of Life. By W. Preyer, Professor of Physiology in Jena. Translated from the original German, by H. W. Brown, Teacher in the State Normal School at Worcester, Mass. Part II of THE MIND OF THE CHILD. $1.50.

Vol. X. **How to Study Geography.** By Francis W. Parker. Prepared for the Professional Training Class of the Cook County Normal School.

Vol. XI. **Education in the United States.** Its History from the Earliest Settlements. By Richard G. Boone, A. M., Professor of Pedagogy in Indiana University.

Vol. XII. **European Schools.** Or what I Saw in the Schools of Germany, France, Austria, and Switzerland. By L. R. Klemm, Ph. D., Author of "Chips from a Teacher's Workshop"; and numerous school-books.

INTERNATIONAL EDUCATION SERIES

EUROPEAN SCHOOLS

OR WHAT I SAW IN
THE SCHOOLS OF GERMANY, FRANCE
AUSTRIA, AND SWITZERLAND

BY

L. R. KLEMM, Ph. D.

AUTHOR OF "CHIPS FROM A TEACHER'S WORKSHOP"
AND NUMEROUS SCHOOL-BOOKS

NEW YORK
D. APPLETON AND COMPANY
1889

EDITOR'S PREFACE.

THE editor presents this volume of the "International Education Series" with some degree of confidence that the reader will find it the first attempt of its kind yet made that proves of real help in the school-room. Although much has been written and published regarding European schools, yet, on the whole, teachers have found little profit in reading it. Vague encomiums on the excellence of methods, sweeping criticisms on features that did not suit the taste of the writer, minute accounts of governmental provision for education, rules and regulations, arrangements for supervision—all these things have wearied the reader without furnishing him new ideas that he could use to advantage. Nor have the descriptions of buildings, statistics of attendance, illiteracy and such matters, although sometimes useful to stir up emulation, satisfied him. Volumes containing immense masses of information compiled from programmes and official regulations have been of still less use. The teacher turns away from such things, and asks for a book that will show him how to do his work of instruction in another and better manner than his own. He wishes to hear of methods, but not in a vague, general way. Let the author show him teachers and pupils at work, and report enough of the essential details to furnish him hints that will assist him in his own efforts.

The lively pictures which Karl von Raumer gives of the work of Pestalozzi and his pupils are remembered by us as model reports of school-work. They enable us still to see with our own eyes, as it were, the method of the famous pedagogue, with its merits and defects clearly portrayed.

This book of Dr. Klemm is not intended as a critical estimate of the school systems of the countries visited. It does not attempt to give the average school nor to exhaust the range of good and poor schools. The author wisely avoids the inferior schools, and adopts the sensible plan of seeking the best and reporting only what he finds noteworthy. He limits himself, for the most part, to what is useful in the class-room. He takes pains to express his preferences quite frankly, and does not expect that the reader will agree with him on all occasions as to the value of the devices that he describes. The reader will, however, thank him for his candor, even when he can not accept his guidance, and feel sure that a less enthusiastic observer would not prove so accommodating in lending the use of his note-book.

The author's readiness with the pencil assists us in seeing many important pieces of apparatus and many processes of instruction that we should fail to understand from a merely verbal description. This is noticeable especially in his account of the industrial and manual-training movements.

He draws attention to the difference between French and German aims in this field of education, and states very clearly that the one seeks to find a direct preparation for the trades in its industrial schools, while the other wishes to get what is educative to the pupil from its manual work.

What is said of instruction in drawing is very interesting, but it leaves the reader in doubt whether the educators in some of the countries of Europe are not looking in a wrong direction for the chief object. For it is not the question of drawing from the flat, or from objects, that reaches the essential point in the educational value of drawing. This concerns the beauty of what is drawn or pictured, rather than how it is copied. If ugly shapes are drawn, either from real objects or from other representations, the taste of the pupil is debased. So, too, if the pupil is allowed to make ugly-shaped objects in wood, like those wooden spoons, boot-jacks, and mallets shown us as products of the Slöjd schools, we feel sure that he is not on the way to a profitable industrial career, for the markets of the world will not receive such goods, but will prefer the more graceful articles furnished by France and Belgium. If instruction in drawing lays stress on the reproduction of ornament and works of art of a high order of taste, it will secure an educative result of universal utility. The taste of the pupils will be elevated, and, whatever the line of industry followed, more remunerative work will be accomplished. Pupils that copy beautiful outlines from the flat will learn a more valuable lesson in form than those who draw indifferent objects from the solid. The cuts exhibiting French and German work in drawing and manual training are for these reasons very instructive to the reader in more than one respect.

A large portion of the book is devoted to what is called "objective teaching." This includes methods of illustrating subjects, and ingenious arrangements for arousing the enthusiasm of pupils to work out and realize their thoughts in deeds. The out-door excursions, described so charmingly, furnish us suggestive hints for new features in our own school-work. It is true that national peculiarity goes for much in the way of determining methods of school management; but each nation should see to it that suitable means are invented to reach all desirable results.

Anglo-Saxon teachers will read what is said of the great Herbartian movement in educational theory with wonder and curiosity. The idea of "concentric instruction," with Robinson Crusoe for the center of interest; the glimpses of earnest and thorough discussions of principles and practice in the light of the subtle psychology of Herbart, the counter-movement of the opposing school of philosophy—what singular phenomena in the history of education, and how suggestive of the originality and thoroughness of the German mind!

Instructive glances at the education of women for teachers in this book make us conscious of the considerable distance that separates our system of educational management from that of the Continent of Europe. Does it seem likely that the latter has begun to move on in the direction we have taken, and that it will follow us in giving higher education to girls, and afterward place women in charge of its schools as extensively as Americans have done?

The school for dullards will suggest to American readers the remarkable educational means employed in the State institutions of New York, Illinois, and some other commonwealths, for feeble-minded children. The methods used in those establishments are so skillful and so highly suggestive for all teachers in the management of their dull or backward pupils, that it seems surprising that we do not often see in our educational journals such descriptions of their processes as Dr. Klemm gives of the school at Elberfeld-Barmen. The trend of educational methods is toward a greater care for the weak and unfortunate. The missionary spirit is more and more manifested in our civilization. While, on the one hand, our institutions make the possession of property more secure, on the other hand we insist more and more that the period of helpless infancy and growing youth shall be devoted to education into the ideals that civilization has found instrumental to spiritual development. Thus, while differences of wealth remain very great, no youth shall be debarred by reason of poverty from his share in the heritage of culture. He shall be made able to help himself in the most efficient manner, and this power of self-help is the best gift that wealth can possibly confer on him..

W. T. HARRIS.

CONCORD, MASS., *July, 1889.*

AUTHOR'S PREFACE.

This book is not, like many official reports, weighed down with statistical data and ponderous descriptions of school systems. It says very little of school houses and sites. The course of study is mentioned only when it is absolutely necessary, and even then in outlines only. The book contains observations in European schools, or "Chips from Educational Workshops." The author has endeavored to offer the reader truthful delineations of the present status of didactics and methodology in the public schools of Germany, France, Austria, and Switzerland. Lessons which he heard are sketched as faithfully as a quick pencil could gather and the memory retain them. Numerous devices in use in Europe are offered in sketch illustrations, and copies of pupils' work where they could conveniently be used. The manual training-schools of Europe are shown in their results; the different systems of drawing and industrial training of girls are compared. Each branch of study of the elementary schools is represented by sketch-lessons, and successful methods of teaching are illustrated by *verbatim* reproduction of model lessons.

The book is written for the purpose of offering a "standard of measurement" for our own schools; a statement of what is done in the schools of Europe, and how it is done. If it should succeed in disproving the opinion that "European methods of teaching can not be adapted to American schools," the author will be most happy. This fallacious opinion is upheld very obstinately. It is heard from the rostrum, found in the educational press, urged in season and out of season; but, since it is merely an opinion, it can be disproved by facts alone, and they are already furnished by hundreds of excellent teachers in this country who adopt and adapt what is good in the theories and practices of their European brethren.

Though the author had frequently advocated methods used in Germany, he had never called them "German methods" nor felt called upon to refute the fallacy of their non-adaptability, knowing that some day he would have an opportunity of answering it more successfully than by entering into controversies. The facts offered in this book, it is hoped, may not seem strange, for they are not decorated with fancies. They can be verified by stacks of pupils' work collected by the author himself on his visits in hundreds of schools of various types. Speculations are rare in this book, though the writer states his opinion freely, and indulges in comparisons perhaps too freely.

He went to Europe with the intention of seeing what was worth reporting. Schools inferior to the average American school he avoided. He strove, during a journey of ten months, to see the best that Europe could offer him, and in this volume he thinks he has pictured the best results, described the most advanced methods, and given a great number of valuable hints that will be serviceable to teachers who have not sunk back into that detestable state of self-sufficiency and satisfaction which is the arch-foe of progress.

The most warm-hearted thanks are due to all who aided the author with valuable advice in selecting "points of observation"; thanks also to the Government officials in France, Prussia, Saxony, Bavaria, Austria, and Switzerland, but particularly to the Minister of Public Instruction in Berlin, Dr. von Gossler, and to the director of "écoles primaire" in Paris, Monsieur J. Buisson. By their generous kindness the writer was enabled to see what few American visitors have had occasion to see.

May this book infuse a little enthusiasm into teachers who consider their professional duties distasteful; may it strengthen others who are earnestly striving to reach a higher level of perfection; and may it contribute its share toward improving the schools of a country which deserves to have the best schools on the face of the earth!

L. R. KLEMM, PH. D.

CINCINNATI, OHIO, *September*, *1888*.

CONTENTS.

	PAGE
INTRODUCTION	1

CHAP.
I. HAMBURG, THE FREE CITY 5
   1. A Master-Stroke. 2. Something for the Little Ones.
   3. Another Device for the Little Ones. 4. Penmanship. 5. A New Scheme for Ventilation. 6. "Homeology" (Heimathskunde). 7. How Literature is taught.

II. DUISBURG, IN RHENISH PRUSSIA 17
   1. An Efficient City School System. 2. "Mittelschule" (Intermediate School). 3. Methods applied. 4. A District Conference. 5. History Teaching. 6. The Principles of this Method. 7. Practical Instruction in Drawing. 8. Learning to shade in Drawing. 9. Female Teachers in Germany. 10. Tenure of Office. 11. Miscellaneous Notes.

III. DÜSSELDORF, IN RHENISH PRUSSIA 41
   1. The Whole Nation a School. 2. Singing in German Schools. 3. A Novel Exercise in Music. 4. "Nature-Description." 5. A Lesson in Botany. 6. Ideal Teaching in Geography. 7. Silhouette Practice Maps. 8. Cause and Effect in Geography. 9. Making History an Experience. 10. The Star-Gazer. 11. Why so few Germans can talk on their Feet. 12. Class-Book of Progress. 13. Promote the Teachers with their Classes. 14. A School of Design.

CHAP.   PAGE

IV. ELBERFELD-BARMEN, IN RHENISH PRUSSIA 73
    1. Proper School Furniture. 2. The First Reformed Parish School. 3. A Separate School for Dullards. A. Object and Organization. B. Results. C. Methods pursued. D. Means of Instruction. 4. A Very Practical Device.

V. CREFELD, IN RHENISH PRUSSIA 94
    1. How English is taught in Germany. 2. A Primary Lesson in Mensuration. 3. Individuality in Teaching. 4. French Pupils in German Schools.

VI. COLOGNE, IN RHENISH PRUSSIA 104
    1. Conservatism and Liberalism. 2. Intermediate Schools. 3. Preparatory Schools for Teachers. 4. Female Teachers' Seminary. 5. Special Instruction for Teachers. 6. Two Conveniences. 7. A Lesson in Physics. 8. A Lesson in Grammar. 9. Girls' Industrial Education, I, II, III, IV.

VII. BERLIN 135
    1. The Old and the New. 2. Position of School-Houses. 3. The Teachers of Berlin. 4. Two School Museums. 5. Correcting Compositions. 6. My Mode of Procedure. 7. Home-made Charts. 8. A Map-Suspender. 9. Length of School Sessions. 10. Normal School for Young Ladies. A. The Building. B. The Practice Department. C. The Normal Department. 11. How not to teach. 12. "Naturkunde" (Knowledge of Nature). 13. A Lesson in Singing. 14. A Lesson in Zoology. 15. A Most Refreshing Sight. 16. A Distinction with a Big Difference. 17. A Rare Case. 18. "Tout comme chez nous." 19. Concentric Extension of the Geographical Horizon.

VIII. HALLE, IN PRUSSIAN SAXONY 182
    1. The "Francke Stiftungen." 2. Concentric Instruction illustrated. 3. The Exponent of the Herbart Move-

ment. 4. The Miser among the Animals. 5. A Lesson on Robinson Crusoe. 6. A Language-Lesson. 7. Miscellaneous Notes from Halle.

IX. VARIOUS OTHER PRUSSIAN PROVINCES 211
1. Schools in Prussia. 2. A Device, not a Method. 3. Mental Arithmetic everywhere. 4. Teaching Decimal Fractions. 5. Arithmetic in a Village School. 6. A Lesson in Botany. 7. Learning to do by doing. 8. Teaching Composition. 9. Criterion of a Model Lesson. 10. Drawing in German Schools. 11. Drawing in a Country School. 12. Compulsory Attendance. 13. Home-made Apparatus. 14. Our "Treasure-Box." 15. Local School Museums. 16. A Prussian Normal School. Introduction. The Building. Biblical History. Literature. Natural History. Drawing and Music. Geography. Arithmetic. Daily Programme. Scarcity of Teachers. 17. Three Kinds of Conferences. 18. Object-Lessons and Sketching. 19. Miscellaneous Observations.

X. LEIPSIC, IN THE KINGDOM OF SAXONY 262
1. Manual Training-School. 2. Appeal to Leipsic's School-Boys. 3. Normal School for Manual Training. 4. The Work done in Leipsic. A. Pasteboard. B. Wood- and Wire-work. C. Wood-Carving. 5. The Germ of the Manual Training Idea. 6. Drawing in Leipsic and other Saxon Cities. 7. Shading in Drawing. 8. A Drawing-Lesson full of Fun. 9. The Best-equipped School. 10. Notes from the Schools of Leipsic.

XI. DRESDEN, IN SAXONY, AND MUNICH, IN BAVARIA . . . 289
1. Examinations in Dresden. 2. Notes from the Schools of Dresden. 3. Manual Training in Germany. 4. Objects made in the Slöjd Schools. 5. What I saw in Munich. 6. An Ideal Course of Study. 7. Cause and Effect in Geography. 8. "Knabenhort" (Asylum for Boys).

CHAP.		PAGE
XII.	PARIS	317

1. Industrial Education of Boys. An Argument. Results. Pupils' Work in using Tools, in Joinery, Metal-work, Turning, Wood-Carving, and Inlaid Work, Modeling in Clay and Plaster. Industrial Work in Evening Schools. Pupils' Work in Building. 2. Industrial Education of Girls. 3. Dinners for School-Children. 4. Gymnastic and Military Drill. 5. Equipment of School-Rooms. 6. Drawing in the Communal School. 7. Sketching. 8. How Geography is taught. 9. French Text-Books. 10. How Reading and Spelling are taught. 11. The "Musée Pédagogique." 12. A Calculating-Machine. 13. Crumbs.—Notes from the Schools of Paris.

XIII.	OTHER FRENCH CITIES	381

1. Making Beauty contagious. 2. Composition-Books in French Schools. 3. More Devices, not Methods. 4. Also a Device, but oh! 5. Ignorance and Chauvinism. 6. Molding Maps. 7. "Ad oculos" Evidence.

XIV.	VIENNA	392

1. A Successful and an Unsuccessful Lesson. 2. An Object-Lesson in the Primary Grade. 3. A Lesson in Grammar. 4. Manual Training-Schools. Introduction. A Work-bench. 5. Pupils' Work in Pasteboard, Joinery, Carpentering, Turning, Wood-Carving, Modeling.

XV.	SWITZERLAND AND ALSACE	409

1. Simplicity in the Wrong Place. 2. Industrial Education of Girls. 3. A Lesson in Philology. 4. Notes from the Schools of Mülhausen.

EUROPEAN SCHOOLS IN 1888.

INTRODUCTION.

THE reader may permit me to introduce the book with an argument. I wish to state emphatically that what is urged in our country, and advocated under the caption "German methods," does not deserve that name. German methods have nothing specifically German about them, so long as they aim at assisting intellectual growth. The faculties of the mind are essentially the same in different craniums. It matters not whether I have to teach the children of a Zulu-Kaffir, or an Indian tribe, or children of English, German, French, or American birth—the leading features of my procedure in teaching them would be the same. It is only matters specifically German, as, for instance, the peculiar form of government and other things, such as customs and habits, that bear upon the government of schools, which can not, and should not, be urged for adoption in our country. But it has never occurred to any one to urge institutions foreign to the spirit of our free institutions as specifically German methods. What is applicable to the education of the human being, not of the German as such, is urged, and that, as was said, is not specifically German.

There can be no objection to such methods, if their object is to facilitate the growth of the mind, the strengthening and steeling of the will, and the skill of the hands, though they be erroneously called German methods, because in Germany they were first applied. To think that there must be special avenues to the mind of the German child, that can not be used for the American, is either the height of presumption, which disdains to use anything not indigenous to the American soil,* or a total disregard of the true definition of the term "method," to wit: "*Method is a way of reaching a given end by a series of acts which tend to secure it.*"

The end in view being the same, why should not the method be the same? I take it for granted that the reader's innate sense of truth permits him to see that the end in view in German and American schools *is* the same, as far as intellectual culture is concerned. For proofs, he may read Comenius's, Pestalozzi's, Froebel's, and Diesterweg's principles and maxims, and compare them with expressions of our home authorities. I will not burden this chapter with them. The lessons I describe in the following pages may convince him that there is nothing specifically German in "German methods." What I find in them is specifically human, and can be applied in any school.

"But," wrote a learned doctor, with whom I had exchanged arguments on this point, "your argument, that the faculties of the mind are the same in different nations and individuals, might lead us to adopt Chinese methods, because the Chinese children's senses are the same as all other children's."

Why should it? We do not wish to adopt and adapt inferior but better methods. If, perchance, the Chinese should hit upon a more direct and profitable method of teaching, I should not hesitate a moment in adopting it. But the Chinese have not developed the art of teaching to

---

* Colonel Parker and other typical American teachers unhesitatingly adapt (nay, adopt) "German" methods, and give due credit to the sources from which they draw. Many of the noted writers in the educational press of to-day have been in Europe to study methods. Thus I found the names of Prof. Larkin Dunton, of Boston, and other Americans, in the register of visitors in schools of Saxony and Prussia.

any high degree, and have not invented or discovered methods worth recommending. Why, therefore, should we adopt their methods?

Any one who travels through Europe as I did for nearly a year, seeing, observing, testing, inquiring, examining in all domains of activity, in society, in schools, in factories, in government offices, etc., would see that in Europe American methods are adopted and applied with an alacrity worthy of a good purpose. I saw applied numerous American inventions, American methods of carrying on trade, of industrial pursuits, of managing public and private affairs, etc., *ad infinitum*. American machines and devices, all that we are justly proud of, are there copied, sold, used, and applied. Why, might I ask, do not the Europeans adopt the Hottentot's methods? It is the same argument, and deserves the same answer: It is the better, not the inferior methods that they want.

Our almost insular seclusion from the other civilized parts of the world should not make us exclusive in thought and action. National pride is a grand virtue; but, when it becomes derogatory to our own interests and shuts our eyes to the progress of other nations, that pride becomes a vice. Not having a standard measure of length, how can we measure a distance! If this book, in a modest way, succeeds in furnishing a standard of excellence by which true-hearted American teachers may measure their own performances, it is all I desire and hope for.

One more word of introduction. Some of my readers may think that this book offers a little too much in the way of illustration. To them may be recommended the perusal of the following article, clipped from "Harper's Bazar" of January 14, 1888. It is here reproduced, partly as a defense and partly for the purpose of preserving the exquisite argument in behalf of illustrations in the professional press and in school-books of recent origin:

"One of the most curious forms of Gradgrind severity is

the crusade occasionally undertaken against all illustrations of school-books. The most thoughtful and carefully designed work in geography, in history, even in arithmetic, is supposed to be sufficiently condemned when it is called a picture-book. Yet it is a period when all works for older persons—dictionaries, encyclopædias, histories, magazines—have brought the art of pictorial illustration to its highest point. Webster and Worcester have alike adopted it. Justin Winsor's monumental 'Narrative and Critical History of America' is crowded with portraits, autographs, *facsimiles*, and reproductions of historic pictures. The later editions of Gray's 'Botany of the Northern United States' have careful delineations of every historical genus. The American magazines have won the admiration of the world by their illustrations of all geographical and historical papers. Mr. Edward Atkinson carries the art of pictorial exhibition even into political economy, and is never quite happy till he can get his proposition embodied for the eye in parallel lines. The United States Census Report resorts to charts and curves and colored diagrams when it wishes fully to elucidate any important general result. All this is done for grown people—for the gravest, the maturest, the most educated. They, if any, are the persons who might fairly be asked to fix their minds clearly and austerely upon words and numerals, without stooping to the alleged frivolity of picture-books. If they do not accomplish this, if the very people who make the criticism are only too glad to eke out their own imperfect knowledge by an illustrated magazine, or an illustrated dictionary, is it not a little absurd in them to enforce such a grim abstinence upon school-children?

"No child can understand from words alone that there is any part of the world which is essentially different from his native town, but his first picture of a glacier or a geyser, a castle or a cathedral, the Sphinx of Egypt or the Eskimo in his *kayak*, opens his eyes to the rest of the globe; he begins to be a traveled man. It is even more true of history:

the most skillful combination of words can never bring a child so near to the Mound-builders or the Pueblo Indians, to the Puritans or the Cavaliers, to the Revolutionary soldiers and the founders of our government, as he is brought by the first good picture he sees. When shall we live up to the strong good sense of Horace Mann, who pointed out that the love of knowledge is as natural to a healthy child's mind as the desire for food?"

CHAPTER I.

HAMBURG.

1. A MASTER-STROKE.

SCENE, a hot, dingy school-room in the Gymnasium of Hamburg; pupils supposed to attend to a lesson in algebra; the teacher a middle-aged, patient-looking man, with careworn features, but remarkably keen eyes and the proverbial square forehead of a mathematician. One of the pupils, a criminally stupid-looking specimen of the genus *homo sapiens*—one of those boys whom Schiller must have had in mind when he said, "With stupidity even the gods fight in vain"—could not see why the difference between plus 6 and minus 10 should be 16. The teacher made it clear by referring to six marbles in pocket and ten lost in the game played "for keeps." The boy persisted in saying the *sum* was 16, but not the difference, confounding in his mind remainder with difference.

I pitied the teacher, but was curious to see the outcome of this tussle with stupidity. The teacher looked up, cast his eyes about the room, ran to the thermometer, snatched it up, and with a triumphant look aimed a last blow at stupidity by demonstrating that the difference between 6° above zero and 10° below zero was 16°, not 4°, as the boy thought. This last stroke was a master-stroke, and the boy's mind yielded to this demonstration *ad oculos*. Further questioning revealed the fact that he had caught the truth and held on to it. I never left a school so thoroughly convinced of the usefulness of the objective method as I did that day.

I have gathered a great many interesting points on my journey of inspection, and shall continue to do so till my purse calls a halt. Most Americans visiting Europe only follow the great high-roads of travel, and care naught for the pleasant by-ways which are studded with flowers of the richest hue. I am wandering with my friend through the country. A small knapsack containing the necessaries for toilet is all the baggage we have. We see much, experience unspeakable pleasures, learn a great deal, and gather honey as we go along. I assure my readers we are the happiest couple of tramps one can imagine.

2. Something for the Little Ones.

This device (see cut, No. 1, below) I found in almost every primer-class in German schools. Its object is plain. It is a

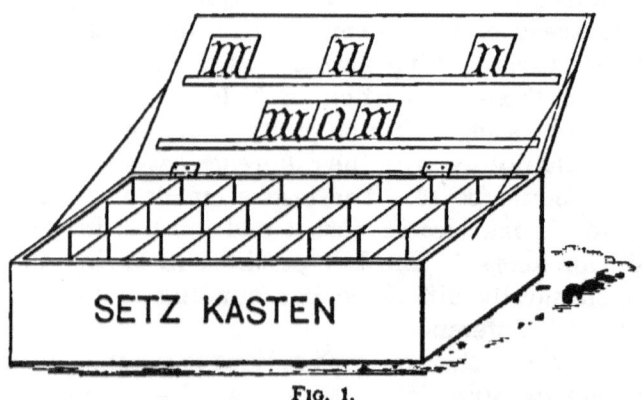

Fig. 1.

box full of movable letters, printed on cardboard, which may be placed on ledges nailed to the lid. The letters are used in teaching young children to read by means of the word and phonic method combined. The letters on stiff cardboard are arranged, according to the frequency with which they are used, like the types in a compositor's case.

Thus, for instance, the word *man* is placed on the ledge and learned as a whole; then the different letters, learned as sounds, are obtained by analyzing the word. After that other known sounds are substituted, for instance, *r* for *m*, which makes the word *ran*, and so on. All new sounds obtained by analyzing words are made into new words, until the child can *sound through any word at sight*. Where the phonic method is used, the "Setz Kasten" may be used very well in English and American schools.

I asked a young lady whom I saw using this device what she would do if she had no "Setz Kasten." She said with determination: "I'd pawn my bonnet and get one at once. I can not teach reading without movable letters. *The reading of an adult person is rapid sounding, and the sounding of the little ones is simply slow reading.*"

Whether this case of letters can be used in teaching reading to English-speaking children is no longer a question, since it has been demonstrated repeatedly. One of my teachers in Hamilton (Ohio) practices analysis and synthesis of words by placing three bright boys in front of the class, charging one to say *m* (the sound *m*, not the letter *em*) when called upon; the next one *a*; and the third *n*. Then by placing them close to each other, so that their shoulders would touch, she makes them sound the word *man* rapidly. The same is done with other words.

Now she separates the boys, the middle one remaining in his place, while the others recede toward the right and left, and every time they make a step the word is pronounced over again, thus separating the sounds farther and farther. After that is done, synthesis follows, and the two "end men" come back to their old position step by step, the three boys pronouncing the sounds as often as a step is made, the sounds being drawn long enough to make them appear one word. Other words are treated in like manner.

Now the teacher changes the boys' positions and asks each to pronounce his sound. Of course, it is at once seen that that does not make the word *man* or whatever word was before the class. Finally, they assume their former position, and once more the well-known words are pronounced. Then these words are found on the chart, on the board, in print and script form, and it goes without saying that the children enjoy these lessons. Call this play if you please. If the children learn more by play than by joyless drudgery, we should prefer play every time. Now, substituting the movable letters, the art of joining letters to make words can be learned quite rapidly even by the dullest child.

"How long does it take an average class to master the art of reading sufficiently to take up the first reader?" I asked several teachers at different places.

"About three or four months, never more. Sometimes a specially bright class gets into the first reader after six weeks." Think of it, and then compare this with the fact that our English-speaking children in America, owing to the incongruity of English spelling, are worried with the words of the primer and charts for more than a year!

3. Another Device for the Little Ones.

A truly ingenious device is the apparatus I wish to describe here. I saw it in Hamburg first and afterward in other German schools. It is used to facilitate the teaching of reading. The two sketches (2 and 3) below may assist me in my description.

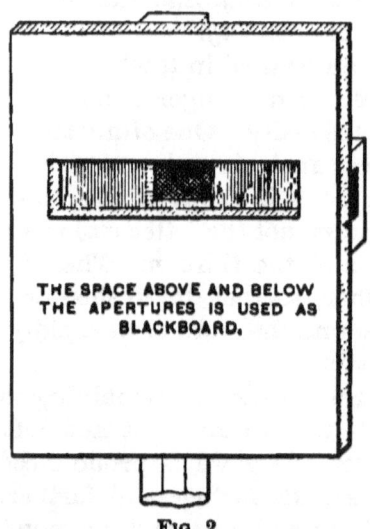

THE SPACE ABOVE AND BELOW THE APERTURES IS USED AS BLACKBOARD.

Fig. 2.

It is a blackboard, two feet square, with three apertures, two of which appear covered by a board in the rear. Into convenient slits are shoved strips of strong pasteboard, on which are printed letters or syllables. The strips containing the vowels are shoved from right to left, or *vice versa;* the slats containing the consonants are shoved up and down.

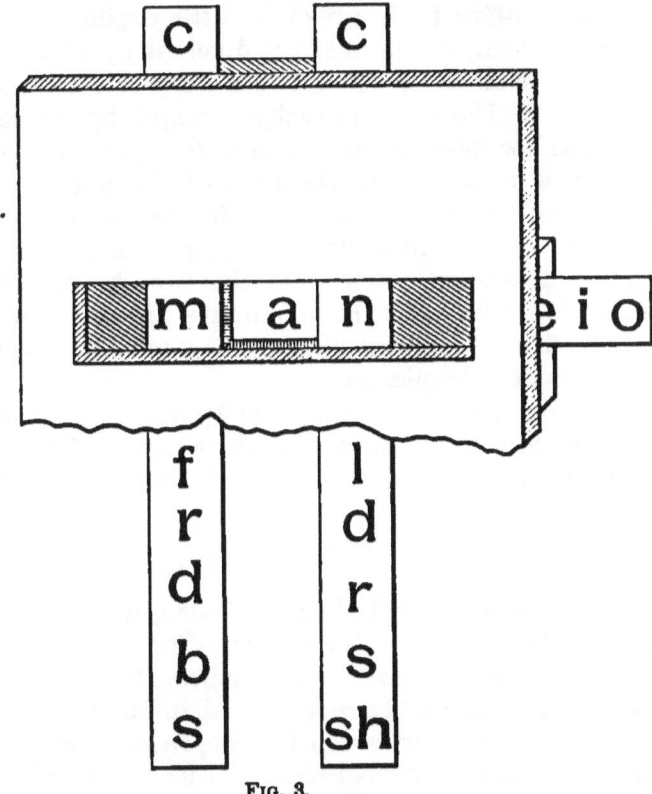

Fig. 3.

Every movement creates a new word, "possible or impossible"; but the characters printed on the strips are exceedingly well selected and grouped, so that their arrangement is made easy.

Of course, a beginner will find some difficulty in handling the apparatus; but it is quickly learned, and the teacher whom I saw use it handled it with such a velocity that no awkward pauses interrupted the lesson. There were a great number of slats, some containing only single letters, some combinations, as *ch, sh, st, ck,* etc.; others containing syllables which are apt to occur often, as *be, dis, in,* etc.

The advantages connected with this apparatus consist in this: 1. It offers to the eye of the little pupils only one word at first. Their attention is not diverted by a large number of words, such as are found on a chart or on a page of the primer. 2. The word is easily changed by changing one letter, as, for instance, *man* to *can, fan, ran, Dan,* etc. This change is made before the eyes of the pupils, who will readily see that the remainder of the word remains the same. 3. It obviates the difficulty of writing whole strings of words on the blackboard. 4. On the charts or in the primer the words are fixed, and the pupils are apt to learn them by heart. This is prevented, since the words in the apparatus change kaleidoscopically.

The apparatus is accompanied by a box containing some forty to fifty slats. (For the convenience of my English-speaking readers I have pictured English letters in my sketch.)

4. Penmanship.

On my tour through German, Dutch, and French schools, I saw only one in which copy-books for instruction in penmanship were in use. Nevertheless, the writing of the pupils was remarkably regular, and in many cases elegant. I found it so everywhere in Prussia, from Hamburg to Mayence. This absence had struck me as well worthy of note. When I did see the copy-book in use, near Hamburg, I thought it time to inquire about it, and the reply was as ludicrous as it was sensible: "My dear sir, my school is under punishment. Because the boys had acquired negligent habits, and handed in poorly written compositions and home exercises, I made them procure copy-books and practice good forms of letters. The boys are fully aware of the fact that they are, calligraphically, 'under a cloud,' and try hard to redeem themselves and regain their former standard.

"As a rule, we do not use copy-books, starting from the principle that the pupils need no special instruction in penmanship, if they write well whatever they write. This is the rule in our school. From the lowest grade upward good writing is insisted upon, and the teachers take good care never to hurry their pupils much in their written work. The teachers themselves never write negligently on the board, so that the pupils have only good models. The result of this practice is so apparent that it needs no emphatic assurance.

"Copy-books are an excuse for bad penmanship. If the pupils write well during the short space of two or three lessons a week, and hurriedly and slovenly during all the remainder of the week, the practice in the copy-book will not produce good penmen. Penmanship is an art which can be maintained only if practiced constantly. Just as little as it will do to be good, kind, and obedient during the early lesson in religion and morals, and unruly, bad, and vicious during the remainder of the day, will it do to permit the habit of poor penmanship to grow upon the pupils."

The answer seemed to me so convincing that I considered it worth quoting. I asked, "What do you do to teach artistic forms, various styles of penmanship, forms of beauty, and fine initials?" The answer was:

"We do not teach them; do not want to attempt such things. If any of our pupils wish to learn them, let them apply to a special school of calligraphy. The teachers in the common school teach what is necessary to a common-school education. All specialties must be excluded."

This answer indicated that the teacher had a correct idea of the end and aim toward which he was steering. I find this generally to be the case in these German schools. Each teacher knows exactly what he aims at. He has his rules and regulations, and his course of study, and he knows them by heart. His thorough professional training enables him to steer his way clear of impediments such as beset the way of any one who is not clear on what he wants. It remains ever true that he who knows *what* he wants will find a way *how* to obtain it.

5. A NEW SCHEME FOR VENTILATION.

When it is found inconvenient to raise or lower the window for the purposes of ventilation, a little device like the one represented in the cut (4) may be applied. I find it in use all over Germany, where many class-rooms are overcrowded, and where the pupils' seats are standing very near the windows. This ventilator is constructed like our Venetian shutters, only that the slats are of glass. Each slat is set in a brass groove which ends in a pin or pivot. The different

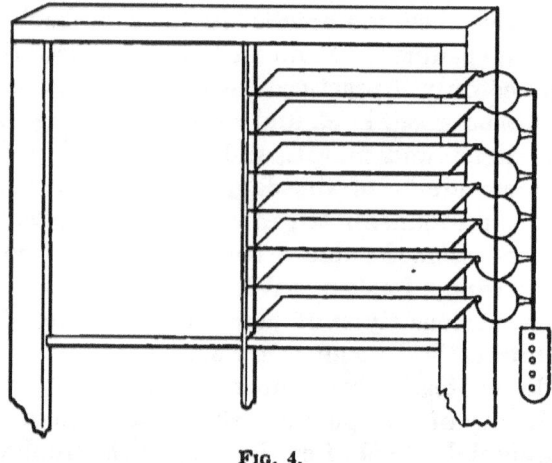

FIG. 4.

slats are connected by a simple device, and may be opened wide, or only a trifle, as may be desirable.

6. "HOME-OLOGY."

"Heimathskunde," knowledge of home and its surroundings, is what they term primary geography in Germany.

In order to give the reader an idea of what is done in the primary grades, a few suggestions may suffice. I heard some lessons in "home-ology" in Hamburg, and enjoyed them very much. I may be allowed to give the results of

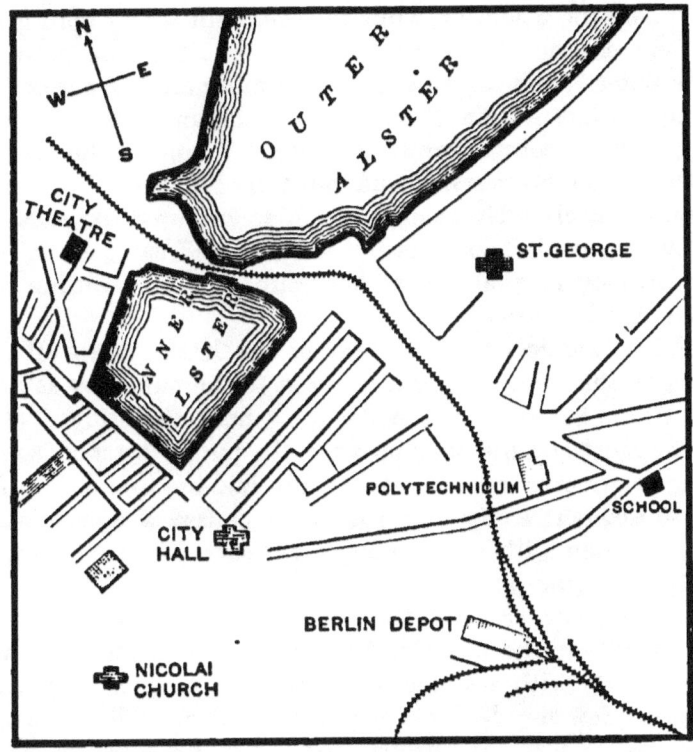

Fig. 5.

the lesson in the form of a sketch-map. This map (5) was made on the board as the lesson proceeded.

Teacher: In what direction is our school from the Inner Alster, or Alster Basin? What street on this side of the Basin? On the opposite side? On the third? fourth? What separates the Inner from the Outer Alster? What bridge? What monuments are erected on the esplanade? In what direction from the Basin is the Nicolai Church?

The new Polytechnicum? The theatre? The Berlin Depot? On what side of the Alster Basin is the new hotel, the Hamburger Hof, situated? and so forth. Some streets were sketched in order to make the picture more vivid.

Every new item was inserted in the sketch on the board drawn by the teacher. Thus the sketch of a city plan grew by degrees, and the pupils drew or imitated this plan on their slates. One can not imagine a more attentive group of young children than these were. Each one was eager to suggest new points known to him. I copied the sketch as the lesson progressed, and hope that its simplicity will speak for itself. No teacher can hide his unwillingness to follow suit behind so flimsy an excuse as "I can't draw," for the drawing of such a sketch presupposes no training nor special skill in drawing.

When the geographical part of the lesson was well disposed of, the teacher gave a new zest to the pupils by asking, "To whom belongs the theatre, the school, the bridge," etc.? In the most natural way possible the pupils learned something of governmental relations, and laid the foundation for the subsequent study of history. It caused a merry interruption when a little boy thought the school-house belonged to Mr. —— (the janitor).

In a higher grade of the same school the geography of Germany was the topic of the day. It was still "homeology," only with a wider horizon. The teacher began by making a few simple lines representing the so-called "mountain-cross" in Central Europe. After first drawing the Fichtel Mountains, the center of the figure (6), he added the Erz Mountains toward the northeast, the Franconian and Thuringian Forest toward the northwest, the Bohemian and Bavarian Forest toward the southeast, the Franconian and Swabian Jura toward the southwest. A few peaks were mentioned, as were also the characteristics of these mountains. Thus, for instance, the silver-mines in Saxony, the dense forests in Bohemia, the lovely scenery in Thuringia, the caves in the Jura, etc., came in for a few well-remembered remarks. The teacher always knew when to stop; he was discretion personified.

Now, the teacher drew the four rivers which rise in the Fichtel Mountains—namely, Main, Saale, Eger, and Naab—showing and indicating on the map into what main rivers

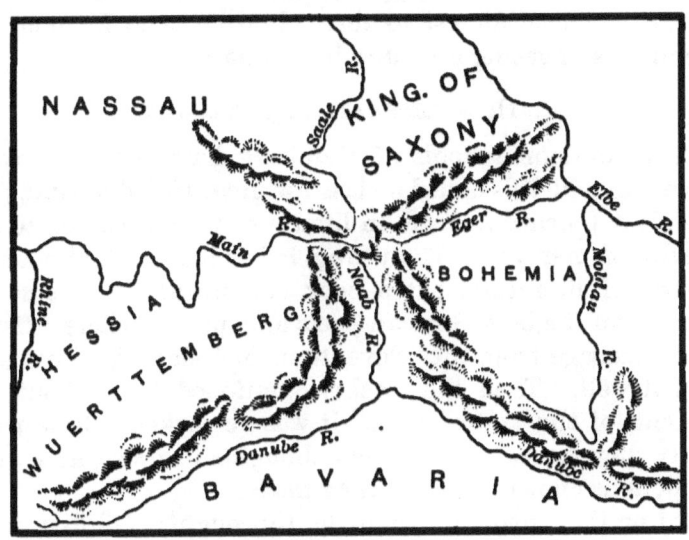

Fig. 6.

they empty. A few important cities and the countries around the cross were named. All this information was partly given, partly asked for, as the case suggested.

Now, the complete map, a printed one, was hung up, and all the information just gained was looked up. Each item was noted, and it made the children fairly glow with enthusiasm when they were able to corroborate the facts of the two maps. In a few points the map on the board was corrected, improved, and completed; then the lesson closed, and now followed the recitation—that is to say, the pupils were called upon to state, in answer to leading questions, what they remembered of the lesson. My heart was filled with joy when I heard them speak out, not like human parrots who had memorized, but like rational beings who had learned by experience. The hour was brought to a close by an imaginary journey all over the section the acquaintance of which they had just made. Many little items of information were added on this journey. Photographic views of rocks and mountain scenery were exhibited, and they proved to be of intense interest to these children, who have no opportunities of seeing a mountain "in nature."

7. How Literature is taught.

The common schools of Hamburg have a seven years' course, to which is added a class for girls, called *selecta*. In this class I heard a lesson in literature which seemed to me worthy of mention. The young ladies had no text-book of history of literature, but a book containing copious selections from the best German poets and prose writers. They read a passage from the "Seventieth Birthday," by Voss, and read it well. Then the teacher questioned them about the contents of the matter read. It was remarkable how accurately they reproduced poetical thoughts in prose, and what a felicitous choice of words they made.

After they had proved to be thoroughly familiar with the substance of the poem, they were questioned as to the kind of poetry it belonged to. And before the pupils made the acquaintance of such words as *prosody*, etc., they had learned a good deal of it. Terms like *epic*, *lyric*, etc., fell like ripe fruit from the tree of experience. After general observations, the characters of certain persons in the poem were reviewed, the old schoolmaster, the wife, etc., and for each discovered trait proofs were searched among the actions and sayings of the person referred to.

Now, the poem was scanned, and the metre was compared with that of others. Repeated references to other poems in hexameters made this part of the lesson particularly fruitful. A vista into the history of literature was then opened by first learning something about the author of the poem under discussion. The information was given by the teachers, and the pupils took notes. Then the surroundings which exercised a beneficial or detrimental influence upon him were mentioned, and in this way the horizon of the pupils was widened. All their knowledge of the history of literature was grouped around a few famous poets.

Before the lesson, which lasted an hour, was closed, another poem, "The Child of Sorrow," by Herder, was read in chorus, and then treated like the first one. Again the poem was made the nucleus around which was grouped the knowledge gained. Since this poem was both in contents and form different from the other, it afforded ample opportunity for contrasts, and thus the knowledge gained was brought into bold relief. Of course, this method needs a teacher of thorough acquaintance with literature, and its history, and one who has the enviable gift of application. All others should keep hands off.

CHAPTER II.

DUISBURG (RHENISH PRUSSIA).

1. An Efficient City School System.

Duisburg, a town of about sixty thousand inhabitants, situated at the confluence of the rivers Ruhr and Rhine, a very busy industrial center, has a most remarkable school system. I will endeavor to sketch it, not because it is worthy of imitation in its organization, for our American school system is, in that regard, much more preferable, but because a description of the system in Duisburg is a typical one, and explains the social conditions of the people. A diagram (7) may assist me:

A is the *People's School*. It consists of two schools, in fact, namely, of A a, five grades of primary schools for both sexes, and A b, four grades of intermediate schools for boys only. This primary or elementary school rounds off its course somewhat—that is, offers its pupils the elements, and abstains from all scientific branches. In arithmetic it leaves off when simple examples in percentage can be solved. The intermediate school takes the boys from the fourth-year grade of the primary school if they intend to stay in school longer, but can not enter a high-school. This intermediate school has a more complete course than our grammar-school, teaching geometry and algebra, natural history and science.

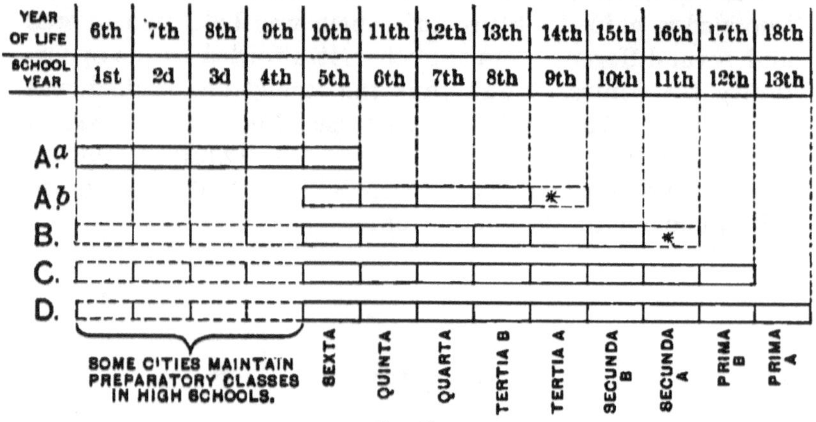

YEAR OF LIFE	6th	7th	8th	9th	10th	11th	12th	13th	14th	15th	16th	17th	18th
SCHOOL YEAR	1st	2d	3d	4th	5th	6th	7th	8th	9th	10th	11th	12th	13th

A^a, A^b, B, C, D.

SOME CITIES MAINTAIN PREPARATORY CLASSES IN HIGH SCHOOLS.

SEXTA, QUINTA, QUARTA, TERTIA B, TERTIA A, SECUNDA B, SECUNDA A, PRIMA B, PRIMA A.

FIG. 7.

Although it is not obligatory to stay during the ninth school year, many pupils prefer to remain till they are fifteen years of age. I have marked that grade with dotted lines and *.

B is the *Girls' High-School*. In other cities it has a preparatory school of its own, and does not draw its pupils from the primary people's school. In many of such schools for girls a seventh grade (a selecta) is added, in which young ladies are prepared for the teacher's profession. I have marked that grade with dotted lines and * also.

C is a *Boys' High-School*, called "Realschule," or "Realgymnasium." It pays more attention to natural history, natural sciences (physiology, physics, and chemistry), modern language, and drawing than does the school marked D. Its graduates are admitted to the universities, but not to all departments. Business men, engineers, and other scientific men prefer this school to D.

D is also a *Boys' High-School*, called Gymnasium. In France it is called Lyceum; in America we would call it the Boys' Classical High-School or College. It pays particular attention to classical languages, and its graduates are admitted to the universities without examination.

Pupils of both C and D, when they have completed the course to lower secunda, pass an examination which abbreviates their three years' term of serving in the army to one year. Such one-year soldiers can be recognized in the ranks of a regiment by black-and-white borders on their shoulder-straps. This privilege of serving only one year instead of three is a tribute the Government pays to thorough and extended education.

I know full well that this separation of children into different schools according to their social standing and worldly circumstances is distasteful to us; I know that we are not apt to imitate this. I also know that this description of the German school system is a digression from my text, but I deem it desirable, if not necessary, to make this explanation, so that my readers may judge more intelligently as to the merits of certain methods and results that I may describe hereafter. The mere statement of this or that being accomplished in this or that school year is not always a sufficient guide, since the material is vastly different in different schools. The people's school contains the poorer, ill-fed children; the others the children of the wealthier and more cultivated classes of society.

Let me add that all these schools are public schools, though tuition fees are paid in all of them. The idea of absolutely free tuition is gaining ground, though, in Germany. In order to complete my sketch, I should add that, in addition to the schools A, B, C, and D, there is another school for boys, called *Bürger School*. Its course is parallel with B (see diagram). But, wherever a Bürger school is maintained, the intermediate school of A is omitted.

2. The "Mittelschule."

It is the intermediate or "middle school" (A b) of which I desire to give an account. While the city of Duisburg maintains a great number of elementary schools, it has but one intermediate school. I spent a whole day in it. Its course of study embraces the following branches:

1. *Religion.* — *a.* Biblical history ; *b.* Catechism ; *c.* Hymns and Bible verses; *d.* History of the Church.
2. *Language.*—Only the mother-tongue. *a.* Reading and literature; *b.* Composition; *c.* Grammar.
3. *Mathematics.*—*a.* Arithmetic completed; *b.* Algebra, elementary; *c.* Geometry and mensuration.
4. *Geography.*—*a.* Topographical ; *b.* Astronomical ; *c.* Political; *d.* Physical.
5. *History.*—*a.* General history in first year; *b.* Prussian history in second year ; *c.* German history in third year; *d.* Review.
6. *Natural History.*—*a.* Botany in first year ; *b.* Zoology in second year.
7. *Physics* in third year; apparatus.
8. *Chemistry* and mineralogy in third and fourth years; apparatus.
9. *Drawing.*—Free-hand, geometrical, decorative, and drawing from solids.
10. *Music.*—Theoretical and vocal.
11. *Gymnastics*, calisthenics, and with suitable apparatus.

A mere glance at this list will reveal the fact that this school, which is equal to our grammar-schools in age of pupils, in organization, etc., accomplishes more than is done in our grammar-schools. First, more in mathematics is offered; secondly, history is offered in four years, while with us it is confined to home history and to one year or at best two years; thirdly, physics and chemistry are taught, and very well, I must say; fourthly, drawing is carried to drawing from casts and other solid models; fifthly, a regular daily lesson in gymnastics is given. Add to all this a daily lesson in religion, which I mention merely to state that it takes time like other branches of study, and it will be clear to my readers that the school offers an education to the lowest classes of society such as is not offered in many American grammar-schools.

I do not pretend to insinuate that this should be a criticism upon our school system, or that I blame our teachers and superintendents; far from it. The reason of this remarkable difference in results may be found in the vast amount of time which is necessarily spent in mastering the outrageous orthography of our English language and in other reasons too obvious to mention; but it is highly instructive to "see ourselves as others see us," or notice what others do and measure our results with theirs.

3. Methods applied.

It is very probable that the methods applied in this school have something to do with the good results achieved. In his famous report Horace Mann said: "In Germany I never saw a teacher hearing a recitation with a book in his hand, nor a teacher sitting while hearing a recitation." This holds good still. I passed through six rooms repeatedly during the day I spent in the Duisburg "Mittelschule," and saw or heard nine lessons or recitations, but not once did I see a teacher with a book in his hands, not even during a lesson in reading and literature. "I expect you to read so that I may understand you instantly," the teacher said to the class; and they did it, to be sure.

Arithmetic was taught without a text-book. After a thorough lesson in division of fractions was completed orally, the order came, "Take your books and solve problems 12 to 18 on page 23." I looked at the book and found it to be a small, primer-like looking thing, filled with problems, and void of all the explanations that swell our text-books of arithmetic. The text-book of algebra was no larger, and for geometry no book at all was used, but the boys entered the results of a new lesson in a composition-book.

I asked for the text-book in grammar, and evoked a broad and humorous smile; but their histories were pretty good-sized books. I found no text-book of botany or zoology, but a valuable collection of objects—dried plants and stuffed animals and finely-colored charts. The apparatus for instruction in physics was in good condition and filled four spacious cupboards. That for chemistry was less costly, naturally so, but complete. Their geography contained no text; it was simply an atlas. Take it all in all, the teachers *taught* and the pupils *saw* much, were obliged to *do* much, and then *to tell* about it orally and in writing.

That is the whole story in a nutshell. In grammar the method was cumulative, not analytic; in physics and chemistry it was experimental throughout; in mathematics it was demonstrative. Nowhere did I find any parrot-like repetition. The only direct appeal to mechanical memorizing was made in literature, for which study a great number of fine poems were learned, recited, dissected, compared, changed into prose, imitated, and, I must say it, enjoyed.

Shall I say more about the methods applied? It is scarcely necessary, if I add that I noticed a truly enviable unanimity among the teachers with reference to their *modus operandi*. Though each teacher is permitted to follow his own methods, there seems to be a tacit understanding or agreement to work into each other's hands.

4. A District Conference.

Rather against my inclination, I went a little out of my way to attend a meeting of a teachers' association in a district of Lower Rhenish Prussia, and I do not rue it, for it gave me a novel experience. It is not too much to say one can not find a finer and more intelligent-looking body of teachers in deliberation anywhere, unless it be the National Council of Educators in America, a body which looks like the Roman senate. One thing was particularly pleasing to me: There was no talking for immediate effect, perhaps because "*feminini generis*" being *non est*.

The three papers read had been selected by a majority vote after the titles of all on the programme had been made public. In other words, the body chose the questions it wanted to discuss, and permitted him "who was primed" to have the first say. The three papers selected were "Principles *versus* Practice," "The Scope of Arithmetic in the Common School," and "Education in America."

The first essay was a masterly refutation of such views as found utterance in our country under the captivating caption, "The Presumption of Brains." It would have done me good to see Superintendent Marble in the audience. The essayist perhaps never heard of this gentleman, but it seemed as though he aimed his words at the author of "Presumption," etc., directly. The discussion was spirited, but a vote of sixty-three to five sustained the position held by the essayist.

The second essay showed that the question lately called up by General Walker in Boston is being ventilated in Germany also; but it was the third paper which challenged my admiration. The referee spoke of our American common schools with a remarkable degree of familiarity, and proved that he had the geography and statistics of our country at his fingers' ends. His statistical items were all very well sifted and true. I could not help sighing when I unwillingly compared this accurate knowledge of America on the part of German teachers with the Egyptian darkness that still prevails in American educational circles about Germany.

Being called upon to address the meeting, I inquired whether the speaker had been in America, that he was enabled to thus speak of the American schools with precision and authority. I was told, however, that he had gathered his data from publications of our National Bureau of Education in Washington; that the library of the association contained a full set of General Eaton's reports and sundry other sources of information.

Again I had to stifle a sigh, thinking of the isolation of thousands of our teachers in America who can be made to read only through persuasion and by the Damocles's sword of an approaching examination. The men present at this meeting were mostly country or village teachers. They looked highly intellectual, but had all more or less care-worn faces and seemed to labor under heavy stress, such as overcrowded school-rooms, poor pay, and perhaps domestic cares.

5. History Teaching.

Perhaps in all my wanderings through the schools of Europe I may never again find such perfect teaching of history as I found in a school of D——, in Rhenish Prussia. Though it is impossible to render the lesson in writing, I will at least give my readers an inkling of it. (Pardon the pun, it was an unconscious one.) There were two such lessons: one was on "The Great Elector of Brandenburg," the other on "Rudolph of Hapsburg." These lessons, I believe, will never fade in my memory. Each was a masterpiece. The classes ranked in age with our C grammar classes, or sixth school year.

First, a biographical narrative was given by the teacher, who spoke in very simple, appropriate language, but feelingly with the glow of enthusiasm and the chest-tone of conviction. He made each pupil identify himself with the hero of the story. The map was frequently used or referred to. Bits of poetry, taken from the reader, were interwoven, and circumstances of our time, as well as persons of very recent history, were mentioned at proper occasions. The attention was breathless.

Secondly, the story was then repeated by pupils who were now and then interrupted by leading questions. The answers were again used to develop new thoughts not brought out by the first narration. Particularly was it cause and effect, and the moral value of certain historical actions which claimed the attention of the teacher. To me it was very instructive to see these children search for analogous cases in human life as they knew it.

Thirdly, the pupils were led to search in their stores of historical knowledge for analogous cases, or cases of decided contrast. This gave me an insight into the extent of their knowledge. When, for instance, certain civil virtues were spoken of, they mentioned cases which revealed a very laudable familiarity with history. But all their knowledge had been grouped around a number of centers—that is, great men. That is to say, their historical knowledge had been gained through biographies.

Fourthly, the pupils were told to write, in a connected narration, what they had just learned. This proved a fertile composition exercise, because the pupils had something to write about—a thing that is not quite so frequent in schools as it seems desirable. I afterward asked the teacher for his principles of method in teaching history, and he gave them to me at length. The following is an epitome of them:

6. THE PRINCIPLES OF THIS METHOD.

It must be the aim of instruction in history to nourish and strengthen all the powers of the soul, *interest, emotion*, and *volition*, so that the harmonious development of the child be assisted and a general interest awakened.

The pupil's *intellect* is increased by making him familiar with historical deeds, and the circumstances under which they were done, with their causes and effects, with various conditions of life, with persons as they are mirrored in their deeds, with the development of the character of persons and that of nations. The intellect is particularly nourished by affording comparisons and making distinctions; by causing keen judgment and correct conclusions. By means of all these, the pupil's thinking power is stimulated and an insight into political and governmental relations past and present is gained, which is important alike for the individual and the state.

The pupil's *heart* is influenced by instruction in history, because many great, sublime, noble, and beautiful actions and motives are presented, which cause pleasure and lead to imitation, unconsciously to the pupil. Again, because history shows, in some abominable examples, that evil is punished as well as the good rewarded; that justice, though slow sometimes, will overtake the evil-doer.

The pupil's *will-power* is greatly stimulated by instruction in history, because he is warmed and inspired by truth, right, and duty, for love of country and his fellow-men. He receives an impetus to imitate great deeds. He takes in some of that spirit which prompts men to act nobly and grandly. The fountain of emotion is the best fountain of volition.

There are, however, some absolutely necessary conditions: 1. That the teacher of history be a person whose heart is full of patriotism, and beats strongly for truth, right, and duty. To him should be said, "Take thy shoes from off thy feet, for the ground upon which thou standest is holy ground." 2. That the instruction be not a mere recital of names and dates, of battles and acquisitions of land, nor dissertations upon abstract ideas and generalities, but, above all, a simple narration of deeds and events, and a glowing description of persons and circumstances. It must be biographical. The most interesting and most ennobling study for children is the lives of great men. Biography is the first step in our historical course.

It is necessary, 3. That the teacher connect the new historical knowledge with circumstances and conditions, such as are either known to the pupil, or are near enough at hand to draw them into the discussion. Relics and other tangible objects, suitable for illustration, should be brought into the class-room, if only in pictures. The teacher must be so objective in his narratives that the events and creations are not only spoken of, but become experiences by natural process of thought. 4. The pupil should not be allowed to remain receptive, but must be induced to be active in this study. In this, as in other studies, practice is wanted. The pupils must be called upon to reproduce, orally and in writing, the matter given them and the thoughts produced in them.

It is necessary, 5. That the teacher should induce his pupils to compare similar and dissimilar actions and persons, and thereby cause judgment upon cause and effect from a moral or ethical standpoint, so that not merely the intellect be developed, but also the heart and the will. Their practical interest is then generated without repressing their speculative interest. 6. That instruction in history be brought into organic connection with the study of language; for this reason, reading is to be brought in as an assistant. Recitations of patriotic poems and ballads can be woven in profitably, and that geography must aid history is self-evident.

During the first three years of school, biblical stories, references to public men, holidays and festivals, legends and stories, and a few biographical attempts are the proper matter there. After that, a biographical history should begin, which may widen with each succeeding year, so that the historical horizon of the child is extended simultaneously with that in other studies.

If the common school gives *that kind of instruction in history*—it need not be great in amount—it is doing much better than teaching higher arithmetic and bookkeeping.

7. Practical Instruction in Drawing.

I doubt not, that it will be of interest to many teachers in the Union to learn how drawing is taught here in city schools. This branch of "study" has so recently been introduced into the American schools, or rather, it has been made an obligatory branch of the curriculum so recently, that it may be said to be still in its infancy with us. Here, in Germany, drawing, as a branch of study, is much older, and more can, therefore, be expected, and better results should be exhibited. But, to speak candidly, when comparing the

SERIES I.—FIGS. 8-17.

drawings exhibited in New Orleans, Madison, Topeka, and Chicago, with what I find here in crowded class-rooms, where seventy and more pupils are seated, I can not say that

Figs. 18-26.

the work is better, certainly not as showy. A standard of measurement is wanting for a true comparison. Still, despite the absence of glittering results and show, I suspect,

30 DUISBURG (RHENISH PRUSSIA).

Series IX.—Figs. 27-37.

PRACTICAL INSTRUCTION IN DRAWING.

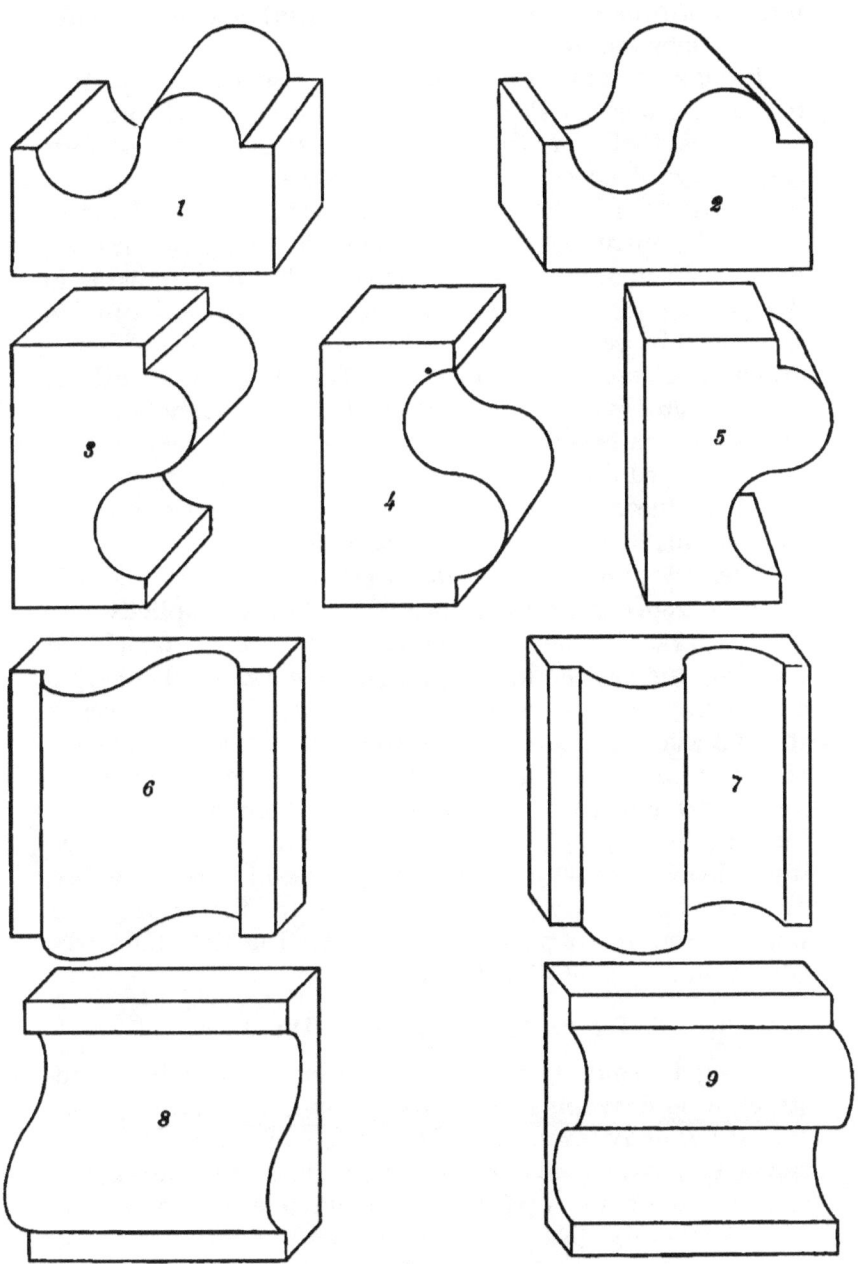

SERIES XIII.—FIGS. 38-46.

more results *en masse*, and a more general and deeper culture are obtained here.

Perhaps I may with impunity say, also, that instruction in drawing here in Prussia is more practical. In order to prove this, I will say that I found drawing of objects quite frequently. The objects used as models are furnished by a Hamburg firm. They are made of hard wood, and are so plentifully furnished that there is one for every two or three pupils. Each pupil draws the object as he sees it—that is, in the position in which it is placed before him. I can not explain this better than by copying a number of series drawn by classes in my presence. The models were all the same in size, given to the classes that day as new subjects. The work was free-hand drawing, and as such very creditable. I copied the accompanying sketches, omitting all construction lines. They are here offered on a smaller scale, so as to permit their insertion in this book.

The series I and IX are the two extremes, so far as difficulty in representing is concerned. Their simplicity certainly speaks for them. I found them used as models for drawing, for clay-modeling, pasteboard work, wood chiseling and sawing in manual training schools. Before I dismiss this subject, I must not neglect to say that the girls are excluded from this drawing of solids. They draw conventionalized leaf and plant forms, and learn their application in knitting, crocheting, embroidering, lace-making, and weaving. Leaves pasted on cardboard are used in great number, and forms of beauty of no mean kind are the result. The reader is referred to pages 123–134, where the girls' industrial education is spoken of at length.

8. Learning to shade in Drawing.

Being thoroughly convinced of the practicability of instruction in drawing solids, I was pleased to find my opinion shared by many teachers in Germany. The difficulty which seems to puzzle many teachers is, to find suitable objects, simple enough to avoid the great obstacle, which consists

LEARNING TO SHADE IN DRAWING. 33

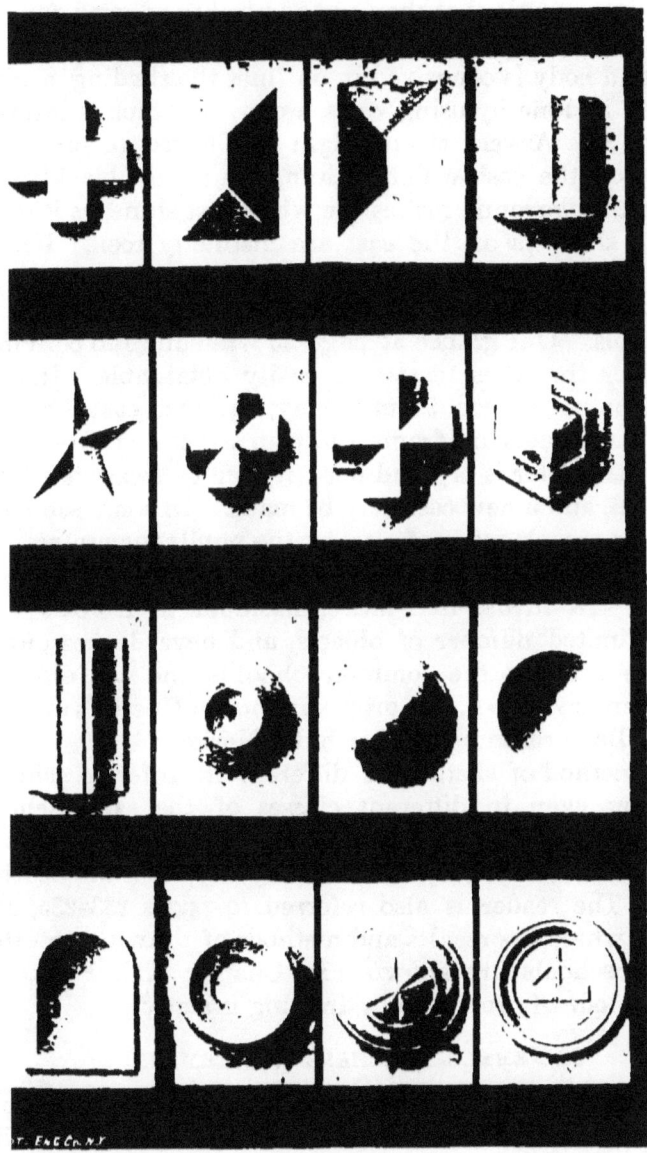

Figs. 47-62.

in the pupils not seeing the covered lines. The solids used here are so simple that they are admirably adapted for the elementary schools.

After a body is conceived in outlines the shading begins, and this is done by using casts, a copy of which is inserted on page 33. A very strong light is allowed to fall from the left on the cast, which is hung up on the blackboard. The dark background makes the white cast shine, as it were, and the shadows on the cast are distinctly seen. I have provided myself with sufficient copies of pupils' work to prove that this drawing of solids is possible in the elementary schools. One glance at page 33 will suffice to convince the reader that these casts are easily obtainable. Indeed, any person may model them in clay, and then cast them, by setting the models in a frame and pouring plaster over them. When the plaster is dry and hard it can be separated from the model, and a new cast may be made. In some schools I found the models made of clay by the pupils themselves.

The system in use here is decidedly more practical than others I saw in use in France, inasmuch as it deals with only a limited number of objects, and never leaves out of sight the fact that the common school is, and can only be, an elementary school. It proves immortal Goethe's maxim: "In der Beschränkung zeigt sich der Meister."

The method of shading is different in different schools, sometimes even in different classes of the same school. While some teachers used lines of various thickness to represent shadow, others, by far the majority, use the leather stump. The reader is also referred to pages 233–235, and 272–281, where the results and methods of drawing in other German schools are shown. In Chapter XII, Paris, the French mode of procedure in drawing is stated.

9. Female Teachers in Germany.

Though I spent several weeks in German schools, I had only heard men teach. But one day I heard two ladies teach, and model lessons they gave. The first was a lesson in reading, according to the word and phonic method combined, or, to speak scientifically, the analytic-synthetic method. An object-lesson on "fish" introduced the reading. When that was closed, oral splitting of the word *fish* into sounds followed. The teacher pronounced the word slowly, thus bringing out each sound clearly, so that the little urchins could recognize and separate them. Then the word was written, copied, and other words were made of material (sounds and letters) previously learned, till at the close of the lesson a great number of new words were read and learned. These were combined into little sentences.

The second lesson I heard a lady give was in religion. The topic was the announcement or prophecy of Christ's birth to Mary, the pious virgin. The children were on an average eight years old, and the teacher a young, sweet-looking girl. I assure my readers that, though the teacher proceeded with laudable tact and much pedagogical skill, the lesson left an unsavory taste, there being too much cant in it to please me.

As a rule, the women teachers in Germany, I am told, teach well in the lower grades, and only there. Middle and higher grades of school are closed to them. During the grand upward start which business took in Germany after the re-establishment of the empire, so many men left the school-room to join the chase after the golden calf, that the Government was obliged to engage women to teach school. At present they are numbered by the thousand.

I inquired whether they could not be promoted, and in due time be elected principals. The inspector with whom I conversed on the subject of women teachers replied with a holy (or shall I say unholy?) horror: "*No*, never, as long as the father is the head of the family. It would be as unnatural as crowing hens. A weak, indulgent man may surrender his breeches to his wife; such cases are found, of course, but these exceptions do not shake, but confirm the rule. Besides, the Government is fully aware that the women can not govern the men, a thing which they would have to do if they were made the heads of schools. Such a thing would be contrary to all precedents, and to the eternal fitness of things, as conceived by us Germans."

Having thus given me a bit of his own mind, he snatched up a paper containing extracts from a recent novel by Walter Besant, saying, "Here is an Englishman with whom I fully agree." I quote:

"There are many points of distinction between the masculine and the feminine mind; as, that the woman is not happy unless she is quite sure and certain, and that the man gets along very comfortably under a sense of uncertainty; also, that any man who disagrees with a woman is, to her, an utterly contemptible person, while to a man, he is only a person with a curious mental twist. But the most distinctive of all these points is, that a woman never invents anything, or wants to change anything, or to improve any methods or ways of doing things. In order to illustrate this proposition, consider the common house-maid, the common household cook, and the household nurse-maid. The first of these has never been known to show the smallest invention in the laying of a fire, nor the second in constructing a dish, nor the third in dressing a baby."

His own metaphors dissuaded me as little as this quotation did, of the natural right of women to rise and take a hand in the government of the world; and that the school, as a world in miniature, is the proper place for women to begin to show their executive and administrative powers. But, being on my guest-behavior, I changed the subject. Strange, however, but true it is, that from the moment I had asked that question, I was looked upon with suspicion, and the confidence of the otherwise pleasant and kindly-spoken man was as though it had dried up.

How deep-rooted the prejudice against female teachers is here in Germany may be seen, also, from the fact that the male teachers club together in the yard during recess, leaving the ladies to amuse themselves. Oh, yes, they speak to them, and politely salute them by uncovering their heads "as they pass by," but no professional discussion, no social conversation, not even a bit of small talk, takes place. All such professional ties seem to be forbidden by an unwritten but well-understood law. I leave my readers to draw their own conclusions.

10. Tenure of Office.

There is one feature of the German schools which deserves attention and imitation—I mean the stability of the teacher's position. After he has completed his course in the normal school, he is assigned to duty somewhere or elected by a community for a two years' probation. Whether he has succeeded well or not, at the end of this time he is called upon to pass his "repetition examination." Having passed that, he is free from all further examinations, and can settle down permanently, since his position is not endangered by political rotation or any other causes, except his own errors, such as neglect of duty, etc.

He lives either in the school-house or in a neighboring dwelling, fitted up by the community as the "schoolmaster's house," as a parsonage is fitted up for the parson by the church authorities. Being thus safely housed, and having no such Damocles's sword as a change in the political complexion of the school board to fear (in fact, there is no school board), his future is assured. Now he naturally begins to "gather moss," like a stone safely imbedded in the loam of the woods. By that, I mean, he increases his library, and devotes his leisure hours to some hobby. Some teachers resort to agriculture or floriculture (every school-house in small towns or villages has a few acres of land for gardening purposes); some raise silk-worms or bees, or start a nursery of trees; others make collections of beetles, butterflies, and minerals. Again, others resort to some kind of manual labor, such as turning, scroll-saw working. A great many choose literature as their leisure-hour occupation. Nearly all foster music, and act as musical directors and conductors of choirs and as organists in churches.

In short, they "gather moss" like an ancient pike in a well-stocked carp-pond. This stability of office engenders a good deal of conservatism, which, queer as it may seem, rarely manifests itself in their methods of teaching; for local, district, provincial, state, and national teachers' meetings, an educational press of most formidable powers, frequent visits of royal school commissioners, and the competition engendered by friendly visits of colleagues, prevent a stagnation in school.

Being curious to know the political proclivities of an old friend of mine, who had become a fixture in a small town of Rhenish Prussia, I frankly asked him. Said he: "Do you know that the Roman citizen was a Roman first, and a Roman last; right or wrong, he was a Roman forever? Well, my friend, I am teacher first, last, and all the time." I accepted this circumlocution for the term "mugwump," and changed the subject.

11. MISCELLANEOUS NOTES.

An Idyl.—Curiosity induced me to visit the place in the country where I gained my first experience in teaching. It was a pretty little village, situated between two industrial centers, and inhabited by vegetable gardeners, who had an average of ten or fifteen acres of land, rarely more. The village had not changed materially within a quarter of a century. The half of a millstone in front of the schoolhouse, serving as a doorstep, was still there, and through its square aperture grew the grass as it did twenty-five years ago. The school-house was as dilapidated as it was then, only a little more so. The church tower had received a new coat of slate, a few new houses had been built, others had been repaired. The same fine linden-trees offered shadow to the school-yard; and, indeed, the picturesque village seemed to have slept the sleep of the Sleeping Beauty, while within sight of the top of the steeple industrial centers had grown from twenty thousand to eighty thousand inhabitants within that time.

The principal teacher, however, was a different sort of man from the morose fellow who used to hold sway there and made my life unbearable. The American can not imagine how peaceful the life of a German country schoolmaster is. He is secure in his position. Nothing but misconduct or gross neglect of duty on his part can remove him. He has no rent to pay, but lives in the upper stories of the school-building, where he has from five to eight rooms and a high garret. Usually a large garden is at his disposal. Let me tell you of the present incumbent.

This teacher's life is a perfect idyl. His young assistants worship him, his pupils love him, his fellow-villagers respect him, call for his prudent advice, and, what is more, believe in it implicitly. He is the universally respected arbiter in all questions of dispute, and is welcomed in every house of the village. In his leisure hours he is a gardener, and the culture of roses is his special hobby. I have seen many fine collections of roses in my life—I even dabble a little in that line myself—but my astonishment was boundless when I saw the results of this man's patient labor. Thousands of varieties of roses, hundreds of colors and sizes, from the lovely carnation centifolia and orange Marshal Neil to the dwarfed pink-colored May rose and yellow Lilliput rose—all were there.

His young assistants and his elder pupils vie with each other in helping him in his work of floriculture, so that there is nothing left for him to do but to direct and supervise. But he never forgets that he is teacher first and gardener afterward. First duty, then pleasure. The man is about fifty years old, and is not married. A housekeeper from the village attends to the duties indoors. Though this idyllic picture is rather out of place in this book, I could not refrain from painting it, to show our American country teachers what is in store for them if they will agitate the question of tenure of office more vigorously.

Herbart versus Pestalozzi.—There is a war carried on here in Germany at present between the disciples of Pestalozzi and those of Herbart—a war which promises to be more beneficial than destructive. My American readers can not conceive of the intensity and earnestness displayed by the combatants. Here in Rhenish Prussia the "Herbartians" are holding meetings, discussing Herbart's and Ziller's principles and methods, and the bookstalls are full of pamphlets, books, and journals, which all refer to the question at issue. Elsewhere, I am told, the same question is agitating the minds of teachers, notably in Thuringia and Saxony.

I attended a meeting of the "Herbartians," to which representatives of Düsseldorf, Crefeld, Duisburg, Mühlheim, Essen, Elberfeld, Barmen, Solingen, Gladbach, and many other towns had been sent. I was deeply impressed with the profundity with which Herbart's psychology and Ziller's concentric circles were discussed from three till after eight o'clock, P. M. What pleased me most was the absence of all personal wrangling, and not a word of disrespect to Pestalozzi and other educational reformers fell from the lips of the speakers. My interest grew amazingly when I examined the shelves of a bookstall later and found no less than sixty books, pamphlets, and exercise-books of very recent origin all discussing and exemplifying the "great question." Well, I own that I left the book-store with an armful of pamphlets and books, and poorer by thirty-five marks.

In the face of such literary activity, such thorough scientific discussion, I heave a deep sigh, thinking of the peaceful mental slumber of thousands of our American teachers, who do not even read an educational journal, and at educational gatherings have nothing to say, but suffer themselves to be read to by essayists, and in the school-room do merely what they are ordered to do. I shall not venture to enter upon the discussion of the disputed question until I have seen the schools of Saxony and Thuringia, and have studied my armful of books. I am like that German professor who was asked for his opinion on a question which he had never approached. His answer was, "I've got to read a lecture on that question before I can answer you." So, then, more anon.

Hospitality of Teachers.—It is no more than simple justice to state that I have found a hospitality among the teachers here which can nowhere be found in like manner except in America. In America, especially west of the Alleghanies and in the South, hospitality is one of the most pronounced virtues of the people, and I know whereof I am speaking, having traveled much in America, and having had opportunities to compare French, Dutch, and German customs with our American customs. Wherever I go here in Germany I find among teachers a truly American hospitality which it is difficult to resist. I deem it just and proper to state this fact in my reports to my American brethren.

CHAPTER III.

DÜSSELDORF (RHENISH PRUSSIA).

1. THE WHOLE NATION A SCHOOL.

My admiration for the schools in Germany grows when I notice the consistent help different institutions for educational and scientific purposes are rendering each other. Thus, for instance, I see in Düsseldorf on the Rhine that the common schools, as well as the several high-schools (the Gymnasium, Realschule, and Young Ladies' Academy), stand in close connection and intimate relation to the management of the Art Academy, the Art Museum, the Zoölogical and Botanical Garden, the Observatory, the libraries, the gymnastic societies, and even the theatre, in fact, with every institution which in some degree may be influential in assisting the work in school.

Plants are ordered for the study of botany at the Botanical Garden. Certain hours are fixed at the Zoölogical Garden for visits of the classes in zoölogy; admission free. Classes in drawing are taken to the art collections and museums, where the teacher of advanced classes gives a lesson monthly. The libraries are open to the pupils on presentation of a membership ticket issued by the rector of the school. Classes in literature go with their teachers to see classic performances in the theatre. The schools having small but very valuable collections frequently exchange specimens with the curator of the museum or even make loans. And so on, to every department of the curriculum, some institution outside of school offers assistance free of charge.

The more I look about me here in Germany, the more am I impressed with the fact that the whole nation is one great educational institution. Churches have their reserved seats for school children; theatres offer classic performances for students; gardens and parks are open to children; playgrounds are provided with flower-beds for children; gymnastic halls and apparatus are erected for the use of pupils of the city schools; in fine, all efforts are made to put public instruction upon a rational basis and to make education contagious. We Americans have much to learn from these "barbarians."

2. Singing in German Schools.

Ah, but what an inexhaustible spring of musical talent is found in German schools! These children sing divinely. Their teachers all play the violin more or less well and have a thorough theoretical training in music, teach the notes, and generally conduct the musical performances of their classes as leaders of orchestras do instrumental music—that is to say, they beat time, keep the different parts in harmony, stimulate here, depress there, and work like good fellows. The results are touchingly beautiful. I heard three- and four-part music in the upper grades of common schools.

Many a time I heard the teacher call upon a single pupil

to sing alone, as we should expect him *to read alone.* They consider this *reciting in music.* In one city on the Lower Rhine I heard a mass-chorus which touched me to the quick. The children sang patriotic airs with an artistic finish which quite upset me. An old gentleman who had accompanied me was moved to tears.

Our American city schools are doing a noble thing in awakening the musical sense of the nation. The adult American, as a rule, is not musical. General Grant used to say: "I know but two tunes. One is 'Yankee Doodle,' and the other—isn't." And if we were to inquire among our Anglo-American friends, we should find that the older generation is not any more musically inclined than General Grant. But in the younger generation a great love and comprehension for music makes itself felt, which is fostered by easy melodious home-made airs such as "Grandfather's Clock," "Wait till the Clouds Roll By," etc. Inferior as these airs may be, it will not do to undervalue their great influence upon the latent musical talent of our American conglomerate. Some generations may yet pass away before we can find such a school in New England as I saw here, where, among four hundred and eighteen pupils, only two were found without a musical ear.

3. A Novel Exercise in Music.

I noticed a novel exercise in vocal music which I deem worthy of mention. The teacher wrote the lines of a pretty little poem on the musical staff painted on the board and called upon certain pupils to compose a new melody. The first pupil looked at the first line thoughtfully awhile, and then struck out, giving a very acceptable air. The teacher asked her to repeat it, and then fixed it by writing it in notes. The second pupil then followed with a continuation which was less acceptable. Another suggested a little but vital improvement which made the line much more acceptable. Again a new line was added, till the four lines were finished. Now the teacher played the tune, suggesting two more, though slight changes, and indeed the melody seemed very pretty.

Now it was harmonized. A pupil was called upon to write the second part (the alto). This he did, with some errors, which were speedily detected by other pupils. Another added a third part (the tenor). Of course, this took longer than it takes me to write about it; but within the short space of thirty-five minutes the three parts were all down on the board. They were tested on the violin and found to harmonize quite well. Now followed a grand rehearsal—that is, the class sang the newly composed song. Again a few changes were found desirable, and again it was tried, till it met the approval of the teacher. There was no need of attention to the order of the room. The order was perfect, simply because all the pupils were intensely interested. The lesson was brought to a close by the request to copy the new song into their manuscript music-books. I have rarely enjoyed a singing lesson as much as I did this one.

The school in which this brilliant theoretical instruction in music was witnessed gave me the pleasure of hearing choruses of wonderful sweetness. The text was sung so well, emphasis or expression was so excellently brought out, that no professional choir could sing better. The fresh metallic sound in the voices of these German youngsters is quite enjoyable.

4. "Nature-Description."

Don't frown at this heading, fair reader. I have put it down for a reason. Our English term "natural history" is faulty, inasmuch as it is anything but history, so far as we teach it in the common school. Whatever criticism may be urged against the teachers here in Germany, they can not be said to be hazy in their technical terms. They do not use such terms as botany, zoölogy, physiology, but German translations which, while they are more precise, at the same time convey a meaning to the child, being grown, as it were, out of German roots: "Pflanzen-Beschreibung" for botany, "Thier-Beschreibung" for zoölogy, etc. So, please, familiarize yourself, my candid and patient reader, with this "odd" heading and follow me into a school representing the sixth school year. Here I heard a lesson in "Thier-Beschreibung" which might be said to be an ideal lesson. It is impossible to give the whole lesson; only essentials must suffice.

Orang-outang and sundry other apes were the subject. *Teacher*, showing the large picture of the orang-outang, and saying that, for want of time, they had only barely touched upon this subject yesterday, asked: "What do you remember having heard of this animal?" A rather insignificant-looking specimen of the *genus homo sapiens* answered: "The orang outang is a monkey which resembles the human being more than other monkeys. But there are more dissimilarities than similarities, I think. He is called orang-outang, because that means 'forest-man' or 'wood-man' on account of his similarity with man. He is very fierce and vicious and of huge strength."

Teacher. "That is about all we said yesterday about him. Now, let us proceed. Let us hunt up some of the similarities as well as dissimilarities between him and man."

Pupil. "His face looks like that of an old man." (Went to the board and wrote under the heading "similarities." "Looks like an old man.")

Teacher. "From this picture it is plainly visible that this must be a young specimen, for the older the monkey gets the more will the jaws grow outward and the forehead recede, so that in old age this monkey will look more like a ferocious beast than like man." Repeat this thought.

Pupil. "John said the orang-outang looks like an old man on this picture. Then this must be a young specimen, for in old age he looks more beast-like."

Teacher. "What changes take place in his face in the course of time?"

Pupil. "His jaws grow outward and his forehead recodes." (Went to the board and jotted down, "Jaws and forehead change with age.")

Teacher. "What other observations?"

Pupil. "He is like man covered with hair; but while man's hair is very short and scarcely visible, the monkey is covered with fur-like hair." (Made appropriate note on the board without being called upon.)

Pupil. "Certain parts of his body are not covered with hair; for instance, the ears and the inside of the hands. In this he resembles man also." (Note on the board.)

Pupil. "I have read somewhere that the teeth of this monkey are exactly like human teeth."

Teacher. "I am glad you tell us that. Then by examining our own teeth we may infer from them as to this animal's teeth." (Now followed a description of the human teeth, size, kind, use, growth, etc., an interesting digression from the lesson of the day, one which revealed some knowledge of physiology and hygiene.) "So, then, we have another point of similarity; what is it?"

Pupil. "He has a complete set of teeth like that of the human being." (Note on the board.)

Pupil. "We can't tell his size from the picture. What is it?"

Teacher. "He never grows any bigger than a boy of fourteen years, but his strength is greater. Now, repeat this statement and make a note of it." (It is done.)

Pupil. "His color is chestnut-brown."

Teacher. "Now some one may repeat connectedly all the points mentioned so far." (This was done, and errors in language were corrected " on the spot." This connected description was repeated by a pupil.)

Pupil. "It appears from this picture that the arms of the orang-outang are very long." (Note.)

Pupil. "His feet are like hands."

Teacher. "True; he has four hands. But what is the difference between hand and foot?"

Pupil. "On the hand the thumb can make a movement

opposite to that of the fingers. This enables the hand to grip or grasp. The big toe can not do that."

Teacher. "What, then, is the characteristic of the hand?"

Pupil. "The hand can grasp, the foot can not."

Teacher. "The monkey walks on his hands, sometimes erect on his hind hands. Sometimes, especially when he is in a hurry, he walks on his four hands. Repeat this." (Whenever the teacher made a statement or a pupil brought out something new, the pupils had to repeat it.)

Pupil. "His arms reach to his ankles, while ours are shorter. The orang-outang can grasp things with his hind hands as well as with the other two."

Teacher. "Yes, an interesting fact is that some monkeys have only two hands. But all who have only two hands have them on their hind-legs, while their two feet are on the fore-legs or arms." (Repeat this.)

Pupil. "I notice that this orang-outang has hair on his arms which grows up and downward. How is that?"

Teacher. "Look at the arms carefully. What do you see?"

Pupil. "The hair on his upper arm grows downward; that on his lower arm grows upward."

Teacher. "What do you infer from this?"

Pupil. "That he must raise his lower arms much."

Teacher. "Yes, I believe we may safely say that. Now, let us repeat connectedly what we heard and mention all the points gathered." (This is done, and with the aid of the numerous notes on the board done very handsomely. These reviews occurred frequently, and they served to "take up loose stitches" here and there.)

Teacher. "He walks erect generally, but has a dragging gait because he has no knee-pans. When pursued he climbs on high trees and hides himself in the foliage. He is not as skillful as other monkeys in climbing, but rather clumsy. He feeds on fruit and birds' eggs. He is here pictured with a stick in his hand, which he seems to use as a cane. It is likely that the orang-outang is often found walking with a stick, perhaps owing to his inability to stand erect long. He makes his nest on high trees, selecting strong branches. On these he lays smaller ones, with thick foliage to make the couch soft. Being very shy, he is not often found. He changes his couch frequently and is unsociable."

Pupils repeat the several new statements and seem to enjoy them. They are again repeated by some in a connected manner.

Teacher. "His home is on the islands of Borneo and Sumatra." (These are looked up on the map.) "The people there—of course I mean the aborigines—say of the orang-outang, that he could talk if he wanted to, but keeps quiet because he is afraid that he would have to work if he betrayed the fact that he could talk. The Europeans know better. His voice is heard in shrill screams and angry howling. It is said, but has never been observed by Europeans, that he drives elephants with a stick. These are probably legends. He can not stand our climate, and if caught and brought north on board of a steamer he generally dies before he reaches Europe. Very few specimens have ever been seen in zoölogical gardens." (This new batch of statements is treated like all the foregoing—that is, repeated, sketched in shortest expressions on the board, and rounded off and polished to secure good style.)

Teacher. "That the orang-outang is an animal of higher type may be seen from his quickness of perception and his skill in imitation. There was one in a zoölogical garden who had been fastened to a chain. At certain stated periods the waiter came to loosen his chain and take him out walking. Of course, the waiter opened the padlock which fastened the chain to the cage. The ape saw him use a key, and one day he took a little chip and tried to open the padlock himself. So, you see, he had not only seen something, but remembered it, and now wanted to make use of this knowledge." (These stories were reviewed.)

Now followed a repetition of the whole description and an occasional reference to other monkeys, of which pictures were exhibited. Then the order was given to write out a composition on the orang-outang. I requested to be shown some of these compositions, for which reason I returned to this class after the lapse of an hour. I was not at all surprised to find that the work was very commendable indeed. A pupil of this age is always likely to express his thoughts well, provided he has any.

In a conversation with the teacher afterward I gathered this thought, worth repeating: " As in the history of the nation or human race it is desirable to group the knowledge around individuals, in other words, make biography the first historical course, so in natural history a single specimen must suffice to group the knowledge of a whole class of animals, plants, or minerals. Now, this orang-outang is a central figure. Let the pupils see more monkeys and then observe and make inferences upon their dissimilarities with the orang-outang. I doubt not they will gather more valuable knowledge, after having some definite knowledge with which they can organically connect new cognitions. *Natural history must be biographical* in the common school. We have neither time nor means to teach more than the elements. A systematic scientific instruction must be left to the higher schools."

I offer this to my readers as a thought worth thinking about. If the lesson sketched above may not seem as brilliant as it was in fact, the fault is mine, owing to my inability to write short-hand. I am afraid many a valuable stitch was dropped.

5. A Lesson in Botany.

In one of the schools of a large city on the Middle Rhine I had the great pleasure of listening to a botany lesson, which seemed to me worthy of being sketched for the benefit of American teachers.

Simple forms of leaves was the subject of the lesson.

The pupils had provided themselves with leaves, either from their own gardens or from the numerous parks in the city; and though every pupil had brought an abundance, there was no litter of branches or leaves on the floor, which proved that good discipline was maintained. I will, in sketching the lesson, omit all introductory and other unimportant things said or done—merely state the essential features.

In the course of a few minutes the teacher made on the blackboard the following figures, which were imitated by the pupils:

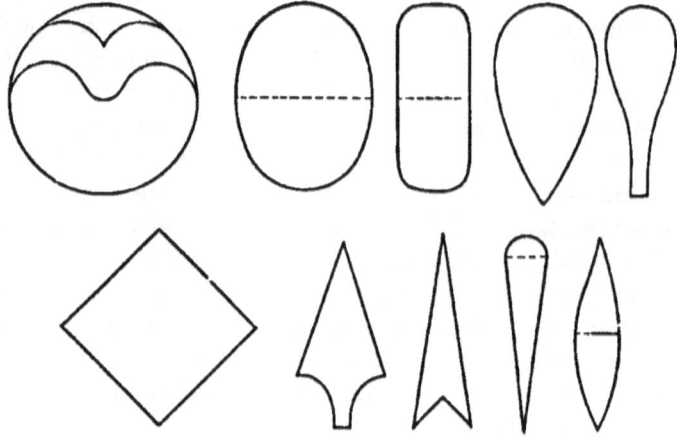

Figs. 63-72.

These forms were named, the terms attached, and the work was accompanied by pleasant conversation, which led to obtaining the proper terms. Frequent references to things previously spoken of made this part of the lesson very interesting. Thus, for instance, the spear-head gave opportunity for referring to the Indians and mound-builders, of which to my genuine astonishment the teacher had a little but a correct knowledge. I must heartily commend the teacher's dexterity and accuracy in sketching the above forms with crayon.

A LESSON IN BOTANY.

When the forms (Figs. 63-72) were recognized and appropriately named as well as copied, the order was given to find leaves among those brought to school which had similar shapes; and now began a busy five minutes. Orderly and quietly the pupils searched for the different forms and for duplicates in order to exchange them for those of which other pupils had plenty. At the close of the five minutes the signal was given to have the work ready for inspection. The teacher and myself went through the class-room and saw how the pupils had arranged their leaves.

Most pupils had *heart-shaped* leaves; only one a *kidney-shaped* leaf; all had *oval-shaped*, both broad and narrow; all had *lancet-shaped* ones, both ending in a point or in the form of a heart. None had a *spattle-shaped* leaf, so the teacher exhibited his specimen. All had *spear-* and *arrow-*shaped leaves, but not one, not even the teacher could exhibit a rue or rhomboid or *diamond-shaped* leaf, and so a mere illustration on the board, hastily yet accurately drawn, had to take the place of an object *in natura*.

Now the order was given to sketch on paper, first the simple figure, then the leaf under it, and I was greatly pleased with the result of the work. It was done quickly. About twenty minutes sufficed for the slowest workers to sketch all the leaves. Care was taken in bringing out the characteristic feature of the leaves. I must say the leaves looked very natural.

While I offer in the above figures my own copy of the teacher's sketches, Figs. 73-81 will be found a pupil's work which was given to me at my request. I hope the reader will find this of sufficient importance to see why I have the neat sketches accurately reproduced for the benefit of those who might like to imitate the lesson. They will show that in this lesson seeing, doing, and telling about it, went hand in hand. They will also bear witness to the skill the pupils displayed in drawing.

No incomprehensible Latin terms were used, much to my delight. *Reniformis* means nothing to the child, while *kidney-shaped* carries with it a meaning, appealing, as it does, to a familiar form in the memory.

Now the leaves were traced to their origin. "What plant has leaves like this one?" "Where did you get yours?" "Was it a tree, a shrub, an herb, a grass?" and so on. What struck me in this lesson was the fact that the teacher led the pupils in an opposite way from the one in which I had seen another teacher lead his class. The other had taken the natural leaf first, and then conventionalized it.

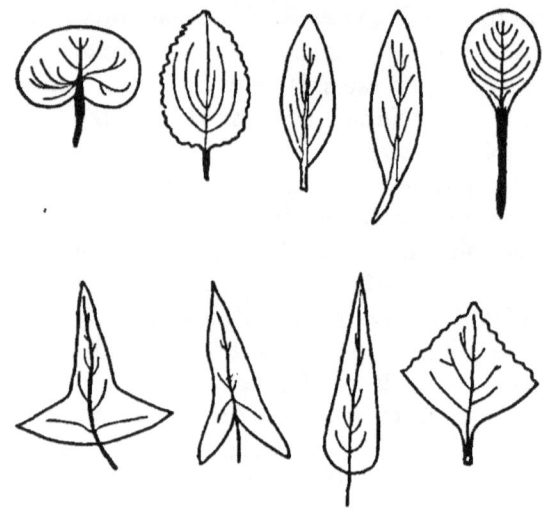

FIGS. 73-81.

This teacher gave the, so to speak, geometrical form first, and led the pupils to recognize that identical form in the leaves. Whether the one or the other may be used, both ways seemed to come to the same point, namely, thorough acquaintance with leaf-forms as well as skill in sketching. Both teachers paid due regard to spelling and language, taking care that the technical terms were duly impressed upon the memory by being written on the board and in the note-books, and by being pronounced in chorus and by single pupils.

I find a great deal of sketching done in the schools of Germany and France, and I take this opportunity to say that this practice has a great educational influence, inasmuch as it develops the sense of form and creates a memory for forms, not to speak of the skill it gives to the hand and the ability to retain knowledge.

"How did you manage to get them to do this sketching so accurately?" was my question. The teacher's reply was characteristic, namely:

"Of course, when we began, many efforts of the pupils were weak and their results execrable; but we persisted, and never let an opportunity for sketching slip by. Nearly every day some sketches of forms are made, and the habit of talking with the pencil is easily acquired. It is just as it is with learning to swim. Plunge in and courageously strike out. Don't try to learn to swim by practicing the movements of arms and legs on the parlor carpet. By persistent practice I accustom my pupils to do this work of sketching. I make it a duty, a pleasure, and even a second nature to them."

The result of such practical teaching is obvious. I see no reason whatever why we should not be able to "go and do likewise."

6. Ideal Teaching in Geography.

It was in a preparatory school in the city of D—— where I saw ideal teaching in geography. The school was provided with all possible means in form of maps. The matter of instruction could be graded just as is done in arithmetic, reading, etc. Geographical knowledge has for ages been wrested from overstocked maps. The child had to search painfully among a bewildering mass of data and facts for those which were to be learned. A systematic or methodical progress step by step was, if not impossible, certainly very difficult. Just as little as a teacher would give into the hands of a child a copy of Webster's "Unabridged" or of Shakespeare's complete works when he begins to learn the art of reading, just as little can it be rational in the teaching of geography to place before him a complete map stocked with a bewildering number of details.

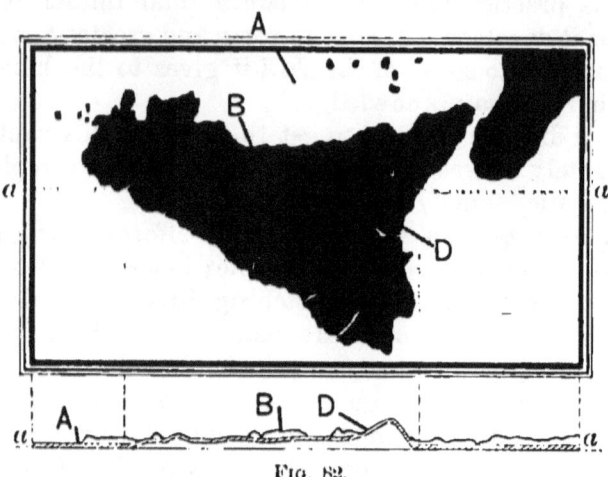

Fig. 82.

This difficulty was removed in the school I refer to. Outline maps were used. First river-maps like the one above (Fig. 82). All the water-courses and the ocean (A) were colored blue, while the land (B) appeared black. Below each map was given a profile, or longitudinal vertical section on certain given lines, as on the above sketch on line a. The pupils drew the map on paper and then inserted the elevations. Then followed another outline map containing the elevations and a few boundary-lines. By degrees more items of information were added, such as cities, trunk-roads, canals, etc. The principle of Father Pestalozzi, "One difficulty at one time," was carefully heeded, and the pupils were not bothered with maps such as we use in America, which blur the children's mental picture by their multiplicity of detail.

Teachers are apt to labor under the misapprehension that a map is a good one when it contains much. This is an error. According to that argument a school reader would be a good one only when it contained the whole literature from Alfred's time to the present day. Outline maps, silhouette maps, and such means for teaching geography rationally, are coming into use here in Europe as well as with us in America.

The school I referred to was lavishly provided with maps and charts. There were outline, silhouette, and complete maps, geographical, historical, physiological, physical, and astronomical maps and charts. What a wealth there was! And what a joy it must be to teach in such a school!

7. SILHOUETTE PRACTICE MAPS.

The *silhouette practice maps* facilitate the grading of the matter of instruction and present opportunities for the gradual up-building of geographical knowledge as gained item by item by the child. Upon these maps (Fig. 83) may be entered as upon a blackboard the data to be learned, first by the teacher, afterward by the pupils, and thus an opportunity is afforded to the child to become a self-active participator in the lesson. When the lesson is completed, all marks or names can be erased with a moist sponge or cloth, and the map is ready for a new lesson or a review.

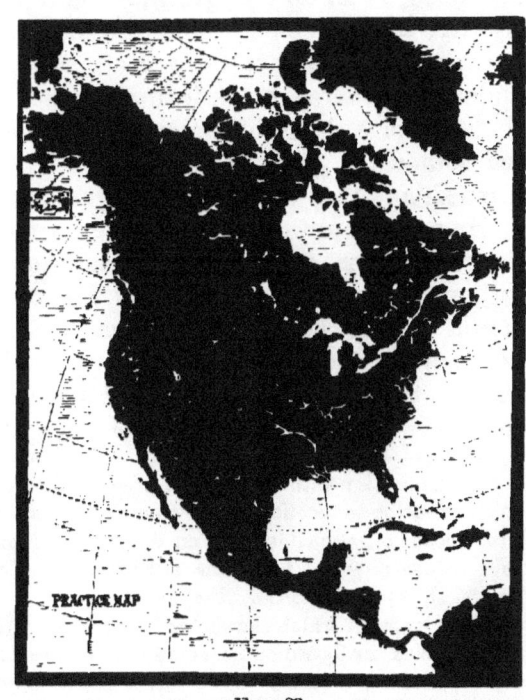

FIG. 83.

The *silhouette practice maps* enable the instructor in history to illustrate with colored crayon changes in political boundaries at different periods. Students of ancient history, as well as general and modern history, can use these maps with great advantage. They do not make common wall maps superfluous, but supplement them.*

8. Cause and Effect in Geography.

The "Popular Educator," of Boston, published in 1887-'88 some excellent contributions which offered in words and pictures the present status of geography teaching in Germany. Those articles leave me little to say on that subject. One thing I can do though, and I do it willingly, namely, to say that the statements made in those articles are correct. German teachers, not only in Saxony, where the author evidently gathered his information, but also in other parts of the empire, do teach geography as there stated; if modified somewhat, perhaps, essentially the same methods are pursued, and that with wonderful results.

How I should like to transfer some of our American teachers hither, who can not imagine a geography lesson without verbatim memorizing of the printed text! How I should like to show them rational teaching! I am fully aware of the fact that we, too, have good teachers, and not a few either; but it can not but please a visitor greatly to find every teacher, good and poor ones, following well-estab-

---

* In connection with the foregoing description it may not be out of place to call attention to an effort of my own which may aid teachers seeking for better means of rational instruction than the overstocked and crowded wall maps in use now. I mean the silhouette practice maps, published by Messrs. D. Appleton & Co., New York.

These maps, of which the sketch in the margin gives an idea, are printed on heavy tack cardboard and covered with a durable *water-proof*, *cleansable surface*, adapted to receive a succession of markings and cleansings. The shaded space represents the water surfaces. Oceans, lakes, and rivers appear in blue on these maps, the land in black; hence their name, *silhouette* maps. They are called *practice* maps because the pupil can on them practice with crayon geography as he does arithmetic.

CAUSE AND EFFECT IN GEOGRAPHY.

lished principles of method. That is the true state of affairs here in the city of D——. Even the poor teachers are not without professional training. There is, however, a deep shadow on this bright picture. Many schools are very poorly equipped with means of instruction, such as maps and charts.

I listened to a lesson in geography lately in a German school where seventy boys sat together like sardines in a box. The teacher had nothing better than a medium-sized wall map made by himself. His mode of marking elevations was very simple and comprehensive, one which is well worth imitating. With pencil or pen he shaded thus (Fig. 84):

Thus he was enabled to represent the topography of a country in a remarkably accurate manner, and this easy method enabled his pupils to judge at a glance as to the height of the land. They saw why certain rivers took such and such a course and no other; why certain cities were cold, others warm; why a river was navigable or not, according to the abruptness of the slope; why certain rivers flowing from great heights had a straighter course than those which had little fall and meandered through the plain; why certain lands are blessed with mild climates, being sheltered on the north side by high and steep mountain-ranges, others had rough climate, being exposed to the north wind.

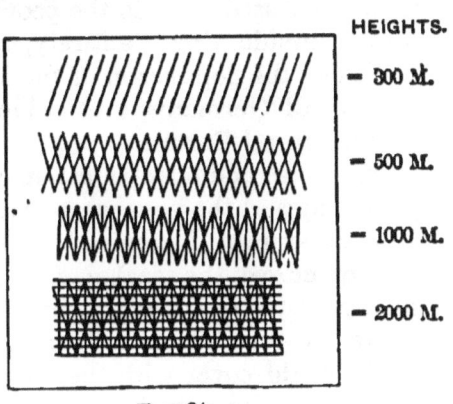

Fig. 84.

The teacher was well informed and gave information in such a manner that it agreed with the children's mental stomachs. *Example:* The Erz-Gebirge (Ore-Mountains) were once full of silver mines. At the time of Martin Luther (at the beginning of the sixteenth century) these mines drew a great number of people to Saxony and particularly to that range of mountains. When the mines ceased to yield, the population, not being so fluctuating as it is now, was obliged to seize upon other modes of occupation. The slopes of the mountains being well provided with various kinds of wood, offered material for a variety of wood-working industries. The slopes being steep, the mountain brooks were turbulent and gave an opportunity to build mills, which were first used for various purposes. Lately, when the textile industry grew, this water-power was utilized to serve that industry. The woods soon disappeared on the Erz Mountains; they were literally used up. So the people had to resort to manufacturing pursuits almost entirely, agriculture being impossible. To-day the population of the kingdom of Saxony is the densest of all Germany, and, aside from that in Belgium, the densest in all Europe.

It was cause and effect constantly, and the attention and responsiveness of the boys were truly delightful.

One other hint I received in this school. When the oral lesson closed, the teacher sent a boy to the blackboard to make a sketch of the map which the other boys were told to make on their slates. Then he showed that distances which he could cover with the span of his hand should be made one inch long on the slate or six inches on the blackboard. Now he measured off certain points on the map by spans, and thus gave the pupils a simple scale by means of which they could furnish a free-hand map which was not out of proportion. This procedure leads the way to a more accurate scale and to the thorough comprehension of scales as such. Afterward even this measuring by spans would be discontinued, I was told, and mere eye-measuring would be substituted. It was a fine lesson, indeed a fruitful lesson!

9. Making History an Experience.

I shall never forget the events of this day, and my readers, I am sure, will enjoy an account of it. Pursuant to a polite invitation I accompanied the teachers and pupils of the Realschule of D——, on an excursion to a neighboring hill about four miles from the city. The school marched in companies behind a drum corps, the teachers acting as captains. The students all wore light grayish-blue flannel suits and a cap, and carried suspended from the shoulders by a strap a tin box called a botanizing drum. This contained a lunch, small hammers for breaking minerals, pincers for dissecting plants, cork and pins for securing beetles, and a drinking-vessel. A few boys carried spades and shovels, ropes and hammocks.

The "regiment" afforded a beautiful sight as it marched from the school-yard between five and six hundred in number. As soon as the country road was reached, the music-teacher began a patriotic song in marching time and the whole school chimed in. Oh, the exhilarating influence that song had! When we came to the villa of a noted philanthropist who had recently given a large sum of money to the school-fund, the regiment drew up in line and gave him a serenade which wound up with three rousing hurrahs. On we went, more singing followed, but never a break in the ranks nor a case of disorder.

When we reached the foot of the hill a rest was taken at an inn, where milk was served and lunch was enjoyed as only youth can enjoy it. Then we plunged into the woods, each class by itself, one botanizing, one looking for minerals, another studying geography, and so on. I joined the history class. The professor took us to the summit of the hill and there gave us a lesson on local history which was interesting to a high degree.

"There it was," said he, "where Prince Ferdinand chased the Frenchmen across the Rhine. Yonder castle is the ancient residence of the Dukes of Jülich-Cleve-Berg, and in that castle it was where the beautiful Princess Jacobea of Baden was murdered. Far in the distance you can see the towers of the Cathedral of Cologne, begun some time during the thirteenth and finished during our nineteenth century.

Yonder is the ancient convent built by the successor of Bishop Boniface; here the ruins of the ancient Falkenburg, the feudal castle in which lived the owner of the land as far as you can see."

Then he drew a vivid picture of the difference between feudalism and modern institutions. The knights and barons in their fortified castles were all robbers, swooping down like hawks on the fords, on the highways, on the moorlands, on the forests, on the little settlements below them, and sometimes on the fortified cities, within the walls of which were fostered the feeble germs of self-government, civil rights, and civil virtues. It was a splendid lesson! The students crowded around him with bated breath. Pencil and note-book were brought into requisition, and within the short space of an hour so many references were made to points studied in the class-room that this lesson proved a profitable review over a month's hard study.

A bugle-signal brought all the different classes together in the Wolfgully. Here the professor addressed the whole school and proposed to make this the scene of the battle of Thermopylæ. About fifty agile, strong boys were selected to represent the Greeks who should defend the pass. Their leader was a fine lad of noble bearing, who played the *rôle* of Leonidas superbly. All the other boys were requested to advance and retreat as Persians. The fight in the pass was not rude, though pretty severe; and the battle could not be fought through with historical faithfulness, since not one of the boys was willing to play the *rôle* of Ephialtes, the traitor, so the teacher had to lead the Persians over the hill on a secret path into the rear of the gallant Greeks, who were disarmed after a most heroic resistance. The historical anecdotes, such as the answer of Leonidas to Xerxes about "fighting in the shade" and others, were woven into the play. This was *doing* history as pupils *do* arithmetic in the class-room.

The supercilious reader, if there be one, may smile over this boyish enthusiasm. Let him! The world owes all its prizes to enthusiasts and nothing to callous men.

After the battle a welcome rest was enjoyed, then vocal music followed. Mendelssohn's "Farewell to the Forest" and similar choruses were rendered charmingly. Now the treasures found during the afternoon were brought forward. Queer-looking specimens of petrifaction, animals, plants, etc., were examined, classified, and disposed of. Gymnastics, climbing of trees, and the tight rope, followed. Class exercises and games occupied part of the time. Certain daring feats were applauded and imitated. The teachers were always among the boys, suggesting and advising, but never showing their authority except when an order came by bugle-sound.

When the sun went down, we all assembled at the summit of the hill and enjoyed the grand sight of a sunset. Then the regiment formed in line and marched toward home, drum corps in front, and the whole school joined in singing and shouting. Another lunch at the inn, and then the march was taken up again. As we approached the city gates perfect order and silence were established, the ranks closed, and by degrees the companies grew smaller, as the boys would, singly or in small groups, leave the ranks, turn into side streets, and go home.

There was never a break or a lull. Every change proposed, every new move made, was so well suited to the occasion, that the whole day resembled a kaleidoscope of beautiful ideas and scenery. I have my well-founded doubts that Young America could pass a day as delightfully and profitably as these healthy German lads did.

The teachers remained together, following the invitation of the rector, and spent the evening at his house, partaking of his choicest vintage and indulging in social and professional talk. I can think of no day in all my professional life that so completely engrossed my attention as this one did.

10. The Star-Gazer.

I had the great pleasure of accompanying a class of boys to the observatory in D——, an institution which is under dif-

DÜSSELDORF (RHENISH PRUSSIA).

ferent management from that of the high-school of the city. Here the whole class, about twenty-four young men, received a lesson in finding the constellations—a lesson given by the astronomer, assisted by the teacher and the astronomer's amanuensis. The class was placed in a row on a veranda, and by means of an ingenious device all the students were enabled to find the stars and constellations instantly. Let me sketch the device. Its name is the stargazer.

It consists of a light rectangular frame, which is suspended by a cord from a cross-beam, a tree, or any other convenient place. There were six of these gazers in use. The astronomer would step behind the line of boys, and with the frame lifted to the height of his eye would look along one side of the frame till he had fixed his gaze on a particular star. A student would then look along the other parallel side of the frame and soon see precisely the same star *which appeared as the vanishing point of the two parallels*. The student would keep his eye on that star, the astronomer would retire, and another student take his place. In a few seconds the whole class looked at the same star; thereby a fixed point was gained from which entire constellations could be mapped out. Maps of the constellations were spread out on a table and were consulted.

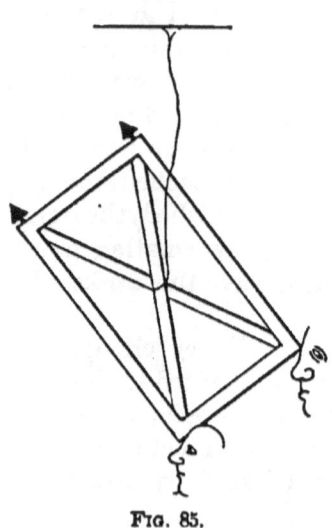

Fig. 85.

Now, the reader may perhaps think this of trifling importance, but it struck me as being worthy of mention on account of its simplicity. The device is also used by Dr. Lander, of Williamston, South Carolina, where I saw it first. I might have forgotten it had I not met with it here and seen its great usefulness for class instruction. Great minds think alike. I hope Dr. Lander will not take me to task for thus giving his invention to the public.

11. WHY SO FEW GERMANS CAN TALK ON THEIR FEET.

I attended a meeting which was held to celebrate the fiftieth birthday of a young ladies' school. It was a pompous affair indeed, but one which betrayed a failing in the German Government officers which could not and, I believe, would not be tolerated in America. There was a privy councilor, a high Government dignitary, who could not speak off-hand without breaking down before he reached the end of a sentence. Not one of his sentences was completed in the style or grammar in which it was begun. When at the close of his miserable speech he decorated the rector of the school with the insignia of the order of the Red Eagle, several gentlemen covered their amusement with an acute attack of violent coughing.

This speaker was followed by a school councilor, who spoke a little more fluently, but mumbling his words wofully, and the audience was heartily pleased when he retired. Then we heard the rector of a similar school and one of a boys' high-school speak. They conveyed the congratulations of sister institutions and dwelt at length upon educational questions.

Well, I must say these speeches caused me to compare the admirable readiness with which American teachers, and in fact average American citizens, speak in public and the awkwardness of these German speakers. They were not average teachers, but noted persons, men who had achieved a reputation in literature and are looked up to as leaders in educational affairs. Think of it that such men have an abiding influence upon the future of the male youth of the empire, young men who are called upon in future to guide the affairs of the state! Not one spark of that natural and graceful eloquence which is one of the characteristics of the public man in America was noticeable; no brilliant rhetoric, not even a commendable elocution.

However, comprehending everything means pardoning everything. The causes are apparent to the naked eye. No wonder our American citizens can talk fluently in public, having so many hundreds of opportunities offered them for public speaking and the practical training they get in their high-schools and even grammar-schools; and then remember that the German "citizen," or, more correctly speaking, the German "subject," has very few such chances and that oratory is not known among the studies of the high-school. Think also of the fact that English is a very easy language; it has no declensions to speak of, and its syntax is of the most primitive kind. In fine, you may build your sentences with unhewn stones; they will, singular as it may seem, always fit well together. In German it is necessary to hew every block before using it. A number of declensions and conjugations and a rather complicated syntax make speaking the language fluently very difficult.

But, despite all this, there are German orators of great talent. When I returned to my hotel I accompanied a lady, who spoke without reserve of this woful want of good speakers in the schools, saying, "If that's a sample of eloquence taught in the Boys' High-School, I don't wonder that the German Parliament is so tame an affair, and that so natural and volcanic an eloquence as that of Bismarck's crushes the men there as though they were mere reeds."

12. Class-Book of Progress.

Whatever you may think or say of the Germans, one thing is indisputable: they are excellent accountants. Systematic in their habits, even in trifling things, as they are, their success in business is not at all astonishing. This same systematic, thoughtful way of doing business may be seen in school. But the reader must not think that these born accountants keep many account-books. A German teacher has only two, or at most three books, which he keeps regularly and methodically. The first is the daily register of attendance; the second a "book of progress," and sometimes a journal is used to enter meritorious cases, or cases of punishment. It is the second book of which I wish to speak.

Each teacher keeps a "book of progress," which contains a broad, convenient column for each branch of study. After each lesson he enters a statement, couched in the fewest possible expressions, of what he did, not of what he meant to do, during the lesson. Let me copy a few items for the benefit of my readers, to show how well the accounts are kept, and with what little waste of time it is done:

GEOGRAPHY. *Teacher:* Mr. ——.

Oct. 17. Mountains of southern Germany, water-sheds and rivers.
" 18. Drainage of central Europe.
" 19. Importance of Rhine, Elba, Oder, Vistula, and Danube for commerce.
" 20. Commercial and industrial cities in central Europe.
" 21. States of Germany. Historical allusions.
" 22. Review.
" 24. Coast-line of Germany compared with that of England and other countries.
" 25. Historical allusions regarding Venice, Trieste, etc.
" 26. Political boundaries of southern Europe.
" 27. The course of the Danube, physical and political geography.
" 28. Review, etc., etc.

As I said, every branch of study is thus treated, and the teacher does not leave the class-room before he has posted up this day-book. This book is of use to himself inasmuch as it affords an easy reference to the ground gone over, and a most convenient means of control on the part of the superintendent. But the curse of our American schools, the daily marking of pupils, the keeping of a class record, the weekly, monthly term, and annual reports, these terrible—but no, there is no occasion to be bitter. Let me simply repeat that, aside from the daily register of attendance and the above-mentioned book of progress, no official accounts are kept.

Despite the absence of daily marking, I find the many pupils of a class in the graded schools more on a level than I ever found them in America. I can in no other way account for this than by the thorough professional training of the teachers, which is a *conditio sine qua non* of holding a position. Do not blame me for mentioning this so often. It can not be said too often, can not be emphasized too strongly.

13. Promote the Teachers with their Classes.

Many of my readers will have observed how detrimental it is to the progress of children that they have to change teachers often. Their mental growth is stunted, though every one of their teachers may be a good one. Before the new teacher has acquainted himself with the peculiarities of each pupil much valuable time is lost; many vital errors are committed, though unintentionally; many points of hostile contact are established, before he is aware of it. Even one new teacher for every year is too frequent a change, as was found by these thoughtful Germans. They hit upon a remedy which, I am glad to say, is in vogue also in America in a few places. It is this:

In the primary grades the teacher is promoted with his class. He steps into the next higher class with all the little ones prepared for promotion. When the second year is over, he takes that class into the third year's work, and in some cities even further up, into the fourth. After that he promotes his class into the intermediate school and steps down again to the new chart class which has just entered school. Here he begins another cycle of three or four years. In other words, he has the same pupils three or four years instead of one year.

The same order of procedure is followed in the next four years, or intermediate school. Here the teacher has his pupils for three years. In this department there is a deviation from the rule, namely, the principal is excluded from this rotary movement. He remains in charge of the highest grade always. I believe this is done to round off and polish the pupils' knowledge before they finish the course of study. It seems hardly necessary to enlarge upon the advantages connected with this practice. They are obvious to any observant witness, although I admit there are disadvantages connected with it, also. On an impartial scale, however, the advantages will outweigh the disadvantages. I am confident of that.

Note.—*Connection of Teacher and Pupils.*—In the "Journal of Education," of April 26th, Dr. L. R. Klemm points out the loss to children from frequent change of teachers, and considers how the change may be avoided. This very important question has not, I think, received the attention it deserves. Speaking of the only schools in which I have worked—viz., the English—I have no doubt that the progress of the cleverer boys is checked by the frequent and sometimes violent changes in methods of study as the pupil passes from teacher to teacher. An able or very hardworking boy will "get his remove" three times in the year; so no "formmaster" has the teaching of him for more than twelve or thirteen weeks. Does it not seem obvious that teacher and pupil are parted just when they are beginning to understand one another?

The Jesuits have, I believe, always adopted the plan recommended by Dr. Klemm. With them the personal influence of the teacher is considered of the highest importance, and the teacher has to make a careful study of the powers, the tastes, and the habits of each pupil. So teacher and pupil must keep together. The same method is common in the great Scotch schools, though without the same motive. This method, with some advantages, must have many drawbacks. In all schools there are, most likely, some weak masters. With us the harm done by this weakness is spread over a large area, but it would be the intellectual and perhaps the moral ruin of a boy to be handed over to such a teacher for the whole of his school life. And how can the same boys be taught together year after year, while the rate of progress of some of them is so much greater than that of others?

I am very glad Dr. Klemm has started the subject for discussion.

R. H. Quick.

Redhill, Surrey, England.

14. A School of Design.

Many months I spent in Germany, visiting schools almost exclusively. I passed through the fairest portions of the empire, through the Free Cities, Westphalia, Rhenish Prussia, Saxony, Thuringia, Brandenburg, etc.; even crossed the boundary into Holland and France, and studiously avoided visiting industrial schools or any other special schools. My first object was to see what could be seen in the elementary schools. Hundreds of schools, more than five hundred class-rooms and lessons I saw, many libraries, collections, school museums, and wherever I found a pearl I picked it up, deliberately appropriating it for the benefit of my American colleagues. I addressed German teachers' meetings, "culture clubs," and other societies, wrote down in leisure hours (sitting in hotel-lobbies, depots, or in my easy-chair of a furnished room) on the spur of the moment what I had seen during the day worth noting down. I wrote, sketched, drew, and copied—and now I am weary.

Though the work is very interesting and exciting, very absorbing, indeed, a holiday occupation such as my wildest dreams of happiness could not have pictured, I begin to believe in Goethe's words, " Nichts ist schwerer zu ertragen als eine Reihe von schoenen Tagen " (nothing is more difficult to endure than a number of fine days). Traveling from one city to another, following suggestions to this and that point in quest of improved teaching, and nowhere enjoying the rest which home alone can offer, I begin to feel as though I deserved a vacation. This I seek in visiting special schools, and, being aware of the commotion in our country caused by the attempt at ingrafting manual training upon the common school, I begin with industrial schools.

The first one of these schools at my disposal, and, as I am told, one of the best in the empire, is a *school of industrial art* (really called art-industry school, " Kunst-Gewerbe-Schule ") at D——. These institutions are a result of the fact that the Germans had recognized the superiority of other nations in the domain of industrial art. In Philadelphia (1876) they found themselves badly beaten by the French, by the Americans, and partly also by the Italians and Austrians. Heroically they set to work to win back the same position in industrial art which Germany had during the middle ages. With the revival in southern Germany of models of the middle ages, a burning desire was felt not to allow the trades to retrograde, but to give them a new impetus. This was found in better models and in more thorough instruction in the industrial arts.

Thus all the industrial occupations were placed on a higher level than heretofore. It was found that, with the enormous extension of machine labor, manual labor was liberated to better efforts and higher, nobler aims. The Government saw that the hands thus liberated by machine-power must be employed, and it did not hesitate a moment in founding schools which directed much of this idle power and talent into new channels. In all industrial centers of the empire schools of industrial art sprung up. They are found in Berlin, Cologne, Nuremberg, Düsseldorf, and many other places, chiefly in South Germany, Saxony, and Rhenish Prussia. These schools are maintained by communal (i. e., local district) and state funds.

While in the common schools manual occupation is introduced to offer the pupils a curriculum in which mental exertion is counterpoised by manual exertion, these *special schools* in Germany have a different object—*they are to perfect the boys in the trades after having gone through the common school*, and to give them that education which fits them to play leading *rôles* in industrial pursuits. The completion of a common-school education is a condition of admission. No pupil is admitted before he has completed his fourteenth year of age, and not even then unless he has entered a workshop as an apprentice or joined an industrial artist in his studio. In other words, he must be a *bona fide* artisan. Academic instruction is only offered in geometry because that branch is not in the course of the common school.

The Düsseldorf Industrial Art School is divided into two distinct departments—the *preparatory* and the *professional*. No pupil can enter the professional department who has not gone through a course in the preparatory department, though special talent will enable him to absolve it in a few months. He must submit to the rigid course which requires of him to pass through all the different preparatory exercises so that he may with wide-open eyes discover his calling and select his trade. In his preparatory class each student draws something of everything—designs for house-building and furniture, designs for gun-, lock-, and tool-smiths and other metalworkers, designs for machine-building and devices, for modeling in clay and wood-carving, for embossing and chasing, for decorative art and engraving, for glass and china painting, and Heaven knows what not.

There is a variety in this preparatory department which at first puzzles many a pupil; but soon he finds his favorite occupation if he had not previously developed a special liking. Toward the end of a year a pupil of this department usually has developed a very decided leaning in one direction, and the professors foster that by giving the pupil work to do that will help him on in his chosen specialty. The main object of this preparatory department is that the student test his strength in all directions and with the aid of the teachers' advice and mature judgment find his calling. It is a process not of natural but of deliberate selection.

Now the student is ready to enter the professional department. Sometimes a student is found to develop such a variety of talents that the professors are obliged to repress and curb him lest he should fritter away his strength in too many directions. I saw many exquisite achievements in the preparatory class; but one thing struck me as highly recommendable—*there was no copying done*. Copies were placed before the pupil; but they had to be reproduced on a larger or smaller scale. If a student is found copying, he is summarily dismissed. Let me say also that a boy who is absent without cause is dismissed without appeal. "We don't want any lazy-bones here," said the rector.

Most of the pupils of the preparatory department are apprentices who ply their trade after school hours; but when they enter the professional department they give up their work in the shop for three years, at least do not work in them steadily. Only models and designs drawn and calculated in school may be worked out in the home shops and brought to school. The school itself has no shops, except studios for wood-carving, modeling in clay and plaster, *repoussé* work, etching, engraving, chasing, and decorative painting. No manual labor in joining and carpentering, etc., is done in this school, but articles are made from models *in natura*, all done at home by the students and professors after designs furnished by the school. These models for joiner-work fill an entire room, and are very costly articles.

The professional department is divided into as many classes as there are trades which can be benefited by designs, the school being in reality a "school of design." I will enumerate the classes:

Class I. Furniture-building (joiner and carpenter work).
II. Architecture.
III. Metal-work (locksmith, armorer, and toolsmith).
IV. Decorative painting (fresco-painting and textile industry.
V. Figural drawing and painting.
VI. Ornamental modeling in clay and wax.
VII. Figural modeling.
VIII. Ornamental and figural wood-carving.
IX. Etching, embossing, and raising in metal.
X. Engraving and chasing (jeweler work).

And several classes of minor importance, chiefly subdivisions. Classes I, II, III embrace instruction in drawing and coloring designs which will further the industrial pursuits of carpenters, joiners, architects, armorers, gun- and locksmiths, etc. New designs are invented under guidance.

Models in "life-size" or in miniature are placed before the pupils. Class IV offers instruction in designing, drawing, and painting of decorations on the plane (surface decoration). Water-colors are used. This class is also frequented by landscape gardeners. Instruction in Class V is made very interesting. Attendance is obligatory for all the students, because the human figure is represented more or less in the work of all trades.

Instruction in Classes VI and VII is perhaps more highly developed here in Düsseldorf than elsewhere. Instruction in Class VIII has special reference to joiner's work, while that of Classes IX and X aims at imitating those costly and valuable drinking-vessels made during the middle ages, the manufacture of which was for a long time almost classed among the lost arts. No matter what class a student has chosen, he is obliged to take part in exercises in perspective drawing, in drawing from casts, and from the nude model. Every student is obliged to listen to a course in anatomy. Particularly talented students are permitted to join several classes.

The daily sessions are from eight to twelve, from two till six, and from seven till nine—total, ten hours. Only Sunday afternoon and evening are free. Tuition fees per annum are ten dollars in the preparatory class, fifteen dollars in the professional department, and five dollars extra for the evening lectures. The building, which was erected specially for the purpose, contains a very large museum of industrial arts, which is open to the students. In America we should consider this school an art-school, but not so here. An academy of fine arts is a totally different thing. While in this industrial art-school everything done is done with reference to industrial pursuits, the art-school confines itself to painting in oil and water-color and to sculpture.

I met a young man from Chicago in the Industrial School who was studying in the class of decorative painting and in the modeling class. He confided to me that he had gone through a similar school in America and then worked as fresco-painter. When he had earned a thousand dollars he had come to Germany and entered this school, confident that he could go through the entire course in half a year. "Well," said he, "I am at the beginning of my fourth half year now, and I am not nearly through yet. What a wonderland this Germany is!" he added, with a sigh.

I spent several hours in rummaging through the accumulated work of the students after having gone through all the classes, and was greatly pleased with what was accomplished. The rector, a young man of great force, told me that the secret of success of this school lay in the fact that the trustees engaged as professors in this institution only men who had proved incontestably that they were masters in their respective departments. "It is not a question of home talent with us, but of merit alone!"

CHAPTER IV.

ELBERFELD-BARMEN (RHENISH PRUSSIA).

1. Proper School Furniture.

In the city of Elberfeld I came across another proof of the careful consideration for the pupils on the part of the authorities such as is not often found in our country. I found a tin scale (see cut on next page) tacked to the door-post with its lower end just one metre above the floor. The pupils are measured frequently and rearranged on the seats with reference to their sizes. Children who measured 110 centimetres are placed on benches numbered VIII. If they measure 117 centimetres, they are placed on a bench a size larger, namely, No. VII, and so upward.

If this is done three or four times a year, each child will have a convenient seat, not too low and not too high. The benches in the schools of that city are all made by one firm, and furnished in accordance with the scale. Some people may consider this pedantic; but the scale being furnished gratis and the arrangement taking little time, there can be no objection to it. I remember with ever-vivid sensation the cramps in my legs and the pain in my back when I as a small boy had to sit on a high bench, my feet dangling and my body swaying, because I could find no convenient rest for the feet or back.

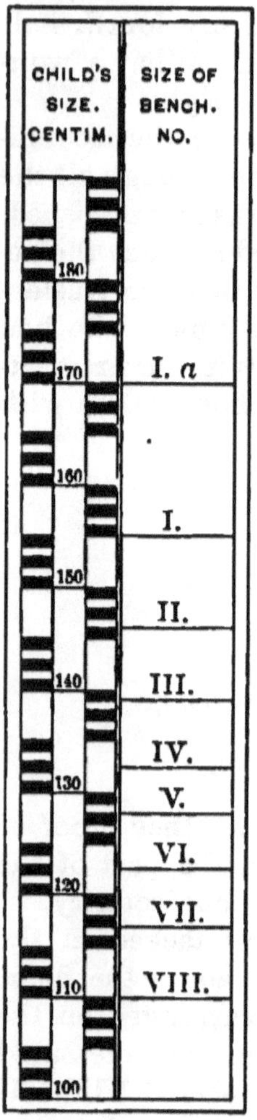

The men in the Board of Education who loftily dismiss any such proposition of the superintendent as changing the desk for hygienic purposes, ought to be condemned to pass a day on such a bench to get a taste of the inconvenience caused by improper furniture. But, then, the schools of some American cities are "governed" by the people for the benefit of political parties, and it is simply ridiculous to expect members of political school committees to consider hygienic principles so long as the question, "Which of the different manufacturers of desks uses most of my wares?" is uppermost in their minds. It is perhaps the very man who "sat down" on a motion of the superintendent to purchase more suitable desks who will, when he gets home, claim the most convenient arm-chair in the house, lean back in it, and tell his wife of the laborious duties of a school committee-man, and expatiate upon his saintly conduct as an immaculate servant of the people. *O tempora! O mores!*

CHILD'S SIZE. CENTIM.	SIZE OF BENCH. NO.
180	
170	I. *a*
160	I.
150	II.
140	III.
130	IV.
	V.
120	VI.
110	VII.
100	VIII.

FIG. 86.

2. THE FIRST REFORMED PARISH SCHOOL.

A historical spot of no mean importance is the school I visited in Elberfeld. During the time of the great Church Reformation this school was a parish school, and when the entire parish severed its connection with the Roman Church and joined the Protestants, this school, being property of the parish, changed its character and name also. Through all the vicissitudes of life during more than three hundred and fifty years the school has remained unchanged save in this, that it is now a city or communal school; but the city authorities are so respectful to the historical reputation of this school that they reserve for it the well-earned distinction of being called the First Reformed Parish School, while all other city schools are called people's or communal schools.

In front of the building, separated from it by a roadway, is an ancient church-yard in which rest the remains of the first Protestants, the first followers of Dr. Martin Luther in this place. From the windows of the front rooms may be seen the tower of the first Lutheran church in the valley, the first church in which the purified faith was preached. Though not a stone's-throw off stands a palatial new Catholic school, a proof of the fact that we live in a different century, this ancient parochial school has kept up its reputation as the best school in town; indeed, a day spent in different rooms of this quaint building convinced me of the powerful influence of historical reminiscences.

I heard a lesson in mathematical geography in the seventh grade (seventh from below), one in language in the sixth, in singing in the seventh, in composition in the sixth, in orthography in the fourth, in reading in the lowest grade, and must pronounce the teaching far superior to that of many other schools. This first reformed school seems to be on the road to reform yet. It protests energetically against all transmitted errors in teaching. The most advanced methods are applied. Thus, for instance, it does not teach to spell (to split words) for the sake of spelling, as is so frequently done in our schools, but teaches orthography (correct writing) chiefly through the sense of sight. This is done in a way which would give an orthodox schoolmaster (or schoolmistress, for that matter) the horrors or make his flesh creep. Let me state how it is done.

The children had read a piece containing a number of difficult words. The teacher ordered these words to be marked, picked out, and written on the board. They were carefully looked at and the difficulties they contained were pointed out. Then the teacher spelled (split) each word in succession. After that a mark was made where the word was divided or broken at the end of a line. Now they were used in new sentences, and some pupils dispatched to the board to write these short sentences. After this the teacher proceeded to erase the words of the lesson, and had them inserted again by other pupils.

After all this was done the entire work on the board was erased and the sentences were dictated. While the pupils wrote them, the teacher passed through the aisles and corrected instantly what errors were met by her sharp, searching eyes. After the work was done on the slates, the pupils were told to erase certain words (the new difficult words of the lesson) and to insert them again after spelling them aloud. Thus an hour was profitably spent in seeing, dividing, writing, erasing, and rewriting words, and the occupation this gave to the children was anything but tedious. Words thus learned in proper surroundings are reviewed next day by merely writing them in columns and using them in sentences orally only.

New words are also taken from the matter in geography, arithmetic, drawing, etc., not only from the reading matter. Words which the pupils should learn, though they are not contained in the reading matter, are purposely thrown at their feet, so that they must either stumble over them or pick them up. This is not done by presenting the pupils with strings of words promiscuously selected, but with their meaning in sentences, for instance, in connection with object-lessons, so that they appear as garments of ideas. They are thus organically connected with knowledge previously gained.

Or, to generalize, a word is not given to find a definition for it, but the thought and the definition are presented and a fitting word is found afterward. First, the object, the phenomenon, the quality, or whatever it may be, then the thought or idea is established, and for that a suitable word, a symbol, as it were, is formed. That word is then incorporated in the child's vocabulary and laid at anchor by seeing it and by writing it correctly. Of course, some words are learned otherwise, but I feel disinclined to state exceptions. What I am after is the rule.

This may seem pale theory to some teachers; but I assure them it takes less time to teach orthography in this way than to dictate incomprehensible words for the purpose of raising a plentiful crop of mistakes. Children loathe incomprehensible words. Spelling in the old-fashioned school was a separate study, and as such no doubt it was a beauty and a joy forever (?). To-day orthography is no separate study, but appears as component part of practice in written language.

3. A Separate School for Dullards.

A. *Object and Organization.*—In such industrial centers as Elberfeld, Barmen, Cologne, Gladbach, Crefeld, Essen, Düsseldorf, Solingen, Duisburg, Remscheid, and others in Rhenish Prussia, the percentage of idiots, deaf-mutes, and other kinds of Nature's step-children, is naturally greater than at places of similar importance in America, where the people do not live so close together. The number of these unfortunates is always smaller where better hygienic conditions admit of healthier life, and beautiful surroundings and the influence of art generate a more moral atmosphere; but it is not of the idiotic children, to wit, those who prove unable to be educated, of whom I will speak. The state and community take care of them in well-regulated institutions as generously as is done in America.

In every graded system of city schools there is a residue of weak-minded children who can not be counted among those unable to learn. In America such children are often repulsed and got rid of by fair or foul means, a thing that can not be done here, where a very severe law prescribes obligatory attendance. The school authorities here deserve the highest praise for not excluding these pariahs, but with infinite care bringing them within the pale of school influence.

Let me have it distinctly understood that I do not mean imbecile children, pronounced idiots, but intellectually weak ones, children who, though in possession of the organic five senses, are poorly endowed in perception, memory, reason, etc., and are therefore unfit to stay among normally endowed children, partly because they deserve a specially slow procedure on the part of the teacher, and are therefore a hindrance to the class; partly also because they are the laughing-stock of their brighter schoolmates, and in consequence of being ill treated lose the last spark of self-respect and ambition.

Here in the district of Düsseldorf, which has more big cities and industrial centers than any other Prussian provincial district, the idea has taken root that these mentally weak children ought to be taught separately, lest in the course of time they might become idiots, but chiefly for the purpose of freeing the common school of a dead weight which impedes its progress.

It was not easy to convince the school committee of the necessity of such a school, but a few of the superintendents took the matter in hand and urged its establishment with all available arguments. München-Gladbach and Elberfeld are the first cities in which such separate or special schools were established. Other cities, such as Cologne, Crefeld, Düsseldorf, followed suit, and in several others the establishment is contemplated, notably also in Basle, Switzerland.

A SEPARATE SCHOOL FOR DULLARDS. 79

Many prejudices of parents had to be overcome. When, some ten or twelve years ago, I urged a superintendent in Ohio to establish such a school, he answered me: "I have a good mind to single out the morally unsound and dangerous elements and put them into an ungraded school by themselves; but I hesitate to single out the dullards." I asked why. Said he, looking wise: "A father or mother is more easily persuaded that his or her boy is mischievous, wicked, and even vicious, than that he is too stupid to make the progress that his schoolmates make. Moral weakness may be attributed to street influence and bad example of others, but the accusation of mental weakness touches the parent to the quick." Similar difficulties had to be overcome here.

One of the rules under which this special school here in Elberfeld operates is that a child can only be admitted after it has attended a public school for two years, and during that time has given ample evidence of its inability to keep up with other children. These are the children that cause anxiety in family and school. They can not be promoted with their schoolmates, but lose courage and finally settle back into a state of hopeless indifference unless placed in the care of a teacher who is particularly well adapted to such work. These children are slow in perception, slower still in reasoning, wofully weak in memory; and their imagination, having been left without food in form of percepts and concepts, is stunted. They can not apply thoughts, and will remain helpless creatures unless special instruction is given them, which will, coupled with infinite patience, awaken thought, nourish the power of abstraction, train the power of application, and generally treat them as objects of tender care.

Some nine years ago a beginning was made here in Elberfeld with twenty-five pupils. A teacher who was remarkably well adapted for this kind of work was sent to special schools for idiots to learn the methods applied there. All desirable means of instruction were placed at his disposal, and the authorities with rare and commendable wisdom gave him free elbow-room—that is, did not hedge him in with a prescribed course of study. No object was fixed in view except to do the best that could be done under the circumstances. The selection of this teacher was a very happy one.

The trial of one year established the indisputable fact that these children were not hopeless cases, but that they could be taught and that they could learn. Some wealthy parents who had children with weak intellects observed the results of this effort and sent their backward children to this school. That removed the reputation of its being a school for outcasts. Poor, prejudiced people thought, "If Mr. Privy Councilor, and Mr. General Agent, and Mr. Banker, and such people, send their children to this school, it can't be a school for outcasts, and we will send ours"; and they did. Soon a second class was started, and the school graded in primary and intermediate class. Still better work could now be done and was done. At the beginning of the fourth or fifth year the opening of a third class was found necessary, and ever since the school has exercised a beneficial influence directly within its walls, and indirectly by freeing the other schools of impediments.

At present (November, 1887) this special school has very commodious quarters, and works according to a curriculum which has been developed slowly as circumstances would permit—a curriculum which is subject to changes as the nature of the pupils may dictate. There is no rigid requirement, no cast-iron rule. Course and method are as elastic and flexible as the individuality of the pupils make it necessary. Some pupils stay beyond the fourteenth year of age. Teachers and inspector keep an eye on those who have completed the course, and help them to enter life to carve out a future. The attendance at present is about ninety pupils in three rooms. If we consider that Elberfeld has one hundred and twenty thousand inhabitants, the number of ninety pupils in this special school is not exorbitant. In the next sections I shall describe the results and the methods observed.

B. *Results.*—It is obvious that this school must in no way be fettered down with rigid rules and regulations, or with a course of study prescribed in schools for normally endowed children. Though it has in due course of time been able to set down in writing what is possible and attainable, its only true guide is—try to attain what is within reach of the individual pupil. The teachers are obliged to change the course and the method frequently so as to adapt them to each individual pupil. If we consider that this school has hardly any models to go by except institutions for idiots, deaf-mutes, etc., and that this is literally a pioneer school, it is easily seen how great must be the difficulties that beset the path of its teachers.

I have, in all my wanderings through schools in America and Europe (and this is my twenty-fifth year of experience in the school-rooms), not found another set of teachers who can compare with these three in inquisitiveness and eagerness to gain information useful to them in their Sisyphus work. One of them told me that he had been sent to a school for deaf-mutes to study methods, and had noticed that, barring the one defect, the children there were normally endowed and had that inspiring desire to learn which flows from ambition. "But look at these young ones," said he; "there is no ambition. All we can awaken at first is a kind of dull or blunt interest in bright pictures. All abstraction is impossible. Many can not conceive of such numbers as 3, 5, 7, and it takes the patience of ten Jobs to 'generate' such concepts."

I find in use here some of Froebel's occupations; not all, but the simplest ones, and even these are modified. I find adapted here methods used in blind asylums, schools for deaf-mutes, and schools for idiots. Suggestions are taken from every source, and readily acknowledged. Of course, the school is not considered a model school of its kind, but I am confident it will be in time to come. Just as carefully as the mind is trained the other powers of the soul are attended to. The emotions, though sluggish, are stimulated; volition, in most cases entirely wanting, is awakened, not crushed; order and discipline are maintained, and thus the foundation is laid for a further development of the moral sense. The pupils' good qualities are lovingly nursed; their bad tendencies are repressed, not violently, yet firmly and consistently.

Pupils who have skill in manual occupations are specially trained in them, so that when they leave school at the age of fourteen years they may be apprenticed to some tradesman; and charitably the school keeps its hand over them for many a year to come until the children are either well enough advanced to carve out their own future or prove incapable of developing further what the school had awakened in them. In the latter cases the State is called upon to take the care, and it rarely hesitates. I have not the least doubt that some day a genius whose mental constitution differs vitally from that of normally endowed children will be found to deserve special treatment in such a special school and find it here. History tells of some such cases who became famous, not on account of their school education, but despite of it. They might have had proper training in such a special school for dullards. Nature is a very queer woman. Who knows but that some of these children may bloom out into full-fledged geniuses who will leave others behind them, astonishing the world with ideas not commonly conceived by the " normally endowed "? According to the established idea, a genius is an abnormally endowed person.

Up to May 1, 1885, thirty pupils were dismissed from this school and sent into the world. May I be permitted to give a few highly interesting statistical data?

I. Number of children who passed the examination for dismissal at fourteen years of age:

Upper Class.—Sixteen boys, six girls.
Lower Class.—Four boys, four girls.
Three were sent away or transferred who proved idiotic;

A SEPARATE SCHOOL FOR DULLARDS. 83

five were sent back who proved well enough endowed to get along in the common school; one moved away from town; one died. Total, forty.

II. Duration of attendance:

Two of these forty children attended this special school one year; three children one and a half years; one child two years; five children two and a half years; two children three years; one child three and a half years; five children four years; three children four and a half years; six children five years; two children five and a half years.

III. Results of the school:

Of the thirty who passed the examination twenty-three could *read* well with proper emphasis, seven only mechanically.

In *writing* seven could only copy; ten could write from memory and dictation; and thirteen could write short compositions, letters, bills, etc.

In *arithmetic* six children could only reckon within the circle of 1 to 20, three within 1 to 100, two within 1 to 200, seven within 1 to 1,000. Three worked with unlimited numbers, and eight succeeded in reckoning with denominate numbers readily and quickly. Only one child learned to work readily with fractions. The reader will please notice that these are results up to May, 1885. To-day the upper class works with fractions, both with common and decimal fractions, and does it well.

In *religion* instruction is given regularly, but only twenty-two of the above-mentioned thirty were admitted to the annual confirmation, three to the first communion, so that of five it must be said that they could not pass the examination in church and were set back.

IV. What became of the thirty children? The following carefully gathered facts will answer the question:

3 locksmiths,	1 clerk in a store,
1 house-painter,	1 messenger,
1 mason,	1 spool-worker,
1 tinsmith,	1 factory-hand (boy),

1 baker,   4 factory-hands (girls),
1 tailor,   6 servant-girls,
1 ribbon-weaver,   3 bodily weak, not working,
1 bookbinder,   3 still undecided.

In other words, twenty-four of the thirty have become useful members of society and possibly three more will be, while three are ill. This certainly is an admirable showing.

C. *The Methods pursued.*—The reader, I believe, will understand why I bestow much attention to this special school. It is something new; perhaps not new in theory, but certainly new in practice. A body of men and women who are looking for modern ideas and advanced methods in teaching must take cognizance of a trial like this, and hear a truthful account of the working of a school which to my mind is destined to cause a revolution in the organization of the entire common-school system in no far-distant time. Follow me, candid reader, and dismiss all prejudice. Let us enter this school for dullards. Rest assured, you will pick up a suggestion here and there which may be of value to you.

We enter the lowest grade. The children here are between eight and ten years of age, but as undeveloped as other children at four. They attended the common school two years, were found unable to learn by means of the methods pursued there, and are treated here with special care. A great number of preparatory exercises are needed which are deemed unnecessary in other schools. There they sit at a Kindergarten-table, nearly all bearing the unmistakable stamp of stupidity on their faces. Some are neatly dressed, being evidently children of wealthy parents; some are clothed raggedly. But the teachers insist upon cleanliness scrupulously. Some have fine features and skulls, but slobbering mouths; others are tall and well built, but have small and abnormal skulls; still others have beautifully chiseled features, but a dull stare in their eyes.

They are learning numbers. Before them lies a heap of pegs of ebony and boxwood about an inch long and half an inch thick. *Teacher.* "See what I do." (Taking three pegs in his hand and placing them in the groove of a frame such as is shown in the cut.) "Do as I do." Pupils take three, one takes four, another two, without seeing their error.

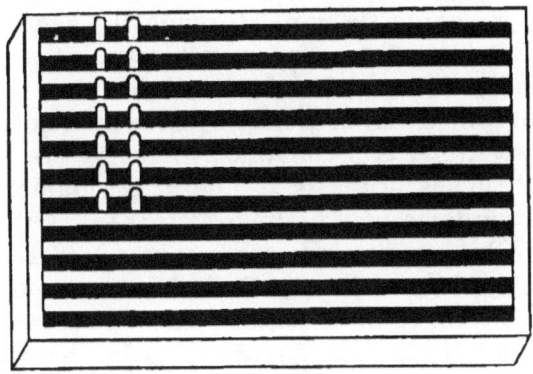

Fig. 87.

This exercise is continued. Its object is to take and set up as many as are shown. After the number has been recognized, the fingers are used in counting. Other objects are used for the same purpose. One little boy thought that *three* meant three pegs always. He could not see instantly that the number three might be applied to other objects. When a number has been recognized, counting it one at a time, of course, it is analyzed—that is, its component parts are found.

Teacher and pupils converse without restraint. Some of the pupils have to be urged to action, being apt to sit in dull contemplation of distant objects. While the teacher is thus busy with the beginners, the other division is working with numbers on their slates. These pupils work aloud, heedless of the disturbance they are causing—in fact, not knowing that they are noisy. The teacher tells us that it is useless to prohibit whispering and talking, simply because the pupils would forget the order, and it does not disturb him in the least, being occupied with the little ones in the farthest corner of the spacious room.

When the lesson is concluded the teacher shows us the means of exemplification he has in form of beans, peas, buttons, sticks, etc. A large cupboard is full of the most ingenious devices, nearly all well known to teachers who believe in approaching the mind through the avenues of the senses. This being the hour for arithmetic, we repair to the middle grade, where the Russian numeral frame is used, and here we find the children pondering over such questions as: "How many times is 9 contained in 28?" "Is 28 a table number?" (That means, Is 28 one of the numbers in the multiplication-table of 9?) "No." "What is the nearest below?" Child, beginning with 9, says, "9, 18, 27," and, ah yes, "9 is found three times in 28." "Is there nothing left if you take 9 from 28 three times?" Again a moment's hard thought and "No" is the answer. Again the whole work has to be repeated, till finally the complete answer comes, "9 is contained in 28 three times and 1 over." A look of joy brightens the child's face, and from the fairly beaming countenance of the teacher he reads his reward and falls back, to let some other child try his luck.

"How many times is 7 in 19?" A dead halt. "Nearly three times," comes the answer at last. "How many are wanting?" "Only two." "Then it isn't three times. How many times is it?" Again the child contracts its brow and studies. At last it says with the air of conviction, "Three times"; and again with Job-like patience the teacher goes over the same ground till the child gets the answer correctly. There is no prompting done by the teacher. All he does is to assist the child in thinking, and approach the mind through the avenues of the senses.

It was in this grade where I detected an error I had frequently heard in German schools. The teachers of this special school being almost faultless methodicians, I venture to mention the error, hoping that it will not be interpreted as hypercritical on my part. I heard the teacher ask, "Tell the ninth part of forty-eight." Answer, "Five and three over." The ninth part could only have been five and one third, for such parts are equal parts. But, fractional expressions being out of the question in this school, he ought to have asked, "How many times is nine contained in forty-eight?" However, this is trifling, and I almost blush for having mentioned it. In all the arithmetical exercises in the two lower grades I find that no abstract example is offered and solved. The pupils *see* the example first in objects as given by the teachers in balls, pegs, sticks, etc., then *do* it, handling the objects—that is, solving it in reality, and, lastly, *tell* about it. Every lesson in this school is a language-lesson.

The singing which followed was rather discordant and inharmonious; but it proved that the school attempts to awaken every latent talent in these children.

Then followed a lesson in biblical history. In the lowest grade this instruction is assisted by beautiful mounted pictures of great artistic value. The narrative under discussion was "Samuel and the High-Priest Eli." I did not enjoy this lesson as much as others, because I saw that these intellectually weak children were unable to imagine themselves back in the time of Eli. This lesson in its incongruity with the circumstances resembled a great bowlder on a smooth prairie. It had no business in this school, and was evidently a mere concession to the intensely religious sentiment of the town. Elberfeld, as is well known, is the stronghold of Protestantism in Rhenish Prussia.

One of the teachers stated that this day was an unlucky day, because the pupils were more than any other people under the influence of the moon, and the moon had just begun its first quarter. I had too often noticed this cause of disturbance in my own schools, to smile incredulously. As long as I had schools to supervise I nerved myself particularly at the time of the moon's first quarter, for invariably at that time pupils were referred to me for correction. The teachers seemed to be more irritable and the youngsters more perverse than at other times.

D. *Means of Instruction.*—" It seems that every thought in these children must be assisted by instruments to come to light," said the teacher. "We can not presuppose a stock of ideas in these children as may be done in other schools. We are obliged to begin in the most elementary way possible. Many of them can not even 'talk straight,' articulation being impaired. Here is a set of charts of simple pictures. See how we use them." Placing a chart on the easel before the class he says, "What is this?" Child, "Chow," giving the c a guttural sound. "No, child, say cow." Child, "Cow." "Again, cow, once more." "Tow." "No, child, look how I say it, cccow." "Chow." "Look again, Cow." Child, "Tow." "Try again, cow." Child, "Tow."

Turning to me the teacher said: "Notice that this is not perverseness, but want of volition. The child has no command over its vocal organs. Anna may say a word correctly ten times. All of a sudden she changes a sound and pronounces it incorrectly and perseveres in it." The charts used were twenty-four in number, each having some sixteen representations of objects, the names of which were arranged with regard to the difficulties offered by the phonic elements of which they were built.

Another set of charts or tablets in use was for the purpose of developing the sense of color. The tablets contained the different shades of color from the brightest hue to the faintest tint. Pieces of pasteboard colored similarly had to be laid on and matched in color. Some of these children did it very nicely, but others were found indifferent to finer shades of color, if not color-blind. A third set of pictures were used to illustrate zoölogy, another botany—that is to say, in other schools they might be used thus; here they could be employed only for the purpose of stimulating the children to talk a little.

Pictures illustrating the trades, the seasons, biblical history, Hey's fables, and geography, were shown. Most were very costly affairs, true masterpieces of art. "Why don't you hang them up and decorate these dreary walls with them? Would it not interest these children and quicken their imagination?" I asked. "My dear sir," was the reply, "every visitor asks me the same question, and invariably I answer, We must not dissipate the attention of these children, must concentrate it upon one point or nothing will be gained. If you could see with what patience we are obliged to proceed, you would understand how anxious we are to keep the children's minds bent upon one thing. Some things can not be comprehended at all, and must be acquired mechanically."

One shelf of the spacious cupboard was filled with a great number of little objects, such as bells, cubes, marbles, keys, bottles, and cheap playthings, each of which is there in duplicate. Specially dull pupils are asked to find a duplicate of an object shown him, and he sometimes hesitates before he decides which to take. After like things have been matched, the pupil is set to find others of the same class. Here the first attempt at generalization is made. Keys of different sizes and shapes are nevertheless all keys, etc. Building-blocks are used to match sizes.

During an articulation lesson I heard, a pupil was found to stutter seriously. He was told to breathe deep every time he had to answer a question. He did so, and it was successful. In order to prove to me that a deep breath taken before the mouth was opened for speech prevented stuttering, the teacher asked this boy several questions in quick succession, and the advice proved good always. Then I took the boy aside and conversed with him without giving him the sign to take a deep breath, and lo! the boy stuttered so that it was painful to behold.

(It may be said, in parenthesis, that the efficient school-inspector, Dr. Boodstein, contemplates the establishment of *a special school* here in Elberfeld *for children with defective speech.* He has recently issued a circular inquiring about the number of such cases in the common school, the kinds of defect, length of school attendance, and home conditions. This inquiry has special reference to stuttering children. Elberfeld is destined to become an educational Mecca if it perseveres in its laudable efforts at establishing separate schools. There is no danger of its going too far in this tendency, for the financial difficulties to be overcome are much too great, and most of these Prussian cities are deeply in debt.)

The children are induced to bring to school whatever gives them pleasure, and the little treasures are well treated and kept in the class museum. Some of these things require paper boxes to keep them in. These are made by the older pupils, who thus get a little practice in industrial pursuits. Lace-work, paper-folding, "figure-laying" (by means of little colored pieces of pasteboard), are done to keep the children busy and profitably engaged between lessons in reading, writing, arithmetic, and religion.

Drawing is hardly attempted; singing is very difficult. Very few of these children are musically inclined. Geography does not extend beyond the nearest hills, simply because this is a study which requires greater imaginative powers than these children possess; indeed, it may be said that in nothing are they so deficient as in the power of abstraction and imagination. The girls learn a little of needlework from the principal's wife, who comes at stated hours.

A form-lesson greatly interested me. I will merely state the results:

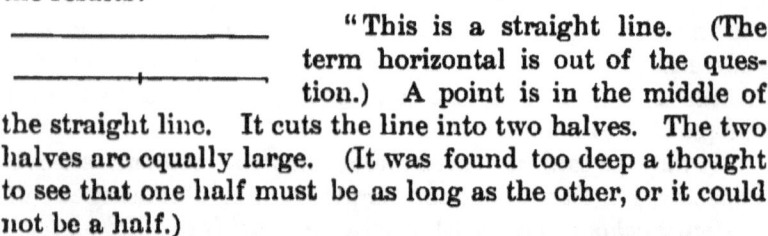

"This is a straight line. (The term horizontal is out of the question.) A point is in the middle of the straight line. It cuts the line into two halves. The two halves are equally large. (It was found too deep a thought to see that one half must be as long as the other, or it could not be a half.)

"There is a point on either end of the line. These are the end points. One point cuts the line into halves, and each half is cut into two equal parts.

"If these lines are lengthened, they will touch and cross each other. One is a slanting line. Oh, yes, both are straight lines. (It was a most laborious task to make the boys see that a straight line is the shortest distance between two points; but at last the truth seemed to dawn upon them.)

"A slanting line 'hits' the straight line. It does so below the line.

"A slanting line 'cuts' the straight line. It cuts it in the middle, etc."

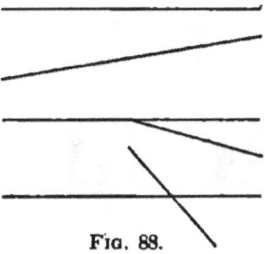

Fig. 88.

These are the results obtained by many minutes of patient questioning and applying the crayon. Many answers had to be corrected and polished before they could be accepted and repeated in chorus.

Verily, thought I, when I left this school for dullards, the patience of ten Jobs is needed to teach here, and that would not suffice sometimes. Not for any amount of money could I be persuaded to try my hand at such Sisyphus work; but all honor to those teachers who attempt what, as Schiller says, the gods do in vain, to wit, fight with stupidity.

4. A VERY PRACTICAL DEVICE.

A very animated discussion regarding the influence of school attendance upon the eye-sight of the pupils has been filling school journals and scientific magazines in Germany for a number of years. A similar discussion is now being carried on in America. It is a timely topic in America, where the evil influence of small type in text-books and of deficient light has been recognized promptly, although it had not been prevalent. Here in Germany the discussion was opened several years ago by Dr. H. Cohn, of Breslau, and has come nearer a final solution than the discussion in America, where some unripe opinions are still uttered and reverently listened to. I had no intention of entering into the discussion, nor have I now; but I must be true to my present vocation, that of a reporter. Dr. Cohn, of whom it

ELBERFELD-BARMEN (RHENISH PRUSSIA).

may be said that he was the instigator of the agitation, has made the most practical suggestions. His last and most practical of all, I believe, will be welcomed in America.

The suggestion has a truly American flavor about it. Its simplicity and practicability are obvious at the first glance.

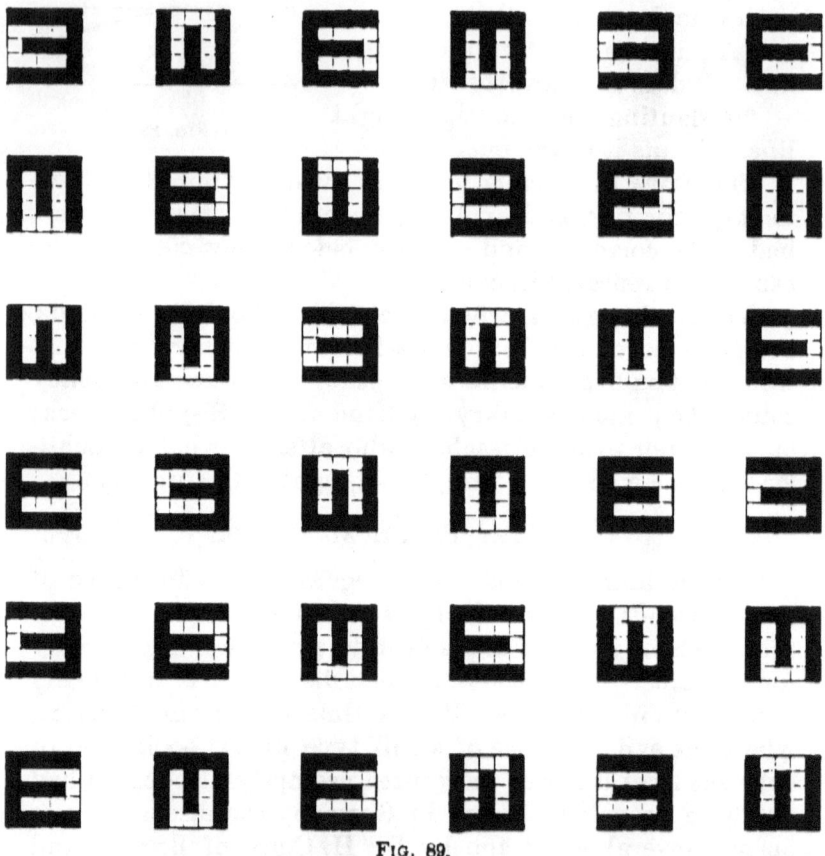

FIG. 89.

He has issued a tablet printed on cardboard, nine by nine inches, which has four brass loops, one on each side, so that it may be hung up on any of the four sides. This tablet is placed on the wall, near a window where the light will be

A VERY PRACTICAL DEVICE.   93

strong. Care is taken to hang it at an average height of the pupils' eyes. The tablet contains the following marks. I send them in their original size, as published by Dr. Cohn, for reproduction by an artist, and hope to see them copied in that size exactly, so that they may be used in the schools of America. I trust some enterprising publisher will reprint a separate edition on immaculate white Bristol cardboard, with a broad margin all around the thirty-six signs. I find the device in use here everywhere.

Tablet to Test the Vision of School-Children.—Dr. Cohn's instructions how to use the tablet:

1. The tablet is to be suspended on the wall near the window, on a level with the average pupil's eyes.

2. The pupil whose eyes are to be tested is placed at a distance of six metres (about six and a half yards). He is asked to state quickly in what direction the figures or signs are open, namely, *above* or *below*, on the *right* or *left* side.

3. All guessing or committing to memory may be prevented by turning the tablet, which is easily done, each side of the square being provided with a loop; or the order may be given to read the figures backward or downward or upward.

4. In order to test each eye separately, the pupil should be ordered to keep one eye closed.

5. *He who can read the thirty-six signs correctly in thirty seconds at a distance of six metres* possesses good eyes—that is, he has the strength of vision called *unity of vision: visus* $= \frac{6}{6} = 1$ (according to the authority of Snellen).

6. A pupil who can read them correctly at a distance of seven metres has a vision of $\frac{7}{6}$ strength; at nine metres, $\frac{9}{6}$ or $1\frac{1}{2}$; at twelve metres, $\frac{12}{6} = 2$, or double strength of vision.

7. He who can recognize the signs and read them aloud in thirty-six seconds at 5, 4, 3, 2, 1 metre has $\frac{5}{6}$, $\frac{4}{6}$ (or $\frac{2}{3}$), $\frac{3}{6}$ (or $\frac{1}{2}$), $\frac{2}{6}$ (or $\frac{1}{3}$), and $\frac{1}{6}$ strength of vision. In such cases a reliable optician will furnish suitable glasses for near-sightedness, being guided by these figures.

8. The weakest concave glasses with which the signs can be seen at a distance of six metres indicates the degree of near-sightedness. The strongest convex glasses with which they can be seen at a distance of six metres indicates the degree of far-sightedness.

9. If a pupil of normal vision (see section 5) can not see the writing on the blackboard at a distance of six metres, the light in the room is insufficient.

10. It is desirable to keep the tablet covered when not in use, to keep it clean. On cloudy or gloomy days it should be hung up or uncovered to test the strength of the light in the room, a pupil of normal sight being the tester at a distance of six metres.

CHAPTER V.

CREFELD (RHENISH PRUSSIA).

1. How English is taught in Germany.

For more than one reason I had studiously avoided teachers of languages; but, in a city where I was well acquainted with the principal of the gymnasium, I inquired about the present status of the method of teaching modern languages, and struck a rich field. I was ushered into a class-room where the boys of "Tertia" were taught English. The Tertia represents the eighth school year or the fourth in the high-school. The teacher had been a tutor in England, and spoke English very fluently. His method did not resemble the ancient Ollendorfian method, nor had it much in common with Sauveur's method. He proved once again that the truth is not found in extremes, but in the middle. It was a decidedly instructive and fruitful lesson. Let me give a meager outline of it:

A pupil told in English the historical anecdote of the Spartan mother who had two sons in the war. When a messenger came to her to announce that both her sons had been killed in the battle, she interrupted him, saying, "I want to know whether the battle was won by the Spartans." "It was," was the reply. "Then," exclaimed the mother, "I rejoice in the death of my sons who have died for the benefit of their country."

This anecdote was repeated several times in the pupils' own English. Errors were instantly corrected. Questions then followed, which caused a different construction of the sentences and idioms. While in the story, as told first, the sentence reads, "I want to know," variations now came, such as, "I wanted to know, I want to find out, I need to know, I do want to know, I shall want information," etc. "I rejoice in the death—" was changed to I am proud of, I am delighted with, I am glad that, etc.

Now, idiomatic expressions, such as, to be delighted *with*, glad *of*, to rejoice *in*, to be exultant *over*, were treated and similar cases looked up, as, for instance, *in* the fields, *in* the yard. After the idiomatic part of the story was finished, the story was repeated orally, and a greater smoothness and elegance of expression was noticeable in its rendition. Now followed a grammatical analysis of certain sentences, notably with reference to the position of the adverb. This part of the lesson was conducted partly on the board with diagrams.

The pupils' familiarity with Latin and German grammar enabled them to compare the rules of the language they were studying with those of others; indeed, they discovered and formulated rules in English grammar which will forever remain a book sealed with seven seals to our American children, who aim at a common English education only. Not that I think these grammar rules are needed to become a good citizen. I am far from claiming that. I only wish to emphasize that in rational instruction one branch of study should assist the other, as the grammar of one language did the study of another in this lesson.

After this exercise in syntax, one in etymology followed,

and here it was where the beautiful simplicity of the English language came to light, while in a discussion of the orthography its darkest spot was revealed.

After the anecdote mentioned above was thoroughly "squeezed" and nothing new could be gained from it any more, the boys were told to get their English readers. Their reading was fluent as their talk was comparatively correct; but the best and most notable feature of this whole lesson was that teacher and pupils conversed almost exclusively in English. Except where new rules had to be formulated, *English was the medium of instruction throughout.*

2. A Primary Lesson in Mensuration.

In one of the largest cities on the lower Rhine I was deeply impressed with the excellent work done in the schools. Nowhere had I seen such harmony between the different teachers and schools. Comparisons are odious; but from the bottom of my heart I wished to have friend B—— (my eternal opponent in the discussion of modern methods of teaching, and withal my dearest friend) with me to show him the results of rational application of the developing method. Among the lessons I heard was one in *measuring*. The pupils could not have been older than eleven or twelve years on an average. I will endeavor to sketch the lesson from notes taken on the spot.

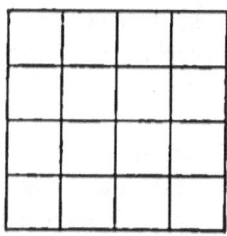

Fig. 90.

The teacher drew a square on the blackboard and divided it into four equal strips; then the strips into four equal parts each, as in the margin. During the entire lesson the pupils drew on their slates the same figures which they saw their teacher draw.

Teacher. "How many of these little squares are there in one row?"

Pupil. "There are four of them in one row."

The pupils always answered in complete sentences, but for

brevity's sake I will not repeat their complete answers. The lesson was one in drawing, arithmetic, and language.

Teacher. "How many of such rows?"

Pupil. "Four."

Teacher. "Have they all the same number of little squares?"

Pupil. "Yes."

Teacher. "Then if there are four in one row, and there being four of such rows, how many must there be in all?"

Pupil. "There must be four times four, or sixteen in all."

Teacher. "Suppose you turn the square so that the top is on the left side, could the measuring be done in the same way? Try it on the slates."

Pupil. "Yes, sir; it makes no difference which way I hold the square."

Teacher. "Now tell me how you measure this figure which is four inches each way."

Pupil. "If there are four inches on one side, it means that there are four square inches in a row; and, there being four of such rows, there must be four times four square inches, or sixteen square inches in the large square."

Other squares of different dimensions are drawn and measured in the same way.

Teacher. "Now measure this four-cornered figure" (Fig. 91).

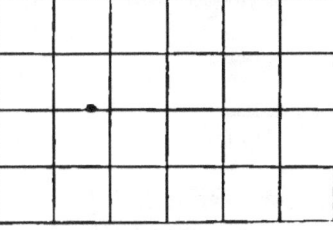

FIG. 91.

Pupil. "It has six square inches in a row and four of such rows; then it must measure four times six or twenty-four square inches."

Teacher. "Count them and see whether that is right."

Pupil. "It is."

Teacher. "Turn your slates so that the long sides of this figure are the side lines. How do you measure now?"

Pupil. "The same way, only that there are only four in the first row; but then there being six of such rows gives the same result. Four times six is equal to six times four."

Teacher. "Is it necessary every time to lay off the whole figure in little squares in order to measure it?"

Pupil. "No; all you would need to do is to measure two sides and multiply the two numbers."

Teacher. "Then let us do it."

Other parallelograms of different sizes are drawn and measured, the pupils rapidly sketched the figures, as the teacher did it on the board.

Teacher. "Let us go back to our first square. Draw a line across it from one corner to the opposite corner. What does that line do?"

Pupil. "It divides the square into two three-cornered figures or into two halves."

Teacher. "Well, if the square measured sixteen square inches, what will one of these triangles measure?"

Pupil. "Eight square inches."

Teacher. "Now, let us divide the square thus. (See figure in the margin and dividing line from left to right.) Is this kind of a half as large as the triangular half?"

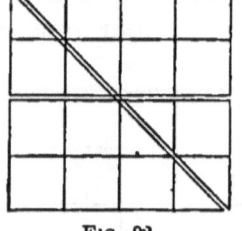

Fig. 92.

(Pupils hesitate.)

Teacher. "If your mother had a gingerbread cake of this shape, and you were told that you might take one half of it, how would you cut it?"

(Pupil indicates that he would cut it on the diagonal.)

Teacher. "Why thus?"

Pupil. "Because I can begin to eat it better."

(A ripple of laughter follows, but it causes no disorder: Proof that the pupils are quite at ease.)

Teacher. "Well, children, what kind of a half would be larger?"

Pupil. "They must be alike. A half can not be smaller or greater than the other half."

By going over the two figures the pupils soon see that it is immaterial which way the cut is made, and that the triangle measures one half of the square.

Now the diagonal is drawn through the parallelogram, and the same truth is discovered. Then follows the rule that such triangles are measured by multiplying the two sides of the rectangular figure and dividing the product by two.

Then the rhombus (Fig. 93) was drawn, and the pupils were told that multiplying the two sides would not do. The teacher demonstrated this in an ingenious way. He took an empty slate-frame (Fig. 21) and pressed it into the form of a rhomboid. When the pupils still doubt-

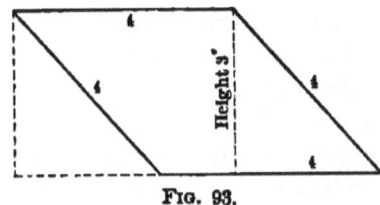

Fig. 93.

ed, he pressed it still more, so that the height was only one inch, and thus showed them that the area of a rhombus made of the four equal lines of a square was smaller than that of the square.

N. B.—No such technical terms as parallelogram, rhombus, etc., were used, except square and triangle.

The measuring of the rhombus was performed as the dotted lines in the figure indicate, and the rule, that it is

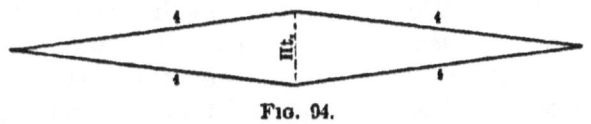

Fig. 94.

measured by multiplying one of the long sides by the height, fell like a ripe fruit from the tree of experience. Just then the bell rang and the class was dismissed. The teacher told me that next day he would take the trapezoid also. That, however, was as far as he cared to go with these young pupils.

General Walker's Echo in Germany.—Being asked why he refrained from using any technical terms, the teacher said: "No; we don't burden the memories of our pupils with technical terms such as trapezoid, rhomboid, parallelogram, parallelopipedon, etc. We call a rhomboid a four-cornered figure and are done with it. The child in the common school is no happier, nor wiser, nor better prepared for life when he has learned these Latin and Greek terms. If a boy enters a technical or a high school and studies geometry, the terms will be given him there. The common school has no business to burden its course with ballast."

Further conversation with the faculty of the school revealed the fact that they all entertained the same view which General Walker in Boston urged lately, namely, that the study of arithmetic had in the course of time become overburdened with matter of a nature unsuited for the pupils of a common school, and that efforts were being made everywhere in Germany to eliminate such things. Said the rector of the school, to whom the assistant teachers all looked up with great veneration, he being a fine-looking, white-haired man: "We sound the battle-cry, 'Elimination,' all along the line. We want to eliminate much from an overcrowded course of study in geography, grammar, and arithmetic, and add more literature and history so as to counteract the vicious influences of bad reading-matter smuggled into the hands of our pupils by, Heaven knows, unscrupulous publishers. We want to do more in manual training, more in the so-called accomplishments, drawing, music, etc., introduce a little of book-keeping, and thus make the common-school education what it ought to be—practical. *We want to teach less for oblivion* than hitherto."

I need not assure my readers how heartily I agreed with him. I felt quite at home among this earnest and enthusiastic body of teachers.

3. INDIVIDUALITY IN TEACHING.

During my frequent visits to schools here in Germany one fact claims my attention with greater force every day. It is the absence of that uniformity in methods so often noticeable in American city school systems. A school superintendent in America, if he be a man of strong principles, firm convictions, and practical experience in teaching, will often unintentionally impress his personal views, his own modes and manners of doing, upon his subordinates. Since the great majority of teachers in American cities are women who have no individual opinion on educational matters, but passively obey instructions without discriminating, and slavishly copy models given them, it is easily seen that the superintendent very often becomes the motive power, or at least the fly-wheel, of the whole machine, the soul and spirit of the entire corps of teachers (particularly of the "corpses"), the domineering character who fashions the instruction of his subordinates according to given patterns. Individuality is in the most perilous situation in such a "system."

No such thing is seen here in Germany. A most refreshing variety in methods is noticeable here, partly owing to the fact that every teacher has professional training, and partly owing to the absence of local supervision. This gives the teachers who are judged by their merits wide elbow-room. It is true, however, that more experimenting is going on here, and perhaps more waste of time and energy upon fruitless attempts; but I can not repress my astonishment at the solid results this great liberty of action has. The German school everywhere has at least one class-room in which an experimental station is established, where new ideas are nursed into full bloom. Germany has been from time immemorial a mine of information on subjects of educational theory and practice—a mine which to me appears inexhaustible.

My note-book is full of sketches and memoranda, and I

can scarcely find time enough to work them out and make them presentable. How it would cure a stiff-necked conservative American schoolmaster who believes in "keeping school, hearing recitation, setting tasks, assigning lessons," to come to these schools and study them as minutely as they deserve it! But, then, they are not English, you know.

4. French Pupils in German Schools.

Despite the bitter hatred Frenchmen entertain against Germany, they are fully alive to the superiority of the German schools and try to profit by them. It is now nearly ten years since the French national school authorities resolved upon a direct acknowledgment of that superiority by sending annually several graduates of French high-schools to attend the last two years of the course in German highschools. No indifferent material is sent, to be sure, but only boys who have won the first prizes. As I have stated elsewhere (in the article, "A Distinction with a Big Difference"), the German secondary schools are well adapted to talented pupils, while weaker ones are weeded out. These French boys, then, coming as they do like "picked nines," are not objected to by German school authorities. They say there is no reason whatever to refuse them admittance, inasmuch as they conduct themselves properly, and usually are a credit to the schools they attend.

These boys are directed to stay a half-year or a year at one school and then go to another. They are not allowed to stay two full years in one town, lest they might enter into ties too close to suit the French Government. They are directed to take board and lodging in private families, and to live exactly as the pupils of German gymnasiums do. The Government pays all expenses during their stay in Germany. At the close of each year the students are required to send in a report of what they experienced and of the manner in which they utilized their time. Of course, the frequent changes of schools and place of habitation are inconvenient, but they enable the young men to see a good deal of that country which ignorant Frenchmen before 1870 thought lay near the north pole!

I had opportunities to learn something of the contents of the reports sent home to the Minister of Instruction, and must confess that they are mostly true to life and tally with my own observations. Most of the young men are very much pleased with the reception they find among the people, the teachers, and fellow-pupils. They praise the delicacy and tact of their German hosts, a fact which the wounded spirit of Frenchmen is apt to appreciate. Some admit that the senseless agitation in France concerning "revenge for 1870" makes their stay in certain places unendurable. All, however, are loud in praising the instruction they get in school.

They are unanimous in saying that the German high-schools are far superior to the French lycées. Especially in mathematics, they think, the German schools prove superior. The way the students are made to work out problems in geometry, trigonometry, oral arithmetic, etc., the self-activity to which the pupils are led, and the independence and self-dependence in thinking, are commended. Instruction in the sciences also is thought superior to that in France. Particularly enthusiastic are the reports about gymnastic drill. This is not astonishing if we consider that the indulgent French youth is not drilled much at home in bodily exercises. An equal share of praise is given to the teaching of music. In referring to this the young Frenchmen speak with animation of the German songs, which they consider very melodious.

As far as instruction is concerned they have but one opinion; but they do not like the rigid discipline exercised in German high-schools. Why, they are not even permitted to smoke, not even in the sanctum sanctorum of their own bedrooms! The slightest deviation from the straight road of virtue is punished severely. They are "not treated as gentlemen," but "as boys," are obliged to doff their hats when they pass a teacher, and are generally treated as unripe youths. Though I can not myself like the rough treatment I noticed here and there, I must admit that the German teachers are consistent in regarding no school-boy a gentleman. However pretentious he may be, he is a minor, and as such can not lay claim to the dignities of a full-grown man. Of course, I full well understand that in a republic this is considered heresy; but we may admit the consistency practiced in German schools where the treatment of pupils is a reflection of the mode of government, monarchical government, in which respect for authority is "learned by doing."

In one particular the German high-schools find condemnation on the part of these French students. They say Germans pay less attention to show—that is, to legitimate show. For instance, they care naught for rhetorical polish, and their recitations are considered good when the essential facts are brought out correctly. The garment of thought is neglected. Their teaching of drawing also is less refined than that in France. This may be true in the high-schools, but I can testify to a wonderful improvement in drawing in the lower schools which has not reached the upper grades as yet. I trust, though, that in ten years that branch of the curriculum will be fully up to the French standard.

CHAPTER VI.

COLOGNE (RHENISH PRUSSIA).

1. CONSERVATISM AND LIBERALISM.

A SPECIAL and very politely worded invitation from the school authorities of Cologne led me once more to this famous city. Things worth reporting, though not in every case worth imitating, are going on here in the shadow of the finest cathedral in the world, a marvel of the middle ages which our nineteenth century was destined to complete. In order to fully comprehend what I shall say about the schools here, I must ask my patient readers to bear certain things in mind.

Consider, first, that this city has a past of nearly two thousand years, having been a German settlement before the Romans fortified the place in 59 B. C. Its name is a corruption of "Colonia Agrippina," as it was called by the Romans afterward in honor of the Empress Agrippina. In a city of that age there is naturally a dense mist of historical reminiscences to overcome. At every movement forward a huge mass of prejudices that have their roots in time-honored customs and laws must be removed. Effecting reforms here is very much more difficult than in American and even in other German cities. Goethe's words, "Es erben sich Gesetz und Rechte wie eine ewige Krankheit fort," are applicable here if anywhere.

Bear in mind also that recently the ancient fortress has been widened, that the old walls are torn down and new fortifications are erected a mile or more farther out, that all this new space is laid out according to the latest most approved styles of European city building and exquisite architecture. Consider the great influx of new elements to the community in consequence of this opening and the application of modern ideas which clash with ancient creeds and meek habits.

We have in all America no such interesting picture of conflict between conservatism and liberalism, no such turmoil of ancient and modern ideas, no such refreshing results of modern exertion side by side with moss-grown, decaying institutions. Though Cologne is the most devoutly Catholic town in Europe, and people here are honestly trying to be more Catholic than the Pope in Rome, yet they are the most light-hearted of all the gay Rhinelanders.

To live here a week with eyes wide open, to be conducted through schools of varied types and characters, through museums, galleries, old churches, new fortifications, dilapidated city gates, crooked lanes of houses built a thousand years ago, and hotels and residences of startling magnificence, new stores and factories only finished yesterday, through ancient crypts and modern zoölogical and botanical gardens, from statues of Bismarck and Moltke of bronze to those of questionable saints in crumbling sandstone—is like going through wonderland, or, to speak in terms of a modern writer, is a liberal education.

I am painfully aware that this is not a "practical" discourse. The American average teacher is supremely indifferent to impressions, and expects in a book like this ideas, suggestions, sketches, etc., all of which are to be immediately applicable in the school-room. I grieve over it, for I am sure I might furnish some readable matter; but I must come to the point. What I said in the foregoing paragraphs was necessary to set in relief what I shall say about the schools of Cologne.

2. INTERMEDIATE SCHOOLS.

The School Inspector of Cologne, Dr. Brandenberg, a most accomplished gentleman and an energetic leader, is engaged at present in reforming the organization of the schools. There are a number of schools here called "poor or free schools," being intended for and frequented by the poor; another number called "district schools," intended for the children of the middle class who can pay tuition fees. Now here in the stronghold of moss-backed conservatism the idea has gained strength that all the schools below the highschools should be made "common schools"; that tuition fees should be done away with; that the upper grades of an eight years' course should be made into what is known in America under the captivating but misleading name "grammar-schools."

Middle or intermediate schools is the name given them here. Among the cities I have seen so far, only Hamburg, Frankfort-on-the-Main, and Duisburg, have intermediate schools. That Cologne should take such a step from which so liberal-minded a city as Düsseldorf shrinks timidly is a proof of the go-aheadness of the citizens of Cologne. It reminds me of the man who heroically pulled himself out of the mire by his own cue.

3. Preparatory School for Teachers.

Another praiseworthy step, and, I believe, one worthy of imitation, is the establishment of a school for boys called preparatory school. Boys and young men who intend to become teachers and to enter one of the royal normal schools (of which there are more than a dozen in the province) are invited to go through a regular course of training in this school. This course lasts three or four years. The students here get thorough academic instruction, and are trained in music, drawing, manual occupations, and gymnastics. Pedagogics and didactics are not taught. These branches are left to the normal school with its three years' course and its practice department.

I was curious to see the working of this preparatory school, and was much pleased to meet there the principal of one of the royal normal schools who had come on his tour of inspection to examine the students. There was a great diversity in age and accomplishments among the boys, some having come from higher schools, others from the people's school; some being fifteen, others eighteen years of age.

I heard a music-lesson, one in the theory of music, and practice on the violin. This instruction was very successful, for the solos and quartets which these boys played were very acceptable performances. No ancient or foreign language is taught in either preparatory or normal school, though the teachers admit that it would have a good effect upon the mother-tongue if the students could take up the study of a foreign language for comparison's sake, if for no other purpose.

A geography-lesson I heard was another indication of the thorough preparation the boys get here. All the matter given was offered in a style and in doses which would indicate how such matters might be presented to other pupils. Though no pedagogical principles were preached, they were practiced. Then followed a grammar-lesson which would have pleased even an Alexander Bain. I intend to sketch this lesson in a subsequent chapter. Now, think that after the students have finished this course they are expected to go through a regular course of three years in a normal school! No wonder Prussia has good teachers!

The principal of the normal school who had come to inspect the institution was a rather irritable man, who after the boys were dismissed criticised the teachers severely; indeed, as I thought, much too severely, harping on trifles and overlooking decided merits. But so well were the teachers disciplined by having served in the army, that they did not change a muscle in their faces while this tirade against trifles was poured over them. No American teacher would have stood this unjust criticism without at least claiming "*audi alteram partem*." I could not help feeling sympathy for one of the teachers, who evidently felt the gross injustice of being thus treated in the presence of a guest. I turned away.

4. FEMALE TEACHERS' SEMINARY.

In another direction Cologne offers an example worthy of imitation. If I am informed correctly, royal normal schools in Prussia do not admit women. Young ladies who desire to become teachers must get their professional education in a private way as well as they can afford; but the Government examines them "just the same"—that is, subjects them to the same rigid and searching examinations as the students of the normal schools. This, it seems to me, is a glaring injustice perpetrated by the state. The city of Cologne is wiser than the state. It has established a normal school of its own for young ladies. The school has a course of four years, and very creditable work is done there, as I hope to show in my next letter.

This school is conducted by the school inspector (or superintendent) himself, who spends an hour a day teaching psychology, logic, and history of education. The first two years are entirely given to academic studies; the third is devoted to theory and practice as well as academic studies; the fourth year is almost exclusively devoted to psychology and experimental teaching. I listened to a lesson in history given by a young lady to a fourth-grade class of girls (the A Primary). Don't shake your head, fair reader; they begin history early in German schools.

Queen Louisa, of Prussia, the mother of Emperor William, was the subject. The following was the rather limited amount of historical facts offered and learned, but they were learned well: "Our present emperor and King of Prussia was born in the same year in which his father became king. The father's name was Frederick William III. The mother's name was Louisa. She was and is still considered the most beautiful queen who ever graced a throne. She was very kind and lovable, disliked pompous court festivals, and devoted her time to her family. Queen Louisa was passionately fond of her sons, the elder of which was Frederick William, who afterward became King of Prussia and died in 1861. The second son was William, who followed his brother on the throne. When the boys were still young the queen wrote to her father one day, 'If I am not very much mistaken, William will be like his father, simple in his habits, true, faithful, straightforward, and sensible.' Indeed, if ever a mother prophesied right, it was Louisa when she wrote these words. When Prussia broke down under the strokes of Napoleon, Louisa had to flee to the extreme eastern end of the kingdom. She comforted her family, completed the education of her two elder sons, and died of a broken heart. Her husband redeemed the old glory of his kingdom when he entered Paris at the head of his victorious army side by side with the Emperors of Russia and Austria, and her beloved son William defeated another Napoleon even more disastrously than his father had done. The Prussian people can never forget that their beautiful Queen Louisa had been personally insulted by Napoleon I."

I give these results only. They may sound rather like

Byzantinism in America; but let us be just and acknowledge that a biography of Martha Washington would be flavored similarly in our schools. "To comprehend everything means to pardon everything." The mode of presenting this historical matter was crude; but the young lady showed that she knew the principles of method, and a teacher who knows them is sure to gain skill.

I also heard lessons given by the professors in mathematical geography. Never did I enjoy as keen a logical train of thoughts in a girls' school as was deduced here; never in a college did I observe better results, or greater diligence either. The most delightful thing I saw here was the course of instruction these young ladies get in industrial occupation, such as drawing, knitting, crocheting, embroidering, sewing, mending, and patching. I shall make that the subject of a special chapter.

A teachers' library of several thousand professional books on general pedagogics, on psychology, on didactics, on methods, on history of education, on special branches of study, etc., graces this seminary. The library is open to all the teachers of the city, and is used frequently. One spacious room is filled with physical, chemical, anatomical, geometrical, etc., apparatus and preparations, and all were in exquisite order, though they are used every day.

5. Special Instruction to Teachers.

One would think that teachers who have enjoyed so thorough a professional preparation as I indicated on page 37, and who have passed all the severe examinations prescribed and conducted by the Government, would be left alone to secure their own success in the class-room ; but far from it. By governmental decree the course in drawing had been changed recently, prescribing that ornamental drawing should be brought into close connection with female home industry. Forthwith the women teachers were called together to spend an evening twice a week in going through a special course in ornamental drawing. It is true this course is free of charge; but think of the hardship of coming from their distant homes after dark to attend lessons, and late, at nine o'clock, go home perhaps unattended! This course is to last all through the winter.

Another governmental order had come making gymnastics an obligatory exercise in a certain grade of schools where it had not been heretofore. Some of the old teachers were not prepared to conduct these exercises. Forthwith the city provided for a special course in gymnastics under the direction of the inspector of gymnastics; and the astonishing fact is that these teachers come and spend their evenings for several months to learn exercises on the horizontal bars, the rope, the parallel bars, the leap-rope, the iron rod, the dumb-bells, etc. Take it all in all, there is a devotion to professional duty here in this modern German Empire which it is gratifying to behold.

When, in the presence of the school inspector, I expressed my astonishment at the munificence the city authorities show in favor of professional training, he said: "Yes, sir, these things may seem strange in the shadow of those ancient churches ; but don't forget that that wonderful cathedral lay unfinished for centuries until our energetic nineteenth century took the matter in hand and finished it. It is so in everything. Side by side with the most intolerable reactionary endeavors our city exhibits the truly heroic spirit of the modern age. Every street here with its modern palaces and old crumbling houses is an example of the dualism of Cologne's institutions. God be devoutly thanked for it that sound modern doctrines take the upper hand in all matters pertaining to the schools. The re-establishment of the German Empire has had a rejuvenating effect upon many institutions, but none has been more benefited by it than the school. Our horizon is wider, our former dream-life has taken a practical turn, and, take it all in all, *we now live a life worth living.*"

6. Two Conveniences.

Here in Cologne I find in general use a kind of wooden blackboard of excellent finish which consists of two leaves hanging on hinges. They can be closed like the leaves of a book. If closed, the board presents only one side; but the two (or three) leaves can be turned easily, so that all four (or six) sides may be used. If the teacher wishes to preserve the sketch of a lesson or illustrations, etc., he can do so by turning the "leaf." For the convenience of smaller pupils the board (or boards) may be lowered, it being set

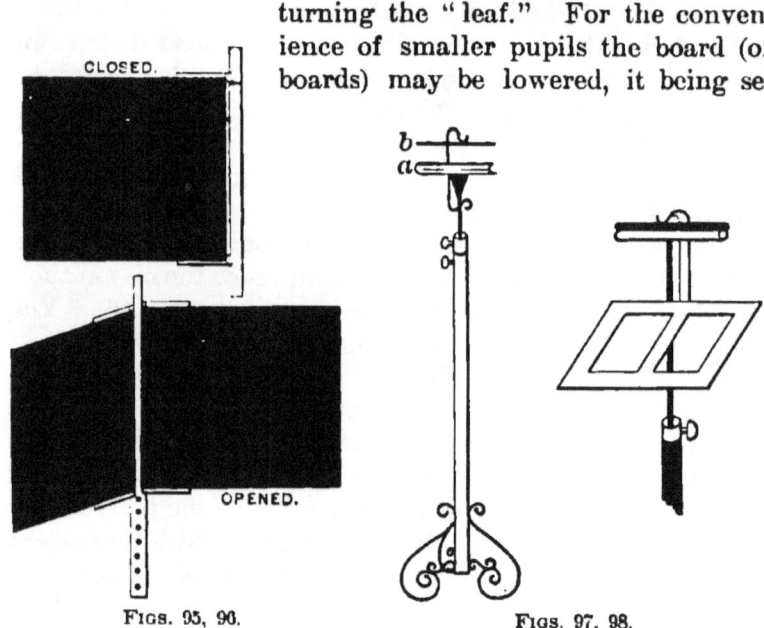

Figs. 95, 96.   Figs. 97, 98.

into a groove and held by an iron pin. This contrivance can be made cheaply, and its great practicability led me to sketch it (Figs. 95, 96).

Another convenient apparatus is a map-stand which can serve several purposes. The upper rod of a wall map is laid into the trough marked a, then a spring in the back is touched and the rod marked b is lowered and presses on the map-rod, thus holding the map securely. The map may be raised to any height one wishes, and can be placed so as to avoid a glare from direct sunlight. Reading, music, and number charts, copies for drawing, etc., can be suspended by the hook without further adjustment. A music-holder may be attached to the stand also. The whole is made of rod steel, and is light enough to transport it easily. I trust some enterprising American firm will profit by the suggestion this sketch offers (Figs. 97, 98).

7. A Lesson in Physics.

It was a grade corresponding to our sixth school year, or second year Grammar, where I listened to an interesting lesson in physics. Optics was the subject. Of course, it would be carrying owls to Athens to repeat the lesson in a book published in America, a country where natural philosophy is taught so well; only I wish to call attention to the fact that it was in a class of the sixth school year, not a high-school, where I heard the lesson.

As we can easily imagine, the teacher proceeded by means of objective teaching and used experiments and illustrations which lay near at hand; as, for instance, when he brought up the question why the sky was blue, he did not, as many a better teacher might have done, explain this by referring to facts of which it was reasonable to suppose that they were known; but, knowing the kind of pupils he had to deal with, he held up a clear pane of glass and placed it against the window. Then he added several more panes, till about a dozen of them stood upon edge, one in front of another. Now he gave the pupils time to deduce the truth from the fact before their eyes. It was literally impossible to see through these twelve or more panes of glass. From that fact to the other, namely, the want of transparency of the great cloak of atmosphere surrounding the earth, was easy. The color in the glass led them on to find the cause of the color of the sky. It was a fine way of teaching, making knowledge experience, to be sure.

Another very taking illustration was suggested by the

question how the color of the evening red was produced. The room was darkened, a light and the janitor's steaming tea-kettle were brought in, and again the boys saw the truth, which was crude as yet and had to be refined by means of leading questions and much critical analysis; but the *beginning* of the truth had been discovered without telling it to or imposing it upon the pupils. When the teacher asked how it came that we saw the morning red much less frequently than the evening red, his face did not betray the fun; but the boys inferred from his question that the morning red occurred less frequently than the evening red. It was a poser. At last a small boy, who must have noticed my smile, suggested that the reason was simply because we lay in bed too late to notice it. What a revelation and what fun!

Let me add briefly but emphatically that no text-book was used, neither had the teacher one in his hand, nor were the pupils required to purchase any. When the lesson was closed, the home task was given out to write a composition on what they had just heard and learned. I venture to believe that the boys had something to say.

8. A Lesson in Grammar.

The lesson in grammar which I promised to sketch (see page 108) treated syntax and as much of etymology as could be touched conveniently without leading the pupils astray. A simple sentence was taken, such as "*Father called.*" First the essential elements of the sentence, subject, and predicate were mentioned.

Teacher. "What question does father answer to?"

Answer. "To the question, Who called?"

Teacher. "If I say father came, would the question be the same?"

Answer. "No, sir; it would be, Who came?"

Teacher. "Is not the interrogative, the questioning word *who*, the same in both questions?"

Answer. "Yes, and that word is always answered by the subject?"

Teacher. "We will note this in the corner of our blackboard thus: Subject answers to the question who? But is that the only question the subject may answer?"

Answer. "If the subject is an animal or inanimate thing, we can not ask *who* does this or that, but must say *what* does? As, for instance, the water bubbles. What bubbles? We can therefore add the word what to the rule, so that it reads, *Subject answers to the questions Who or What?*" (Teacher does so.)

Teacher. "Why do you say who *or* what? Why not who *and* what?"

Answer. "Because it can not do both; it can only do one of the two."

Teacher. "Are there any other questions to which the subject of a sentence may answer? Let us see. Open your readers on page 17. Read, John."

John reads: "The sun shines. Sun, the subject, answers to *what* shines?"

Fred reads: "The physician hurried to the spot. Here the subject answers to the question *Who?*"

Other sentences are looked up. All the pupils agree that who and what are the only questions to which a subject may answer.

Teacher. "Then we have found a means by which we are able to detect the subject of any sentence."

Pupils are then led to state that the nominative case is the Who or What case, and that the subject is invariably in that case. A note is made of the fact.

Teacher. "To what question does the predicate give an answer?"

Answer. "It answers to the question, What did father do?"

Teacher notes in the corner of the board: "Predicate answers to *What does* or *did do?* Are there any other questions to which a predicate may give answer?"

Answer, after a few leading questions: "Yes, it may answer to the question *What is?* as for instance in this sentence: My father is a carpenter."

Teacher. "Well, we will make a note of that, too. Any other question."

Answer, after some searching : "Yes, it may answer to *How is ?* as for instance in the sentences, My father is well; the violet is fragrant; the door is open."

Teacher. "To prevent loss of time by useless searching, let me say that these three questions—(1) What does, (2) What is, and (3) How is ?—are the only ones a predicate can answer. Such questions as, What did, or has done, or will do, etc., are only variations of what does, being merely changes in the tense or mood of the verb."

Pupil. "Do I understand you to mean that the question What does ? is always answered by a predicate consisting of a verb ?"

Teacher. "Yes, my boy, I meant to come to that. Now, having found that much yourself, tell me of what the predicate must consist, if it answers to What is, and to How is ?"

Answer. "A noun and an adjective."

Teacher. "In what case must the predicate noun be ?"

Answer. "In the nominative, because it answers to what ?"

Teacher. "Then we have a new rule. What is it ?"

Answer. "That the predicate noun, like the subject noun, is in the nominative case." This is verified by examples.

Teacher. "Change the sentence, The emperor is William, so that the predicate becomes the subject, thus, William is the emperor; are the cases the same as before ?"

Answer. "Indeed, they are." Several other sentences are thus twisted, and the rule is confirmed and noted down.

Teacher. "Let us see: some one said that the predicate is an adjective when it answers to How is ? Is blue an adjective ?"

Answer. "Yes, sir."

Teacher. "Then the rule, I am afraid, does not hold good. I may say, My favorite color is blue. Blue here answers to What, not to How."

Answer. "In this case blue is not an adjective, it is a noun."

Pupil adds with some satisfaction : " I believe you may leave that rule as it is; it is well enough."

Teacher, laughing: " As you please. Let us go on. Our original sentence may be enlarged by saying, John's father called, or my father called; what addition do I make ? "

Answer. " You state *Whose* father called."

Teacher. " Does this in any way limit or modify the predicate ? "

Answer. " No, it modifies the subject and states definitely whose father called."

Leading questions reveal the truth that *John's* and *my* are attributive elements, or, briefly stated, attributes.

Teacher. " Can you think of any other attributes which are not nouns like *John's* in the possessive case, or possessive pronouns* like *my* ? "

Answer. " We might further limit the subject by saying, My *old* father called. *Old* answers to the question *What kind of* ? "

Teacher. " Find the attribute in this sentence, The cathedral of Cologne took six hundred years to build."

Answer. " Of Cologne is the attribute. It answers to the question *Which* cathedral ? "

Teacher. " Then we will note down, attributes answer to the questions *Whose* ? *What kind of* ? *Which* ? " (The teacher confided to me afterward that in the next course he would further enlarge this topic by drawing in cases of apposition.)

Teacher. "Now, if you had a long sentence, such as, ' Yesterday at eight o'clock in the morning the sixty-ninth regiment of the Prussian army marched through our town with waving banner and a brass band,' how would you find out the subject, predicate, and attributes ? "

Now followed an application of the tests which had been learned. Other sentences were treated likewise, and the rule was put to the proof in many ways.

---

* My readers must not forget that this was a lesson in German grammar.

A statement was formulated which fixed the fact that an attribute answering to whose? and consisting of a noun, must be in the genitive case. Also another, that an attribute may consist of a noun in the dative being dependent upon a preposition governing that case. But all such considerations must be left out here in view of the fact that I write for people who speak an almost grammarless tongue, according to Superintendent Sill. I will do justice to the teacher by saying that he did not once forget his end in view.

Teacher. "Suppose, now, that we enlarge our sentence still further, so that it reads, 'John's old father called the dog.' What shall we call this new element?"

Now followed a statement as to the questions which objects may answer; in what case they are found; of what words they may consist. My readers may imagine, with the aid of the foregoing, how this part of the lesson was conducted.

Then followed a similar consideration of the adverbial elements, and that brought the lesson to a close. At the end of the lesson the blackboard contained these notes, which were copied by the boys:

I. *Subject* answers to *Who* or *What?* always nominative.

II. *Predicate* answers *What does? What is?* or *How is?* if a noun—always nominative.

III. *Attribute* answers to *Whose? What kind? Which?* If a noun—possessive, or with a preposition which governs its case.

IV. *Object* answers to *Whom* or *To Whom? What* or *To What?* In answer to the first—dative; in answer to the second, accusative case.

V. *Adverbial* answers to [(a) Time]: *When? Since When?* and *How long?* It states present, past, or future of an action. [(b) Place]: *Where? Whither? Whence?* [(c) Condition]: *How?* Degree, intensity, and other adverbials were omitted for want of time. [(d) Cause]: *Why? What for?*

The home lesson given out was to furnish a sentence from

the history or reader which would illustrate those rules. For a lesson to beginners in grammar it was a very fruitful lesson—indeed, rather too fruitful, as I suspect; that is, it offered too much for one lesson. "Less would have been more," I believe. Still, I must say I enjoyed it, and the boys did so, too ; that was obvious.

9. Girls' Industrial Education.

I. Every city I have visited here in Germany, has its own local flavor, its own peculiar bias caused by its history. A German city can not shake itself free from its reminiscences and strike out into new domains of human exertion. It is commonly thought that America has cause for congratulation because it has no ruins and no history. But the opposite idea is worth defending. The inhabitant of Cologne, for instance, though he be a beggar, resembles the descendant of an ancient family, while the most respected citizen of one of the Western mushroom cities in America is like unto the man who " has no grandfather."

While thus it would seem as though I envied the fate of a Neapolitan, or Cologne, or Parisian beggar, I beg to state emphatically that for myself I prefer the fate of that highly respected citizen in yonder Western mushroom settlement, for reasons too obvious to mention. But my individual predilection, and your fancy, my dear reader, are not questions to be considered here. I mean to show in this letter that a glorious city history dating back through the middle ages, and farther back into antiquity, must of necessity influence school legislation, and the action of executive officers and teachers of such a city. Even if it be desirable to free instruction of all such influence (which would be heresy), the very stones here in Cologne would speak out and protest.

Imagine yourself back in the middle ages, and think of the exquisite altar-covers, embroidered by the wives and daughters of the famous citizens of Cologne. Think of the splendid garments with which they used to adorn their saints in church and home. Think of the splendor of silken gowns of bright colors worn during the middle ages. Think of the costly points and laces of those times, and of the knitted jackets worn by the men under their armor. Think of the close confinement of the women formerly, and their endeavors to beautify and adorn homes in their own inimitable way, and then bear in mind that these ancient customs are traceable in the churches, in the museums, in public and private houses of Cologne, even to this day.

It stands to reason that among such surroundings female manual occupations are considered at par in importance with intellectual training. And though, under the high pressure of our "modern age of ready-made clothing," the ideals, customs, and laws of Cologne have changed, we still perceive their influence. There is a *causal nexus* between the past and the present which, though subtle and indefinable, is none the less strong and determinate.

Thus we see the women teachers of Cologne teaching the girls knitting, crocheting, embroidery, weaving, sewing, lace-making, mending, and patching not only as I saw it done in other cities—that is, in a sort of practical crazy-quilt fashion, but under the direct influence of beautiful models and according to the best pedagogical principles and methods. With mute astonishment I followed them (teachers and students of the girls' teachers' seminary) through their "stores." A whole, good-sized room was filled with things finished in one year's course. Every object was neatly wrapped and labeled with the pupil's name, and the dates at which it was begun and finished. Everything was scrupulously clean. This exhibition proved the admirable methodical skill of the teachers, to say little, and the profound wisdom of him who had framed the course so as to bring this department to so high a degree of perfection.

Although I can, under high pressure of necessity, sew on buttons which will *stay on*, and mend a seam, I am afraid of betraying a woful ignorance with woman's accomplishments if I attempt to sketch the course laid down and carried out. I will therefore merely say that the course begins with knitting with two needles a broad strap about a foot long. On this strap are taught the various stitches—plain, double, reversed, etc. This is the work of the first year's course. The course begins in the second school year at the age of seven. It ends within six years with embroidery, lace-making, and sewing shirts, chemises, and artistic bedclothing. It includes a complete garniture of tidies, embroidery of letters, point-lace-making, and thorough instruction in cutting out.

While the course is inflexible as to the *what* is to be done and as to the number of pieces required to be finished, it affords ample elbow-room for the employment of the pupil's own taste and ingenuity in designing. I was determined to follow the saying *nil admirari*, and refrained from praising except as much as could be fittingly expressed by a satisfied grunt; but when I came to the mending and patching department I forgot my resolution. That loosened my tongue. Imagine, my fair reader, square patches, star-shaped patches, circular patches, laid on the sleeve of a shirt, patches that looked as handsome as though they were not to hide a defect, to wit, a vulgar tear, but to beautify the sleeve. A tear in the common form of a Roman V I saw mended with such exquisite exactness, by following the woof and web of the linen, that I could not help expressing my deep-felt gratification. The teachers laughed heartily and said: "How like a man! Things that cost a hundred times more ingenuity and skill than that leave him cool as a cucumber, but when he sees this patching and mending he breaks loose in high praise."

Well, I acknowledged my resolution and was absolved. I have seen many beautiful school exhibitions, but none that was so genuinely true an expression of what is actually done in school daily, hourly. Though most of these things were very beautiful, there was nothing there among all those treasures which had no practical bearing and could not be made use of in any household, rich or poor. White yarn is used in knitting, bright colors in embroidering, white linen in sewing, so as to accustom the pupils to the most scrupulous cleanliness, for it is a rule that no finished thing is to be washed. In case it gets soiled, it must be renewed.

Side by side with each year's course goes a course in drawing and designing of patterns which lifts this instruction from a mere practical, bread-and-butter exercise to a study of no mean importance. In this study and practice of drawing can be traced with infallible certainty the models of former ages, the influence of beautiful surroundings, and of a culture of centuries. This secret power of the beautiful has an ennobling influence, one that can not be overrated in America and must not be underrated.

I argued with the teachers, saying, "Many of these things need not be learned in our age of machines and ready-made linen and clothing." The answer came: "Just as much as the artisan stands in need of a complete knowledge and a great deal of skill to understand the entire bearings of his trade will it benefit our girls to be able to make all the things you see here. Think of the many thousands of girls who make a living by working for shops. Suppose them to be trained like so many miserable, discontented machine-hands in shops only to do one kind of thing, to learn one knack and nothing more. If they are dismissed, they are at the mercy of Heaven knows whom! No, sir; knowledge, thorough, systematic knowledge, and high artistic skill never lose their value, be the conditions of life whatever they may."

These female manual occupations are taught in some schools in America, but nowhere so methodically as here. As the children are disciplined by class-work in writing and reading, etc., so are they disciplined by knitting. Whole classes here knit as the teacher beats time. This exercise is part of every lesson in manual occupation. Many a lady teacher of manual training in our country is a good seamstress, can cut out, embroider, crochet, and knit well; but, having no professional preparation as teacher, she works out her own course and method, usually a very erratic one, to put the most favorable estimate on it.

But see these women teachers at Cologne and hear them state principles for every action, every step of their six years' course, quote authorities, reason with you from an unassailable vantage-ground of pedagogical authorities, with clear insight into the conditions of life, with one eye in the future and one in the past, and one can not but acknowledge their superiority.

Being constitutionally free from envy and jealousy, I can well afford to praise others, knowing that, though the American school lacks this admirable and desirable accomplishment I have described above, it has other virtues which redeem it in the eyes of every impartial observer. However, I respectfully suggest to school authorities to try and lift this particular branch of instruction to a higher level. It pays, as is seen in the thrifty industry of German women. But if these manual occupations in school did nothing else than temporarily lead the pupils from excessive brain-work to something equally valuable, that alone would be a sufficient cause to foster them. But first teach the teachers!

II. On a previous page I referred to the fact that, side by side with the course in manual occupations for girls, goes a course in drawing which lifts this branch of the curriculum to a higher level than it can otherwise reach. In previous chapters I have paid attention to the boys' drawing, particularly to their course in drawing from solids, and gave a number of copies illustrating this, and I am confident that I can in no better way illustrate the course in ornamental drawing laid down for the girls than by offering a few samples which may prove:

1. The very systematic and thorough treatment the subject receives;

2. The practical bearings this kind of drawing has upon the manual occupations; and,

3. That the results of free inventive drawing or adaptation of elementary forms in complicated composition are not to be despised.

Not being an artist, I am naturally constrained to select

simple specimens, for I am utterly unable to follow the students to higher ranges of art and produce copies of drawings with many intricate combinations. What I offer in the following cuts I saw done by pupils. Instead of giving them in their "life-size," I copy them in reduced size from

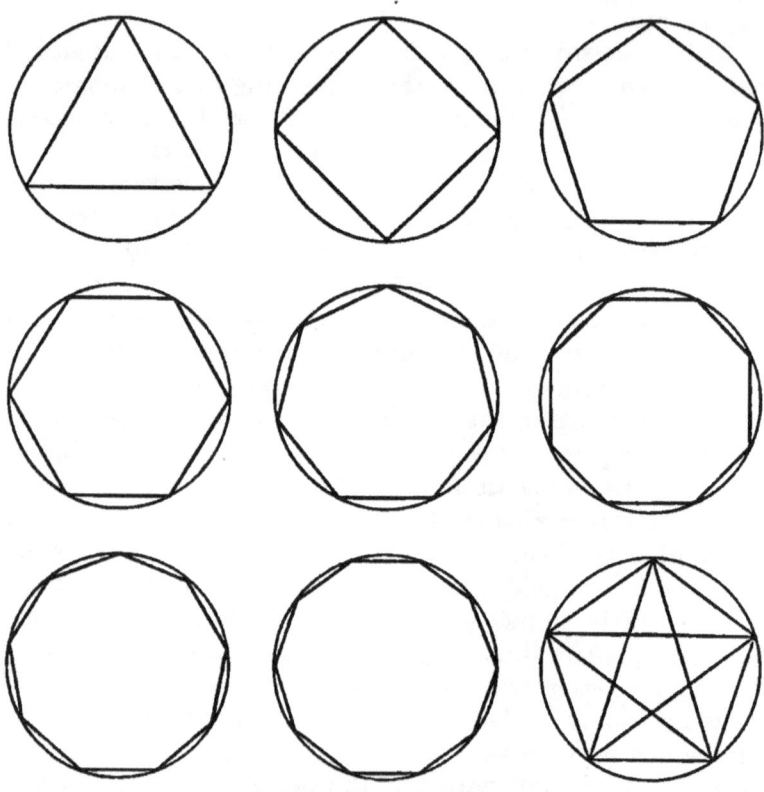

Series I.—Figs. 99-107.

a course laid down for the guidance of the teachers. This work is used in several cities, and contains thousands of models, all systematically arranged, following each other in genetic order. I trust that my readers will readily see from this scanty selection that the models are adapted to be applied in work with yarn, cloth, linen, lace, etc.

Another batch which follows this one may give evidence to the development of the sense of beauty. But of that, more anon.

Series I consists of polygons in the circle and the simple stars that may be inscribed. These do not, by far, exhaust

SERIES I.—FIGS. 108-116.

the series. They are only a few selected ones. There are still hundreds of possibilities for combinations. Of course, in drawing them the ruler and compasses are used. The compasses are introduced during the sixth school year. (See Figs. 99-125.)

One of the objects of the teachers in the upper grades is

that the pupils may be led to invent new forms from given lines, curves, and measurements. This is not as hard as it would seem. Children here display a great deal of ingenuity. Of course, these invented forms are only reinventions,

SERIES I.—FIGS. 117-125.

for there is hardly any ornamental form that has not been produced before by others. But that does not lessen the value of the pupil's own work. Such work is formative to a high degree. I add two of such reinventions to show the conceptive power of a developed sense of form and beauty. (See Figs. 126, 127.)

Fig. 126.

Fig. 127.

Series II, which follows on page 129, is a reproduction in miniature of drawings which I saw beautifully colored in sepia, green, yellow, blue, etc. (See Figs. 128–135.)

I sincerely hope none of my readers will think it superfluous to have these specimens cut in wood. I trust they will be heartily welcomed by the women teachers, especially at a time in which manual training for the boys is so ably and masterly defended. To reverse the proverb, "What's sauce for the gander ought to be sauce for the goose."

Series III. The drawings I submit in this series are from the same course to which the others belonged. From plain geometrical figures the course leads over to a more independent use of the curved line. The combinations are all very fine. Conventionalized animal and plant forms are brought in, and the way is paved to free invention of new forms. The schemes of geometrical figures are the common property of all the nations that ever tried to conventionalize forms. But every civilized nation which has established a national self-dependence *turns to certain forms as its favorite ones*, and develops these in vulgar as well as in fine art, and often succeeds in opening new vistas into undiscovered realms of art. *Thus national styles originate.* Think of the straight line and the triangle, and you have the ground-form of Greek architecture; think of the half-circle, and you have the Roman form; think of the two arcs meeting in a point, and you have the Gothic; and so I might go on through a chapter of the history of art. (See Figs. 136–138.)

But I fear that an essay on that subject would be written *pour le roi de Prusse,* as the Frenchman says. The author would have to let it die an ignoble and cruel death in the waste-basket. Suffice it to say that *styles* are taught here in school in a most practical way "by doing." Besides, every one of the rosettes I copied may be found chiseled in stone or carved in wood, by inspecting the Cathedral of Cologne, or the elegant portico of the city hall, or the ancient tower of that hall, or the stained-glass windows found in almost

GIRLS' INDUSTRIAL EDUCATION. 129

Series II.—Figs. 128-135.

COLOGNE (RHENISH PRUSSIA).

Series III.

Fig. 136.—Modern Style.

Fig. 137.—Gothic Style.

every ancient building, especially in the cathedral. The selections I offer here are so different in conception that they indicate the vast variety possible.

I add also two applications of animal and plant forms, representing two distinct styles, the one modern, the other Gothic. I select these because I found them beautifully re-

FIG. 138.

produced in lace and embroidered tidies. If I find more sets of such drawings I shall with pleasure copy and insert them.

Series IV. The drawings submitted in this series are taken from courses pursued in various schools of Germany. I insert them because the forms, despite their eminent beauty, are

Series IV.—Figs. 139-148.

SERIES IV.—FIGS. 149-154.

COLOGNE (RHENISH PRUSSIA).

Series IV.—Figs. 155-160.

simple and can be reproduced in crocheting and in other ornamental needlework, as I saw it done ; also because few hand-books for girls' industrial education in our country contain models of this kind. Of course, I do not intend to publish such a manual, but I sincerely hope that the models here offered may be of service to teachers and give them a standard with which to measure their own efforts. (See Figs. 139-160.)

CHAPTER VII.

BERLIN.

1. THE OLD AND THE NEW.

FROM Cologne, the ancient, I went after a short interval to Berlin, the modern city of the German Empire, and the move proved a very happy one, for I could thus notice the fundamental difference between the two cities and compare the impressions they made upon me. In one thing Berlin has the advantage over Cologne and many other old cities of the empire: its school system is a rather recent growth. Not that I mean to say Berlin has not had communal schools as early as the beginning of this century, but the city authorities had allowed the private-school calamity to grow to an insufferable degree, so that the communal-school system had degenerated to a system of poor or pauper schools. But when, under the overpowering influence of the rejuvenation of the empire, Berlin became an imperial city, and Dr. Falk, the liberal-minded lawyer, was appointed Minister of Education, soon after 1871, the city school system took an upward start, such as can scarcely find a parallel, unless it be the sudden establishment of a system of "board-schools" in London.

Berlin has no more old school-houses. No such iniquities as dedicating an ancient, musty convent to school purposes are tolerated by the Berlin city fathers. If, in any part of the marvelously expanding city, a school-house is needed, no old relics of former glory are used, but a new house is built. The many private schools that used to flourish like mushrooms have shriveled up and disappeared; even tuition fees are a thing of the past in liberal-minded Berlin. And the state encourages this with all its might. Its own institutions in Berlin, the royal seminaries, the universities, the technical and art schools, are improved and rebuilt on a grand scale.

One day I went to see the mausoleum of Queen Louisa, at Charlottenburg, and on my way I noticed a building in Florentinian palace style of graceful beauty, immense dimensions and exquisite finish, situated on a public boulevard. I inquired of my "Murray" what great personage lived here, and read to my delight that this was the new Polytechnic University. Well, I had my *passe-partout* in my pocket, and on my return from the mausoleum I entered this palace (my pen hesitates to write school-house), was shown all over it, and enjoyed the sight of what modern ideas of school architecture had accomplished. It lies outside the province of my reports to say anything of what I learned here or in the university and museums of Berlin. It is but just, though, to mention the proud efforts of state and community which vie with each other in producing something that will mark the time of the Emperor William as an era of unparalleled exertion in all domains of education, art, science, industry, and military defense.

Another signal difference between Berlin and such cities as Cologne, Mayence, Strasburg, etc., is the absence of statues of saints, popes, and similar personages in Berlin. One sees here the heroes of the people: the Great Elector Frederick William, King Frederick the Great, the famous field-marshals and generals of the Prussian army; the great men of science, Humboldt and Leibnitz, the poets and painters, and numerous symbolic statues, mostly formed after classic models, statues of rare beauty in bronze, marble, and sandstone.

Shall I generalize and say, Cologne and other old German cities offer reflections of the devout aspirations and efforts of the middle ages; Berlin, a child of the modern age, exhibits in all its doings a practical turn of mind. In nothing have the two cities expressed their character better than in their city halls: Cologne's quaint and incommodious city hall, with its moss-grown old Gothic tower of rare architectural beauty, a structure which seems to point upward; and Berlin's "brand-new" city hall, with its overpowering grandeur and square, massive, yet withal beautiful tower which appears to plant itself squarely and say, "Here I am, and I've come to stay."

My journey, with its many professional excursions, is expensive, but I do not rue the cost. What a multitude of ideas this journey is furnishing me at nearly every turn of the road; what a world of scenery; what a taste for the beautiful!

Before I enter upon the individual work of the teachers, I must mention the school-houses in Berlin. It is customary to judge from outside appearances. I do not wish to fall into the same mistake, but I venture to say that in houses well ventilated and warmed, well arranged and even adorned, the educational influence of the school is more refining than where all these desirable things are wanting. Now it is but true to say that we Americans have not much to learn, if anything, in regard to school-house architecture. We are far ahead of the Europeans in the arrangement of space, in ventilation and heating, but not in adorning the school-houses. Our plain, whitewashed walls are ugly.

There is one other consideration in which the Berlin school authorities give their brethren of New York, Philadelphia, and other populous cities a shining example; it is in the position of their new school-houses. This is so unique, so well calculated to meet the circumstances of a large town and the well-founded requirements of school, that it is worth while to call attention to it.

138   BERLIN.

2. Position of School-Houses.

My readers who live in smaller towns, where the school-house is the most prominent building surrounded by large, shady yards, must understand that their standard of a school-house can not be realized in a city like Berlin. Open spaces are rare in Berlin, almost equally rare are trees. But the

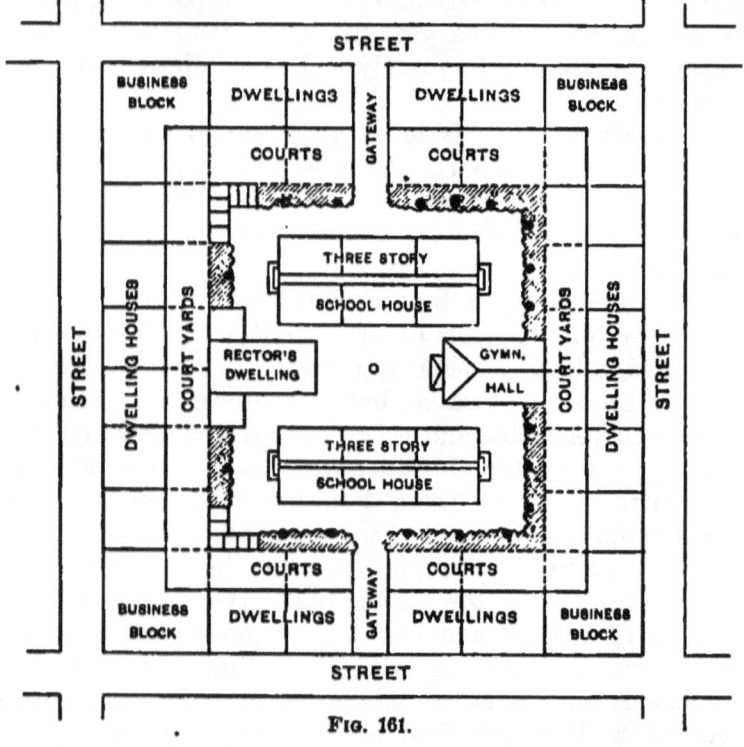

Fig. 161.

school authorities have hit upon a solution of the difficulty which is worth reporting. New school-houses are built in the inner court-yard of a block of houses surrounded by four streets. Two gateways lead to the school-yard. The above sketch, made from memory, may explain the plan.

The dotted lines are to represent low walls which inclose the courts belonging to the dwellings surrounding the square.

All around the yard is found a row of trees and flower-beds, of which more anon. The school-houses are three-story buildings built of pressed brick, but have the look of very substantial architecture. The first and second floor each contains six school-rooms; the third floor contains the session-room (*aula*) of the school, which is used on festive occasions and for meetings. Sometimes, when there is no special building for the rector on the grounds, a dwelling is found on the third floor.

Usually two buildings, one for boys and one for girls, are found on these school-grounds. A third building, one story high, is used for gymnastic exercises. This latter building is never wanting. Hardly ever is a school-building found facing a street, except in the older part of the town. One may wander through many a street without seeing a school-house. The market-halls are built in the same way, in the inner square of a large block of houses.

In most of the yards of the schools I visited I found flower-beds, and I heard that they were used by the teacher of botany quite extensively. The children are here induced to study leaf-forms and observe the growth of plants. If a row of trees is planted, care is taken to select as great a variety as can be conveniently placed. The sense of ownership which is fostered in the children with regard to these flower-beds, shrubs, and trees, is perhaps the best protection that can be applied. Compared with American school-yards, those in Berlin are small, but that even on them a small portion is set apart for a school-garden is laudable and deserves to be imitated in large, crowded cities; in smaller towns of the West, where every family has a garden of its own, it may perhaps be superfluous, although in the interest of rational teaching it may not seem so.

3. The Teachers of Berlin.

I had not been in Berlin quite five days, when I had occasion to compare notes with a colleague from Norway. I told him I had seen six schools (three common schools, one gymnasium, one higher girls' school, and a private school), in each of which I had spent two or three hours; six museums (the National Gallery, the old and the new museum, the wonderful armory with its Hall of Fame, and two school museums); had heard two operas and attended three meetings, namely, one of the Teachers' Social Club, one of the teachers of the third school district, and a banquet. He thought that was making a business of pleasure, but I assured him that this was the only way which would enable me to accomplish what I had come to do.

Mr. Olsen, the Norwegian School Councilor, agreed with me that the teachers of Berlin are a remarkable set of men, in aspirations, in skill, in results, professional as well as social and political. Berlin has so many teachers who have ideas and are not slow in giving utterance to them, that it is worth associating with them. They have a number of clubs, societies and so many official and private conferences, that it was well-nigh impossible for me to attend them all. Some urgent invitations I was sorry to decline, but circumstances, such as great distance from my hotel, demanded it.

The teachers here maintain a daily paper of their own, several weeklies, and support with literary contributions many professional journals outside. Think of maintaining and supporting their own press! Yet they are not clannish, only they stubbornly defend their professional interests, and their *esprit du corps* has done wonders, for nowhere in Germany are the teachers paid so well as here in Berlin; nowhere do teachers occupy so high a rank in society as here, where they support their demands by numerical strength and claim respect by their talents. I assure my readers, the teachers of Berlin are factors on which the city fathers reckon.

How I should like to see the teachers of New York, Boston, Philadelphia, Chicago, Baltimore, Cincinnati, St. Louis, etc., maintain their rights with the aid of the ballot-box and a press of their own! How soon some miserable wretches of political tricksters who find their way into the

Board of Education would vanish from the surface! As circumstances are now, his Satanic Majesty must have a broad grin on his face, reaching from ear to ear, when he sees some of the vilest of men, men who can not even write their names, lifted by the grace of popular vote to the dignity of members of the Board of Education!

Comparisons are odious, it is said. That may be; but they are very instructive. When I see a school system maintained by wise, conservative legislation, governed by men of unquestioned wisdom and unsullied reputation, and in that system a body of teachers every one of whom is a professional teacher, I can not refrain from comparing what is with what might be in our country.

I had only one fault to find with the teachers of Berlin. Many whom I visited in their school-rooms soon after I appeared dropped the lesson of the day and began to review, bent on showing what their pupils knew and could do. Of course, to see what could be accomplished was very interesting, but it was not what I had come to see. So, one day when I was called upon to address a gathering of teachers, I took occasion to ask them to show me *how* they taught, not *what* they had accomplished.

From that day my visits were more fruitful to me than before, and, when I left Berlin after three weeks of hard work and much sight-seeing, I had a note-book full of the most interesting notes.

4. Two School Museums.

In Cologne I had seen a well-stocked Exposition of Means of Instruction, supported by private exertions. Here in Berlin I found two school museums, one maintained by the city, the other by voluntary contributions of the Berlin Teachers' Association. The City School Museum is situated in the hall of the forty-sixth common school, on Stallschreiber Street. It contains many thousands of bound books on pedagogy and kindred sciences. The hall is very well adapted for the purpose. The books are arranged on two rows of black-walnut shelves neatly carved. The shelves are found all around the room. The upper row is approachable by iron stairs and a balcony which leads all around the hall. On the long side of the hall spacious alcoves or side rooms open, which are filled with apparatus for physics and chemistry, collections for the study of physiology, botany, zoölogy, mineralogy, maps, charts, general and special maps and devices for suspending them, apparatus for the study of geometry and drawing. In fact, it is a valuable collection, such as every large city could well afford to have, but the like of which, I am sorry to admit, can not be found in America.

The city pays four thousand marks every year for repairing and new purchases. This is not much, but with good management it goes a great way. Many a valuable book, stuffed animal, bust, map, etc., is presented to the museum, and thus the institution can keep pace with the modern requirements of our professional science and art.

The other museum is not as well supported; but it is a specialty such as can not be found anywhere else except, perhaps, in Switzerland, where "The Pestalozzi-Stuebchen" may vie with this museum. The peculiar charm of this one is its unique arrangement prescribed by its object. The owners emphasize the historical development of popular education. There is, for instance, one section which contains every publication and device concerning the study of geography, arranged according to historical stages of development of that science so far as it comes within the pale of the common school. Another section represents the methods of teaching language. This contains only books and a few charts which provoke a smile at the oddities into which human ingenuity can be misled. Again, another section has reference to object-lessons. A very valuable section this is. Another is devoted to arithmetic, and here I could not control myself. I broke out into laughter when I observed the queer machines and contrivances made to assist the teacher in arithmetic. Since most of these things are antiquated, it does not pay to sketch them.

Of late the managers of this private museum have undertaken the task of collecting everything available and obtainable with reference to Diesterweg, the Horace Mann of Prussia. This is a most interesting section. At present a Harkort section is being made.

Take it all in all, the Berlin common schools are anything but a stagnant pool. There are life, exertion, enthusiasm, ambition, literary skill, successful teaching, and good results. The administration is similar to that of American schools. There is a school commission (a committee of the City Council), a general superintendent (called school councilor), seven assistant superintendents (called inspectors), a rector at the head of each building, and many associate teachers. Only those teachers who are not engaged definitely as yet are called assistants. These have to prove their fitness during a probationary term. After that they are fixtures and can not be removed except for cause.

5. Correcting Compositions.

In a class representing the seventh school year of a district (or communal) school in Berlin, I heard a lesson which I shall not readily forget. The teacher had a stack of composition-books on his desk, and the boys sat with eager expectation before him. The compositions had been corrected with red ink, and the teacher now took one after another and discussed mistakes he had found several times. His mode of criticism was very interesting. An error in orthography was corrected by asking the offending party to spell the word orally and write it on the blackboard.

The subject of the composition was Schiller's "Lay of the Bell," which had been read and thoroughly treated. The teacher was rational yet withal charitable in his criticism, for he never needlessly wounded the spirits of his pupils till he came to one where his patience seemed to forsake him. He broke out, saying: "How could you be so stupid as to write such things? No," he added, "I'll take that back. Stupidity is not your besetting sin, but criminal negligence." It was a study to see the face, which showed defiance at the accusation of being stupid, soften when the teacher did him the justice to acknowledge that it was not stupidity but negligence which lay at the root of this worthless work. The boy bowed his head in shame and said: "Please, sir, I was hurried when I wrote this work. I'll do it over again if you'll allow me. I am sure I can do it better next time."

Sentences which were faulty in construction were written out in full after being corrected orally. Then they were repeated in chorus, and thus the correct construction made a more lasting impression. I nowhere find incorrect words or sentences spread on the board in German schools, and I am induced to think that this is more beneficial than the sight of numerous mistakes. An error which had its root in dialectic speech was weeded out thoroughly by making a number of pupils repeat the correct form, while the incorrect form was heard only once. Thus the frequent repetition of the correct obliterates the incorrect form. Like the teachers in Rhenish Prussia, those of Berlin have to fight constantly with the wretched dialect of the lower strata of the population. The teachers of Thuringia and the provinces of Saxony and Hanover have an easy time of it compared with the Sisyphus work of their colleagues in Berlin and Cologne.

Well, this work of correcting went on, and the teacher dealt out his commendation and reproof with the spirit of a true educator who knows every one of his pupils and gives his doses according to the nature of the disease. This lesson closed, and at the stroke of the clock the next followed. It was a unique one, to say little. On the programme it was marked "Miscellaneous." The teacher explained that this hour was reserved every week for the boys' "spontaneous efforts." Each pupil was permitted to prepare a contribution of his own, the reading of a composition on a topic chosen by himself, or the recitation of a poem of his own choice, or an oral description of scenery viewed, or a narration of an event witnessed by himself, etc.

This was a very instructive lesson to—the teacher; yes, instructive to him, for it gave him an opportunity of studying his pupils. They unconsciously revealed their true nature, partly by their choice of a subject, partly by their mode of rendition, partly by the reception their work found among their schoolmates.

"You see," said the teacher, "this is my special study-hour, and the notes I take during this hour spent in listening to voluntary contributions are of incalculable benefit to me." I spent a day in this school in several class-rooms, and traced among the entire corps of teachers the influence of this excellent rector.

6. My Mode of Procedure.

I must not repeat myself, and can therefore not sketch many of the lessons I saw in Berlin, because they very much resembled the lessons I sketched on previous pages. This time a statement of my mode of procedure may take the place of a description.

Early in the morning, before eight o'clock, I call at the office of the rector, hand him my *passe-partout*, and am received with courtesy. He places before me his daily programme, which contains a summary of all the daily programmes of the whole school—that is, of all the class-rooms in the house. Upon inquiry after special meritorious cases, I get the information I want and select the lessons I desire to hear; but I am careful to select several for every hour of the school day, so that, in case I may have made a poor choice, I can retire to another class-room. If I "strike a gold-mine," I stay; if, on the contrary, I find indifferent teaching (which, to do honor to truth, happens rarely), I usually advance some plausible pretext for retiring. Thus I am enabled to see a good deal. Though it is exhausting work, it lasts only till twelve or at most till one o'clock. (For reasons, see No. 9 below on school sessions in Berlin.) The afternoons are left to pleasure, sight-seeing, and attending teachers' meetings.

One day I followed an urgent invitation to a private school. I had spent about an hour in it, and had gone from room to room without seeing anything that could entice me to stay, when I took French leave and went in search of another school. My usual luck favored me. I came to the Coelnische Gymnasium, and was greatly elated at finding that the rector was Prof. Dr. Kern, the famous grammarian, a man who has recently published a number of books on a new mode of treating grammar, and a text-book on pedagogy, for young teachers. I had a charming interview with Prof. Kern, and shall remember his school.

On the programme was trigonometry in Lower Prima, taught by Prof. Hermes, author of well-known text-books on mathematics; and, since I was desirous to compare the teaching of such a man with that of others I had seen, I expressed that desire. Prof. Kern said, "You seem to know where you may expect something worth seeing." Well, he took me up to that teacher, and I was very glad of it afterward.

The professor, a fine, old, white-haired man, took no notice of us after the introduction, and I had the best opportunity to observe him and his students. A very difficult and knotty problem was given out, and a few moments were spent in hard thinking. Then a student was called up who began to demonstrate. At a deviation from the mathematical logic, the professor followed up this thread and proved its absurdity, then led the student back to where the break had occurred, and again the student started out. He did not rise from his seat, but, while solving the problem orally, made the algebraic figures with astonishing velocity in his note-book.

Another student was called who got through the whole solution without a break. A third was called to the board to demonstrate the problem by drawing the figure, and it was a sight worth seeing as the boys sat there watching the demonstrator. The professor was an excellent methodician. He never did for the students what they might do for themselves. His memory was simply prodigious. When, after about ten minutes of demonstrating, a student mistook the letter *m* for *n*, the professor, without looking at the board, said, "Look again, you are mistaking one angle for another." I was convinced that these students learned mathematics thoroughly.

Though I heard many fine lessons in Berlin, I missed the methodical skill I had found in some schools in the western part of the kingdom. Herbart is not considered in Berlin the great apostle which they make of him in Saxony and Thuringia.

7. Home-made Charts.

In a school in Berlin I noticed a number of charts that had been made of common dark-blue packing or wrapping paper. This paper had been pasted on a light wooden frame. The teacher had then written on the paper or sketched his illustrations with pointed white and colored crayons very neatly (they had reference to botany, zoölogy, physiology, physics, etc.), and then, in order to preserve them for future use, he had covered the paper with fresh (unboiled) milk. The soft, spongy paper had absorbed the fluid, but the milk formed a sufficiently strong coat of varnish to preserve the crayon-marks. The paper, when dried thoroughly, was stretched tight, and lost its former flabbiness, so that the charts when hung up for use would not collect dust any more than any other smooth surface. The charts can be dusted with a feather or hair dust-brush without injury to the illustrations ; the only thing which will injure the charts is moisture, for that will warp them.

I inquired whether the wooden frames were necessary, and the reply was, "Yes, lest the paper become warped during the process of drying after it is soaked with milk." But one frame will do for a good many charts. After one is thoroughly dry, it may be cut out of the frame and hung up for use, or secured in a portfolio. Then a new chart is mounted, covered with illustrations and writing, and then "milked" to give it a coat. The milk must not be spread over with a brush, but poured over the sheet. The teacher who had hit upon this device was a handy draughtsman, and had prepared a great number of charts for plant analysis and other studies, and he adds a few charts to his stock every year. Some of those I saw were ten years old, but they were as fresh-looking as though made yesterday.

8. A Map-Suspender.

Sometimes a teacher neglects to hang up a map during the lesson in geography, because it is inconvenient to handle the large, unwieldy wall-map. To be candid, in some schools no devices for suspending maps easily are found. In Berlin, in a school for young ladies, I found a device which deserves to be mentioned. Here is a sketch of it:

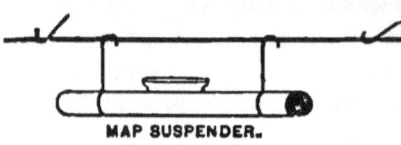
MAP SUSPENDER.

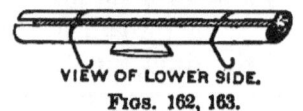
VIEW OF LOWER SIDE.
FIGS. 162, 163.

An iron rod is fastened close to the wall; from that is suspended by two hooks a tin cylinder, which has a slit one third of an inch in width. Into the cylinder is shoved the upper rod of a mounted map while the map passes through the slit. A handle soldered on to the cylinder affords an easy handling. The young ladies used the apparatus dexterously, and changed the maps without loss of time.

9. Length of School Sessions.

In Berlin the daily school session opens at eight o'clock in the morning and usually lasts till one o'clock, rarely till two. The primary classes are dismissed at twelve o'clock. In the afternoon only such classes as were dismissed at one or at twelve have one more lesson, but this is a lesson in gymnastics, drawing, and industrial pursuits. No absorbing brain-work is done in the afternoon. From eight till one o'clock are five hours; that is considered enough for one day's brain-work. But notice that this five hours' work takes place six times a week, the pupils having, as everywhere else in Germany, no whole holiday on Saturday, but are free on two afternoons, namely, Wednesdays and Saturdays. Since the afternoons of the other four week-days are occupied with gymnastics, manual work or drawing, the fact remains that the pupils here do a solid day's brain-work, of five hours each, six times a week.

It may be claimed that five consecutive hours is too much for one session. That is true, but the difficulty is obviated by giving the pupils a recess after each hour. There is a short recess of five minutes at nine and at eleven o'clock, and one of ten minutes each at ten and twelve o'clock. These frequent recesses prevent an undue exertion of the brain. Though the order which makes the boys do six days' work is very ingenious, I doubt whether our independent American youth would submit to the arrangement which would virtually wipe out their time-honored privilege of enjoying a holiday on Saturday.

As to vacations, they have here one week at Christmas, one at Easter, one at Whitsuntide, and three weeks at harvest-time in the fall (usually in September); total, six weeks. Deduct this from the fifty-two weeks of the year, and you have forty-six school weeks left, as compared with our forty. Few city schools in the United States have a longer school year than forty weeks. It stands to reason that a school can accomplish more in forty-six weeks of six days each, than one in forty weeks of five days each, all other things being equal.

10. NORMAL SCHOOL FOR YOUNG LADIES IN BERLIN.

A. *The Building.*—My former connection with the Cincinnati Normal School has left a special liking in me for schools of similar character. I saw one in Cologne, and have mentioned my experiences there in former letters. Here in Berlin I had occasion to see and thoroughly inspect another normal school for women. Comparisons are odious, and I will therefore refrain from comparing this school with similar institutions in America, though I am sure the comparison may in some instances turn the scale in favor of American schools, notably if the munificence with which they are founded and supported is taken into consideration.

The school I wish to speak of is not a city institution like the one in Cologne, but is supported by the state exclusively; in fact, it is the first state institution of this kind in Prussia. In one of my former letters I said that the state as such offered no professional training to young ladies who intend to become teachers. This is not quite correct. The state partly supports a few such normal schools; but their number is not in just proportion to the number of normal schools for young men. It is perhaps two or three to one hundred. This seminary in Berlin, together with its extensive practice department of over fourteen classes, is known as the "Augusta School." It enjoys the "protection" of the Empress Augusta, whose bust, in over life-size, adorns the large session hall, of which more anon.

The school-house is a magnificent building which has cost five hundred and fifty thousand marks, or about one hundred and ten thousand dollars, to build. It consists of an enormous main building and a wing. Pressed brick and stone facings make the building look very handsome. A fine vestibule and massive gates lead to a roomy stair-house. Pillars of solid sandstone and a broad marble staircase, finely carved gates and doors, wrought-iron railings and partitions of exquisite workmanship, stained-glass windows, fresco-paintings, and heavy cornices of immaculate whiteness inside, make the school a thing of beauty and a joy forever. The school-rooms are small as compared with what I consider the proper size of a school-room.

The practice department of the Augusta Seminary is a complete common school of nine grades (nine school years), with several parallel classes, in none of which are found more than twenty pupils, and the seminary proper has a course of three years. The class-rooms for all these classes are on the first and second floors. On the second is also found the hall for physics and chemistry, with amphitheatrically arranged seats, the library, the school museum, the office of the rector, and the conference-room of the faculty. On the third floor is the art-room and also the "aula" or session hall. This is the most splendid school-room I have seen in twenty-five years. Think of frescoed walls, of a ceiling of carved oak-wood, of stained-glass windows, of marble facings and an inlaid floor, a grand organ and commodious settees!

The marble stairs and mosaic floors of the corridors are protected by a strip of linoleum, and the cleanliness in this school reminds the visitor of fairy tales. Not a speck of dust anywhere—a fine testimonial to the efficiency of the janitor. The visitor, accustomed to criminal negligence and dirt found in so many German schools, feels inclined to step softly here. The system of ventilation and warming is so perfect that no vitiated air is noticeable after several hours. They have steam-heating and automatic ventilation happily combined. O, happy children who can spend their youth in such a school!

B. *The Practice Department.*—Having expressed my desire to see the young ladies of the senior class teach, I was conducted through the eight rooms of the four lower grades, where I heard lessons in primary arithmetic.

The course I saw in actual operation was: First half-year, operations in addition and subtraction of numbers between 1 and 10 and counting to 100; only oral work. Second half-year, all the four fundamental rules applied to numbers between 1 and 20; here begins written work. First half of second year, all the operations with whole numbers between 1 and 100, counting to 1,000. Second half of second year, same with whole numbers and simple fractions; also some denominate numbers. In this, the beginning of the second half of the second year, I heard problems solved, such as "Sixteen thirds, how many whole ones and thirds?" The answer came instantly, "Five whole ones and one third."

Fractions were also written by these children, who handled them "with ease and elegance," as though they offered no difficulties whatever. At the close of the second year the children must have mastered the multiplication-table, and they were just at work with the tables of eight and nine, which they recited in this wise:

(a) 8, 16, 24, 32, 40, 48, 56, 64, 72, 80.
(b) 80, 72, 64, 56, 48, 40, 32, 24, 16, 8.
(c) $1 \times 8 = 8, 2 \times 8 = 16, 3 \times 8 = 24$, etc.
(d) $10 \times 8 = 80, 9 \times 8 = 72, 8 \times 8 = 64$, etc.

This recital backward and forward made the pupils very dexterous in the use of the tables.

The third school year completes multiplication and division with large numbers, and the fourth adds denominate numbers and a more thorough treatment of fractions. In the third year it was where I found such problems as "Find one sixth of 68, one eighth of 91, one seventh of 86," etc., solved very quickly. All this may seem to many of my readers like a tale from fairy-land. Even I who had claimed that more could be done in our schools if the fundamental rules were treated from the beginning—even I was dumfounded when I saw the chapter of fractions completed in the A Primary (or the fourth school year); but, when I considered the material these teachers worked with, I fell back into my *nil admirari*. The pupils were children who came from very refined homes, the so-called "Geheimraths-Viertel," and spoke almost faultless German. The Sisyphus work of correcting their mother-tongue or dialect did not retard the teachers in their work.

In this school I found a very simple and useful apparatus for illustrating the combinations in arithmetic between 1 and 100. It consists of a small blackboard two feet square into which small smooth holes are bored. Into these holes white ivory buttons were inserted, such as shown in the cut. These buttons are easily removed and replaced, and can be handled by the pupils. (See Fig. 164.)

The so-called Russian numeral frame also is greatly improved in this school. On both sides of the frame is a strip of black board, behind which the balls that are not used in an operation are hidden.

From the second half of the first year a series of blank books is used in arithmetic, the leaves of which are covered with a net of lines intersecting each other at right angles. The work entered upon these pages was remarkably neat and very correct.

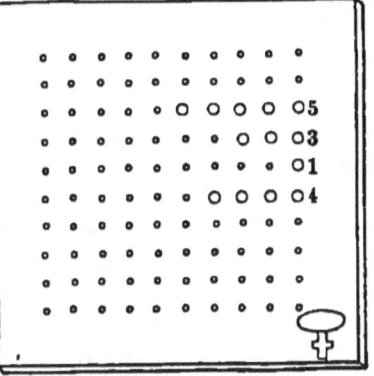

Fig. 164.

The students were well trained in teaching. I inquired how that was accomplished. "Simply by thorough theoretic preparation and by giving them much free elbow-room—that is, allowing them to remain in charge of a room for several weeks. After the charm of novelty is worn off, they are visited by their schoolmates and by the practice teacher, and then their work is criticised," was the answer.

C. *The Normal School-Work.*—"What preparation do you require of these students before you admit them to the normal school (or seminary)?" "The results of a higher young ladies' school, which has a course of nine years. They may get that education anywhere, or privately, or in our Augusta Practice School; in fact, wherever they please. But we admit none except those who pass the examination for admission."

For once my customary luck forsook me in this school. The rector, Mr. Supprian, well known in German educational circles as author of popular text-books and readers, and a good speaker, was ill and off on a furlough; but he was well represented by other men of the faculty. One of these gentlemen gave a lesson to the students of the senior class on the history of methods of teaching reading, which lesson I wish all those American teachers had heard who are now killing rational teaching in the bud by insisting upon the pure, unadulterated word-method.

The students were very well acquainted with the entire history of the phonic method, with all its phases of development. Good old Ickelsamer, the first inventor of it, would have chuckled in his grave could he have heard the lesson. Stephani, the Bavarian school inspector, too, received his full share of the fame as reinventor and as promoter of good teaching. The whole lesson was like an Axminster carpet, rich in colors, exquisite in form and design— that is, full of interesting historical data, alternating with arguments as to the merits of this, that, and another method. The course in methodical treatment of sounds, open and closed syllables, etc., was well established. All enjoyed the lesson—the teacher, the young students, and, more than all, myself.

There was no difficulty in finding my way from room to room, for in the corridors could be seen on every door what class was engaged in the room, and the daily programme was suspended under glass outside, so that one need not enter the room to inquire what was going on inside. This seemed to me so useful a thing that I resolved to mention it.

Well, I found my way to the art hall, in which drawing was taught. It was a magnificent room, fully sixty feet long by thirty wide. High windows with north light made this room especially fit for the purpose. I will not go into details, but only mention an idea I gathered here. The students, about forty in number, represented the tenth school year or the first in the normal school. Part of the lesson was devoted to a class exercise in drawing from solids, the same that I have described before. When that was concluded, the teacher ordered the students to turn to their individual drawings. Some drew from plaster casts, some from relief ornaments, some from plain wooden geometrical bodies, some even turned to plain copying and learning to shade with the stub.

I inquired after the cause of this variety. The answer was characteristic and well worth recording: "The gifts of nature, such as the sense of form, or the musical ear, or the eye for color, the skill in working out forms by means of modeling—in fine, all those talents which may, perhaps, be uniformly developed when the millennium approaches—are not, at the close of our nineteenth century, as yet the undisputed common property of everybody. Much variety is still noticeable. Some human beings are far more gifted than others in music and in the art of representing form on the flat surface. Now, it would retard the progress of many of these young ladies to keep them back in order to keep step with their less gifted sisters.

"So, you see, I divide all my lessons by first giving class-instruction in the course in drawing they will be called upon to give to little children after some years; but when that part of the lesson is finished I give each student wide elbow-room to turn to her favorite pursuit in art. This is never without the most gratifying results, as you may see by going through the aisles. You will have noticed that I tied the students down to a rigid performance of duty so far as the course prescribed is involved; after that I say, let them have the liberty to work out what accomplishment Mother Nature has given them."

This was common sense, decidedly. That it was, besides, obedience to the pedagogical maxim, "Individualize!" did not decrease the value of the common sense one iota.

During a lesson in physiology sketches of the circulatory system were drawn on the board, and a very forcible distinction was made between *sketch or schematic illustrations and perspective copies from nature.* I append a few samples, which will illustrate the distinction. (See Figs. 165, 166.)

Of course, the heart was there *in natura* also—that is, a perfect preparation of papier-maché.

The last lesson I heard was a failure, because it was a lecture. Lectures are out of place in a young ladies' school. The professor was a very learned man, but a poor teacher.

His subject was the history of gymnastics. The young ladies began to seek diversion in whispering, giggling, and writing, while the worthy old man talked louder and louder

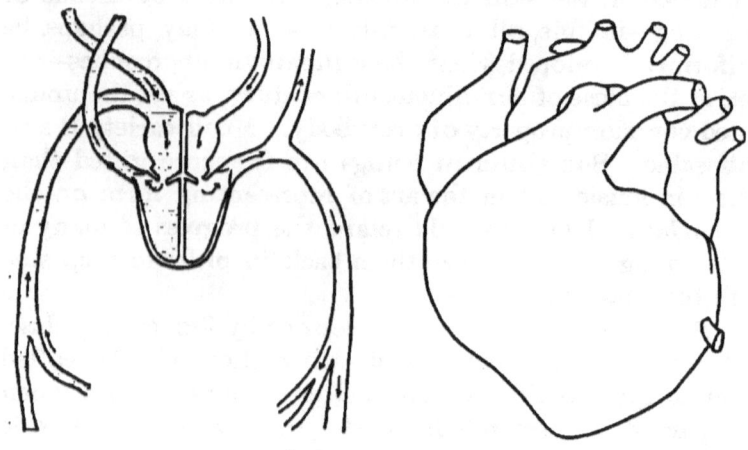

FIGS. 165, 166.

to overcome the increasing noise. The spectacle became so unpleasant that I preferred to leave. This one unpleasant experience could not, however, mar the deep impression I received during the other lessons. I had spent a day most profitably, as I hope to have proved in this chapter.

One word more: English and French are taught here, and taught well, I assure my readers. Only, the English *th* was a stumbling-block to some of the pupils, and will perhaps always remain so, as the German vowel *ue* (ü) is to Americans and Englishmen.

11. How not to teach.

One day I was on my way to a school in the outskirts of Berlin, when, riding on the tramway, I espied the sign, "Royal Teachers' Seminary." On the previous day I had inspected a similar institution for young ladies, and the desire arose to see this one, evidently a normal school for young men. A comparison, I thought, would be very instructive. I acted upon the impulse and entered the building. The rector received me kindly and handed me over to the next in command, because he himself had to leave the building to conduct an examination in another part of the city. This teacher was engaged in giving a lesson in church history. I thought this a very good beginning, and was about to pat myself on the back for my luck, metaphorically speaking, when, lo! I abruptly paused in my self-congratulation, for the teacher was a *scold!*

He was a massive man, a strong man, a man who exercised a power of command which might have been better fitted for military exercise than for the school-room. He was utterly void of tact, and trampled upon the children's dignity as though his massive foot stepped upon pebbles. He made his importance felt so severely that he confused his pupils. He intimidated them by his glance, by his mode of questioning, and his seemingly compassionate smiles, which seemed to imply, "I know you can't grasp this, but I'll ask you, nevertheless, to make you feel your utter worthlessness." His reign was a reign of terror.

No answer was left without severe criticism, and every time he got through with a boy, after severely squeezing him (metaphorically speaking), and ridiculing him when occasion offered, I saw the boy take his seat with a woe-begone countenance that reminded me of Lady Jane in "Patience," when she sighs, "Crushed again!" When the substance of the answer was correct, the teacher found fault with its form. When the form was correct, but the answer did not fully cover the subject asked for, or when the boy, in his anguish, tried to branch out and reach over as much ground as he could, to satisfy the teacher, sarcastic remarks followed, which were positively ugly. The boys, on an average about fourteen or fifteen years old, resembled so many sheep in a thunder-storm.

But mind well, my patient reader, the teacher was not coarse; not a nickname, not a word escaped him which might have been interpreted as a direct insult. But his manner of applying reproof was so icy, so penetrating, so chilling, and the reproof was given for such trifling things, that it took my breath away. There was not a word of commendation, not a look of approval during the whole lesson, not one friendly, helpful glance—it appeared as though the teacher considered it beneath himself to waste such things on a gang of criminals. I did not sketch the lesson. My attention was entirely absorbed in studying how not to teach.

It will ever remain true that we are apt to copy our own teachers in our mode of teaching, and therefore the best teachers and educators are barely good enough as normal-school teachers. This lesson chilled me through and through, and I left the building. From other teachers, upon very cautious and veiled inquiry, I heard that the one I had listened to was an exception; but I can not help pondering about the anomaly that a man of his caliber should teach the religion of love, Christianity. He certainly acted like a veritable Peter Arbus in very transparent disguise. I am happy to say I did not find another specimen of a cruel scold like this one during all my visits in the schools of Berlin or elsewhere, but I insert this description to point out a glaring contrast.

12. "Naturkunde"—Knowledge of Nature.

"The world do move," so the President of the Lime-Kiln Club says, not to mention a more illustrious authority for that expression. I was reminded of it when I saw here, in Germany, the girls in the communal, or people's school, study physics; here, where the people cling stubbornly to the prejudice that women need not, nay, must not, rise to the lofty realms of thought in science and art, that their sphere precludes scientific pursuits, etc. (I will not repeat the threadbare argument which American women have so successfully refuted by ocular evidence.) Yes, "she does move," thought I, when listening to a lesson in physics in a girls' school in Berlin, in a class of the eighth school year.

"NATURKUNDE"—KNOWLEDGE OF NATURE.

Electricity was the subject, and the method pursued by the teacher so rational that I resolved to sketch it.

The school was well provided with apparatus. A little ball of elder pith, suspended by a linen thread from a brass holder; another suspended by a silk thread; a gutta-percha rod rubbed with a woolen cloth; a glass rod rubbed with a silk cloth—were the first objects viewed and used in experimenting.

After each part of the apparatus was well understood, the teacher took the gutta-percha rod, rubbed it, and *approached* the little ball on a silk thread without touching it; after that, the one on a linen thread. The girls put in words their observations, by simply stating the facts observed. Then the teacher took the glass rod, rubbed it, approached the balls, one after another, and again the girls simply but correctly stated what they had observed. The little balls acted very differently. So far, in short steps, the lesson had progressed, when some of the girls were about to jump at conclusions. But the teacher cautioned them not to do so, but await the results of further experiments.

Again he rubbed rod No. 1, and this time *touched* the little balls. The results observed made those girls who had worn a victorious smile on their faces, as though they had discovered the reason of the ball's action, lean back with knitted brows. The observations were again clearly stated. Now the rod No. 2 was used in a similar manner, and the opposite results were attained. Then all the eight different phenomena were once more repeated in quick succession, and the teacher summarized them, and after that "submitted the case to the jury."

An insignificant-looking specimen of *homo sapiens feminini generis*, but with a pair of eyes that seemed to be able to look outwardly and inwardly, then said: "The fact that the same rod acts differently upon the two balls can only be explained by the difference of connection between the balls and the holder. In other words, the electricity issuing from the rods, and seeking its way through the balls to the brass holder, finds a conductor in one of the strings and a non-conductor in the other thread. Hence the opposite actions of the balls."

Space forbids to go into further details, save to say that the fact of positive and negative electricity, also that electricity acts on the surface, not inside of bodies, and other facts, were well established at the close of the lesson. I must not forget to state that the teacher showed great presence of mind when at one stage of the lesson an experiment failed, to wit, one of the balls remained indifferent instead of being attracted. He candidly stated that he was nonplused, and proceeded to examine the apparatus. Seeing the brass rod of the holder covered with a thick coat of dust, he quickly polished it, and tried the experiment again, this time successfully. A few remarks concerning the evil influence of dust impressed themselves upon the girls' memories. The class was large, but all the pupils participated and were frequently called to repeat statements of observations or experiments made before their eyes.

I inquired what difference, if any, the teacher noticed in teaching science to girls and to boys. The answer was: "The girls are much quicker in coming to conclusions than the boys. They almost jump at them, and do not sufficiently investigate facts. The boys arrive more slowly at conclusions; they insist upon trying various experiments before they form a judgment. Another very decided difference is, that girls forget scientific facts sooner than boys. It seems as though the boys' power of retention is greater. And a third (to me the most vital and significant) difference is found in the fact that it is difficult to retain the girls' attention long. They get tired much too soon. While the boys can hold out a solid hour in physics without getting mentally exhausted, I am obliged to branch off into some different subject to offer the girls a distraction from the severe strain of continuous thought."

I offer these statements as they were given to me. Since they come from a highly successful teacher, one who has been rector of both a boys' and a girls' school for many years, his words ought to have some weight.

13. A Lesson in Singing.

A lesson in vocal music that I heard in one of the communal schools of Berlin very vividly impressed itself upon my mind. During the recess between two lessons, while promenading with the rector in the corridor, I made the acquaintance of a young man of great promise. I took a liking to him, and followed him into the class-room, where at the stroke of the bell two classes of girls filed in to take a singing-lesson. The teacher offered me the choice between practicing songs that had been studied, and the study of a new song. I chose the latter offer, and was well rewarded, for what I heard was a model lesson. The rector selected a song from a book not in the hands of the pupils—a song which was strange to the pupils and strange to me.

As quickly as possible the teacher copied the soprano part on the board which was ruled for music, and had this part read by the whole class. The pupils *read* D, F sharp, G, A, A, A, etc., then *sang* the notes thus. The length of the notes was then marked, and the pupils beat time. Now the words were substituted, and suitable places for breathing were marked. Again a halt was made, and signs of expression were called for where the pupils thought fit to place them. Thus the whole melody was treated. All the pupils sang the melody, and the teacher, being rather a fine violinist without being a professional musician, played the second or alto part, thus accustoming the ear of his pupils to the harmony.

Now the alto part was written, and the class called upon to practice a few intervals, such as from the second to the fifth tone of the scale, etc. When these preliminary exercises were finished, the part was sung without the leading melody. Though the part was not without difficult passages, the class sang through it bravely. Now it was repeated, and the violin took up the melody. This made the alto singing easier. The pupils were seated in three groups—soprano, alto, and second alto. (Perhaps we might call them upper and lower soprano and alto.)

Now the order came for the soprano voices to sing their part and the alto voices theirs, while the violin played the third part. It was interesting to see the girls who were to sing the third part attend closely to catch the run of their part which was not written yet. This was written last, it was easy, and offered no difficult intervals. The signs of expression had to be the same in all three parts; and after the third part had been read and tried aloud, the three parts were sung together. The song was rendered charmingly and without the least error. Time of lesson, thirty-five minutes.

Many questions on the theory of music, on the length of the notes, on signs of expression, on time, on signature, on keys, etc., now followed, and I was highly pleased with the results, for the pupils revealed considerable familiarity with written music. The age of the pupils was twelve to thirteen years, the class being on a level with our intermediate or grammar grade. At the close of the hour a few songs previously learned were sung. It was three-part music throughout, and well rendered. The expression was fine, the harmony exquisite, and it seemed as though the pupils vied with the teacher in producing something that was worth hearing. What pleased my rather fastidious musical ear were the beautiful *crescendos* and *diminuendos;* the voices swelled so evenly and gradually from the gentlest *piano* to a strong *forte,* and again decreased to *mezzoforte* or *pianissimo,* that I could have listened all day. What a source of musical wealth their school must be to these children! And how they hung on the lips of their teacher!

14. A Lesson in Zoölogy.

It was in the same school that I heard a lesson in "description of nature" (not to call it zoölogy), which was very pleasing. I will endeavor to give the gist of it. It proved to me beyond controversy that, while in English and American schools much valuable time is spent in learning the fabric of the garment of thought, the English language (spelling, grammar, etc.), these German children get more substance of thought. While we, perhaps driven by the nature of our language, are making our pupils think *about* the language, the German children think *in* their language. They gain more knowledge, useful, practical knowledge in physics, physiology, hygiene, natural history, history of man, geography, etc., than we can offer our pupils. In sketching the lesson I must confine myself to the essentials as I noted them down. Subject, "The Whale." A large picture of a whale was placed before the class.

After a description that was partly deduced from previous knowledge and from the picture before the class, the teacher entered upon a more instructive part of the lesson by proposing, where occasion offered, questions about cause and effect.

"How does it come so," he asked, "that the animal emits vapor through its nostrils, and not streams of water?"

"What is the most vital difference between the tail of the whale and that of fishes?" The answer, that "its position is horizontal instead of vertical," led to the other question:

"Have we an example of horizontal rudders on our boats or skiffs?" The boys all agreed that a boat's rudder must be vertical. Then the question came, "Who knows what is meant by sculling a skiff or canoe?" Up went two hands of boys, who described the use of an oar both as propeller and rudder.

The teeth of the whale, especially their fringe, puzzled the children. They saw that, if their own teeth were as soft as felt on the edges, they could not last. It was soon decided that the animal does not use its teeth to bite with, but as a sieve. The teacher then explained—what could not well be seen on the picture—that the animal turns these "teeth-bones" on their axes after preparing to swallow. He showed this by turning three rulers, which were first held with the edges toward the class, so that the broad sides were seen. Thus the teacher taught objectively without ostentation. He seemed to discover means for appealing to the senses where others could not use anything but the word of mouth. A simple gesture of his often sufficed to make things clear.

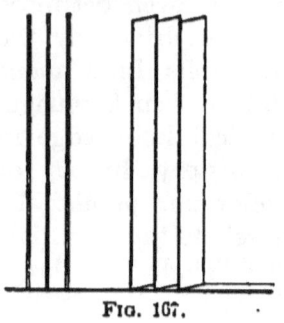
Fig. 107.

When the whaling or whale-hunting was described, the question, "Why are the whalers sure of catching their prey, if a single harpoon has struck?" led to a vital difference between whale and fish, namely, the organ of respiration. The existence of parasites on the skin of the whale led to the question why the animal permits them to grow and lodge in his skin. This was a poser. At last a pupil said: "I can understand that monkeys can pick off their parasites; that birds can free themselves of them by means of their beaks; that a buffalo or a dog can rub himself on the bark of a tree or other suitable object; but I fail to see what the unwieldy whale should do, having neither hands nor beak to pick off his parasites, nor any hard substance in the sea on which he might rub himself."

Thus the lesson went on—a lesson which furnished knowledge and awakened thought. It wound up with a neat description of the animal's mode of life, thus:

The home of the whale is in the northern seas, where they are free of ice. Where the ocean offers food in abundance they can be found in great numbers like herds of cattle. Now they dive to considerable depths, and there move in quiet majesty, like huge ship-hulls, and soon after appear on the surface, "sailing" with the velocity of steamers. Now they play like merry giants' children, rear like horses or make somersaults and stretch their tails out of the water, or whip the water with their tails till the surface is covered all around them with white foam, and again float as though dead on the surface, and permit water-birds to alight on them.

It was a fruitful lesson—fruitful in many ways to the pupils. The harvest of language was rich, the exercise of judgment in discovering the why and wherefore of things very lively. Altogether the lesson was a proof of the fact that a good teacher is not made but born.

15. A Most Refreshing Sight.

Berlin is a big city, no doubt my readers know that ; but its size became very obvious to me one day, when I attended a meeting of the teachers of Section III. Berlin is divided into several (I believe, seven) school sections, each of which has a section superintendent, called inspector, while the general superintendent, called Schulrath, is the general-in-chief. The rectors, associate and assistant teachers of this section —some two to three hundred in number—had a conference in the session-room of the one hundred and seventh communal school. The hall was magnificent, lofty, spacious, well warmed and ventilated, and exquisitely decorated with fresco, paintings, marble and plaster busts, and carved wood. It was very obvious that I was in the capital of the German Empire, in a city which is known for its inexhaustible collections of art. An art-loving community like that of Berlin can not leave the schools of the children unadorned, and if we consider that many children attending the lower schools never see a beautiful room—unless it be in school—it seems like investing money well to decorate the school-rooms. Æsthetic education is not the result of teaching, but of impressions.

The hundreds of teachers present on this occasion (I am sorry to say there were no women among them) were a fine body of men, indeed, I rarely, if ever, saw so many fine heads assembled as I did here. I had an opportunity to see the Reichstag (German Congress) assembled a few days afterward, and I was somewhat disappointed. Venerable as many of its members were, I could not help seeing that as far as intelligence, ready wit, oratory, and parliamentary skill were concerned, the teachers of Section III surpassed the members of the Reichstag. The inspector of this section took the chair, and conducted the discussion in a very commendable way.

The subject of the day was *Efforts in reforming Instruction in Natural History*. And again, as I had noticed in Rhenish Prussia and Westphalia, the battle raged about Herbart *pro* and *contra*. Though the name Herbart was not once mentioned, it was obvious to me that the views of the two authorities—Pestalozzi and Herbart—were at the bottom of the whole commotion. It may seem presumptuous to render in English the theses which were discussed, but, since they offer in synopsis the course of the whole discussion, I will give them. So here are the theses:

I. In the study commonly called natural history our object should be to lead the pupils to a better comprehension of *life* in nature.

II. The present status of science should be considered, in which the *system* is not the main point, but the train of changes which culminated in the present artificial systems of classification. It can not be urged too strongly that we must not go beyond the pupil's faculty of comprehension.

III. Direct observation of life in nature, both in botany and zoölogy, must take the place of description of absent objects. To this end class-excursions into the country should be arranged, work in the school-garden and lessons in observation alternate with excursions.

IV. It is not sufficient to have the physiological organs of natural objects named. Of greater importance is the relation between the organs and their functions.

V. In order to get a clear insight into the life and growth of plants and animals, it is necessary to observe and discuss their characteristic momenta. Dead specimens may afford opportunities for description and study of forms, but they offer no chance for seeing the organs in action.

VI. The influence which the surroundings have upon

the peculiar development of the object in life should be emphasized so far as the children can comprehend it. This can best be studied during excursions.

VII. Instruction in natural history has also a practical object, to wit, to prove the importance of natural objects to man in commerce, in industry, or as food and ornament. This should be considered in the selection of objects for study.

VIII. In higher instruction this elementary observation of forms, organs, and their functions should terminate in systematic grouping and the observation of phenomena in formulating biological laws.

The young teacher who was the chief speaker read a paper first in which he defended these theses. He opened the discussion formally. For three hours opinions, couched in short, five-minute speeches, followed each other, and the chairman selected the speakers always with a view toward fairly dividing the time between the *pro* and *contra* sides.

The whole discussion was based upon a work of recent publication called "The Village Pond" (by Fr. Junge, published by Lipsius & Fischer in Kiel). Humboldt once said, "Nature is reflected in every corner," and the village pond was considered by the author the most convenient corner to study nature. Botany, zoölogy, and mineralogy are studied while studying the phenomena observable in and about that pond. It is a wonderful book, quite in harmony with the teaching of Herbart—a book which has created a sensation among the teachers of Germany such as can only be compared to the sensation created by Pestalozzi's " Wie Gertrude ihre Kinder lehrt." If I had the time at present I should translate the book for my American colleagues; but I apprehend that when I return home to settle down again I shall find it on the market in America in English garb. It is altogether a sensible book, one which is destined to mark an epoch in science-teaching.

A few more remarks about the discussion. In all the many addresses and impromptu speeches of the day there was not an unpleasant word said directed at any one in particular, not a breath of suspicion as to the motives of any speaker, nor an allusion which might in any way have been interpreted as containing a sting. All criticism (and there was much of it, and severe criticism to boot) hit the system or the method in vogue, never the person. All evidences given in support of ideas and opinions were well selected from personal experiences, and when at last a committee was appointed to work out a plan for applying the principles and practice of Junge in city schools, the work of the day left no bitter feeling—not often the case after a heated debate. No little of the success of the day was owing to the masterly directive action of the chairman, who was what every presiding officer should be—a true moderator, not a despot.

I had had the impression that parliamentary rules were nowhere better understood and applied than in our land of parliamentary government; but I have had several occasions to modify my judgment concerning that point. The presiding officers of several meetings I attended had a knack of disentangling conflicting questions, laying motions before the assemblies, and a simplicity in deciding and taking votes, which fairly astonished me and would have graced a legislative body in America. Time was when parliamentary usage was very rarely found in Germany; but the granting of universal suffrage has set into activity latent parliamentary talents which are not to be despised.

When the conference closed we repaired to a fashionable restaurant, where a commodious hall was reserved for us for a banquet. Think of this body of men on a Saturday evening, after a heated debate, peacefully enjoying themselves with songs, toasts, and something for the inner man! A chorus of select voices rendered fine vocal music. The words of the songs that were to be sung by the whole assembly were passed around on printed slips. They had been composed "especially for the occasion," and were full of happy allusions to the events of the day. The toasts were good, and joy reigned supreme till the small hours.

16. A Distinction with a Big Difference.

Generally I prefer to visit the so-called people's schools here in Germany, because it is more probable that in them I can pick up suggestions of value to our American common schools. The gymnasiums and other secondary schools partake more of the nature of colleges and special schools. The instruction offered in them is more scientific, the courses of study much more rigid, and the schools as such too exclusive to suit my taste. Still, for the sake of proper comparison, I go to see higher schools in every city in which I stay longer than a day or two.

The general impression I received in these higher schools is not a very favorable one. I find much more inferior teaching in them than in the common schools; but let me not be misunderstood. The teaching would be very good for mature minds who can and are willing to follow the lecturing teacher with undivided attention. The instruction, be it demonstrative or not, is almost always addressed to the best and brightest pupils. Weaker ones are merely dragged along and go to the wall when the annual reckoning takes place.

This is one of the causes why the higher schools have the dropsy in the lowest and the consumption in the highest grades. To see one or two graduates in a school of six or eight grades (from the tenth to the nineteenth year of age), with an enrollment of four to five hundred, is not a rare case at all. It does not seem the object of the faculty to do the greatest good to the greatest number, but to prepare a selected few for the next higher grades and suffer the remainder to stay and "try again" or drop out of school. Nowhere is Darwin's theory of the survival of the fittest more forcibly illustrated than in German secondary schools. I am aware that this is very harsh criticism, but it is based upon "ocular inspection" and several private conversations with noted school-men, who agree with me both as to the fact and its causes.

They are not reticent about this weakness of the system, but speak without reserve. One gentleman of national reputation said, when I mentioned this anomaly: "It is only too true that the improvement in didactic practice in the higher schools does not keep step with that of the lower schools. The state requires the teachers of the lower schools to have attended a normal school, while those of the secondary schools are raw university men who may have learned much but do not know how to teach.

"A normal school graduate may not know so much of the sciences of mathematics, physics, chemistry, philology, archæology, history, etc., but he knows how to apply what he did learn, and, what is of still greater value, he has learned by actual practice in the school-room how to discipline and educate, not merely how to teach. Many a young university man addresses his immature pupils as though they were college students. He can not stoop to their level of comprehension, and it is a comparatively small number of these candidates who ever get to be good teachers. Do you know, I invariably send my young university men to some renowned teacher in the people's school that they may observe how to teach methodically before I intrust a class to their care?"

Now, much of what this good man said is applicable to American college graduates, I thought. Here in Germany it is fashionable to send the boys to a secondary school instead of allowing them to mix with "the rabble." So long as social distinctions are as high here as they are, it will be considered a privilege to attend a gymnasium, or a Realschule, or a Bürger Schule, and, to be sure, it is a distinction with a big difference.

Before I close this criticism, I wish to have it distinctly understood that I do not mean to say there are no good, excellent teachers in the secondary schools. I am far from saying that, for I have witnessed lessons in such schools that were model lessons in every way; but I mean to say the good teachers are fewer in number there absolutely and relatively than in the people's schools. I mean to emphasize also that there is too much waste of good material and the number of graduates in disproportion to the number of pupils entering secondary schools.

Furthermore, I maintain it to be a lamentable error to allow the pupils to begin a number of higher studies and languages without ever being able to make any headway in them when they could obtain a well-rounded elementary education in the people's school which would fit them for life much better than that half-and-half education which offers a little of everything and nothing of anything. The secondary schools in Germany are not so much educational institutions as they are seats of learning. Therein lies the distinction and the difference.

17. A RARE CASE.

In one of the communal schools of Berlin I confided to the rector that it was so difficult to make the teachers understand that I had not come to inspect the school with a view toward ascertaining *what the pupils knew*, but *how the teachers taught*. He was not astonished, and said: "We rarely see visitors in our school. When an inspector or school councilor comes, he is usually bent upon examining into results." He suggested that he had several teachers whom he could place at my disposal. He introduced me to one of them who happened to enter the office at that moment. One glance at him convinced me of his genius. The rector asked him: "Would you kindly take a class in geography instead of Mr. So-and-so on the spur of the moment?" "Certainly," was the answer. "What subject shall I take?" "The class is studying the map of Asia." "Very well." "Or would you mind taking my class in physics while I take the other class?" "With pleasure. What is the class studying?" "We are at the chapter of electricity." "That would please me very much."

I engaged the young man in conversation during recess, and found he had a perfect sample card of studies on his daily programme. He taught natural history, physics, geography, history, grammar, gymnastics, and music, and the rector confided to me that he taught all these branches well. "He is a most valuable man to have in a school," said he. "He is obliging, always ready on the spur of the moment to jump into the breach, a perfect mine of information, and a most accomplished methodician. Every pupil in the school likes him. Every teacher acknowledges his superiority. Young as he is, he has already passed the examination for a rectorship, and I am seriously afraid I shall lose him, for the authorities will soon appoint him to a rectorship. What a power he might be in a secondary school! But, then, that is out of the question, he being only—a normal graduate. Despite his profound learning he has something child-like about him. He can play with the boys in the yard, and laugh and romp with them to their hearts' content, yet in the class-room he is a strict disciplinarian. He much resembles the iron hand under a velvet glove. In all my thirty years of experience I have never discovered so unmistakable a born teacher as he is."

Well, I saw that teacher engaged in several lessons and owe him many an inspiration.

18. "Tout comme chez nous."

Cheating in examination. The "Berlin Gazette" recently published an account of an attempt at circumnavigating the dangers of a final examination which deserves to be reprinted in America. A paper one day contained the innocent advertisement:

"Wanted, a young man who either has passed the final examination in a gymnasium or is about to go through the ordeal. Wanted for an innocent purpose. Employment for two or three weeks. Salary, seven hundred marks. Applications, accompanied by a '*curriculum vitæ*,' to be sent to this office addressed to A. P., No. 101."

A student of the university in Berlin who thought the advertiser needed coaching to get ready for his examination, applied and received an answer of the following purport: "A certain aristocratic young gentleman who intends to enter the army as officer is required to pass the final examination (which is a sesame for both the university and the army), but, having been ill for some years, is too poorly prepared, and desires to find a substitute who will under an assumed name pass the examination for him. This is done easily, no risk whatever."

In order to catch this cheat, the student entered upon his plan, but notified the public prosecutor, who caused the arrest of the young aristocrat after sufficient proofs were collected.

Will my readers have a moral? It is this: This one case has made a profound sensation upon the people of Germany. They ask with holy horror how it is possible to conceive of such an infernal idea, and clamor for protection to honest students by prohibiting the admission of any one to the final examination in a high-school who has not been a student in that school for a year at least. The Germans do not hastily legislate, but, when they do, their laws go straight to the root of evil.

19. Concentric Extension of the Geographical Horizon.

It is always attended with a feeling of satisfaction when one observes an idea consistently carried through the different stages of the curriculum, especially if that consistency is in strict compliance with educational maxims and principles. Here in Berlin a truly refreshing example of consistency is offered in the school-book used in the study of geography, which book is an atlas pure and simple, not a text-book. It may not be without interest to read an account of what that book contains, for it is got up with undeniable skill. The reader must kindly bear in mind that the atlas is made expressly for use in the elementary (or communal) schools of Berlin. The idea which is so consistently carried through in it is expressed in the above heading.

174   BERLIN

Fig. 168.

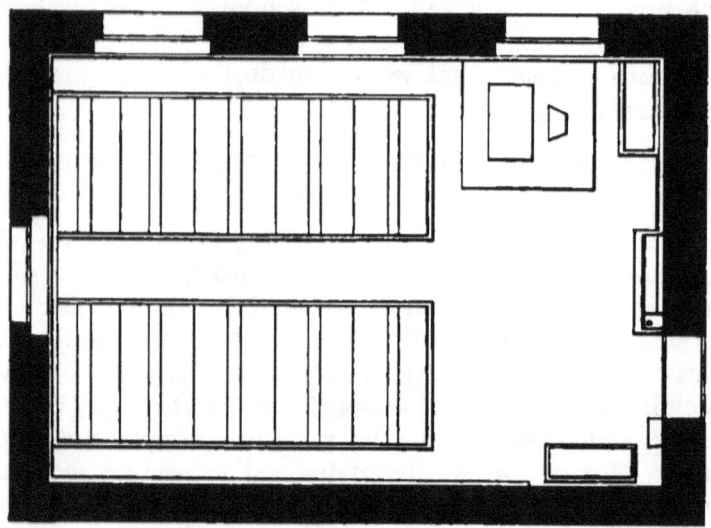

SCALE 1:100.

Fig. 169.—Map-Plan of the School-Room.

THE GEOGRAPHICAL HORIZON. 175

Page 1 contains six pictures and plans. The first (Fig. 168) is a perspective view of the inside of a school-room, and side by side with it is a map-plan (Fig. 169) of that room. This is nothing new in America. Many American textbooks of geography contain a similar illustration. It is here reproduced for no other reason than to present an unbroken chain of methodical links. Notice that the atlas does not begin with the hemispheres. The picture, with its attendant, the plan, represents the first circle of the pupil's geographical horizon, and is drawn on a scale of 1 to 100.

Then follows a perspective view of the whole school-house (Fig. 170) and a map-plan of the building (Fig. 171). These form the second circle. Scale: 1 to 300. The bird's-eye view of Fig. 171 is certainly an ingenious contrivance.

This is followed by a perspective view of a portion of a city and its map-plan. The school-house is again found on this map. (See Figs. 172 and 173.) These form the third circle of the pupil's horizon. Scale: 1 to 1,500.

Page 2 contains a larger perspective view of a landscape, accompanied by a map-plan. The artist had to reduce this view to adjust it to the size of the page. The original in the atlas is much larger. The reader will find the same school-house and portion of the town represented in Figs. 170 and 172. This forms the fourth circle. Scale: 1 to 7,500.

Page 3. This extension of the horizon is followed on page 3 by a picture of an imaginary landscape which is inserted for the purpose of teaching the most vital topographical ideas. This picture also is accompanied by a map-plan.

Page 4 contains a minute city plan of Berlin, which forms the fifth circle of the horizon. Scale: 1 to 36,000.

Page 5 is Berlin and vicinity, the same city plan but much reduced in size and surrounded by the many villages, hamlets, etc., within a radius of twelve kilometres. This forms the sixth circle. Scale: 1 to 100,000.

Page 6 is a map of the governmental district of Potsdam,

Fig. 170.

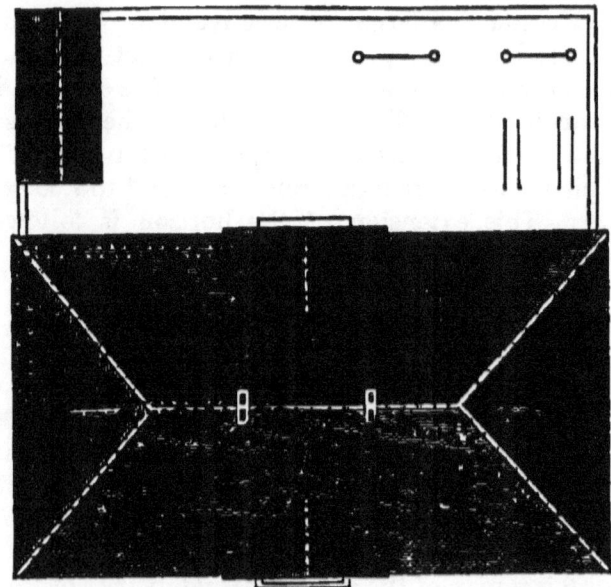

Fig. 171.

Fig. 172.

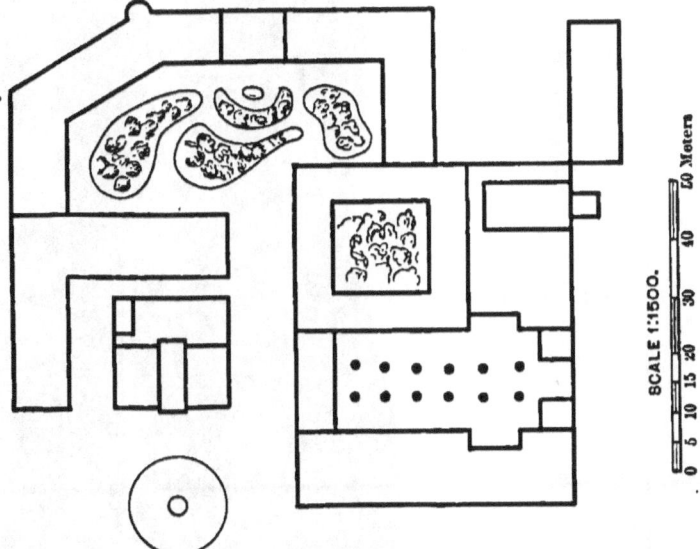

Fig. 173.—Map-Plan of School-House and Vicinity.

178　BERLIN.

Fig. 174.

THE GEOGRAPHICAL HORIZON. 179

Fig. 175.—Map-Plan of the City. Scale 1:7500.

in the center of which Berlin is situated, this being the seventh circle. Scale: 1 to 1,000,000.

Page 7 is a physical map of the province of Brandenburg (center Berlin). Eighth circle of horizon. Scale of map: 1 to 1,260,000. Map contains also a local map exhibiting the railroads entering Berlin.

Page 8 is a political map of the same province. Scale the same. Local map of the city of Potsdam.

Page 9 is a physical map of Germany. Ninth circle of horizon. Scale: 1 to 4,000,000.

Page 10 is a political map of Germany. Same circle, same scale. Local map of the Thuringian principalities.

Page 11 is a physical map of Europe. Tenth circle of horizon. Scale: 1 to 15,000,000.

Page 12 contains the political map of Europe. Same circle, same scale.

Page 13 contains the map of Asia. Scale: 1 to 50,000,000.

Page 14 contains the map of Africa. Scale: 1 to 40,000,000. Local maps of the Nile-Delta, the Cape Colony, and Cape Town.

Page 15 contains the map of North America. Scale 1 to 35,000,000.

Page 16 contains the map of South America. Same scale.

Page 17 contains the map of Australia and Oceanica with local map of Victoria Land, and an illustration of the formation of coral reefs. Scale of main map, 1 to 50,000,000.

The foregoing five maps may be considered the eleventh circle.

Page 18 is again a local map, namely, that of Palestine, a map which is very useful to teachers and pupils in the study of biblical history.

Page 19 contains the twelfth circle of geographical horizon, namely the Eastern Hemisphere.

Page 20. The Western Hemisphere. Scale not stated.

Page 21 directs the pupils' look upward to the heavens. It contains a representation of the northern sky, with the most important constellations and the milky way.

Page 22, the last one in the book, is devoted to mathematical geography. It contains illustrations of the eclipses, of the earth's orbit, the solar system, the phases of the moon, and various very useful devices of similar nature.

The whole book costs a mark, or twenty-five cents, which price is a standing reproach to our publishers, who ask a dollar and a quarter to a dollar and a half for a book containing on an average not any more maps than this one; for the useless ballast which makes them unwieldy and induces ignorant teachers to make presumptuous prattlers of our pupils, is not worth the paper on which it is printed.

These, then, are the contents of the elementary geography in use in the city of Berlin. The reader will perhaps advance objections to this, that, or another item; will object, for instance, to the picture of the quaint city (which the artist has minutely copied), as being foreign to our pupils' surroundings. I repeat, for his benefit, that the atlas is not made for American children, but for the children in Berlin. I should think it might be possible to present a series of pictures and accompanying map-plans which could be used in large cities such as New York, Philadelphia, and Chicago.

The reader may, perhaps, consider it somewhat of a strait-jacket to be tied down to such a course, one which will not give the precocious child a chance to look beyond the "board fence of the circle." To him it may be said: There is no objection at all for any precocious child to look at the next pages and ask questions about them, but the regular, methodical course is here prescribed according to the principle "From the near to the remote." If he desires to deviate from the course, he may skip a few pages, and return to them whenever he sees fit.

But the consistency with which the principles of education that presuppose concentric growth are carried out, deserves commendation. We are too often talking of principles and shunning to apply them. Here is a sample of that consistency which does what it preaches. Whether we like it or not, we may at least be just and find it praiseworthy as such.

CHAPTER VIII.

HALLE (PRUSSIAN PROVINCE OF SAXONY).

1. THE "FRANCKE STIFTUNGEN" IN HALLE.

I MUST refer the reader to the history of education, and ask him to look up Francke, and to read what heroic efforts he made in charitable institutions. To-day—two hundred years after he began to look about for means to establish an orphan asylum—a small city looms up within the city of Halle, built mostly by him without governmental aid; and, though he has been dead for the last century and a half, his work still lives and thrives, governed by almost identically the same rules which Francke, the man with the large heart, and active sympathy for the poor and needy, laid down. Suffice it to say that he was the most noted benefactor the poor in Saxony and, in fact, all Germany, ever had. He had no millions to bequeath, but, on the contrary, began with *seven dollars*. According to a report of 1883, issued for the benefit of the Emperor William, who during that year visited the institution, it embraced then :

	Founded in—	No. of pupils in 1883.	No. of pupils since beginning
1. A boys' elementary school..............	1695	221	9,300
2. A girls' elementary school..............	1695	225	9,500
3. A boys' intermediate school	1695	584	23,000
4. A girls' intermediate school	1695	469	15,700
5. A boys' preparatory school..............	1845	239	1,743
6. A Latin school	1695	775	23,257
7. A high school for boys	1835	454	6,400
8. A high school for girls	1835	370	2,100
9. An orphan asylum for boys.............	1695	115	5,276
10. An orphan asylum for girls............	1695	16	1,501
11. A boarding establishment for outside pupils of the high schools...............	1697	285	10,000
12. Same for students of the Royal Pedagogium.................................	1696	54	4,387
13. A normal school for young ladies.......	1879	23	88
14. A " Seminarium Praeceptorum "	1696	12	4,395

THE "FRANCKE STIFTUNGEN" IN HALLE. 183

Connected with the institution—which, is in fact, a small town within a town—are several undertakings, called "the money-making additions," namely :

(1) A *Publishing House*, founded in 1698, with an annual sale of 200,000 marks ; (2) a *Printing House*, founded in 1701, with an annual earning of 130,000 marks ; (3) a *Drug-Store*, founded in 1698, with an annual sale of 45,000 marks; (4) a *Bible House*, founded in 1710, with a capital of 150,000 marks, 6,200,000 Bibles have been sent out since 1710; (5) an *East India Mission*, founded in 1705, with a capital of 246,-900 marks ; (6) the "Streit Fund," for the purpose of supporting German Protestant congregations in Pennsylvania, founded in 1755, with a capital of 29,900 marks.

The entire institution embraces seventy-five acres of land, of which seventeen acres are covered with buildings. The buildings are insured against fire to the amount of one million and a quarter marks.

The reader may think these statements out of place in a book like this. I insert them to show that a spirit which succeeded in erecting, independently of state aid, such a grand and imposing temple of charity, finds its expression in independent educational enterprise. In our age of associated charities, the original intention of gathering the orphans of the realm has become too narrow. The institution has become the center of all efforts of reform in school education in Germany—an experimental colony, so to speak. For it is not dependent upon the state funds or taxes, and is therefore not governed by rules and regulations issued from the governmental green-table, but has its own director, who thinks it quite in harmony with Francke's principles and charitable intentions to make these schools the *pioneer schools of Germany*.

Director Dr. Otto Frick, since Prof. Ziller's death the foremost leader of the Herbartian school, advocates Herbart's principles and Ziller's practice, and selects his teachers exclusively with reference to their fitness to teach and educate. He is not tied down by narrow courses of study and regulations, nor are his tongue and pen tied by considerations of state reason or bread-and-butter interest. Consequently he is, to state the situation metaphorically, "the best-hated pedagogue of Prussia, a vigorous pike in a carp-pond."

I spent several days in this "city within a city," and more than once sat in speechless admiration at the manner of teaching and the results I witnessed. Of course, I was to some extent, prepared for what I saw; but when I noticed the absence of that rigorous discipline under which other schools suffer ; when I saw the children converse with their teachers as though speaking with a friend; when I saw them working with their hands, and giving intelligible accounts of what they had seen, heard, and experienced; when I noticed that they learned as though by means of play—I felt as though the millennium was near at hand. And again, when I considered that, after all, this band of teachers was in the most hopeless minority, that there may be an approximation to this kind of procedure but never a perfect imitation in the vast majority of teachers in the world ; that, after all, this was a mere oasis in a vast desert—I seemed to feel the millennium recede.

I own frankly that I felt myself very small, a mere mite in the presence of these men who so completely and willingly lost their character as teachers, as it were, and meant to be nothing but companions of their pupils. Yet, despite this apparent disappearance of the teacher, he was here, always suggesting movements, aiding efforts, leading the way, feeding the imagination, directing invisibly the education of the pupils under his charge. He reminded me of the iron hand under the velvet glove.

It would have led me out of my way to visit all the grades of school that are here represented up to the university and beyond it. That would have necessitated a stay of weeks, a condition which could not be complied with. Suffice it to say, each class has its "Gesinnungs-Stoff" (matter appealing to the sentiment). In the higher grades of the elementary schools it was biblical history, in the lowest it was a collection of "Maerchen" (popular tales), such as Andersen's and Grimms'. The principle of concentric circles in education is applied in every branch, every class, every school.

I spent much time in a third grade (third from below). Everything done there in the day was in organic connection with the central topic, Robinson Crusoe. Geography was learned by molding maps in the sand and tracing his journey; by molding his island, etc. Manual work was linked with the pupil's intellectual efforts. They made pots like Robinson, wove baskets like Robinson, etc. The compositions written on slates had Robinson's exploits for their subjects. All seemed like a natural growth. All instruction had a common center. Robinson Crusoe had to these children both a centrifugal and a centripetal power, and wielded them as Old Sol does his powers, unseen, unfelt, yet very effectively.

2. Concentric Instruction Illustrated.

It would be tedious work to lead my readers through the labyrinth of conflicting interpretations of the Herbart-Ziller movement now stirring up the pedagogical world of Germany as a leviathan does the quiet depths of the sea. I have been spending my leisure hours in railroad-cars, in hotel-lobbies, and by the light of my faithful student's lamp in studying both sides of the question; have seen lessons given according to the prescription of these latter-day apostles, have conversed with men of great experience, and young, ambitious, and striving teachers; have heard lectures on the subject—in fine, I have honestly striven to climb up to a point of view from which I might judge impartially. After several months of intense study, I believe that I am ready to pronounce judgment. But I will reserve it till I have offered my reader a few more lessons which may illustrate the principles. Perhaps he will then be able to form his own opinion.

One thing I must note at once: *We* are apt to talk of a

man's *method* of teaching. The disciples of Herbart shun that word where they can consistently do so. They speak of this or that *principle*, of this or that *type* of instruction, and thus set an American schoolmaster wildly groping for something to hold on to in the labyrinth of conflicting opinions. One of these principles of teaching is, that each branch of study should have a logical and, if possible, a tangible, at any rate an organic connection with, if not *all*, at least with as many other branches of study as possible, to make the whole course of instruction one organic growth. This, it is claimed, will facilitate mental growth better, than by keeping the different disciplines apart. Of this principle I saw an illustration in print by Mr. Lehmann in Halle which I will give in full, omitting all explanatory remarks which he offers for the benefit of his readers.

The lesson was a lesson in drawing, entitled "The Ivy-leaf."

Object.—Boys, hitherto you drew leaf-forms from copies in print, or from forms I drew on the board for you. To-day the copy is wanting, and the natural leaf is given to you to draw from. (Each pupil has an ivy-leaf on his desk.) From what plant are the leaves taken? If our former drawing was called drawing from copies, what may we call this kind? If our object were merely to learn to *draw* the form of the ivy-leaf, I should have given you printed copies; but we must learn something besides drawing. You know that the leaves of different plants show in their outlines distinct geometrical figures or forms. Mention a few. Now, what geometrical form do you discover in this maple-leaf? (An irregular pentagon.) Yes, you might also find in it the isosceles triangle and the trapezium. Show them. You also know that every plant has (aside from a few so-called root or radical leaves) one form of leaves which is consistently repeated, though showing slight variations. It is so with the ivy. Our notion of an ivy-leaf is a very distinct one. It is the type of ivy-leaf form. Among all the different forms of ivy-leaves I have furnished you *in natura*, you will have to

CONCENTRIC INSTRUCTION ILLUSTRATED. 187

find that type. This is the other object of our lesson. Our objects, then, are (1) to find the typical ivy-leaf form, and (2) to learn to draw it.

I. Since we have discussed and drawn other leaf-forms, I suppose you can find some things yourselves. First, tell whether the ivy-leaf belongs to the simple or complex leaves. State the respective order. When is a leaf called simple? When complex? When lobate? Show that the ivy-leaf is lobate. Describe the different lobes as to their number, relative size, and position. Repeat what we have said of the leaf so far. (This is to establish connection with botany.)

II. What geometrical figure do you recognize in this leaf? (Holding up a perfect ivy-leaf.) Who has a leaf which shows a perfect pentagon in its outlines? Show a leaf in whose outlines a pentagon is only suggested, not clearly worked out. Has any one an ivy-leaf which does not exhibit the geometrical ground-form of a pentagon? There are but few. What, then, seems to be the typical form of the ivy-leaf? What kind of a pentagon is it? What leaf may be said to be a regular pentagon? Describe the irregular pentagon your leaf represents: (a) the sides, (b) the angles. Who has found this confirmed in his leaf? In what way does yours differ? Now repeat in connection what we have so far said about the ivy-leaf.

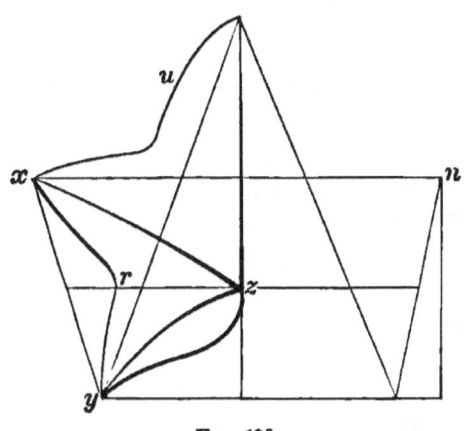

FIG. 176.

The irregular pentagon of the typical form shall be drawn afterward. First we must take some measurements. Suppose a straight line be drawn from the apex to the base of the leaf. Under what angle and in what point would that strike the base-line which connects the two lobes? In what proportion is this base-line to the length of the perpendicular? Now suppose the points of the two middle lobes connected by a stright line. (See Fig. 176, points x and n.) What angles would this line form with the perpendicular? At about what point would the two lines intersect each other? Now, one pupil may repeat what was said concerning the geometrical ground form and the construction lines, while another goes to the blackboard and draws the construction lines as the other pupil dictates. As we found in the maple-leaf, we may accept two geometrical forms, the trapezium and the isosceles triangle. (This part of the lesson establishes connection with geometry.)

The outlines or contours of the lobes remain to be sketched. What do you notice on the large one? It shows a line on each side which is curved or waved; especially in the middle a large curvature outward is visible. Draw the outline on the board as you see it in your leaf. You will find it difficult to determine the outlines of the other lobes from your natural leaves. Let us compare other leaves. What did we discover in the leaf of the horse-chestnut? The contours of the lobes of that leaf are similar. Here is the maple-leaf. In how many extremities of that leaf is the similarity of form unquestionable? But even in the two lower ones we have recognized the ground form of the other three. What alone could lead us astray?

Hence it is apparent that it is a peculiarity of plant-leaves that forms repeat themselves in them. Let us see whether that is also the case in the ivy-leaf. Who has a leaf in which the outer form of the middle lobe is found in the side-lobes? State how the outlines of the different lobes are joined, whether in a sharp angle or a curved line. I now add the outlines of all the five lobes to our sketch on the board.

Here follows a review, which summarizes the points gained.

III. Here you see three ivy-leaves (Figs. 177-179). In what particular does II differ from I? Show the rudiments of the lower lobes. Who has a natural leaf that resembles this one? So, then, it is evident that in the ivy-leaf the forms repeat themselves also. II proves it. Compare II with part *x*, *y*, *z* of I. Only at one place a difference is seen. Where? Now you will also be able to recognize the contours of a lobe in the imperfect leaves of III and IV. What part of II is similar to IV? Where would the fourth and fifth

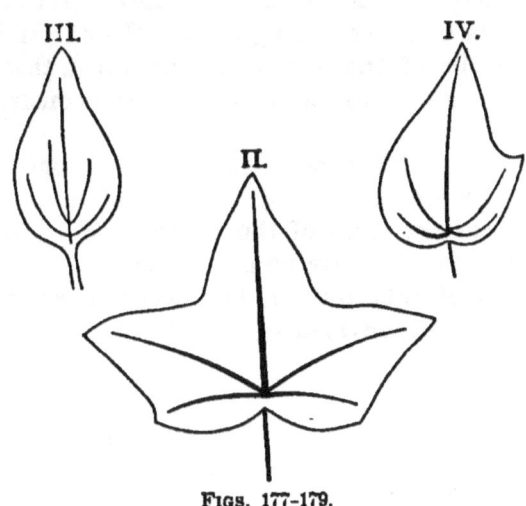

Figs. 177-179.

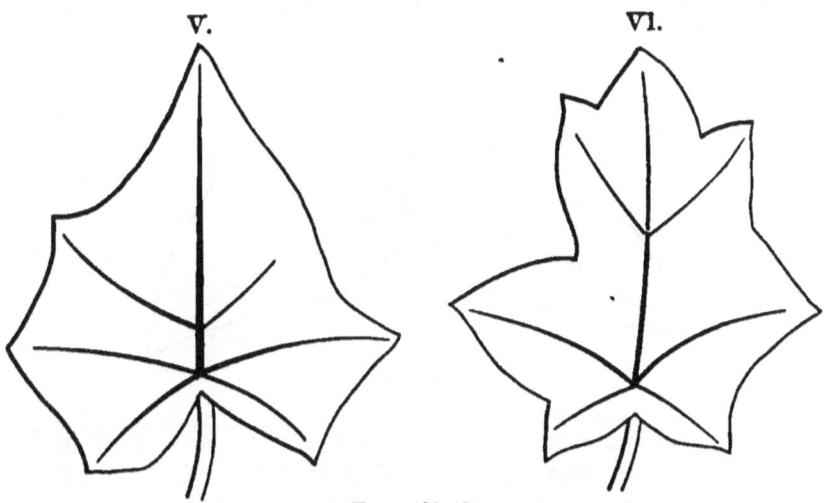

Figs. 180, 181.

lobe be if they had developed? How do you determine it? Who has a leaf similar to IV? What part of I shows similarity with III (r, y, x)? Also in III the division into five parts or lobes is suggested. How? It is plain, then, that the ribs of the leaves are important, that indeed they determine its construction or rather the construction of the single lobes.

Now if I were to let side ribs go out from the main rib, where would that be? Then you understand the swelling in the contours of the leaves. (Pointing to u in Fig. 176.) What would develop in this place? A new lobe? This is no impossibility indeed, but occurs frequently, as V and VI (Figs. 180, 181) show.

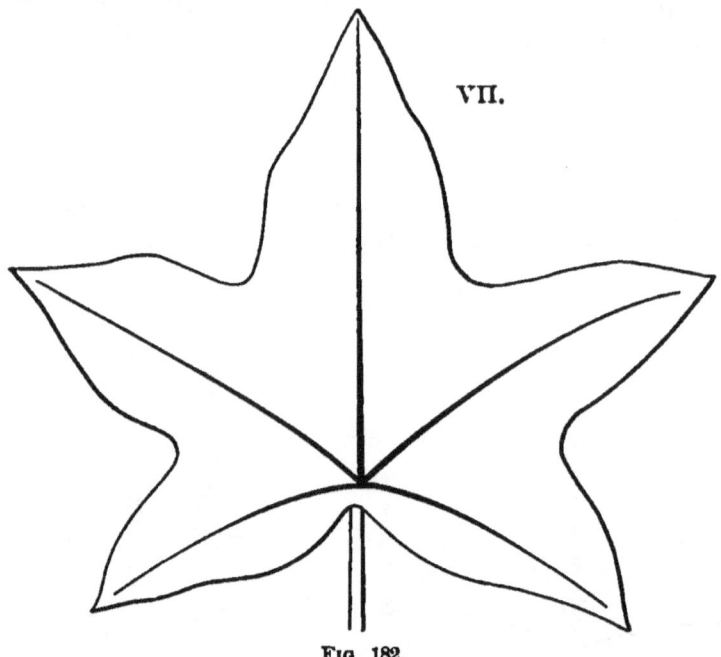

Fig. 182.

IV. The perfect ivy-leaf is now shown in a copy and compared with the natural leaf (Fig. 182), and the matter discussed is thoroughly reviewed with the aid of this leaf.

V. After that the pupils draw the ivy-leaf from the natural leaves before them. Construction lines are permitted at first; they are discarded at a second attempt.

3. HALLE.—THE EXPONENT OF THE HERBART MOVEMENT.

In previous chapters I have lightly touched upon the great movement going through the educational world in Germany known as the "Herbartian revival." Hitherto I have studiously avoided to state my opinion as to the merits of the so-called "Herbartian school." I reserved it until I had seen some schools which followed Herbart's principles and Ziller's practice. Even now, after having seen such schools, I hesitate to decide. It is a case where fools are apt to rush in though angels fear to tread. Not that I mean to insinuate that I feel very angelic, but that I am not foolish enough to jump at a conclusion. I sincerely doubt that the Herbartian school offers the recipe which will improve our schools without delay. I grant willingly that, if all our teachers were like the brilliant teachers I saw at work in the "Francke Stiftungen" at Halle, we might unconditionally advocate the adoption of the principles and practices of the Herbartian school.

A simile may help me to explain this. There are two ways of smoothing a board—the hand-plane and the planing-machine. I should trust my dexterity in handicraft to make use of a hand-plane, but I should hesitate to use the planing-machine with its destructive cutter-heads that make three thousand to four thousand revolutions a minute. I should hesitate to risk the board as little as my fingers to that most efficient and useful device. It is even so with the Herbartian practice. It is most intricate, yet withal so wonderfully simple that one can not but stand in mute astonishment when seeing it applied.

The essential idea underlying the practice is this: Everything taught during a day, a week, a month, a year, should all be organically connected. In the center of all stands a "Gesinnungs-Stoff" (a matter appealing to the heart and interest). Thus, for instance, I found in the third school year Robinson Crusoe as the central point from which issued all the interest, and to which was referred back all else. All language-lessons take their material first from the narration of the day, then from other sources. All written work is in some natural or artificial way brought into some connection with Robinson Crusoe. Arithmetical problems, I thought, were excepted from this rule. But no, even they primarily referred or alluded to him. As, for instance, Robinson had so many sheep or goats; he took sixty with him. How many were left on the island to shift for themselves? He had been on the ocean so-and-so many days; he counted the marks that told him how many days he had spent on the island and found them to be so-and-so many. How long had he been away from home? etc. In reading, the pupils started with Robinson, and their interest in reading was kept alive because each boy identified himself with Robinson and thus read much and well. I do not mean to say that all the children learned was saturated with the narrative of Robinson; but the teacher employed their intense interest in that hero as a starting-point in nearly every lesson.

These Robinson Crusoe lessons were exceedingly fruitful in many ways, for they gave opportunities for stimulating self-activity which without them would have remained dormant. Thus, for instance, they gave rise to a desire to imitate Robinson in making pots of clay, ladders and furniture of wood (all in miniature), fish-hooks, tools, and many other things. The best specimens are preserved and serve as illustrations in review-lessons. I was present during the last Robinson lesson of the year's course given in this class. The subject was Robinson returning home. Something was said about sailing-vessels and steamers, and the teacher remarked, "Well, you never saw a sail or an anchor, so I must draw them for you." He did so, and next day several boys brought sails *in natura* and anchors made of lead. (See ROBINSON CRUSOE LESSON, No. 5 below.)

Religion proper is not taught in this grade, but the narration of Robinson offers occasions in great abundance for teaching morals. Moral precepts are thus very effectively learned because they are drawn from the children's own experience, for they experience Robinson's trials and apply them to every-day occurrences.

I asked Dr. Otto Frick, the director of the "Francke Stiftungen," to what extent Herbart's principles and Ziller's interpretations were adopted in the different schools of the "Stiftungen." He replied: "We have absolutely no compulsion with regard to the methods of teaching. I am not autocratically inclined, and like to leave to each teacher the choice of his methods. Of course, I advocate Herbart, and in our own teachers' meetings we discuss his works thoroughly. His ideas have found their way into our schools with the impressibility of truth. There is still opposition among my numerous teachers against Herbart, and that will perhaps not end so long as there exists a peg to hang an argument on; but, while I am happy to be able to say Herbart is gaining ground, I am rejoiced also in noticing that the wholesome opposition (which, of course, never turns into hostility) acts like a clarifying element in the Herbart camp."

4. The Miser among the Animals.

An ideal lesson in natural history I heard in the "Francke Stiftungen" in Halle. It was in a school in which I least expected such a result, namely, in a free school (school for the poor) and in a class of the third year. The subject was the hamster, or German marmot. A stuffed specimen

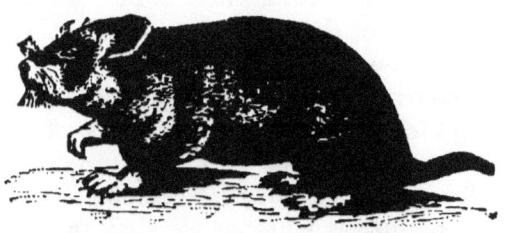

Fig. 183.—The Hamster, or German Marmot.
(*Cricetus Frumentarius Pallas.*)

was exhibited and also several chromo-lithographic pictures. I will omit the description given both by pupils and teacher, it being much like the one I sketched in the article "Nature Description." There was more in this lesson worthy of note. The children, eight to ten years of age, spoke with conviction, because they spoke of experiences, having been out in the fields with their teacher and explored a hamster's burrow.

It is a maxim of this teacher never to allow a positive statement on the part of the pupils unless it is the result of actual observation and experience, or of conviction, and as such the result of correct reasoning. This will appear more distinctly in the course of this sketch. The reader will please bear in mind that I offer only a few phases of the lesson.

"What is the reason the marmot is called a miser?"

"All summer he gathers food and hoards it up in his cave. He carries home grain in his spacious cheek-pockets."

"How do you know that?"

"We saw some grain in the cheek-pockets of the one we caught, and his den was full of it like a barn."

"But it can not be right to call him a miser for collecting food and providing for the winter. We do that, too, by keeping potatoes in the cellar, flour in barrels, and so forth. The bees, too, provide for the winter. I should think it unjust to call the animal a miser for what appears to be nothing but wise, provident saving."

"Ah, well, but a miser is he who saves for himself only, and will not share his stores with others. We are expected to share our provisions with others. The bee never gathers for its own use, but for the whole hive, while the hamster won't let anybody else have any of his hoarded treasures; he lives alone, and eats the stored-up grain himself. We call him a miser for that reason."

"Let us see whether we shall not find other reasons for calling him a miser. Does a miser let everybody know that he has money saved?"

"No, he hides it in a safe place where no one but himself can get at it. And that is exactly what the hamster does.

He hides his treasures in the ground, in a cave dug by himself. It is difficult to get at him and his treasures."

"Do you think a miser would fill his safe with copper pennies?"

"No, as soon as he has a hundred of them, he has them changed to a silver mark, for that takes less room and can be hidden better; and when he has ten of them, he has them changed to a gold piece, which is still smaller, and worth as much as a thousand pennies. Copper and silver would fill his safe too soon."

"Well said. The hamster does not fill his cave with bulky potatoes, turnips, and roots, that take up much space, but with yellow wheat and oats. But tell me what the miser does if his money-safe is attacked?"

"He defends it, and so does the marmot. Don't you know, when I reached with my hand into the hole, he bit me badly? We had to use a spade to get at him."

"Hugo, you may tell us what you remember best of our excursion to the hamster's cave."

"When we arrived at a place where fresh loose earth was piled up around a hole, we thought it must be the entrance of the cave of a pretty good-sized animal, at least as large as a cat. After the animal inside had bitten Paul's fingers we knew we should catch him. You thought it might be a hamster. Some of us watched the holes—the one on top which we had some difficulty in finding, and the one we had discovered first—so that he could not come out, while the other boys went for Mr. H——'s dog. Oh, we could scarcely wait for him we got so excited! Once we saw the hamster come to the opening, but he darted back. When Packan, the dog, came (you'll remember it was the young one with the crooked legs, called badger-legged dog), he was told to enter the hole. He sniffed at the hole for some time, and then boldly entered. Presently we heard a yelling and snarling in the ground, and, not long after, Packan appeared again with bloody snout at the opening of the tunnel, and we knew he had killed the animal. Now you told us we might dig for the animal, but to do it carefully, lest the earth should cave in and cover up what we were anxious to see. So we dug and dug, following the tunnel, and I tell you it was hard work; some roots of a tree were in the way."

"Yes," cried other boys, "it *was* hard work; we dug for it till the sweat rolled down our faces!"

"At last we saw the cave or burrow, and then you took the shovel to open the hole carefully. Yes, there he lay, Mr. Hamster, stone-dead. We laid him aside, for first we wanted to see his house."

(Boy went to the board without being told, took the crayon and sketched while he continued to tell the story.)

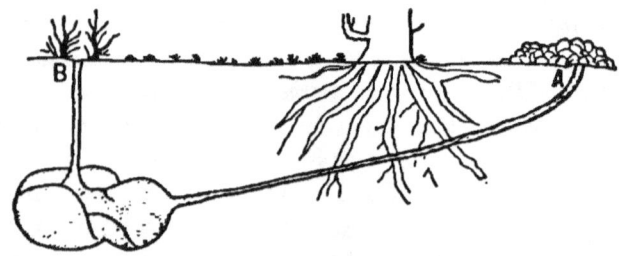

FIG. 184.

"The cave was almost egg-shaped, and had several parts or smaller caves, nearly all filled with gold-yellow grain. It was like a house with many rooms in it. The tunnel through which the dog had entered was slanting and quite long. On the top of the cave there was the second tunnel which went almost straight up."

"Very well done, my son. Did you see that the little dog found it difficult to squeeze himself through the hole? I wonder why he was not killed by the hamster."

"Oh, I suppose the tunnel was wide enough for the dog to creep into. You see it must be pretty wide, for the hamster has to turn around in it."

"Did you notice that, around the hole we saw first, loose earth was piled up?"

"Yes, that was what called our attention to the opening."

"Was the hole B discovered as easily?"

"No, we had to search for it for some time. At last we found it, almost hidden and covered with dry leaves. But there was no loose earth around it."

"That must have had some cause; can you, or any one of the class, think of it?" Another boy says:

"The hamster must have begun to dig here" (pointing at A), "and thrown the earth behind him. I believe he dug the tunnel farther and deeper in a slanting way, till he thought he had dug deep enough. Then he began to widen out a cave. He carried or rather, shoveled, the loose earth with his hind-feet, or paws, out through the tunnel till his burrow was wide enough."

"Yes, that is likely the way he did, but that does not explain why the edge of tunnel B was so clean without any loose earth around it."

That was a poser for the boys, and the teacher did not feel disposed to help them. After some hard thinking, one boy's face lit up, and he said: "I believe I can tell the reason why the edge of that perpendicular tunnel was clean. You notice, from Hugo's sketch, that this tunnel was a little wider below than above; that it looked funnel-shaped. I think the animal did not begin to dig on the surface, but from below. The earth he loosened he shoveled with his paws out through tunnel A, and continued digging upward till he had reached the surface. Thus, no earth was collected around the hole B, for it fell inward."

"Very well said, Fritz. But I am curious to find out why he made that tunnel at all. It must be very inconvenient to use it. If he entered that hole B, he would instantly fall down into the cave, and such a fall would not be pleasant enough to try it often."

"Ah, well, he must have a place for the air to come in, or go out. Without the hole B, the cave would soon smell bad."

"That is a pretty good reason, my lad, but for that purpose the tunnel might have been slanting, giving him *two* convenient ways to get in and out. There must be another reason, I think, so try again."

"Is the hamster a fighting animal like the wolf ?

"No, my son, he is not. Though he is very ferocious, he fights only when attacked."

"Then, I believe, I can guess at the cause of that vertical opening. You remember the entrance to it was almost hidden under bushes. I believe that the marmot uses that hole to reach his den only when he is pursued or chased ; and through B he can reach it quicker than through A."

"No," interrupted another boy, "you mean he can disappear from the sight of his pursuers more quickly by entering the hole B than he can do it going through A."

"Indeed, Fred, that must be the reason. Hunters tell me that hamsters sometimes disappear at quite a different place from that in which the entrance of their den is (point A)."

This is only an episode of the lesson I heard. Some of my readers may be disposed to doubt the report of this conversation, and I do not vouch for the exact choice of words and expressions, but essentially the report is correct.

I heard that lesson, and noted down on the spot the manner and method. Teacher and pupils conversed as though under no restraint, yet an interruption of a speaker occurred seldom, and then it seemed quite in place. Not an inattentive child was seen ; all were deeply interested.

When again the stuffed animal was viewed, and the pictures were compared, it seemed as though a class of highschool students, not little fellows of nine and ten years, recited. The fact is, they said nothing but what they really had seen, or could pronounce as the result of their own hard thinking. In the course of the lesson the feet of the marmot, his teeth, his whole build, were compared with those of the mole, the rat, and other animals, and the whole family of rodents. In other words, the knowledge these children accumulated was organically connected with previous cognitions.

Oh, how I wished to be a child again and go to school

here! All the teachers in the "Francke Stiftungen" are proud of that colleague of theirs. His name is Koehler. If any of my American brethren should visit Europe and should chance to go to Halle, let them call on Dr. Frick, to get permission to hear this teacher.

5. A Lesson on Robinson Crusoe.

The reader is referred to previous chapters to understand the importance of these lessons.

Teacher. "Well, my children, we heard that Robinson had at last found means to return home. He was ready to embark in the ship, the captain of which was willing to take him across the ocean. What do you think he took along with him?"

Pupil. "I think he took his parrot."

Teacher. "Why?"

Pupil. "Oh, he liked the bird, and he thought it would be a nice present for his mother."

Teacher. "Indeed, my child, he was sure to have taken his parrot, and I am glad he thought of that dear mother of his. Would you have thought of your mother first, if you had been in his place?"

Pupil. "Yes. Don't you know he had nearly broken his mother's heart by running away from home?"

Teacher. "Well, what else did he take with him?"

Pupil. "I think he took Friday. He could not have left him alone on the island. He owed him thanks for being his companion."

Teacher. "True, we must never forget a debt of gratitude. He who in fortune forgets a friend is not worth having a friend. What else did he take?"

Pupil. "He took his self-made clothes and parasol, to show how he had helped himself."

Teacher. "Yes, it is likely that he took them. Anything else?"

Pupil. "I think he took the tools he had made, and some of the pots he had formed and baked."

Teacher. "The tools, yes, but hardly the pots, for he would have found it very troublesome to travel with them. So then, they took leave of the island. The sun shone brightly, and the birds sang as though they meant to say good-by to Robinson and his black friend. They both went on board the large sailing-vessel, where they were well received. Now the anchor was wound up." (Teacher draws an anchor, pupils explain its use.) "The sails were hoisted" (sails were drawn on the board, by pupils likewise on slate), "and the wind began to move the vessel onward. Robinson stood on deck and looked back to the island on which he and Friday had spent so many weary months. Both remembered the many hardships they had suffered.—Now some one may tell the story so far."

Pupil. "When the captain of the sailing-vessel had agreed to take Robinson with him to Hamburg,* Robinson said to him: 'Let me take my friend Friday. He has been my companion for many months and years, and it would be ungrateful if I should leave him here alone on the island.' The captain was willing to take the black fellow also. Then Robinson took on board what was dear to him, his parrot, his tools, his clothes of goat-skin, and other things which he wanted to show at home. He intended to give the parrot to his dear mother, the poor lady who had grieved for her bad, runaway boy. Both Robinson and Friday took leave of the places on the island where they had found shelter, and by taking the captain along on their tour of leave-taking they showed him the island and many of the objects that had served them. When they stood on the deck of the sailing-vessel, they looked back upon the island. The sun shone upon the gently swaying palm-trees, the goats were capering among the rocks, and the birds sang and twittered as though they meant to take leave of Robinson," . . . etc., with delightful childish particularity.

---

* Remember this was a German school. Another deviation from Defoe's original is found in the substitution of goats for llamas.

Now another pupil told the story, somewhat differently, a proof that each pupil thought his own thoughts. Then this part of the narrative was entitled "*Robinson's Departure from the Island.*" This heading found a place on the blackboard under I.

Teacher. "For the present, children, we must leave Robinson on the ocean, and let us hope he will not meet with another storm such as had wrecked the ship on which he had left home. We have a gentleman with us who has been on the ocean several times. He comes all the way from America. Ask him how long it took him to cross the mighty ocean."

Pupil. "Oh, no, he can not have come from there; he is not black or red like Negroes and Indians." Some boys laughingly agreed that the teacher's statement could not have been right. But others looked sober, and one of them said : "My cousin went over to America some time ago, and when he comes back I hope he will be white yet. People don't get black there who are not born black." That sobered the others at once, and now they believed that there might be white people in America. After this fact was acknowledged the boys said to me, "Do tell us how long it took you to cross the ocean."

"It took me thirteen days and ten hours, but you see, I came in a large steamer. Had I been in a sailing-vessel, it would have taken me much longer—at any rate, several weeks."

Pupil. "Why, that's nearly two weeks! Did you not see any land on the way ?"

"Yes, on the tenth day we hailed the coast of England, and after that we hardly ever lost the coast out of sight, till we reached Hamburg."

Pupil. "Well, how long does it take a sailing-vessel to cross the ocean ?"

"If the wind is favorable, about five weeks. But it may take seven weeks."

Pupil. "Hooh! seven weeks ; why that's, forty-nine days, just think of it ! Did you see any fishes ?"

"Yes, my dear, we saw large fishes, called tumblers, who jumped from one wave into another, following the steamer to eat what was thrown overboard. They are called hog-fish, because their flesh looks like fresh pork, rosy and fat."

Pupil. "Did you have any storms on the sea?"

"Yes, a storm that lasted three days, and we had much fog, in which we could not see the bow of the steamer when standing at the stern." Other questions with which I was pelted I will omit here, and proceed with the lesson.

Teacher. "Let us see, boys: our story tells us that Robinson had a passage which lasted nine weeks. If you remember where Robinson's island is situated, west of South America, the voyage was very swift." (Map is shown, and distances are compared.) "The vessel met with no storm or fog, and the weather was fine. The fishes in the sea could be seen playing in the sunshine. Robinson and Friday made themselves useful on board by helping to set sails and doing other things. At last they reached the coast of England, but did not land. The vessel glided along the shores of England, France, Holland, and Germany, and finally up the river Elbe, and entered the harbor of Hamburg. Some one may tell the story of '*Robinson's Voyage across the Ocean.*'"

First one, then two others, told the story, mentioning time of voyage, comparing it with that of a steamer. The fishes, sunshine, wind, sails, work on deck, and other points were touched with a faithfulness truly astonishing.

Teacher "Let us proceed. Tell me what was done when the ship was fastened to the dock?"

Pupil. "The people left the ship and went on land."

Teacher. "Leaving everything under deck they had brought with them?"

Pupil. "No, they unloaded the freight."

Teacher. "What may that have consisted of?"

Pupil. "Well, the ship had been in the South Sea, and may have been loaded with oranges or other southern fruit, perhaps with cocoanuts."

Teacher. "What other things are brought from foreign countries?"

Pupil. "Petroleum, wheat, dye-wood, wild animals, hides, dried fish."

Teacher. "Think of some things that do not grow in Germany."

Pupil. "Coffee, rice, tea, cane-sugar, cotton, tobacco."

Teacher. "Very well. Our story does not say with what the ship was loaded; but, when it was fastened to the dock, all the freight was carried out and wheeled into the big magazines along the dock, where the merchants came to buy. Shall we stay at the dock and see the freight unloaded, or follow Robinson and Friday into town?"

Pupil. "Let us follow Robinson."

Teacher. "All right; it must have taken several days to unload the ship, and Robinson wanted to hurry home to see his dear old mother. How do you think Friday behaved when they reached the harbor?"

Pupil. "Oh, he must have been very much astonished, for he had never seen a city. The many ships, the high houses, the many white people, and the smoking chimney-stacks of the steamers, the cranes for unloading ships, all of it must have looked very queer to him."

Another pupil. "The strangest things the savage saw must have been the horses drawing wagons. 'Look, Robinson,' he cried, 'look at these animals! Did you ever see such strange things?' And when they entered a horse-car and noticed the long rows of houses with the many many windows, the thousands of people on the streets, and all the many objects of interest flitting by, he sat in dumb amazement."

Teacher. "Very well told, my boy. I see I need not tell the story myself; you can tell it as well as I can. What happened when they left the street-car?"

Pupil. "Oh, Friday saw so many new things he had never seen before that he stood still every minute to ask Robinson to look at this and that." *Other pupils.* "Yes;

and when they came to a big shop-window he wanted to know what everything seen there was for."—" He reached out his hand to take some of the things to look at them closer, but was much astonished to find he could not do that on account of the thick pane of glass between him and the articles."—" I wonder how often he cried to Robinson, who was urging him on, to stay and look at a new article he had never seen ?"—" I believe he was afraid when he saw the first dog. He may have thought him to be a wild animal, such as a panther."

Teacher. "We will call this part of our story ' *Their Arrival in Hamburg and Friday's Astonishment.*' Some one may tell me the story." It is repeated in a connected manner by several pupils. Then the teacher said: "Before we hear what Robinson found at home, let us repeat the three parts of our story. This section shall tell us of his departure from the island; the second section may tell us all about his voyage across the ocean; and the third of their arrival in the harbor and Friday's astonishment at the new sights he beheld." It was surprising to see how faithfully they recalled the different incidents spoken of and how well they expressed their thoughts.

Teacher. "At last they reached the house where Robinson was born. He looked at the door-plate, which used to bear the name ' Daniel Crusoe,' but now bore another name. Robinson rang the bell. A servant opened the door and asked whom he wanted to see. He said, 'I want to see Mr. and Mrs. Crusoe.' 'They do not live here any longer; but wait a moment, I will call my master. He may tell you where to find them.' The gentleman came and looked at this strange couple, Robinson not having had time to shave his long beard and cut his hair, and Friday, the black fellow, must have looked odd enough in this city of white people; and then remember that they were laden with queer-shaped things and a jabbering parrot. Robinson asked anxiously after his mother. The gentleman of the house asked them in, offered them seats, and then told them all about the old people.

"Robinson's mother had grieved so much over her runaway boy that she fell ill, and, when news reached her that the ship in which he had sailed for foreign lands had been wrecked, she died of a broken heart. Think of the bitter tears of repentance Robinson cried when he heard that that dear, gentle, loving mother of his had died of grief! He was a strong man now; but the hot tears trickled down into his long beard, and for some time he could not control himself. Friday, seeing his friend's great distress, began to weep too; but the parrot that was intended for a present to the old dame did not know what to make of it. At last Robinson controlled himself enough to ask after his father.

"He was still alive, the gentleman said, but he had retired from business and lived in a small house near the harbor, where he sat, lonely and forsaken, to watch the ships coming in and leaving the harbor. Robinson thanked the gentleman kindly for the information and left the old house, to look up his father. After many inquiries along the wharf, he found the house where his father lived. They hurried up-stairs, and in a tidy little room they found the old man. His hair had become white, his eyes dim, and his voice trembling. Robinson threw himself on his knees before him and told him he was that bad, runaway boy. He had been saved, and had come back to him never to leave him again. The old man laid his hands on his son's head and thanked God for having given him back his boy."

My readers may believe me if I say the pupils sat there spellbound, tears in their eyes, and many of them were sobbing. The teacher had told the story so touchingly that the children's sympathy had been aroused. Not an incredulous smile, not a sneer was seen, not a word was heard from them for some moments after the teacher had closed his narrative. It was one of those moments in which it is said an angel walks through the room. At last the teacher roused the children from a deep reverie by asking them to repeat this part of the story, which he termed "*Robinson's Bitter Repentance.*" It was done with touching simplicity and great accuracy. Again the entire lesson was reviewed, partly by questioning the class, partly by allowing them to narrate portions in a connected manner. Many new incidents were added, and, when at last the lesson closed, the story of Robinson Crusoe was finished to the satisfaction of all concerned.

This narration furnishes the "Gesinnungs-Stoff" (material for the sentiments) of this class as other tales do in lower and biblical history does in higher grades. Besides offering food for the sentiments, these lessons increase the pupil's knowledge, give opportunities for employing their hands, and polish their language. Much of what is offered in a connected manner in the above account was given in conversation; but a *verbatim* repetition might have been tedious to the reader.

6. A LANGUAGE-LESSON.

It was in a boys' school of the "Francke Stiftungen" that I heard a lesson in reading and language preparatory to a composition exercise. The subject was that well-known poem of Chamisso, "The Sun brings it to Light." The poem was read in parts, and the contents were grouped logically in four divisions: 1. The master and his wife in the workshop; 2. The wife's efforts to get at the secret; 3. The betrayal of the secret; 4. The consequences. All who know the beautiful poem can understand how interestingly it can be treated. I will therefore only say that the teacher succeeded in bringing out all the points that could be of assistance in writing the composition—that is, in transposing the poem into prose.

But there was an epilogue to the lesson which proved a revelation to the class. Let me sketch it.

Teacher. "How do you think a poem is suggested to a poet?"

Answer. "He sees something beautiful and gives the feelings it creates in him expression in rhymed words."

Another answer. "He may hear of a praiseworthy act, or read of it in the papers, and may be much moved by it, so much, indeed, that a desire is awakened in him to preserve in poetry the memory of the brave act; or, instead of an act of heroism, it may be any other memorable occurrence."

Teacher. "It so happened that Chamisso read of this case of murder and of the discovery of the guilty party, and then set it in poetry. But do you think the poems produced thus accurately describe the cases as given in newspaper accounts?"

Answer. "No, not exactly. They often differ very much in names, in descriptions, in regard to time and circumstances, etc. The poet is likely to 'decorate' the occurrence, and often supplies a poetic luster which the occurrence itself does not possess. Thus, for instance, the poet Schwab could not have known what the great-grandmother, grandmother, mother, and child said and thought just before the lightning struck them. Yet in his poem, 'The Thunderstorm,' he makes them say and do things as though he had been present and seen and heard it all."

Teacher. "Well, then, what is your opinion with regard to this poem of Chamisso?"

Answer. "What Fred said, I think, holds good in this case. The poet evidently supplied description and sentiments, and only the essential facts are the same as in the account he read."

Teacher. "We will see. I have here the account which induced Chamisso to make the poem that we read to-day. I will read you the account. Notice what changes the poet made."

And now he proceeded to read an old popular narrative which bore such striking resemblance to Chamisso's poem that the boys were much surprised. Such words as "malt zitternde Kringel an die Wand," "plagt ihn mit Hadern und Bitten," occurred in the prose narration, even the name of the master was the same. Altogether it was the most faithful and minute transposition of poetry into prose that one could imagine. "What now, boys?" asked the teacher when he had finished reading the account.

15

Answer. "What a surprising similarity! How the poet must have labored to preserve the particular expressions, and how he could mold the entire account into metric feet and rhymes without omitting one detail or changing even the characteristic expressions of the prose! Or have you been making sport of us by reading a prose rendition of the poetry? I feel disposed to ask which is the older production, the poem or the prose narration?"

Teacher. "No; the prose narration is the older. It is the very account the poet transposed. But what do you infer from the fact that the two show such a remarkable similarity?"

Answer. "I think that enhances Chamisso's value as a poet. If he could so wield the language as to preserve all the beauties of expression found in this prose narration and add to them by molding them into poetry, he must be a genius of no low type."

Teacher and pupils all agreed with that, and when the boys began to write their composition they resolved to preserve the felicitous choice of words which makes the poem so popular. They went to work, indeed, as though they meant to produce a masterpiece in prose, a determination which I traced back to the innocent but effective device of the teacher.

7. MISCELLANEOUS NOTES FROM HALLE.

Among the several schools in the "Francke Stiftungen" in Halle in which I spent some time, was a normal school for young ladies. It had thirty-three pupils, between eighteen and twenty-one years of age. These young ladies were very much more healthy-looking than the average pupil of the Cincinnati Normal School and other similar institutions in America with which I am acquainted, but they were not so handsome and not by far so intelligent as the American young ladies. The lesson I heard was one in psychology and logic. It seemed as though this was the most difficult study under the sun, although the teacher was a perfect master of the science and art of teaching.

In a girls' school in Halle I heard a lesson in percentage in a class similar to our D Grammar (fifth school year). The pupils handled the subject clumsily, as would be expected, but to think that, at the close of the fourth year, the subject of fractions is finished, is astonishing. I found this in several places in Germany and France, and can explain it only by the fact that the ponderous chapter of denominate numbers is omitted. In countries where the metric system is used the measures are taught along with numeration and notation.

A lesson in geography that I heard in an upper grade of a girls' school is also very vividly remembered. The teacher discussed continental climate, its causes and effects. Every conclusion the pupils arrived at was found by themselves by comparison of facts. All the teacher did was pointing out the topographical conditions of each continent. Our American scorching summers and cold, blizzard winters were accounted for, and I could not help but admire the teacher's intimate acquaintance with America, and the girls' intense interest and keen intellect.

One observation made in every class-room of the "Francke Stiftungen" is, that the teachers make a halt every now and then during the lesson, and carefully go over the work by calling upon pupils to present in a connected manner what conclusion was drawn, and upon what premises it rested. They thereby prevented a great deal of reviewing; they allowed the matter to sink in deeper; they enabled the pupil to look back over the entire road on which they had arrived at their conclusions. These "part-reviews" are most desirable also for the reason that the pupils get conscious of their reasoning and are enabled to reproduce it in writing, which task follows nearly every lesson in these schools.

It is natural to suppose that in an institution like Francke's, industrial work of the girls is much thought of. It would be a useless repetition, though, to describe it, since I have dwelt on that subject elsewhere at length. (Compare pages 120-126.) Suffice it to say that I noticed an effort

210 HALLE (PRUSSIAN PROVINCE OF SAXONY).

at economical cutting of linen and shirting in the getting up of undergarments which is characteristic. A blackboard

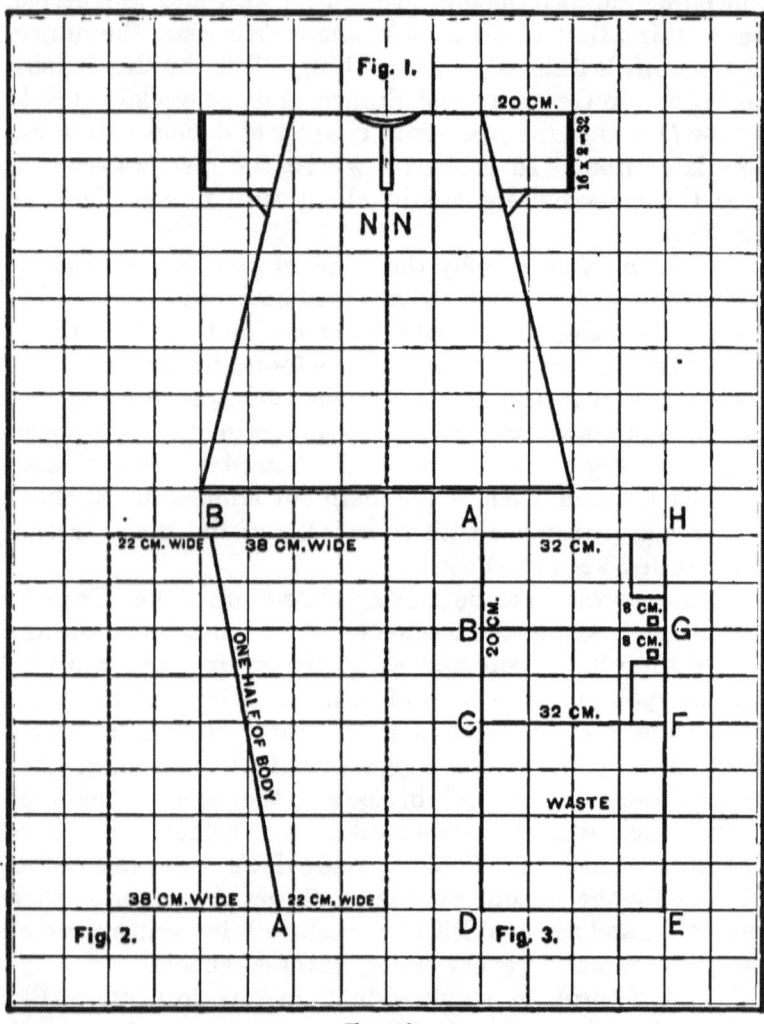

Fig. 185.

covered with a close network of lines was used to draw first the piece of linen according to exact measurements; every square on the board represents a square decimetre. Then the body of a chemise, for instance, was cut out, the sleeves, the triangular sides, squares for the arm-pits etc. The foregoing sketch shows the mode of procedure.

CHAPTER IX.

FROM VARIOUS OTHER PRUSSIAN PROVINCES.

1. SCHOOLS IN PRUSSIA.

THERE are four classes of public schools in Prussian as well as in other German cities. It may be of interest to learn their distinctions:

1. *People's Schools*, either Catholic or Protestant, but both maintained by state and community. These people's schools have an eight years' course. Children of *both sexes* enter at six and leave at thirteen or fourteen years. No language but German is taught, and this almost entirely without the aid of grammar, simply by careful training in the use of the language. Arithmetic is carried on not quite so far as we do in our common schools. History is taught, both German and universal history, chiefly in biographies. Geography, topographical, political, mathematical, and physical—within a limited compass, of course. Physics and natural history are taught during the last two years of the course, only in an elementary way, not quite so far perhaps as Paul Bert's recent book shows, which has been presented to the American public lately. Drawing, singing, and gymnastics are all taught to a greater extent than is done in America. In their readers the pupils find more solid knowledge than is found in the flimsy conversations of our English-American readers; the books contain masterpieces of all kinds of prose and poetry, instructive and amusing. Composing in words and pictures goes on at every step, and is developed to a very astonishing degree.

2. *Bürger Schools*, Citizen's Schools so called in contradistinction from the People's Schools, which are elementary in this respect, that they teach the elements of knowledge and abstain from scientific presentation. These Bürger Schools attempt more than mere elements. Their course is about ten years, beginning with the sixth and ending with the sixteenth year of age. The first three years are considered the preparatory school. After that the semi-scientific course begins, which embraces besides the common branches also French and a little Latin. The natural sciences are treated more thoroughly in the higher grades, and drawing leans toward industrial pursuits. The Bürger Schools are only for boys.

Side by side with these schools are the

Higher Young Ladies' Schools, of which I can not say much, not having visited many. I only know that they terminate in a post-graduate course for young teachers. The Bürger and Young Ladies' Schools resemble in their higher grades our city high-schools. The Bürger School does not prepare for the university. It may be said that this class of schools was established to offer an education more advanced than can be given in People's Schools, and less extended than a preparation for the university would necessitate. All religions and denominations are admitted, and religious instruction is given in these schools by specially appointed clergymen, both Catholic and Protestant. The Young Ladies' School is mostly for Protestants, while for Catholic girls the higher convent-schools are open. In the People's Schools religion is taught by the regular class teachers and the pupils are considered ready for graduation when they are ready to be confirmed in church.

3. *Higher Schools*, which may be said to be on a level with the majority of our colleges. They are all for boys. Among these schools there are three distinct divisions:

I. *Gymnasium*, or Lyceum, or Classical School. These schools prepare for the three learned professions—law, medicine, and theology. Much emphasis is laid upon Latin,

Greek, and Hebrew, as well as history and archæology. While modern languages and sciences are not neglected, they can not be said to be the most important branches of the curriculum.

Its course is fourteen years, from the sixth till the twentieth year of life.

The teachers are all graduates of universities.

II. *Realschule*, also called Real-gymnasium, pays more attention to modern languages and the sciences than to the classical languages and archæology. Much attention is given to drawing and the mathematics. Students of medicine, engineering, and business men are prepared here.

Course, fourteen years. Teachers all university men.

III. *Special Schools*, are either industrial or art schools, or teachers' seminaries. Among the latter a few are, under certain restrictions, open to ladies.

The course of all these special schools varies so much, that a statement as to its length can not safely be made.

The teachers of art and technical schools are artists, enginers, artisans, etc.

Only large cities in centers of industry maintain special schools of this kind, while normal schools or teachers' seminaries are state institutions and mostly found in small towns.

4. *Universities*, the work of which is so well known in America that I need not say anything about them.

2. A Device, not a Method.

Business led me to the little town of V—— in Holland,* near the German boundary, and having a few hours to while away in waiting, I called at the elementary school, where I found a bright, blue-eyed young man busily engaged in teaching about fifty pupils between six and ten years of age.

---

* This being the only school I saw in Holland, I insert the article in this chapter, being aware that the Dutch teachers to a great extent copy their German brethren.

He did not ask me the customary American question, "What would you like to hear?" but, after offering me a seat, proceeded with his work as if no stranger was present. I liked that, and soon my liking for the young man grew into admiration, when I observed with what loving-kindness he treated the youngsters, and in what a masterly way he handled a class and taught his subjects.

The pupils were young, and the class before him at the board may have averaged eight years. They were wrestling with *fractions*; yes, dear reader, fractions! Not such as $\frac{111}{117}$, but familiar ones, such as $\frac{1}{2}$, $\frac{1}{3}$, $\frac{1}{4}$, etc. The teacher used a very interesting contrivance to illustrate the parts of a whole. I will sketch it.

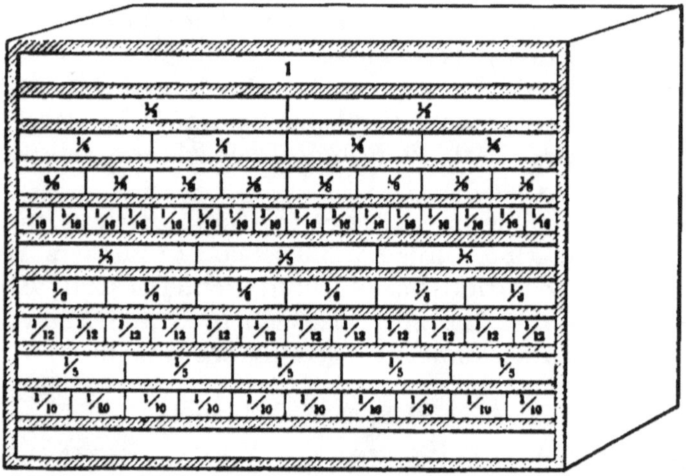

FIG. 186.

The above is to represent a chest of shallow shelves, into which boards fit snugly; the boards are cut accurately into parts, as indicated in the cut, and each part is labeled. A glance at the above sketch will suffice to reveal the purpose of the contrivance. It speaks for itself.

The teacher had removed the thirds, fifths, sixths, and others, and now showed that a whole was equal to $\frac{2}{2}$, $\frac{4}{4}$, $\frac{8}{8}$,

½. Then taking one of the halves out, he asked how many fourths, eighths, and sixteenths made one half, etc. Reduction, ascending and descending, was thus thoroughly exemplified and practiced.

The same exercise was had in thirds, sixths, ninths, twelfths, and the pupils were led to work with these fractions themselves; that is, "do," not only "see" or "hear." It was a great pleasure to observe the little Dutch boys and girls "do" fractions. Their cheeks glowed with excitement, and they noticed the stranger as little as did the teacher.

When, after singing a pretty little song, they were dismissed, I inquired of the teacher how long he would use this device. "Only a few times," was the reply, "for it would weaken the children's comprehension, or rather their power of thinking, to have the objects always before them. It is my intention to lead the pupils from the object to its symbol as soon as possible. But if I were to use the symbols—that is, the figures—at once, without the objects they represent, I should be putting the cart before the horse. To-day, the children learned by actual observation that $\frac{2}{4}=\frac{3}{6}=\frac{4}{8}$, etc. To-morrow, they will learn to write these fractions while having this device before them. The next day will bring easy combinations, both *in fact* and *in figures*. Thus, I think, in a week they will handle with ease and accuracy simple fractions, such as are illustrated by these boards. And then is the time when I shall put the device away. But I mean to build on solid rock, on a firm basis of sense-perception."

"Did you invent this contrivance?"

"Oh, bless your soul, no! It was invented by a Japanese schoolmaster, and our commissioner to the New Orleans Exposition brought the idea to us. He saw the device in the Japanese school exhibit."

"Have you had special preparation for the profession?"

"Yes, sir; I am a graduate of the Royal Normal School, at ——."

3. MENTAL ARITHMETIC EVERYWHERE.

The great advantages of the metric system in the teaching of arithmetic are obvious everywhere here in Germany. Arbitrary measures, such as ours, are a hindrance in school. Pound, gallon, bushel, yard, etc., all have a different number of parts, while the division in tens, hundreds, thousands, makes reckoning remarkably easy. This enables the teacher to conduct mentally eighty per cent of all the practice in arithmetic. It is very interesting to see pupils of the third and fourth school years use numbers mentally which would take our pupils' breath away. The latter can not handle the arbitrary measures, such as yards and inches, gallons, quarts, and pints, bushels and pecks, pounds, ounces, and grains, etc., simply because the variety of divisions makes a number of tables necessary whose committal goes beyond the capacity of young pupils.

As soon as the German child knows the notation and numeration up to 1,000, he is made to apply numbers to metres, litres, and grammes. The divisions are the same in all measures, namely, deka, hecto, and kilo, multiples of one, and deci, centi, and milli, parts of one. It is always 10, 100, 1,000 of one, or $\frac{1}{10}$, $\frac{1}{100}$, $\frac{1}{1000}$ of one. I assure my readers that only one half-hour daily is spent in arithmetic here, and that mostly in mental or oral arithmetic. In the fourth school year the chapter of "Fractions," both common and decimal, is completed, and the fifth school year takes up simple proportion, the so-called rule of three. In the sixth school year percentage and most of the business rules and mensuration are treated, things which with us are reserved for the eighth school year.

I am fully aware that we can not help this, being hampered by the voluminous chapter on denominate numbers during the fourth and fifth school years. Here in Germany they do not treat that chapter as a separate and highly important one. The pupils need not study tables, for the measures are taught right along with numeration and notation. As the pupil's horizon in notation widens, his knowledge of the measures increases. It is a fact that almost the entire ground in arithmetic gone over in the eight years' course of the American common school is here completed in six years. This is not astonishing, and must not be attributed to a greater intellectual power of the German children, for they are not as quick in perception and application as our shrewd American youth, but rather of a slow but sure kind.

The reason is to be found solely in the use of the metric system and the prevalence of mental, or, more correctly speaking, of *oral* arithmetic. A third-year class in Duisburg solved these problems in the twinkling of an eye : "One sack contained 5 kilogrammes, 7 hectogrammes, 3 dekagrammes, and 8 grammes ; another 2 kilogrammes, 3 dekagrammes, and 5 grammes. What was the weight of both ?" "A man divided 21 marks, 25 pennies, equally among five boys. What was each boy's share ?" And it was done without the aid of pen or pencil.

Much of what we teach in our American schools under the captivating title of business rules is prohibited here by the regulations laid down by the Minister of Instruction ; as, for instance, compound interest, stocks and bonds, taxes, exchange, etc. The course prescribed is eminently practical, to say the least, and much may be learned from it.

4. Teaching Decimal Fractions.

Teachers in countries that have adopted the metric system have an advantage over American teachers in this, that they have at their disposal means for illustrating which we can not apply. While our measures—*foot-rule, yard-stick*, etc.—are very convenient for illustrating *common fractions* (twelve and thirty-six being oftener divisible than ten), the *metre* is the ideal means for illustrating *decimal fractions*. In H—— I observed a teacher introduce the subject of decimal fractions to, what seemed to me, very young pupils. First, he reviewed numeration : "Ten ones make one ten. Ten is the tenfold of one. Ten tens make a hundred. A hundred is the tenfold of ten, and the hundred-fold of one"; etc. "One place farther to the left increases the value of the digit tenfold; one place farther to the right decreases it to the tenth part. As the tens are obtained from the hundred by dividing by ten, and the one from ten by dividing by ten, so the fractions are obtained in the same way. Thus, by dividing one by ten, we get ten tenths, and, by dividing one tenth thus, we obtain ten hundredths, etc. This was further illustrated by using the "metre and its divisions."

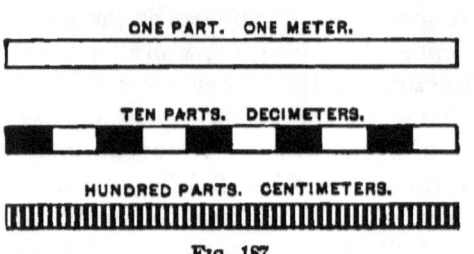

Fig. 187.

A metre-measure (pardon the tautology) was sketched on the board in "life-size." It was made three times, as the cut shows.

The children knew that 1 metre = 10 decimetres. So the teacher made them *see* and *say* that 1 decimetre = $\frac{1}{10}$ metre. Similar expressions had preceded when common fractions were treated. But the teacher was very thorough in his mode of procedure. He now made the pupils *see*, *say*, and *write* as follows:

1 dm. = $\frac{1}{10}$ m. $\frac{1}{10}$ m. = 1 dm.
2 dm. = $\frac{2}{10}$ m. $\frac{2}{10}$ m. = 2 dm.
3 dm. = $\frac{3}{10}$ m., etc. $\frac{3}{10}$ m. = 3 dm., etc.
9 dm. = $\frac{9}{10}$ m. $\frac{9}{10}$ m. = 9 dm.
10 dm. = $\frac{10}{10}$ m. = 1 m.   1 m. or $\frac{10}{10}$ m. = 10 dm.

Then exercises like these followed:

2 m. 1 dm. = $2\frac{1}{10}$ m.
2 m. 2 dm. = $2\frac{2}{10}$ m. and so forth to $2\frac{9}{10}$ m.

When this was sufficiently practiced, the decimal notation was introduced. They knew, from preceding exercises, that every place farther to the right would decrease the digit to the tenth part. Now they were asked to write:

$$2 \text{ m. } 1 \text{ dm.} = 2\tfrac{1}{10} \text{ m. or } 2.1 \text{ m.}$$
$$2 \text{ m. } 2 \text{ dm.} = 2\tfrac{2}{10} \text{ m. or } 2.2 \text{ m.}$$
$$2 \text{ m. } 3 \text{ dm.} = 2\tfrac{3}{10} \text{ m. or } 2.3 \text{ m.}$$

The use of the decimal point was not necessary to explain, it having been taught in connection with notation of *marks, groschen,* and *pennies,* as is done in our country with *dollars, dimes,* and *cents.* The result of this lesson is that 5 metres 6 decimetres may be written 5.6m., just as 5 marks 6 groschen may be written M.5.6.

Now the hundredths were treated like the tenths by writing whole strings and columns of common fractions. Thus the centimetre was brought in:

$$1 \text{ cm.} = \tfrac{1}{10} \text{ dm.} = \tfrac{1}{100} \text{ m.} \qquad \tfrac{1}{100} \text{ m.} = \tfrac{1}{10} \text{ dm.} = 1 \text{ cm.}$$
$$2 \text{ cm.} = \tfrac{2}{10} \text{ dm.} = \tfrac{2}{100} \text{ m.} \qquad \tfrac{2}{100} \text{ m.} = \tfrac{2}{10} \text{ dm.} = 2 \text{ cm.}$$
$$3 \text{ cm.} = \tfrac{3}{10} \text{ dm.} = \tfrac{3}{100} \text{ m.} \qquad \tfrac{3}{100} \text{ m.} = \tfrac{3}{10} \text{ dm.} = 3 \text{ cm.}$$

Then followed again:

$$3 \text{ m. } 4 \text{ dm. } 1 \text{ cm.} = 3 \text{ m. } 4\tfrac{1}{10} \text{ dm. or } 3.41 \text{ m.}$$
$$3 \text{ m. } 4 \text{ dm. } 2 \text{ cm.} = 3 \text{ m. } 4\tfrac{2}{10} \text{ dm. or } 3.42 \text{ m.}$$

Again, notation of money was made use of. Thus they wrote 5 mark, 4 groschen, 3 pennies=M.5.43.

There was nothing startlingly new, if anything new at all, in this lesson. I sketch it for the sole purpose of showing that familiarity with the metric tables will assist in the teaching of decimal fractions. If there was anything else in this lesson which commended itself to me, it was the systematic and thorough treatment. There was no skipping, no jumping at conclusions, but a steady movement which reminded me of Nature's own unhurried manner of growth.

5. ARITHMETIC IN A VILLAGE SCHOOL.

After having roamed about the Siebengebirge (the seven mounts, a little way up the Rhine from the university town Bonn) and thoroughly enjoyed the views, we concluded to inspect the school of a hamlet not six miles distant from the summit of the "Drachenfels," and visible from there. The reader of my "Chips," perhaps knows that the writer has a singularly keen eye for defects in school-wook, a quality which amounts to a fault, where it should be an object to see "naught but good." Well, we had seen Dutch, French, and German city schools, schools mostly in populous cities, and were so deeply impressed with the excellence of the work done in them that the perverse spirit of envy made us long to see something to criticise severely. The school in the hamlet mentioned, we thought, would prove to be, like that of an American backwoods settlement, primitive in the

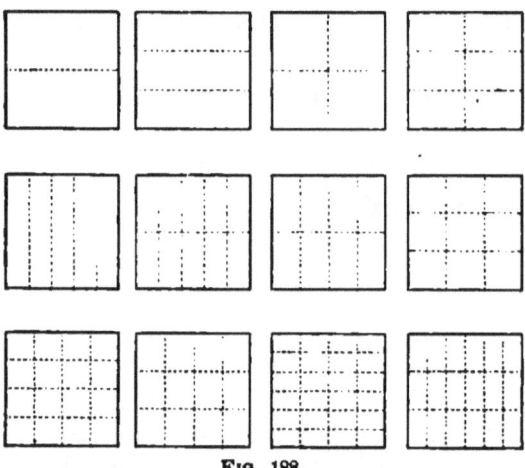

FIG. 188.

extreme. But we were greatly mistaken. What we saw was admirable work.

One device particularly struck me, since I had advocated its use myself in the educational press of America. It was the use of *paper squares* of uniform size (six inches), but of different colors. These squares were *perforated* like sheets of postage-stamps, but so as to divide them into different parts, such as halves, thirds, fourths, etc. In order not to be misunderstood, I will sketch them (see Fig. 188). The

ARITHMETIC IN A VILLAGE SCHOOL.   221

squares were used to *illustrate fractions*, and both teacher and pupils were liberally supplied with them. They had been procured at a paper-mill, and cut and perforated by a printer.

The pupils learned the process of reduction ascending and descending very rapidly. The terms of ⅓ multiplied by 2 gave ⅔, and it was *done* by folding the sheet of thirds so that each third was folded to make two of six equal parts of the whole. The opposite way was just as easily shown.

The squares were of different color: halves, fourths, eighths, and sixteenths were pink; thirds, sixths, ninths, etc., green; fifths and tenths, yellow. This afforded an instant selection of the proper sheet when a problem was given out. The paper had the thickness of ordinary writing-paper, and the pupils could write on it with pencil or ink.

One problem particularly interested me, since the pupils received no help whatever in its solution. I had given it out myself, prompted by a spirit of mischief. Example: Multiply ⅔ by ¼. A few seconds sufficed for the brighter pupils to do the work *in* paper and *on* paper. Being asked to select a pupil to demonstrate this problem, I selected a sleepy-looking youngster, who arose, and much to my surprise turned to me, saying:

"You can not multiply by a fraction, since multiplying means repeating. You can not repeat fewer times than once; ¼ not being even 1, it is clear that you meant to say ¼ of ⅔. Now take a sheet of twelfths." I did. "Fold ¼ under, leaving ¾ of the sheet visible." I did. "Now fold the ⅔ into four equal strips. By thus dividing ⅔, you also divide the third third folded under. You really divide each third into fourths, or the whole sheet into twelfths."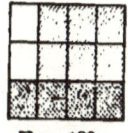

Fig. 189.

I did as indicated in the margin (Fig. 189). "Then ¼ of ⅔ equals 2/12 or ⅙." Thus spoke the youth, and sat down.

My admiration grew when examples in division were solved. The teacher, a thorough master of his profession, did little talking, but instead, permitted the children to work with hands, brains, and lips, not caring to repress whispering, knowing that this was the inevitable attendant of earnest work. The school was a regular country school. It contained about forty pupils of all ages between six and thirteen, nicely graded in four grades.

6. A Lesson in Botany.

My companion and I had missed the Rhine steamer one day, and were obliged to stay overnight at the foot of a vine-clad hill, on top of which one of the grandest piles of ruins—that of a feudal castle—spoke louder than any orator could of the victory of modern ideas over feudalism, and of civil virtue over absolutism. It was a pretty little town where we were thus detained, and we enjoyed the night's rest at a quaint old inn, where we had the best attention possible; indeed, the landlord took great care to make us feel at home. I had spent several days at the gorgeous Kimball House in Atlanta, in the Palmer House in Chicago, and other costly hotels in the Union, where the rates were sixteen to twenty marks a day, and had not enjoyed the conveniences which here were offered for three marks. The steamer was due at one o'clock, and so we found our way to the school-house as a duck finds its way to the water.

The house was as quaint-looking as the town. It had low ceilings, small windows, and was poorly ventilated, but somehow the thought that perhaps a score of generations of children had been educated in this building mitigated our disgust. My faithful companion made friends with the schoolmaster's wife, who was trimming vines in the garden, and I began to mine for methods. I praise my good luck for having missed the steamer. The teacher of the "upper class" gave a botany-lesson. Botany was something I had not had occasion to "see," and I determined to get the most out of that lesson.

The teacher explained to me privately that, when he had been young, botany had always "given him the creeps," he had so abhorred the deadening influence of learning technical terms, and classifying plants and flowers according to the Linnæan system. When he was appointed to this place, he determined to make botany liked by his pupils. In order to understand the situation, the reader must remember that this was an elementary school, not a high-school.

The pupils were plentifully provided with leaves which, according to directions, they had gathered on their way to school. Now they learned to classify the leaves according to their edges. It was interesting to notice how skillfully the teacher combined with this botany-lesson (*a*) spelling, (*b*) language, (*c*) drawing. He enlarged the pupils' vocabulary by placing on the board every new word used ; then it was spelled, and then copied into the note-book under the drawing or sketch made, which served as illustration.

Not a single Latin technical term was employed, all were German, and that struck me as eminently wise. Such words as *serratum, dentatum, crenatum, repantum, sinuatum, ciliatum*, mean nothing to the children. You may as well say *setarum* for *serratum*, it is all the same to them. But if called "saw-like, tooth-like, notch-like, slope-like, bay-like," etc., the words convey a meaning. Ideas arising from such instruction abide in the memory, because they are, as it were, the organic growth and outcome of sense-perception. Catch me using the outlandish botanical names again in schools below the high-school ! I won't do it !

This is the way the teacher proceeded : He selected a number of leaves, the edges of which were all "saw-like," and then sketched them on the board. There were four different kinds. Of the fourth kind no sample could be furnished, so he had to reproduce it from memory, but every pupil nodded, indicating thereby that he had seen it somewhere. The German technical terms were added, spelled, copied (as were the sketches), and then the momentous question arose, what plants have this kind of leaves, say "fine saw-edged," or "double saw-edged leaves ? "

These facts were added to the notes already taken. When an honest difference of opinion arose between two pupils, the teacher asked them to go into the garden and determine who was right. In a few moments they returned with specimens, which set the matter at rest.

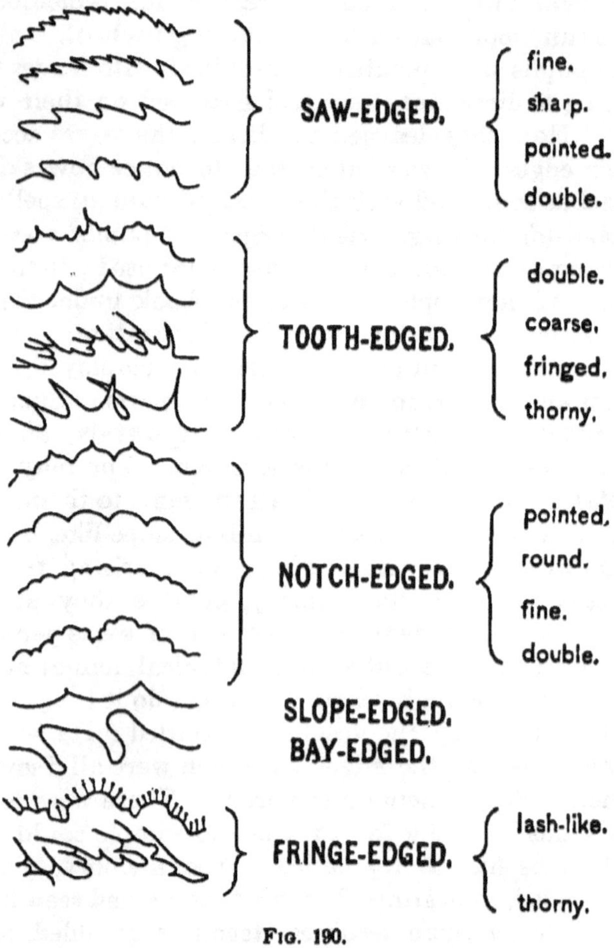

SAW-EDGED. { fine. sharp. pointed. double. }

TOOTH-EDGED. { double. coarse. fringed. thorny. }

NOTCH-EDGED. { pointed. round. fine. double. }

SLOPE-EDGED.
BAY-EDGED.

FRINGE-EDGED. { lash-like. thorny. }

FIG. 190.

After the saw-edged leaves had been disposed of, the tooth-edged ones came up for a hearing, then the notch-edged followed, and so on through the whole list. In one thing the teacher acted masterly. He made the pupils suggest technical terms, and usually the right term was among the ones suggested; then he quickly reviewed all, and by degrees made the pupils see why that particular term was the best to select. Of course, it found the sanction of the class and was adopted. It took about an hour before the end of the lesson was reached. At the close of the lesson I was invited to pass through the aisles with him, and have a peep at the work done by the pupils.

Well, I must pronounce it very creditable work on the whole, far exceeding my expectations. I selected the work of a sweet-looking, modest girl, and requested her to let me copy it for my readers in America. She looked startled, when I explained I would set an artist to work to make an engraving which I would have printed. What a beam of joy shone forth from those dark-blue eyes! And the teacher was as happy as a rare, a very rare, word of appreciation and commendation could make him. He suggested that Louise might cut this leaf out of her book and present it to me, so as to save me the trouble of copying it. Readily the request was granted, and the above is the work, dear reader. I cut off the German technical words and substitute their literal translation in English. I was invited to stay and hear other lessons, but I declined, because I had to return to the hotel, get a dinner, and be ready for the steamer.

7. Learning to do by Doing.

I struck "a gold-mine in the cellar," or something very much like it, the other day. When entering a German school I found the teacher giving a botany-lesson. The art of sketching quickly was here developed to a high degree. I begged to be allowed to take some of the sketches made by pupils for the purpose of having them cut in wood and thus presenting them to American readers. The request was readily granted.

These leaves were studied, named, classified, and then drawn from nature. Some of them are, perhaps, not absolutely correct, but they are remarkably "life-like." The pu-

226 FROM VARIOUS OTHER PRUSSIAN PROVINCES.

Figs. 191-201.

pils of this school can talk in pictures better, perhaps, than in words, and they are induced and urged to sketch quite frequently. Scarcely a lesson is given without some opportunity for sketching. It was amusing to see a boy called upon to recite, seize a pencil, and, while talking, assist his demonstration by a few sketchy lines.

The curriculum of this school does not contain a course in drawing which necessitates the use of drawing-books; but from the primer class through all the stages of the curriculum drawing is a medium of recitation just as talking and writing are. To give an outline of the lessons in botany I heard, and of which the accompanying sketches of leaves are results, would be useless, since they differ in no way from rational lessons given in our schools in America. I hope sincerely that the reader will consider these sketches worthy of his attention. They will speak louder than many columns of text.

8. Teaching Composition.

In many schools of Germany I find a consistent course prescribed for exercises in composition. Instead of detailing this course, I prefer to state the principle upon which it is based. It starts with the presumption that one can not prepare a good beef-soup without meat or without a soup-bone—that is to say, thoughts must be at hand to express thoughts. The dressing of the thoughts may vary in different compositions, like the flavor of the soups in different pots. Individual tastes and available means decide that. Hence all practice in composition-writing in the upper grades is based upon some thought-bearing study—that is to say, each composition is a summary, an extract, as it were, of some lesson given in geography, history, botany, zoölogy, physics, etc. Yea, even arithmetic offers suitable subjects for composition. A perfect analysis of a problem worked out orally is sometimes fixed in writing, and the teacher thus hits two flies with one stroke—he fixes in the minds of his pupils a logical train of mathematical thought and assists language by exercising it.

Such a composition lesson is not a terror, as it is so frequently in schools where compositions are required without the wherewithal to make them. Abstract topics are no better than no thoughts and topics at all. They tell a disgusting story of the women in a tenement-house in Paris. One of them called to her neighbor across the court-yard to lend her her ham-bone for a soup. Her sick husband was "mortally bad" that morning and needed something strong. The answer came that Madame Somebodyelse had borrowed it, but as soon as it was returned it would be at madame's disposal! Every time I see an attempt at making compositions on abstract topics foreign to the children's range of thought or at making compositions without a plentiful array of facts, that ham-bone occurs to my mind. Whether these German teachers ever heard that ham-bone story is immaterial. One thing is certain, their pupils make compositions upon subjects with which they are familiar and express thoughts which, if they are not their own originally, at least have become their own by mental digestion and assimilation.

The pupils learn the use of capital letters and punctuation-marks, headings, and paragraphs, etc., by studying these difficulties in their readers. Sometimes a perfect piece is put on the board, and all the paraphernalia of composition are carefully reviewed—why a comma is placed then and there, why a paragraph here, why a capital there, and so on. One day—it was in a school of Thuringia—I found an old joke of mine (I mean a joke that I had used often). On the board was placed the following stanza, without punctuation-marks:

> There is a lady in our land
> Who has ten nails on every hand
> Five and twenty on hands and feet
> All this is true and no deceit

The children were allowed to laugh at these lines to their hearts' content, until one of them suddenly stopped laughing, grew sober, and raising his hand said, "Teacher, I know how to make it right." The teacher allowed him to do it, and, quickly stepping forward, he punctuated the lines thus:

> There is a lady in our land
> Who has ten nails, on every hand
> Five, and twenty on hands and feet.
> All this is true and no deceit.

It was a pleasure to see the disappointment of those who "hadn't seen it" and the triumphant mien of him who had. The lines were allowed to remain on the board during the lesson, as a memento of the importance of punctuation-marks.

Wherever in Germany I listened to a lesson in history, botany, or some other thought-bearing (hence thought-awakening) study, the teacher wound up by saying, "Now write out an account of this lesson." This was done in the class-room or at home as circumstances determined. The composition-books I saw gave evidence of the fertility of this kind of instruction. Not every composition written or prepared is entered in the composition-book. Many are merely written on the slate or on a slip of paper; but weekly, at least, one is recorded on the pages of the blank book. I saw but one school in which this was overdone, namely, in which a composition was written in the book every day.

It seems to be a rule here to correct the written work of the pupils with red ink; but most teachers have adopted the universally known proof-reader's marks, which not only simplify the work of the corrector, but also require of the pupil to do the actual correcting himself.

As to the course, I only need to say that it begins with copying and dictation work in the two lowest grades. Then follows free reproduction of given models, such as fables. Thus by degrees the power of producing is strengthened, until at the close of the sixth or seventh year's course the pupils are well trained in giving an account of a story they read, or write out a description of a scene or a phenomenon they saw, or reproduce a train of thoughts developed during a lesson. I could give my readers a very convincing proof of the good results of this work by copying a few of the compositions from the books I inspected; but even the least skeptical of my patient readers might suspect me of having selected exceptionally good work. Besides that, as a matter of self-evidence, I should have to render them in English, and I am afraid I am unable to imitate their " pristine youth and beauty." Cause enough, therefore, to resist the temptation; but let me ask my colleagues to try the experiment of making bouillon of a soup-bone with marrow in it and a good deal of meat on it.

9. CRITERION OF A MODEL LESSON.

In "Lehrproben und Lehrgaenge" (a publication, mentioned elsewhere in this book) a number of questions are offered by a normal-school teacher, which with their laudable conciseness may serve as test-questions for any teacher who does not consider himself finished and has not acquired that self-sufficiency which is the arch-foe of all progress. I will render the article in English, hoping to meet the approval of teachers who work in isolation and desire a reliable standard of measurement:

I. *Selection and Arrangement of the Matter of Instruction.*

1. Did the amount of matter stand in proper proportion to the given time ?

2. Was the matter sifted sufficiently, arranged in methodical unities, and well distributed ?

3. Was the disposition apparent and transparent ?

II. *Mode of Treatment (Method).*

1. Was a consistent and suitable method pursued ?

 a. In preparing the new by organic connection with previous cognitions ?

 b. In bringing forward the new by developing it from the old ?

 c. In bringing it to a clear comprehension by means of assimilation, proofs, consolidation, and review ?

 d. In applying it by practice and inculcation ?

2. Was the matter offered objectively, developed logically, worked out systematically, practiced sufficiently, infixed firmly?

3. Was the teacher's mode of forming questions correct? Did he apply the principle of consolidation—that is, did he establish points of connection with other domains of knowledge? Did he distribute his questions well among his pupils?

III. *Personality of the Teacher.*

1. What was the teacher's attitude? Was he vigorous, animating, lively, without injuring his dignity?

2. Did he govern his class with the power of his eyes and his voice, or did he have to resort to "heroic means"?

3. Was his language correct, well articulated, distinct, and used sparingly? His reading perfect?

IV. *Discipline.*

1. Did the teacher employ the whole class?

2. Did he question only the better pupils, or did he give too much of his time and energy to the weaklings?

3. Did he employ proper means, such as pauses, speaking in chorus, rising, bodily exercises, to refresh the attention?

4. Did he correct errors or transgressions of his pupils, or did he leave them unnoticed?

V. *General Results and Impressions of the Lesson.*

1. Was a decided gain noticeable in the pupils—that is to say, was it obvious that the pupils had profited by the lesson?

2. Did the teacher show improvement in teaching and in discipline?

3. Did the lesson appear to be a "chance lesson," or was it well prepared?

10. DRAWING IN GERMAN SCHOOLS.

Whenever I had the chance of inspecting the instruction in drawing and its results, I took especial pains to inquire into the methods applied. Not often did I get the chance. Oh, yes, results evidently touched up by the teacher, were readily shown, but rarely did I see a drawing-class in operation. It is natural, though, for according to the old proverb, it is "A fool who shows half-finished work." I suspect Superintendent Bright, of Englewood (Chicago), Ill., sketched the truth in bold, conspicuous outlines, when he said : "The children make their drawings, and we revise them. Then they draw again, and we revise. Then they draw again. Then we marshal ourselves before the superintendent of drawing and await our turns like candidates at a barber-shop, in order that our re-revisions may be revised by the highest authority. Then the children take another turn at the drawing." I know that to have been the case in Cincinnati, and, since the weaknesses of mankind are about the same everywhere, I could fully appreciate the European teachers' hesitancy to give drawing-lessons in my presence. But a little obstinate insisting prevailed, and I can now judge upon the methods applied. In several cities I found the old copying process in vogue—that is, flat-surfaced copies were set before the pupils, and they copied them, the work being corrected by the teacher, who passed slowly through the aisles. But there is a revolution going on in the teaching of drawing in the common schools of Germany as well as America, and I trust the movement will be successful.

In several schools of Rhenish Prussia I found the old method discarded contemptuously, and drawing or sketching "from nature" substituted. It was not done heedlessly, but with a methodical skill truly admirable. I have neither time nor inclination (the space of a book would be needed) to explain minutely the first steps taken ; suffice it to say that very simple geometrical bodies, such as cube, pyramid, cone, cylinder, sphere, etc., are placed before the class, and each child is made to draw the object *as he sees it*, which affords a great variety of views. The objects are made of different materials, some of pasteboard, many of wood painted white, a few of plaster, or even of china.

In one school (in the province of Westphalia, east of

Rhenish Prussia, where I stayed a few days with an old schoolmate of mine) I found this system of sketching "from nature" perfected to a high degree. I sketched some of the objects in the order in which they were used there for the benefit of my readers (Figs. 202-209). These were made of wood. They are imitations of plant-stems:

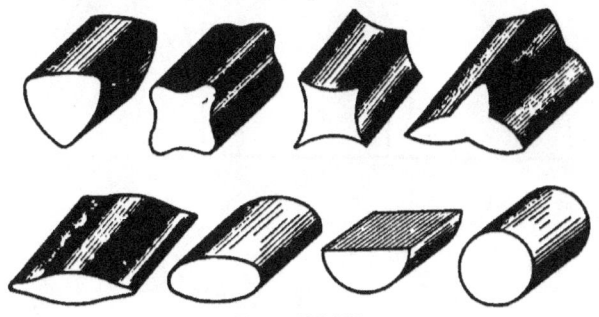

FIGS. 202-209.

The following objects (Figs. 210-216) were made of milk-glass or china, and are characteristic forms of blossoms:

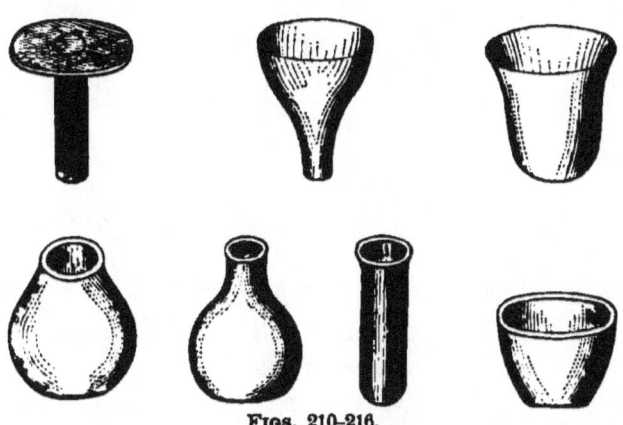

FIGS. 210-216.

It was remarkable to see the results exhibited in portfolios and spread out for inspection. I could scarcely repress my envy, when I compared such results with the abortive endeavors of the pupils under the deadening influence of the copying system in vogue in America. In a primary school—fourth school year—the teacher had a number of leaves which he exhibited and then sketched on the blackboard, showing the differences in form, and conventionalizing them as he proceeded. I was so charmed with

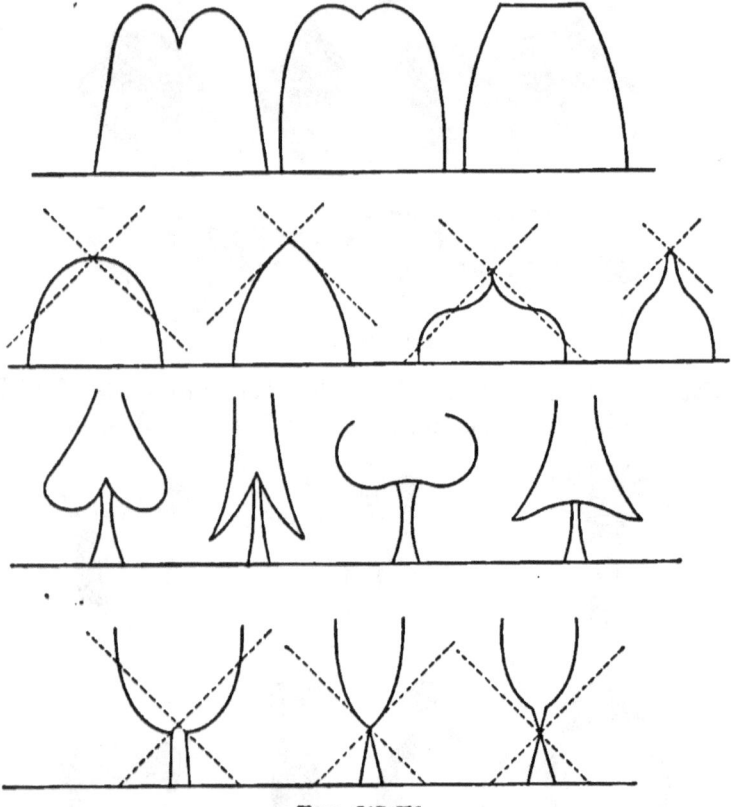

Figs. 217-230.

his skillful treatment that I sat down among the youngsters and sketched like a good little boy. I showed my work to the teacher—like the other little boys—and was gently praised for it. Oh, the fun that caused among the children! I submit the result of the lessons (Figs. 217-230).

What a splendid preparation for the study of botany! What a beneficial awakening of the sense of form! What an opportunity for obtaining skill in the use of the utensils! I can well understand why I find such a decided opposition among German teachers against industrial schools *as special schools*. They bend all their energy upon making their common schools the best on earth, and are willing, nay, eager, to adapt and adopt whatever of industrial pursuits can be adapted to and adopted in their course of study.

All branches of study which may have a practical bearing upon life are made to reflect life. Thus, not only drawing, but geography, is made practical, the latter by imaginative journeys. Putty and clay are used to mold geographical formations in imitation of nature. Mensuration is made both attractive and practical by handling geometrical bodies, not merely by imagining them. They are made of pasteboard, and are home-made by the pupils—another opportunity for manual occupation. Kindergarten occupations I find in almost general use in the lower grades. Of course, much more advanced work is done—in modeling, for instance—than is done in a Kindergarten.

In composition work I find letters, notes, bills, receipts, petitions, etc., written, such as the pupils may be called upon to write after leaving school. Arithmetic is taught rationally, and the problems have bearings upon the child's everyday experience. In one school a lesson in buying and selling greatly interested me. One boy was made storekeeper, and great glee was occasioned by an error he made whereby he lost a few pennies while making change. This lesson was an object-lesson, it was a language-lesson, a lesson in arithmetic, a composition and reading lesson—it was all that and more; it was something which organically connected school-work with life's demands.

Among all the schools I have visited so far—and I saw some in France, some in Holland and Germany—I am ready to pronounce those of Lower Rhenish Prussia the most advanced in methods and results. But it is perhaps too soon to discriminate, having really only begun my tour. I may greatly change my opinion after having seen the famous schools of Berlin and the kingdom of Saxony.

I must not burden these pages with reflections upon political and social questions, or with impressions gained by traveling through this continent, much as I should like to, for I am here for a purpose, and these articles are written for a purpose, not to speak of the amiable reader's disinclination to read a guide-book. I think it due to myself to state this fact.

11. Drawing in a Country School.

The teacher of a small country school I visited in Germany seemed to be an inventive genius of no mean kind, for home-made appliances of various kinds on shelves and on the walls, on desks and window-sills, gave evidence of it as well as of a skill in workmanship not to be despised. I noticed a number of geometrical objects (cubes, pyramids, cones, etc.), made of white pasteboard, and asked whether he taught geometry. "No, sir," said he; "these are used in drawing."

My curiosity being aroused, I asked him to show me how. He began a drawing-lesson which would have been a revelation to many teachers who follow one of the established systems of copying from the flat-surfaced copy. The pupils did the work on slates; drawing-books seemed to be *non est*.

The teacher placed a pyramid before the class and asked the pupils to draw one side of it. They drew a triangle rapidly but very neatly. Then the teacher said, "Complete the figure *as you see it*." These (Fig. 231) are some of the results as I sketched them in my note-book:

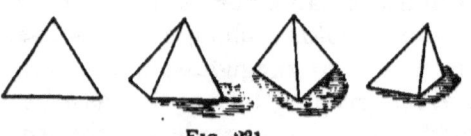

Fig. 231.

Each pupil seeing the object from a different point of view, no two figures were alike, but each was a correct sketch of the object from the point from which the pupil who drew it had viewed it.

Then a cube was placed before the class, and the pupils drew first one face—that is, either a square or a parallelogram, according to the pupil's position. After that, the other visible faces of the cube were drawn, as each pupil saw them. These (Fig. 232) are a few of the results:

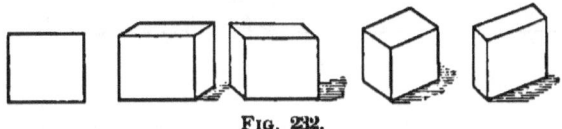

FIG. 232.

Then a truncated cone was drawn. Of course, the figure in the first position was alike in all cases, until the cone was placed in different positions. Here (Fig. 233) are some of the sketches I saw:

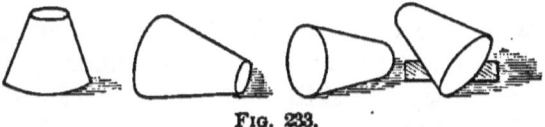

FIG. 233.

Now a disk followed (Fig. 234) in different positions:

FIG. 234.

After that followed a wheel, a cart, a box, a table, and the lesson closed with the drawing of a house. This was drawn from dictation (Fig. 235). Thus: "Draw a rectangular figure." "Complete a block by drawing the right and top face." "Put on an overhanging roof, and erase superfluous lines." "Add a kitchen to your house in the rear." "Put on a chimney, and provide the house with doors and windows." "Place a tree and a pump where you please." I copied the work of a sweet-looking, flaxen-haired girl as minutely and as accurately as I could do it on a small scale, and here it is:

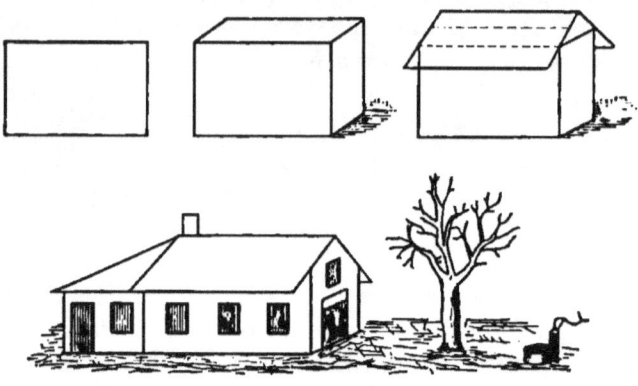

Fig. 255.

I do not wish to add any reflections, sorely tempted as I am at this point, but I must say that the pupils did this work with great accuracy and skill, and that they seemed to enjoy doing it. The slate-pencil lines were easily erased in case they proved inaccurate. In order to get a clear view of the object before him, the pupil would shut one eye and keenly "eye" the object before he drew the lines.

"Can these pupils sketch from memory?" I asked. "Yes," was the reply, "if the objects are not too complicated." "Then let them draw a candlestick or a lamp." It was done. The figures exhibited were different from each other, some were faulty in perspective, but all represented unmistakable candlesticks, or lamps, as the case might be. Other objects were called for, and a few seconds sufficed to sketch them. Then the teacher asked for forms of leaves and flowers, but I noticed that he refrained from calling for forms of animals. Justly so, I thought; for the results so far shown proved to be more than satisfactory for a country school in a remote mountain hamlet.

This little school appeared to me a real gold-mine of devices and methods for illustrating, and I may return to it.

12. COMPULSORY ATTENDANCE.

Except those in Hamburg, I have not yet seen any other than Prussian schools in Germany, but have reason to believe that what I say here holds good in all other German states also. The daily register of attendance in Prussian schools is a valuable legal instrument; in fact, it makes the schoolmaster a power in the state. Careful keeping of this register is a necessity for the teacher, not on account of the reports he has to make to superintendents or inspectors, for very few statistical reports are made in these schools, but with this daily register stands or falls the law regarding compulsory attendance.

Whenever a pupil is marked absent for a week, inquiry is made as to the causes. If a valid excuse is given, well and good. But if a willful absence is noticed, or the parents' authority proves inadequate, or if the parents themselves have taken it into their heads to defy the law by sending their child to the factory before he is thirteen years old, the teacher reports the case to the police authorities with an exact statement of the number of days of absence, and there is no "going behind the returns."

The father is summoned before the police court and is called upon to explain. If no satisfactory explanation is forthcoming, the father is fined. This fine is increased twice in cases of backsliding, and finally ends in imprisonment.

The school law, I understand, makes the limit of compulsory attendance eight months per year, between the ages of six and thirteen. If there is a case found of inability to send children to school, owing to extreme poverty, the state or community provides for necessaries, such as clothes, shoes, books, etc. In cases of defective parental authority, the boys are sent to reform-schools. In cases of worthlessness, such as a drunkard father, the police authorities, of which the justice of the peace is one, give the children into custody of guardians, who act *in loco parentis* for a nominal remuneration, provided for either by the state or local benevolent societies. The law of compulsory education works so successfully that in Rhenish Prussia not three tenths of one per cent of the young men called in for military service are found to be illiterate. Verily, the whole nation is a school!

13. Home-made Apparatus.

We have certainly made commendable progress in our common schools, especially in some educational centers. Dr. Seeley is quite right in saying that the whole foundation of our common school is adapted to carry a greater, loftier, and more substantial structure than that of the German school. But there are certain features in German schools which are worthy of imitation. We have unquestionably developed our graded school systems in cities to a high degree, but the country schools, to be candid, are in a lamentable state of deficiency.

How different in Prussia, and I suspect in other German states, where the country school is doing excellent work, owing to the fact that every teacher employed is either a graduate of a normal school or college, or has during a searching examination, conducted by the faculty of a normal school in presence of the school inspector of the province or state, proved and demonstrated that he has not only the required knowledge, but also the ability to teach clearly! Nowhere among the four great civilized nations is the business of education in country schools pursued with such utter lack of systematic preparation, with such complete, unsympathizing, self-dependent isolation of efforts as with us in America. And I say this advisedly, for I have seen enough country schools in Ohio and other States, and observed their fruit when sent to the city schools "to be finished," to know whereof I speak.

It is with an unpleasant sensation, bordering on envy, that I observe how many village schools here in Germany are supplied with an outfit for object-lessons in natural history, physics, etc. Many teachers, for want of means to purchase, make their own contrivances, and an apparatus thus procured gives to the instruction an impetus which can not be overrated. I have in mind one particular school, in the neighborhood of Solingen, in which I found a book-case with glass doors filled with a set of physical apparatus as complete as seemed necessary for the scope of physics as a study can have in a country school.

A few of the pieces had been bought or procured by a judicious exchange of "commodities," such as rare birds or plants, but most of them were made at home. The latter looked clumsy, but were very serviceable; they were made of such material as was at the disposal of the maker. I desired to sketch the whole set, to show the ingenious skill of the maker, but gave up the task when I thought of the space it would take. Only two contrivances (see cuts below) may be shown. They were rudimentary hydrostatic presses made of materials indicated below:

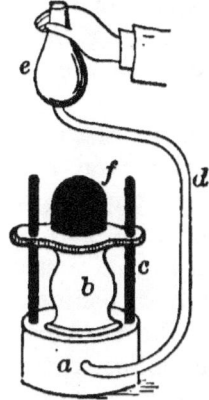

FIGS. 236, 237.

a, wood. b, e, leather.
c, brass rods. d, rubber tube.
f, bowlder or weight.

a, boards. b, leather.
c, bamboo. d, tin funnel.
e, rock or weight.

Now, the impartial reader may compare this with the indescribable poverty of most of the country schools in Ohio or elsewhere, especially in the South, where school trustees not unfrequently refuse to provide the school with a blackboard. Of course, every picture has its shadows, and so perhaps has this bright picture of a German country school. Not every country school here is as well supplied with an enthusiast as this one ; but, judging from the many fine specimens I have seen, it is reasonable to conclude as to all. I may safely say, without danger of being contradicted, that the average German teacher is imbued with professional spirit, with devotion, energy, and natural capacity deserving the most cordial praise.

14. "OUR TREASURE-BOX."

In a school in Westphalia I found a cabinet of ebony-wood hanging on the wall. It was elaborately carved, and appeared to me a piece of exquisite workmanship. An inscription in gilt letters, "Our Treasure-Box," indicated rather obscurely what its object was. The teacher explained it to me. It contained the school registers of the last seventy years, the "day-book" or journal, the class composition-book, the accounts of the school savings-bank, and sundry highly valued relics connected with the school's history.

The journal is a book for daily entries of cases of discipline, meritorious cases of good behavior, and excellent work. The "primus" of the class, the best pupil in studies and conduct, has charge of it. The account-book of the school savings-bank is, in fact, the ledger of that institution. The teacher receives the funds in the form of pennies, takes charge of them, and receipts for them in the bank-books of the pupils. Every week he transfers the collected funds to the city bank, where the whole school has one account. The bank pays the teacher three per cent for sums left a year, while he pays two per cent interest to the pupils, thus giving him an income of from fifteen to twenty dollars a year for this additional trouble. Any one who is acquainted with the low salaries paid to teachers in Germany will understand that twenty dollars additional income per year is an item not to be despised.

But the class composition-book claimed my attention most. There was a novel idea, and I hasten to submit it to my readers. The school wrote a composition every week. The relatively best one was ordered to be copied into this class-book, which was thus made an incentive for the pupils to do good work. They would, as it were, immortalize themselves on the leaves of this gilt-edged book. At the same time the book was a record of what the school did, not only in composition, but in all branches of study, for the subjects were chosen from the matter of instruction of object-lessons treated during the week.

I saw some excellent penmanship in this book, and, considering that these were childish efforts at composition, I think them very commendable thoughts expressed in plain but clean garments.

A lady of this town who did fine work in wood-carving, I was told, had presented this cabinet to the school, and was at the time at work in making a pendant to it which they would call "Our Medicine-Chest." The teacher meant to collect in it such medicines and chemicals as are likely to be used in cases of emergency.

15. Local School Museums.

The teacher who presides over a school in a small German town or village is a fixture, and naturally the custodian of the school museum. Most German schools have a museum—that is, a book-case or two full of books, and many shelves full of objects necessary for illustrating the instruction in natural history, geography, physics, etc.

There was a time in Germany when the principle of object-teaching electrified every schoolmaster from the Rhine to the Vistula and from the Baltic to the Alps. It was thought that objective teaching was the panacea for all educational diseases. All order and system was abandoned, and objects were brought into the school-room till it looked like a pawnbroker's shop. No broken horseshoe was left lying in the street; old boots were eagerly gathered for the leather they yielded; no ant's hill was safe from the destructive hand that gathered ants' eggs, and the life of every snail innocently creeping across the road was imperiled. Everything was carried into school—animals, plants, and minerals. There the objects that would keep were neatly labeled, numbered, classified, and stored up.

The children had good times then. The paper boxes, moles' skeletons, minerals, stuffed birds, samples of wood, dried plants, and the like, went from hand to hand, and, to be sure, half a school-day was often passed in contemplating the treasures of the museum; and the teacher quieted his conscience by thinking this to be an object-lesson. The children were also taken to observe the cabinet-maker; they went to the locksmith's shop; watched the shoemaker and tanner at their work; they "studied" all the different kinds of leather, wool, wood, cloth, and metal; they knew the name of every tool—in short, they failed to see the woods on account of the multitude of trees!

Now, this was a craze. To-day the fever has abated considerably. A reaction followed, and to-day the school-children in some places have not the remotest idea how a mill or a foundry looks inside, how the weaver works, and the tanner and the furrier, etc. The museum in some schools has been moved to the garret, and all the many objects of interest lead a contemplative existence in closed boxes on shelves and under a cover of dust.

If the teacher needs a mineral, or an air-pump, or the Leyden-jars, he is obliged to give a week's notice to the janitor, so that he may search for the objects and make them presentable. The swallow's nest and the ostrich-egg yawn at each other. The miniature plow rests securely in the lap of a miniature spinning-wheel, and both play the rôle of The Sleeping Beauty. The spiders have covered the mole's skeleton neatly with their fine threads, and the dust has changed the nets into a gray skin. To be sure, it is a dreary spectacle. As the first wild craze was one extreme, this indifference is the other.

On the whole, it may be said that the pendulum swinging backward and forward is sure to come to rest at the point of a golden mean; and, so long as the teachers are secure in their positions, the moss gathered in the form of museum collections for the benefit of rational objective teaching will accumulate. When I compare the utter absence of anything like museums or libraries in our schools, I heave a sigh; but, when I recollect the insecurity of position under which our teachers in America are suffering, I can see a complete chain of cause and effect.

16. A Prussian Normal School.

Introduction.—In previous articles I have taken pains to state repeatedly that the excellent results of the Prussian system of people's schools are to be attributed to the proper preparation of the teachers. The teachers' seminaries, or normal and training schools as we are accustomed to term them, are state institutions. With the exception of the Augusta School in Berlin and a few similar institutions elsewhere, they are for young men. Every one of the twelve provinces of Prussia (I am not speaking of other German states, though I suspect they follow the Prussian example) has a sufficient number of such special schools. They receive their pupils from a limited number of preparatory schools such as I described in my letter from Cologne. All the seminaries in Prussia are following the same course of study. The central directive power is found in a department of the Ministry of Public Instruction in Berlin.

Most of these schools are situated in small towns of four to eight thousand inhabitants; indeed, I know of none situated in a large city except the one in Berlin. The reason of this is found in the desire to keep the young would-be teachers free from the temptations of a large city. The schools are all boarding schools—that is, the students live in the school-building and are kept under rigid control all day long.

Connected with the institution is a practice department, consisting of an entire school of six to eight grades, in all of which the students are expected to gain their experience in teaching. The course lasts three years, and is divided into an academic and a professional department.

The Building.—I took occasion to thoroughly inspect such a normal school. In a quiet, sleepy little town, connected by railways with large industrial centers, the Government had erected a large building with two spacious wings for the special purpose of giving the normal school of the district a suitable home. The structure is very fine, and reminds one of true American school architecture. It is large, handsome, commodious, well ventilated, and surrounded by extensive yards and gardens. The stairs and halls are covered with linoleum, the windows are generous, the walls delicately tinted, and the general session-room (used as a chapel) decorated with beautiful fresco borders and other ornaments.

Altogether the building is a worthy habitation of a teachers' training-school, particularly because it impresses the students with a correct idea of what a good school-building is or ought to be.

Biblical History.—I passed a day in this school, and was well repaid for getting up at six o'clock A. M., on a raw winter day, traveling an hour on the railway, and calling on the rector before eight o'clock—that is, in time for opening school. The first lesson I heard was one in biblical history. The rector had announced on the previous day that he would give a model lesson to young pupils, in presence of the senior class of students. I begged of him not to change the programme. Indeed, it was a model lesson in more senses than he had understood that technical term. How I wished that lesson had been given in presence of a large class of American Sunday-school teachers! Subject of the lesson was : The wise men from the East following the star and coming to Jerusalem to inquire of King Herod where the new-born King of the Jews might be found; then being told to go to Bethlehem, and there finding Jesus, giving him their presents and worshiping him.

The rector told the whole story in plain, unassuming words such as the little pupils could understand. By such simple means as describing the mode of traveling in the East; the poor, modest dwelling of the Holy Family, etc., he succeeded in creating vivid mental pictures. Then he questioned the little ones on a part of the story, namely, on the journey to Jerusalem and the inquiries of Herod. The rector's skill in the art of questioning could not be adequately conveyed except by a stenographic report. After this part of the story was well worked over, and every incident explained or called forth by leading questions, two pupils had to repeat the part, and they did it with singular faithfulness as regards facts and expressions. Errors of speech were corrected on the spot, but never in a humiliating way, nor so that the thread of the conversation was broken or tangled.

Then the second part—Herod's inquiries, the mention of the prophet Micah, the journey to Bethlehem, and the finding of Jesus—followed. In this part of the story the insincerity of Herod and his evil intentions were dwelt upon, and a holy horror could be noticed on the faces of the youngsters when they heard that a king should so debase himself as to say one thing and mean another. Again, all the minute details of this part of the narrative were brought out by skillful questioning, and the answers were very faithful, both in regard to facts and expressions. Again, as before, a review was had in connected repetition.

The third part was treated likewise, and here the presents, gold, incense, and myrrh, gave rise to a pretty explanation, child-like but all-sufficient. When this part was repeated, a general review followed. One little boy told one part, another the second, a third the last; and the singular faithfulness with which they repeated whole sentences with almost identically the same words could only be attributed to the consistency with which the rector had clung to these expressions all through the lesson. Then he wound up by showing a handsome, illustration in which the Holy Family, the wise men, the servants, the camels, the star, the presents, etc., were shown. This fixed every item of the whole story in the memory of the little ones.

All through the masterly lesson the seniors sat apparently with bated breath, making notes now and then. When the little ones were dismissed, the students were questioned as to what they had heard. Object of the lesson, means employed, psychological references, methods, principles of method—I know not what words to use to give my readers an adequate idea of how that model lesson was dissected. The rector gave the students free scope to express their judgment. It seemed to me that if any of these young men did not take away treasures of knowledge, of skill in handling a class, and methodical treatment of matter, it certainly was not the fault of the rector and his youngsters.

Literature.—The second lesson I heard was a lesson in German literature. It began with the reading of a composition upon Lessing's "Minna von Barnhelm," the first distinctly German drama. Though the diction of the student was faulty at times, the composition was unquestionably an original effort of rare merit. The professor (not the rector) proceeded in his criticism with that delicacy which is the distinctive sign of a thorough-bred gentleman. It was obvious that the most friendly relations existed between him and the students. Nevertheless, he spoke very much to the point, and the students assisted him in correcting with praiseworthy zeal.

The vistas which were opened to the students in the realm of German literature were wide and pleasant. There was nothing of that gnawing at the shell, or of that splitting of hairs, which is sometimes observed in the teaching of literature, where the students never get to see the forest on account of the multitude of trees. In short, the lesson was characteristic, inasmuch as it was free from that petty annoying criticism indulged in where conformity with the exact text of the book is the criterion of successful study. This professor was a master in the art of questioning, such as I had rarely met in my life. Altogether the lesson left a pleasant impression, and I concluded that the students would later in life do very well to copy their teacher.

Natural History.—The next lesson I heard was one in zoölogy, and here again, as so often in Germany, I saw the principle illustrated that observation is the foundation of cognition. Birds were studied like that proverbial fish of Agassiz. Stuffed birds were available in large number; colored pictures assisted where objects were wanting, and the lesson proceeded as one would wish every lesson in zoölogy to proceed : 1. Actual observation established percepts ; 2. Several of these formed concepts; 3. These then were grouped by collecting the essentials and dropping minor items to establish clear-cut ideas. The latter were well expressed. When a number of them were available, conclusions were drawn from them. Thus the process of gathering knowledge and strengthening the thinking power was successfully exemplified. Some of the steps taken were superfluous, it seemed to me, in a class of adults, but it was the evident desire of the professor to make these young men learn in precisely the way in which they are to cause young children to learn afterward.

It was with much curiosity that I heard the students state their observations of domestic birds. We are very apt to think that we know all about them, and that in zoölogy the attention should be directed to the birds which the children are never likely to see. This lesson converted me to the opinion that we know much less of domestic birds than we think we do. It was with much curiosity that I heard the students state the difference in the mode of drinking between pigeons and chickens, to wit, that the pigeon sucks water by keeping its beak almost closed and causing a vacuum in the throat, while the hen dips or ladles water with the lower part of the beak, and then raises its head to let the water run down into the craw. The causes were looked for and found in the peculiar build of the beaks of the different birds. Monogamy among the pigeons, polygamy among the fowls; the peculiar flight of pigeons, swallows, and other birds, which was traced to the form of the wings and feathers; and various other things of great interest were brought out, all of which gave opportunity for tracing effect back to cause, and to judge from cause to effect.

This kind of instruction is very interesting, and as different from the old-time zoölogy-lessons as day is from night. No text-book in zoölogy, botany, or mineralogy was used, but each pupil had an atlas which contained at least several thousands of exquisite illustrations of natural objects, accompanied by a few pages of print containing a table of contents and a key to pronunciation.

I have but one fault to find with this and one other teacher, in the institution. They were overbearing, and would humiliate a student for a slight slip of the tongue. This seems to be a general fault in normal schools in Germany. Whether it is done intentionally, in order to make the young teachers as humble as possible, or what is the reason, I don't know. But, if that is the real motive, it has the opposite effect, for nowhere have I found a more fearless set of teachers than here in Prussia. One cause of this fearlessness may be the fact that there is a scarcity of teachers at present, of which more anon.

Drawing.—The drawing-lesson I saw was poor, and the results meager. This department was evidently the weakest point in the institution.

Music.—A lesson on the church-organ I heard gave me a fair sample of the thoroughness with which the students are prepared for organist's service in church. Each student, as his turn came to play a hymn, was told to play a prelude of his own composition. Thus, for instance, if the hymn was written in D major, he would start in E major, and, by way of septime-chords, try to reach D through A. Or, beginning at C major, he would go upward through D into G, and then through A into D. These were some of the easiest preludes. This practice made the young men free and easy at the instrument. But the pedal proved full of pitfalls, as it naturally will to beginners. After three years of daily practice, good results are obtained.

Geography.—Then followed a lesson in geography, in which a professor illustrated the principle of concentric instruction, by drawing into this lesson history, physics, meteorology, etc., and thus making the lesson have connection with many other branches of study. Through all my visits in German schools I had not had the chance of hearing a lesson in the geography of the United States. Here luck favored me, and my readers may imagine my pleasure when I heard Washington pronounced Uâshington, and not *Vashington;* New York, not *Noy York;* Maine, not *Mine,* etc. It was a very pleasant surprise to me. I inquired whether the teacher spoke English, and, upon receiving a negative answer, I inquired how it came that he pronounced the English and American geographical names correctly. The answer was:

"We are careful in looking up the pronunciation, for we insist upon pronouncing each name correctly. As there can be but one correct pronunciation of the name of the river Spree, namely, *Spray* (else Berlin would be constantly 'on a spree'), so there can be but one correct pronunciation of Ohio, namely, Ohio, not *Oheeo,* as we Germans might be tempted to pronounce it. We are aware of the fact that English-speaking nations anglicize all geographical names. This we consider wrong. We follow the golden rule, 'Do as you would be done by.' Of course, ignorance may excuse a man's mispronunciation; but a teacher who pleads the baby-act, by claiming not to know how Frenchmen pronounce their geographical names, or Americans theirs, deserves to be dismissed."

A review of the political geography of the Union led to a historical outlook upon its rapid growth, and there teacher and pupils revealed a familiarity with American history which brought the lamentable ignorance of the average

American teacher regarding German history into bold relief. Our almost insular isolation makes us rather exclusive, and it is well to call attention to it, and make us measure ourselves by the standards of others. As a rule, I find less ignorance concerning America among teachers in Germany than among French teachers—a statement which, I trust, is readily believed. The teacher in this grade was a gentleman of the highest type, who treated his students like gentlemen, and never intentionally or otherwise wounded their sensibilities.

Arithmetic.—Then I heard a lesson in arithmetic. Percentage was the subject of discussion. Problems were solved orally with a rapidity which fairly left me behind. I asked permission to put a few questions to the students, and among other things asked them to tell me how they would begin the study of percentage, and at what stage in the course. The answer was very gratifying, to wit, expressions couched in the term *per cent* might be taught in connection with reduction of fractions. Thus, for instance, the children might be taught that one fourth is equal to twenty-five hundredths, or twenty-five parts of one hundred. The subsequent practice of percentage would thus receive an early foundation. The professor in this room was rather harsh, and, like many mathematicians, punctilious, but not unfair nor overbearing.

Daily Programme. — As I passed through the hall, I copied the characteristic items of the daily programme to give my readers a fair sample of how to get sixteen hours' work out of twenty-four:

6 —6.30. Rising, dressing, washing.
6.30—7.30. Preparing lessons under supervision.
7.30—7.50. Breakfast.
7.50—8. Opening exercises in chapel.
8 —1. Lessons and experimental teaching.
1 —1.30. Dinner.
1.30—2. Playing and walking in the grounds.
2 —5. Lessons in academic department.

5 —6. Practice in instrumental music.
6 —7. Outside exercises.
7 —7.30. Supper.
7.30—9.30. Working in class-rooms under supervision.
9.50—10. Evening prayer.
10. Turning into bed.

Scarcity of Teachers.—One thing seemed to me incongruous. The building was designed to accommodate no less than one hundred and twenty resident students, but there were only forty-two enrolled. Inquiries revealed the fact that all the royal seminaries were suffering from want of students. In this institution thirty-five to forty could have been admitted last year, but only twenty-three had presented themselves for admission, and of these only seventeen had proved competent. The young men do not see why they should sacrifice their whole life on the altar of popular education for 800 to 1,000 marks ($200 to $250) a year. Prussia needs more teachers, and they do not come unless paid better. Since Germany has made such wonderful forward strides in all domains of art and industrial pursuits, young men can earn more in other professions; and it is not a mercenary motive either which makes them shun the teacher's profession, though much work and responsibility, and poor, niggardly pay, are causes enough to frighten away even the most willing of young men.

A great number of country teachers in Silesia and other provinces are paid 810 marks per annum, and free rent and fuel—total, a little more than 1,100 marks, or $275. It is literally impossible for a family to live on such a pittance. After twelve years of service, an additional sum of 60 marks ($15) is paid, after twenty years 180 marks ($45), making a maximum of $320. In cities, of course, the salaries are better. They usually have a fixed scale, which increases from 800 to 2,000 marks ($200 to $500). This explains why the country teachers flock to the cities. The number of applicants for places in cities is incredible. In Frankfort-on-the-Main a rectorship with a somewhat reasonable salary became vacant lately, and no less than 487 applicants offered their services!

How necessary an increase in the number of teachers in Prussia is, may be seen from these numbers: In one province alone the number of pupils in the people's schools is 682,-139, while the number of teachers is only 7,959; this gives 85 to 86 pupils to the teacher. Yes, in densely settled districts the number of pupils in many school-rooms varies between 100 and 110. The Government tries various experiments to increase the number of teachers, but so long as the only real inducement—better pay—is not resorted to, all palliative remedies will be of no avail. Lowering the conditions of admission to normal schools is not a means to be recommended, and founding preparatory schools will prove futile; for as soon as the young men are old enough to have their eyes opened to the fate that is awaiting them, they will desert, and enter business or industrial schools. It is, indeed, a sign of the times when one sees the number of pupils in industrial schools increase beyond the capacity of the schools, and the seminaries empty. The Government can no longer be blind to that fact. And now that Prussia has entered the happy family of states which liquidate their national debts, it is reasonable to suppose that the Prussian Government will begin to alleviate the starving condition of the teachers.

17. THREE KINDS OF CONFERENCES.

The principal of a normal school I inspected held conferences with his students outside of the hour reserved for academic studies. These meetings were so full of interest that the students would rather have suffered martyrdom than stayed away from them. There were three kinds of conferences he held with his students:

I. *Practicum.*—In the conference thus called the young would-be teachers submitted plans of the lessons they were going to give in the practice department. They were either sketched in outlines only, or painfully worked out in every detail. These dispositions were submitted, and the master would suggest an improvement here and there, or would submit a difference of opinion to the decision of the class, but he could never be brought to an expression of his judgment as to the practicability or impracticability of the plan. He held that "the proof of the pudding is in the eating thereof." These meetings had the advantage of letting the entire class know what each student, as his turn came, intended to do. When the lessons were given, the class again met under the supervision of the master and in presence of the model teachers of the school. This second lesson was called the

II. *Criticum.*—Now the lessons given were criticised and the master took care that not an unpleasant allusion was made, not a word was uttered which might in any way tend toward wounding the feelings of the student whose lesson was under discussion. The students were not sparing with their criticism, but, if any one proved unable to base his criticism on a well-understood principle, he was told not to let his emotions run away with his judgment. When the students had had their say (sometimes it was approval and even warm-hearted praise), the practice teachers gave their opinion, after which the master summed up and generalized the points gained. The *criticum* I heard was perhaps more exciting than most others, since two students got into a heated discussion as to the value of certain methods, and each claimed that his interpretation of the principle was correct. When the master afterward interpreted the principle, and in a logical train of thought convincingly proved that neither of the two had clearly comprehended the principle, the occurrence gave rise to some hilarity. The third kind of conferences held in this normal school was the

III. *Scholasticum.*—It was held with the faculty and the students, and consisted of lectures given by the master. These were invariably professional, and gave rise to fruitful discussion. Most of them have been published, and they have created much comment and well-deserved praise. The normal school in which these conferences are in vogue is a school of national fame.

256 FROM VARIOUS OTHER PRUSSIAN PROVINCES.

18. Object-Lessons and Sketching.

The reader will remember that I dwelt at length, in one of my previous chapters, upon the sketching done in German schools, and stated that, though no regular daily lesson in sketching was given, it was part of every lesson which

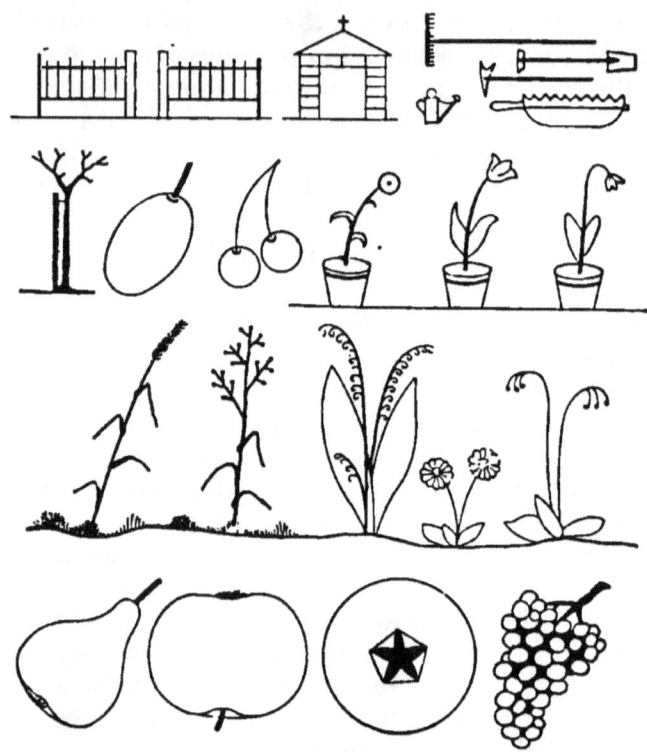

Fig. 238.—The Garden.

needed illustrating. I offered a few samples of pupils' work, and desire now to still further illustrate my statement by samples. Object-lessons without objects are like the play of "Hamlet" with Hamlet left out, or like a bladeless knife that has no handle. I have seen or listened to such lessons here in Germany and in America, though rarely.

OBJECT-LESSONS AND SKETCHING. 257

Usually the teacher has something tangible to begin with, be it a twig and a few leaves with which to give a lesson on the woods; be it a pot-plant for a lesson on garden-

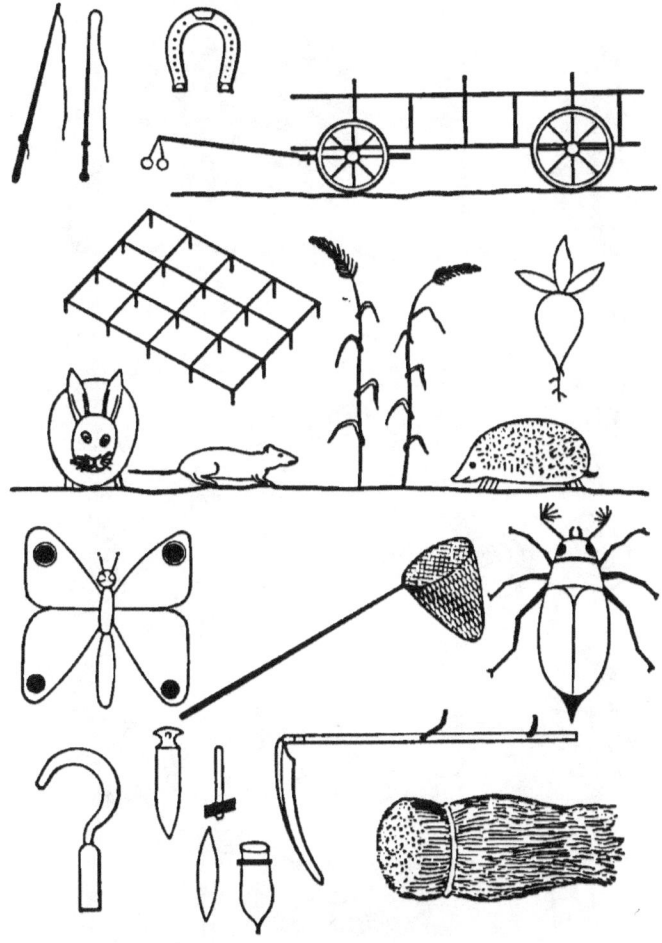

FIG. 239.—THE FIELD.

ing, or a stalk of corn for a lesson on fields. From that he branches out, and by means of the crayon enlarges the circle of observation and asks the pupils to sketch the objects as he goes along. Some of these efforts on the part of the children are mediocre, but most are quite commendable, and betray a skill not to be despised.

Fig. 240.—The Woods.

One day I visited a school where, to my amazement, there were four blackboards. Usually the authorities furnish only one, about four by five feet. The boards I saw here were a new contrivance. They consisted of huge plates of black glass, ground so as to facilitate the writing and prevent the reflection of the light. Three of these boards were covered with sketches, which, I was told, were used and made during the lessons on objects and common things and in language-lessons. They were simple, but very characteristic and easy to draw. I inquired whether they were original.

The teacher said: "No, sir; I copied them from a book on objective teaching by E. Jordan, teacher in the practice department of the city normal school at Vienna. I own I am not a handy draughtsman, and therefore help myself as well as I can, for to give object-lessons without frequent sketching would be absurd."

Now, I am not an artist myself, but I venture to copy some of the numerous simple models given in that book, and I group them exactly as the teacher had grouped them on his boards. One group was called "The Garden," the second "The Field," and the third "The Woods" (see Figs. 238–240).

It is easy to trace the course which the teacher had gone with his class through garden, field, and woods, by looking at these sketches. The group entitled "The Woods" was very fine. I asked to see the pupils' copies, and their slates were produced, and lo! here for the first time in Germany I saw double slates in use. Very neat and accurate were the sketches of these youngsters, who were in their second and some in their third school year.

19. Miscellaneous Observations.

It is not easy to go through the schools of a foreign country, appear interested, and yet search critically for good and bad points without losing the confidence of your hosts. However, not one of the many teachers I saw at work in Germany, France, and Holland objects to me as a reporter.

My note-book is brought into requisition only when a sketch is to be made, and I do that in such an unostentatious way that it does not irritate the teachers; but the first thing I do after getting to my hotel is to note down the leading points of criticism, or those of a lesson or of a conversation held with teachers. I find my memory very faithful. It retains interesting matter, and loses unimportant things as though it were a sieve.

I will close this chapter with a few stray ears that I glean from various pages of my note-book.

Nowhere in Europe do I find *daily marking of lessons* resorted to. The teachers are not marking-machines, but are earnestly engaged in teaching, helping, suggesting, asking, directing, watching, etc. There is a total absence of that detestable immoral competition which so often plays havoc with our pupils in America. *Reports (Zeugnisse,* testimonials) are sent home at the close of every term ; but they express the grades of the pupils in such terms as very good, good, satisfactory, poor, very poor, or similar ones. The prevalence of such terms as "very good" and "excellent" stamps the report No. 1. If the greater number of submarks is good and mediocre, it is called No. 2, and so on. Reports such as are given out in America, that express shades of differences by tenths of a per cent, are wholly unknown here.

Blackboards I find fixed in grooves like window-sashes, hung by weights, so that they may be adjusted to the height of the pupil at work before them. In some schools I find the board standing on easels, but rarely are the walls changed into blackboards, though the cumbersome easel is being done away with in most places. The long, slender, dustless crayons used in America are found here also; but in some country schools I noticed chunks of chalk just as they were broken out of the quarries.

In France I saw one school in which the children used *no slates.* The tops of their desks were *white marble,* and the children wrote with soft lead-pencils, thus avoiding the injury to the eyes resulting from writing on black; but the marble tops needed thorough cleansing and an occasional renewal. I am afraid, though, that if our Young Americans had marble tops on their desks, they would have to be replaced "semi-occasionally."

In many villages in France, Holland, Lower Rhenish Prussia, and Westphalia, I find the children coming to school in wooden shoes, which are placed in a row in the corridors or slipped under a low shelf. In school the children sit with bare feet. In winter they wear these wooden shoes over their leather ones, and even line them with straw or hay to keep the feet warm. Many of these pupils are obliged to walk great distances to reach school.

Silentium! Silence-hour. An odd name, is it not? But an appropriate one, as we shall see. In large, crowded cities (and there seems to be a big town at every turn of the road here in Rhenish Prussia) many children come from homes where quiet mental work is impossible. Tenement-houses are very frequent. Home lessons can not be expected unless the conditions of undisturbed work are offered. The teachers of some high-schools solve this difficulty by alternately spending one hour, from 7 till 8 P. M., at the school-house and helping the pupils prepare their home lessons. This hour is called *silentium* (silence). No pupil is permitted to talk aloud; only whispering is allowed. When the noise increases beyond regulation height, the teacher shouts, "*Silentium!*" and the noise subsides to a mere humming. The teacher sits at his desk and gives in subdued tone the assistance asked for by a pupil who steps up to him. Since there is no study-hour during the day's work—that is, within the daily programme—this silence-hour becomes a necessity. Of course, it imposes additional work on the teacher, but, since each one is called upon to spend only an hour every fortnight, the burden is not great.

CHAPTER X.

LEIPSIC (KINGDOM OF SAXONY).

1. LEIPSIC. MANUAL TRAINING SCHOOL.

BEFORE I describe this school and state its results, it seems essential to emphasize the principal difference between this (the German) manual training-school and those in Paris.

In Paris, skill in some trades seems end and aim. In this school in Leipsic (and in those of more than two dozen good-sized towns in Germany) the manual occupations are "part and parcel" of a "harmonious, all-sided education, which aims alike at intellectual growth, increase of will-power, and skill in the use of the hands and tools. This difference is the principal one, but, as is readily seen, it is also a difference in principle. The French motive-power is utilitarianism; that of the Germans is, as Froebel has it, "to make men—whole, complete men—men who can observe, learn by experience, and act up to their convictions."

In nothing is the difference so clearly seen as in the things which the pupils here in the ancient Thomas School manufacture. In subsequent pages of this report this will be more clearly seen. From the illustrations I gathered in Paris (see p. 325), it will be seen that no complete thing is made. Each object furnished by the pupils is an exercise, as it were. Not a door is made, but a corner-joint of a door; not a drawer, but the dovetailing joint of two boards; not a window, but a window-cross, and so on.

I can in no better way explain the work in Paris than by comparing the manual work of the boys there with the *études* and exercises on the piano, practiced for the purpose of gaining that dexterity of the fingers which may be necessary; but to confine a pupil exclusively to such practice would be making a little rebel of him in a short time. Besides, it is claimed by people who ought to know whereof they talk, that that dexterity can be gained equally well by practicing musical "pieces." Another simile drawn from our professional art is that the Parisian *travail manuel* schools teach the grammar of manual work, while the German schools teach the work itself, which includes the grammar.

Another very essential difference between the French and German manual training schools is found in this: the French boys do work which ought to be reserved for adults —the details of a door-joint are foreign to a child's range of experience; while in the German schools the boys learn to make things such as they find use for. This causes a certain satisfaction, while details leave the working boys unsatisfied. Nothing in the German schools is made that has not in itself a value for the child. The educational value of the German manual training school is well characterized in the following:

2. Appeal to Leipsic's School-Boys.

Listen to what we have to say, boys. It concerns every true boy. Every one of you who wants to become a true man likes to watch diligent workmen and wishes to do like them—that is to say, use the hammer and hatchet, the tweezers and gimlet, the plane and saw, the file and rasp, the bolt and solder, the blow-pipe, the modeling-tool and carving-knife, etc. Every boy who is a real boy tries to use these tools. He will find opportunities to do so in our manual training-school.

We don't want to make artisans of you, for your leisure hours would not suffice for that; but we want to make you more skillful and clever than boys usually are. How many can drive a nail without hitting their fingers? How many can make kites that balance and fly well? How many, when the skates get shaky on the ice, can help themselves and need not run to the locksmith? Yes, many of you can not even point a pencil well, or put a wrapper around a school-book without making it look clumsy.

Your parents mean to benefit you when they present you with a toolbox at Christmas. How many of such boxes are shoved into the corner, where the tools rust and the box is covered with dust? You must have some one who teaches you how to use tools. Or you get a scroll-saw, and, after breaking a number of saw-blades, you succeed in sawing out of cigar-box boards a few clumsy patterns. Then you go to a joiner to have them glued and adjusted. He is the one who does the real work. Yet you give these things away as your work. It isn't right, boys! It can't be right!

We must talk plainly, boys. Most of you do not know how to use tools. That needs to be learned. Most of you spend too much time in reading, and spoiling their precious eye-sight. When you are called to do a manual job for your mothers, you are at a loss how to go at it. Oh, what would have become of you had you been in Robinson Crusoe's place? You would have perished miserably. Come, boys, think of it!

Things should be different. When school is over and home tasks are done, a true boy spends an hour happily on the playground and in summer takes a bath in the river. In winter he may learn to work with his hands at the work-bench and the vise. After many hours of brain-work he uses his strength in planing and sawing, hammering and chiseling. He learns to see and admire lines of beauty in drawing, and working out his drawings in models. He furnishes models in clay and carves wood. He makes physical experiments, and works neat Christmas presents for his dear ones at home.

And when, outside, the winter storms rage and the snow-flakes fall, our pupils come together in a warm room and work like good fellows to produce something, and laugh, chat, and sing in company, while book-worms sit in corners like hermits. Our pupils have had such pleasures for several years. Come and join us.

But, remember, we don't want any "lazy-bones." If any of you like to shirk work, and after a few weeks, when the work gets harder, thinks he has a toothache, or perchance some other ache, don't let him come. We don't want him. We want diligent boys. All who like to work are welcome. Ask your parents. They will allow you to come for an hour or two where they know you are well looked after.

Life is full of work, boys, now more than ever. Prepare for it. A true man learns to help himself, and we will show you how. So come, and be welcomed by

THE MASTERS OF THE TRAINING-SCHOOL.

This appeal was printed in 1883, and hung up in the corridors of the several common schools, and in consequence five hundred and seventy-five pupils were enlisted in the manual training school.

3. NORMAL SCHOOL FOR MANUAL TRAINING.

Leipsic has become the center of the manual training movement in Germany. A wise provision of the people there was to establish a normal school for manual occupations. It was argued that, so long as teachers were wanting and artisans had to be employed as teachers, the instruction would go astray as it did in Paris; it would inevitably end in special apprentice school work. To make manual training an essential part of public education, it must be brought into harmony with all the other educational exertions of the school; itself must rest on educational principles.

How deeply the want of a seminary for manual training teachers had been felt all over Germany, could be seen from the fact that, when this school was opened, fifty-five students, mostly teachers, applied for admission from all parts of Germany, Austria, and one even from Russia. They were delegated by state governments and city councils, by school committees and societies, provided with the necessary means by public and private efforts. All of them had some skill in the use of tools, and therefore attended the first course of the new institution very profitably. Ever since this first course the time of the courses has been extended, so that now every department of manual training, so far as approved to come within the pale of public education, is taught, namely:

1. Pasteboard and bookbinder's work.
2. Joiner's and carpenter's work.
3. Turner's work (wood and other materials).
4. Carving in wood and plaster.
5. Modeling in clay, and casting.
6. Wire-work and tinsmithing.
7. Lock- and tool-smithing.

The old Thomas School, a building which is perhaps four hundred years old, and in which Sebastian Bach used to be cantor, has been entirely given over by the city authorities to the Society for the Introduction of Manual Training. In the afternoons and evenings the lower floor contains hundreds of little fellows hard at work, and on the third floor is the normal school. Here are seen men of forty or fifty as pupils, using the file or the hammer and saw. It looks odd yet natural. Every normal school pupil must make a masterpiece before he can graduate. I saw a beautiful money-safe made by a middle-aged man, whose long waving beard showed streaks of gray. He hoped to graduate upon the strength of this safe.

I spent a day in this quaint old school-house, and found it as instructive as it was amusing. There are two sitting-rooms for the students, furnished handsomely and provided with a piano. Here the students converse, read, and sing, during the pauses between lessons. Chorus singing, under the leadership of a musician from their ranks, is indulged in, and the work is thus made pleasant. Several halls are filled with the work of the pupils, an exhibition of rare merit. Dr. W. Goetze, the rector of this institution, seems to be the leading spirit of the entire movement in Leipsic.

4. The Work done in Leipsic.

And now I will proceed to show what kind of work is done in Leipsic. Among the many hundreds of objects made of pasteboard and paper I will sketch a few typical ones.

The wood-work (joiner-work) is essentially the same as that done in Vienna. The reader is requested to compare pages 401–409. But the children in Leipsic make a number of pieces of apparatus used in physics; many of them are very exact. I insert some models on page 268.

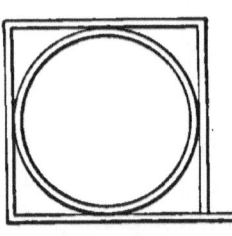

Fig. 241.

In wire-work this school does more than any other I saw. Truly ingenious devices are made with soft and hard wires. The first step in this department is making geometrical figures. After that a great number of objects of use in the house are made, such as button-hooks, lamp-chimney clean-

THE WORK DONE IN LEIPSIC.

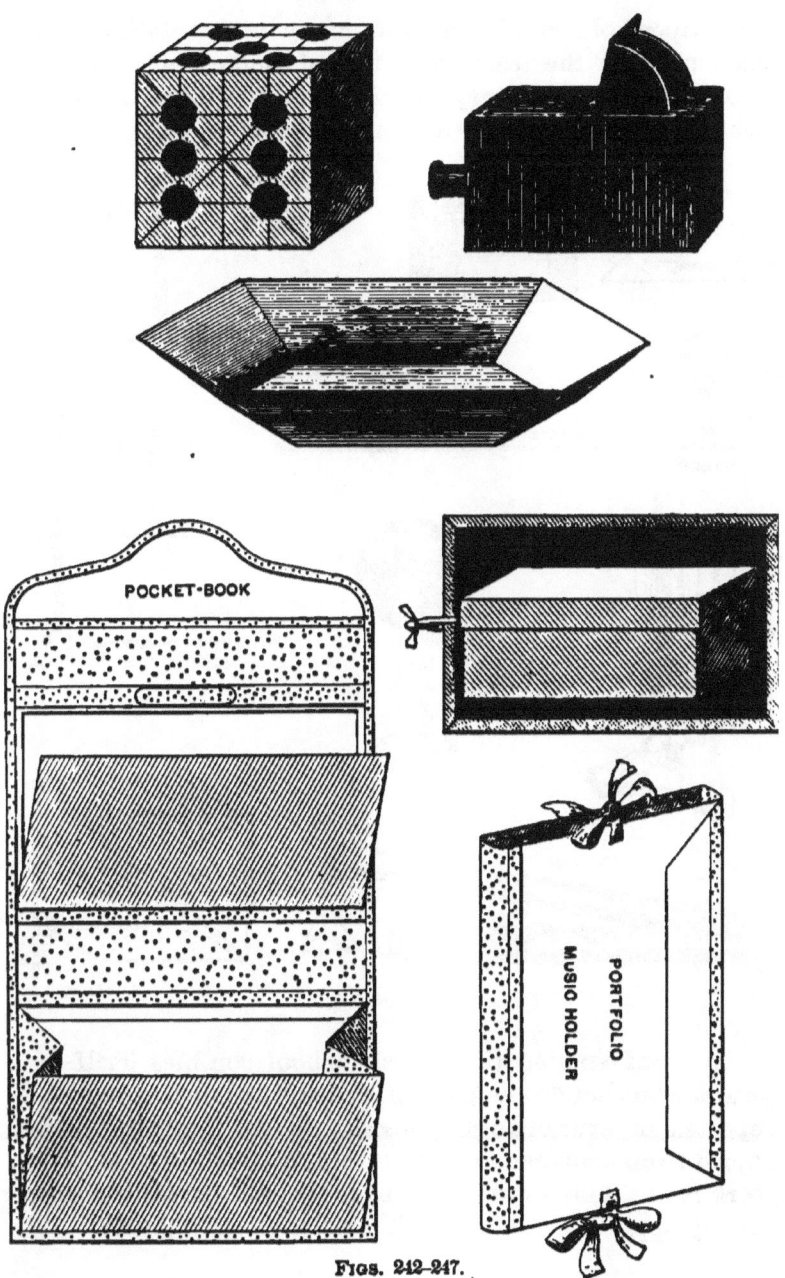

Figs. 242-247.

268 LEIPSIC (KINGDOM OF SAXONY).

ers, paper-holders, chains, and many others. The handbook used by the teachers is full of suggestions. The tin and zinc work has a very "useful look." Quite a number of neat things are made of tin, zinc, and copper.

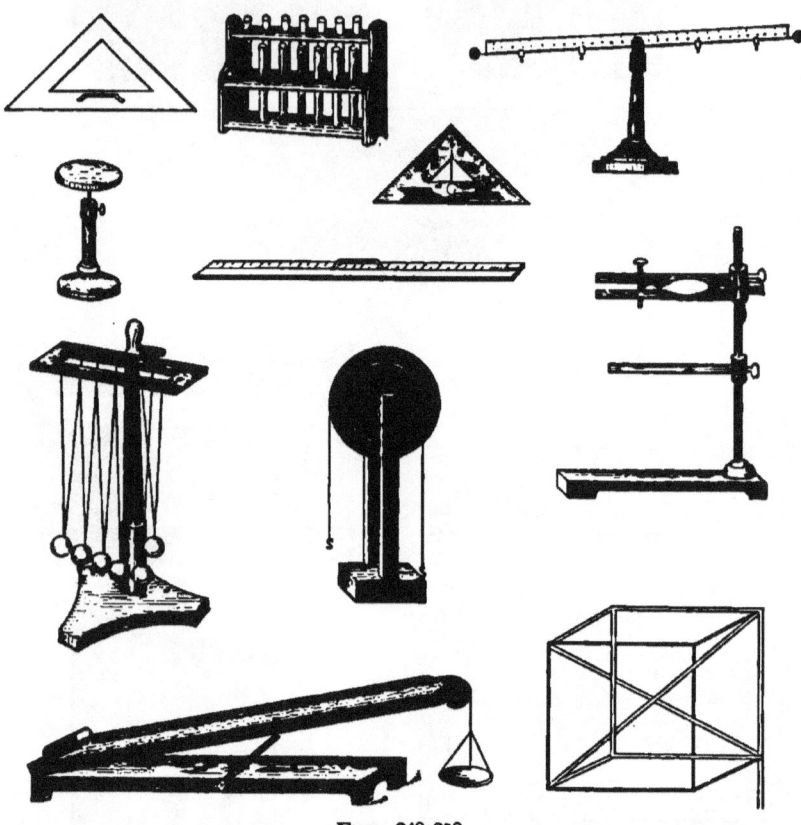

Figs. 248-258.

In *wood-carving* the Leipsic school confines itself to a peculiar but handsome pattern, called "scallop cut," which is repeated in ever-changing forms. A few typical sketches copied from ornamented furniture may illustrate this. This work is not done as exercise only, but each new form is instantly applied on some useful article. (See page 269.)

The work in modeling in clay also is vastly different from that in Paris; while there ornamenting is the chief

Fig. 259.—Wood-Carving.

aim, here in Leipsic it is forming objects, beginning with geometrical and ending with forms of life.

But in one thing all the manual training-schools I have

seen follow the same method. No article, no exercise is done in material, be that clay, plaster, wood, metal, or pasteboard, unless a drawing is first made by the pupil.

Characteristic of the object of this Leipsic school is the condensed announcement of its rector, in which he says: "Instruction in our workshops aims at developing the boys' practical common sense, training their senses, making them skillful in the handling of tools, giving their creative activity opportunities for application and the overtaxed brain a chance to recuperate by means of manual work, which is in itself an innocent recreation and pleasure, while it strengthens the body. No aimless play-work is permitted, nor tedious exercises with no apparent object. A boy who begins an article must know what he intends to produce, and then bend all his energy to secure that end. Boys who thus learn to work respect labor in any form, and are not ashamed of it."

To sum up: I prefer this German school, with all its inconveniences, to the magnificently equipped manual training halls in Paris with their tedious exercises.

5. The Germ of the Manual Training Idea.

In the month of January, 1888, died the noted school reformer of Finland (in Russia), Uno Cygnaeus, rector of a normal school at Iyväskylae, on Lake Paijene, Finland. The news of his death was scarcely noticed beyond the confines of Finland. Yet the name of that man deserves to be remembered in every civilized country. Cygnaeus was the father of that practical instruction in manual training which is now taking its conquering course through the civilized world, and is being recognized as a regular and legitimate branch of study or occupation in the boys' schools of Finland, Sweden, France, Switzerland, and Germany. In viewing the life of this man it may be seen that America has contributed its mite toward developing an idea which will prove a salvation to thousands and hundreds of thousands of boys, not to mention the benefits it offers to education in general all over the civilized world.

Cygnaeus was born at Tavastehus, on the 12th of October, 1810. When he had completed his school and college studies, he prepared himself for the ministry and accepted a position as preacher in the state-prison at Viborg. But in 1839 he left his native country to follow a call to Russian America (now Alaska). Among the Russian settlements of extreme Northwestern America there were a number of Finnish families that needed a minister of the gospel. Cygnaeus was assigned to that duty. In order to reach his post he took the long way around Cape Horn, and landed at Novo-Archangelsk in May, 1840.

He brought with him embryonic thoughts on education, and, thrown upon his own resources for intellectual company among the semi-savages on the coast of the Pacific in Russian America, he began to construe the world's needs in his own inimitable way. He was a man of active intellect and fertile imagination. Here in this northern wilderness it was that the idea of Finland's school reform was conceived and born. It was a feeble germ, though. For here it was nurtured in its infancy by no more food than the brain of a man who was cut loose from the civilized world, like a convict in the mines of Siberia.

Otto Salomon, the rector of the Swedish Manual Training Seminary at Nääs, says of him: "Cut loose from the world of culture and thought, surrounded by human beings who were half savages, the young preacher, in his lonely walks from one settlement to another, and by the lamp in his hermit's study, was seized by an unconquerable desire to benefit his race; to find suitable means for lifting men to a higher level of existence; to discover ways and means of reform in intellectual and moral education. Few books were at his disposal, but among them were Pestalozzi's and Froebel's works. These he studied in his lonely hours, and soon the fructifying spirit of Froebel awakened in him the germ of that idea which afterward took that definite shape in which we know it."

The study of Froebel's works particularly strengthened

him in his determination to devote his life to the cause of education of coming generations. Five years he spent in studying his favorite authors, and in framing his plans. Then he returned home by way of Okhotsk through Siberia and Russia. From the year 1846 till 1856, for more than ten years, he lived among his countrymen at St. Petersburg, acting as religious adviser, and made himself and his educational reform plans known to others through the press.

When, in 1856, Emperor Nicholas died, and with Alexander II an era of reform began not only in Russia proper but also in Finland (the people of which are more Swedish than Russian), Cygnaeus thought the time had come for the realization of his plans. Alexander II was crowned as Grand-duke of Finland, and came to this province, where he declared, in a memorable session of the provincial senate, that Finland should enjoy the blessings of a common-school system. Wisely the emperor left the execution of that order to the home government, and the senate called upon the councilors of the three consistories (at the time regents of church and school in Finland) to make propositions for a system of schools which would come up to the emperor's well-emphasized decision. These propositions were published, and subjected to public scrutiny.

This gave Cygnaeus a chance to forward his plans in connection with a dignified criticism of the councilors' propositions. Among the essays submitted to the Government was that of Cygnaeus, which made the most favorable impression. With that tolerance for the opinion of others which will always commend itself, Cygnaeus discussed the propositions and suggested his own plans. In the senate his ideas found favor at once, and it was thought that a man who could thus consistently lay open his plans and so well sustain them, was the proper person to execute them.

He was rewarded with the entire confidence of the authorities, and was charged with framing the plans for a system of schools which offered room for manual training. But, in order to enable him to present the best results of study and observation, he was sent to central Europe, to inspect the schools there. This he did, and, after studying the ideas of German educational reformers and observing their practical results, returned home, embodied what he had learned into his own plans, and then submitted his new plans.

They were unanimously adopted, and he was appointed Inspector-General of the People's Schools of Finland, and rector of the normal school at Iyväskylae (situated on the woody shore of Lake Paijene, in the center of the province). In this position he was able to execute his favorite idea of introducing manual training for boys, and other far-reaching plans of reform, without opposition. The fact that he found little, if any opposition, may be attributed to his lovable character and charming temper. It is said of him that he disarmed opposition with his saint-like smile, his unconquerable determination, and wonderful strength of argument.

His chief points of reform consisted in introducing Pestalozzi's objective teaching and Froebel's occupations into the schools, supplementing both by manual training for more advanced grades. The principle upon which his system was based was, that education of the young must aim not at one-sided intellectual training, but at the harmonious strengthening and exercise of man's inborn powers, *with constant consideration of practical aims in life.* The whole life of this man proves again what a power a man can be who has an idea, and the strength of will to pursue and realize it.

6. Drawing in Leipsic and other Saxon Cities.

Prof. F. Flinzer, the famous illustrator of "Die deutsche Jugend," author of "König Nobel," and inspector of the drawing department in Leipsic, had the great kindness to devote a day to the task of initiating me into the method pursued in the teaching of drawing in that city and other places of Saxony. He is the leader of one of the four principal systems employed in Germany. A simple statement of the differences in the systems or methods will not come amiss in this book.

There is, first of all, the Hamburg system, of which I made frequent reference in previous pages. It has been modified somewhat to adapt it to existing circumstances, and has recently been officially introduced in all the schools of Prussia. Prof. Stuhlmann, rector of the industrial art-school in Hamburg, is the author. It may be said that it is spread over more territory than any other system, simply because the largest and leading state of Germany—Prussia—has adopted it. This system applies geometrical forms from the beginning, and presents the child in due course of years with a wealth of beautiful ornamental forms, a few of which are found on previous pages. Like other good systems, it avoids printed copies, and requires teacher and pupils to work out, to develop forms from others. It begins with drawing in net-lines, and ends with perspective drawing of solids.

There is, however, a serious error in the Prussian or Hamburg system: it permits—nay, requires—the use of instruments, ruler, compasses, etc., and ties down the child to the use of measures, such as ruler, paper-strips, etc. It never quite emancipates the pupil from artistic measures. He measures his construction-lines on every grade of the course, and he is, even at a time when his eye should be sufficiently trained in measuring without aids, such as paper-strips, required to verify his estimates taken by the eye. If this error is eliminated, I think the system is destined to a great future.

Opposed to this Prussian or Hamburg school is Flinzer's system. It is known in Germany as the Leipsic system. Flinzer never allows an instrument, but practices the eye to measure accurately. He discards drawing in net-lines, but begins with free-hand drawing, and continues it through the entire course. Drawing from solids, geometrical bodies, casts, busts, etc., begins in the third grade, and compasses and ruler are excluded rigidly and mercilessly from the entire course. I believe it is permitted only where mechanical engineering is taught in the high-school. Naturally Flinzer's course is much slower than Stuhlmann's.

The third system in vogue at many places in Germany is the one I mentioned also in one of my previous reports (see page 233). It consists of drawing solids at once, and discards flat-surfaced copies. This system is rather in a primitive state of development, and may perhaps, in years to come, grow more methodical. Where industrial, so-called, manual training schools are established, this system of drawing finds many friends.

The fourth system is the well-known copying from flat-surfaced models, which never develops self-activity, but keeps the pupil dependent upon copies. I am sorry to say that this system is still in general use in America. Here in Germany it is fast disappearing. Of all the systems I saw in operation here in Europe, that of Prof. Flinzer recommends itself to me most favorably. I have gathered about forty specimens from his own pupils representing the ages from nine till fourteen years, and shall endeavor to have them reproduced by the photo-lithographic process.

This Leipsic system is in harmony with the principles of the modern science of education. It seems to seek the aim of free-hand drawing in the general aim of the school, that is, in intellectual growth, not merely in dexterity of the hand and correct representation of form. Each of its steps may be, and I believe is, founded upon a basis of psychological reasoning. It aims at the development of an "intellectual eye," at conscious seeing. Manual dexterity is considered of secondary importance ; indeed, it acknowledges the latter only when it gives evidence of an actual comprehension of the form to be produced or reproduced.

Perhaps in nothing is Flinzer's procedure so fruitful as in strengthening the power of judgment and creative activity. Never during the entire course does Flinzer touch a pupil's drawing to correct an error. By skillful questioning and the simplest but most effective tests he makes the pupils see their own errors—and having recognized the errors the correcting of them follows easily. There is no show, no aiming at glittering results, in his manner of teaching. It is a fact which can be fully comprehended only by having seen the system in operation, or by comparing the results with those of other systems.

The Leipsic system is logical—proceeds from the simplest to the most complicated forms; that is, it proceeds genetically. By means of analysis and synthesis it develops forms; in short, it proceeds precisely in the world of forms as the good teacher does in the world of ideas : observation, percept, concept, idea, judgment, follow in proper succession, and the power of imagination is wonderfully nourished.

Again, there is no confusion; the course is concentrically arranged. Everything new stands in organic connection with previous cognitions. And above all stands the fact that Flinzer makes his pupils productive; not a form is taught which is not used to produce new ones in ever-varying applications. A boy who has gone through this course is never at a loss how to present forms, both flat-surfaced ornaments and solid bodies. This productive application is so peculiar a merit of this system that it deserves special mention. No pupil of Prof. Flinzer, after leaving school, has dropped drawing, but continues the practice. It is a preparation adapted alike for artisan and artist—a quality which can not be claimed by any other system.

I trace this back to the noteworthy fact that, from the very start, instruments are rejected, and the pupil is required to rely entirely upon himself. No artificial measuring is allowed; the eye alone must do the measuring.

7. Shading in Drawing.

Pupils are apt to think that the light falls in parallel beams on all objects, and that therefore the side on which the light falls should be represented in white, while others not struck by direct beams of light might be shaded. In the beginning of the course in shading this may suffice. But it is no more true than it is to say "the sun rises or sets." Illumina-

SHADING IN DRAWING.

tion by parallel beams does not occur in nature anywhere, for all things visible to the eye are struck by beams of light which stand at different angles to each other. The following sketch of one of Prof. Flinzer's lessons is highly instructive:

Suppose that $a\ b$ in the following illustration be a window through which strong light falls upon a sphere beyond its equator, namely, as far as line $c\ d$. The lowest beam of light which can strike the sphere perpendicularly is the one marked $b\ e$, the highest that marked $a\ f$. The space, or angle, between these two lines is filled with beams each of which forms a "pole of light." To these are added a great number of parallel beams of which those that strike the sphere may be considered first. We will call the parallels belonging to each other a system. Now, it is plain that an innumerable number of such systems of beams strike the sphere, and their poles illumine the space between e and f. Each of these systems has its equa-

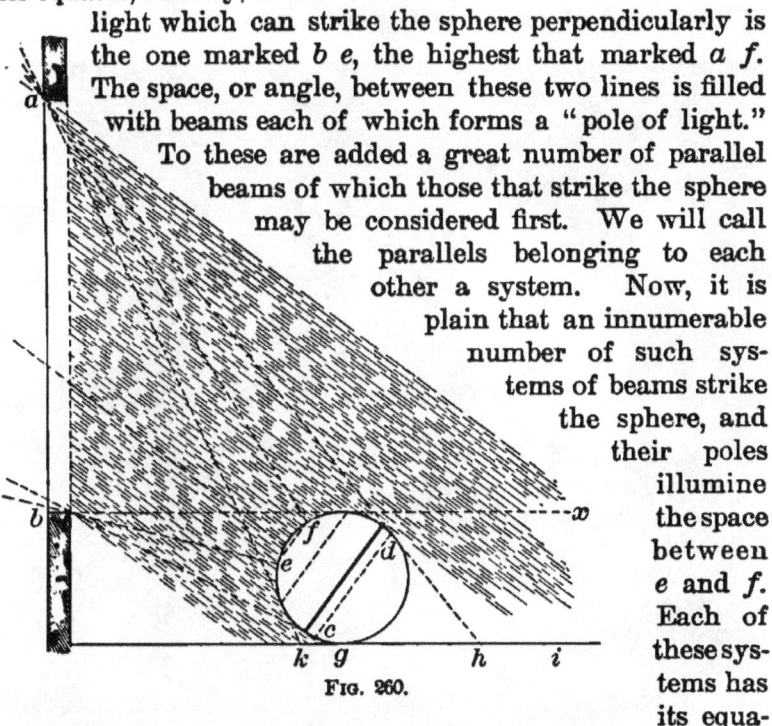

Fig. 260.

tor, that is, its circumference; but most of these circumferences are destroyed or obliterated by the beams of other systems, since they too illumine a space. The boundary-line of shadow which in case of parallel illumination would be congruent with the equator of the sphere is now moved beyond the equator, or as far as line $c\ d$, that is, to the tangents $a\ d$ and $b\ c$. The impression this makes on the eye is that the equator has receded.

Hence it is obvious that the greatest amount of light is found on line ef, and that on the zone formed by lines ef and cd the light becomes less clearly defined until line cd is reached, where dense shadow will prevail if reflected light does not strike even the lower part of the sphere and make it visible to us. The zone between ef and cd must therefore be shaded; beginning at ef, the shadow must be represented as increasing till the darkest portion is reached.

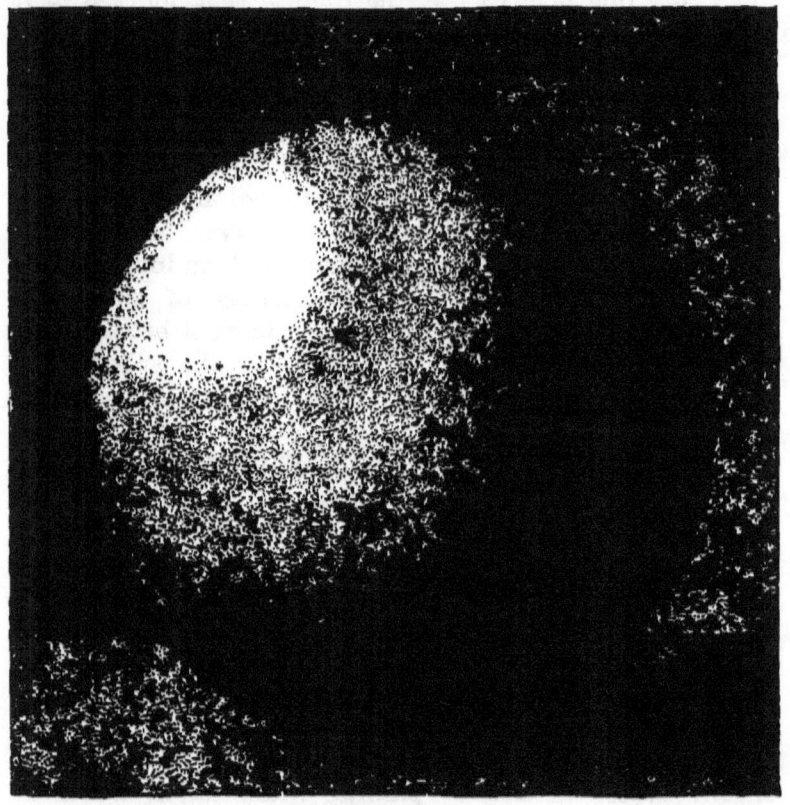

Fig. 261.

The foregoing cut is a reproduction of a shaded sphere, a drawing of which I saw done by pupils of the schools in Leipsic.

During the lessons I heard Prof. Flinzer give, I noticed two ingenious devices that appealed strongly to the senses. The first was a white board on hinges, which could be placed in front of a window to catch the direct beams of light. Its dazzling whiteness was well observed; then the teacher turned it slightly, say at an angle of twenty degrees. The difference in the tone of the color was at once noticed.

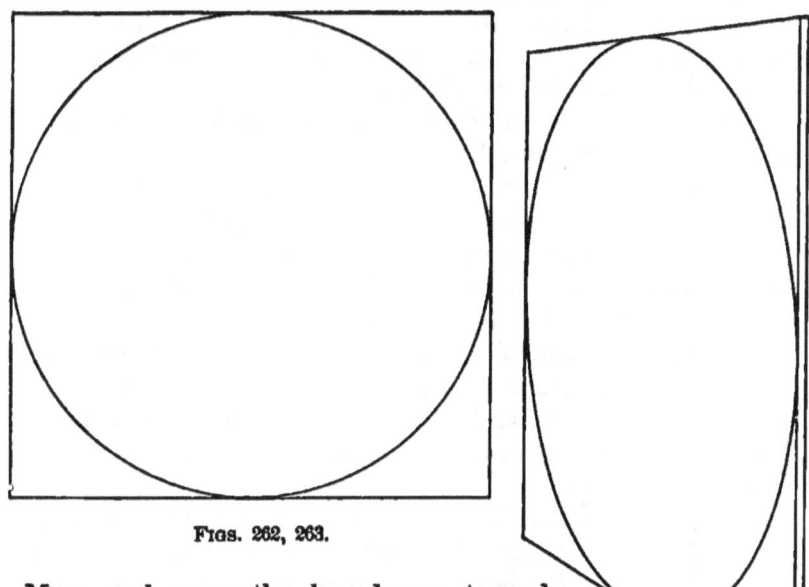

FIGS. 262, 263.

More and more the board was turned away from the direct beams of light; and when, finally, it was turned at an angle of ninety degrees, the decrease of light on the board was sufficient to convince the boys of the necessity of shading it, in case they had to represent the board in a drawing. This gradual change showed them what tone to apply in shading.

The other device consisted of a square blackboard showing a large circle in white oil-color. This board hung on hinges also. When it was turned to the left, the pupils saw the circle shortened and changed into an ellipse, as the foregoing cuts show.

8. A Drawing-Lesson full of Fun.

Drawing-lessons are generally rather prosy affairs. They are not apt to employ the brain; weighty arguments, hard thinking, quick responses, flashes of wit, and a pleasant flow of humor, are usually not characteristics of the drawing-lessons as I know them to be in many schools. In Leipsic a bit of genuine fun is mixed with the unavoidable drudgery of the drawing-lesson, which bit of fun, after all, has a solid foundation of earnest intention on the part of the instigator, the teacher. The latter—Prof. Flinzer—told me that a pupil might test his sketches of live forms by blackening them to make them appear as silhouettes.

"Draw the outlines of the human body," said he; "they may seem to you correct; then fill out the outlines, and you will instantly detect where the lines are faulty. Or, you may instinctively feel yourself that the outlines are faulty somewhere, but you may be unable to detect where the errors are. All you have to do is to make a silhouette of the form you sketched in lines. The errors made will cry out their grievances, and you will hasten to redress them. This has led me to give my pupils from time to time a lesson in silhouette-drawing.

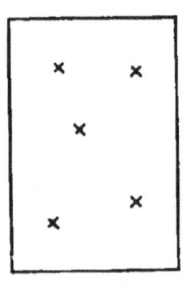

Fig. 264.

"No special methodical steps are planned for this kind of work. I merely use it as a test-lesson, but the boys enjoy it as much as going to a circus. Thus I proceed: A boy is called to make five dots on the board, and to designate which of the five is to be the head of the figure. Then a pupil is called to the board to draw a human form within these five dots, two of which are to designate the place of the hands, two the places of the feet, and one that of the head. He is not permitted to choose the latter for himself. If a pupil of much imaginative force is called, very interesting-looking figures are the results. The five

A DRAWING-LESSON FULL OF FUN. 281

points in the frame in the margin, for instance, would instantly suggest the picture of the crucified. This being class-work, all the pupils learn to give shape to the forms they imagine. Even poor draughtsmen do commendable work.

"Sometimes we take five crumbs of bread, or five grains of sand, and let them fall on the drawing-paper. Where they chance to come to rest, faint dots are made, the teacher having previously stated that the upper left, or the lower right, or some other corner, designates the position of the head. Of course, chance determines the position of these dots. It exercises the ingenuity and imaginative power to determine what kind of figures should fill the frame.

"The fun which grows out of this kind of work is exhilarating, especially when the order is given to make the head

FIGS. 265-268.

in the lower left corner. This difficult problem was solved nicely by representing an acrobat lying on his back and playing ball with his feet."

I offer to the reader some of the work done by the pupils of Prof. Flinzer. These sketches will speak for themselves. They are not of equal perfection; nor is any of them perfect, but as the work of boys of the age of twelve to fourteen years the figures are meritorious. Perhaps the best recommendation of this kind of lessons is the consideration that it stimulates self-activity to a greater degree than copying

282 LEIPSIC (KINGDOM OF SAXONY).

drawings or models. The practice is at least worthy of an honest trial now and then, and may be used as a stimulus which has the enviable quality of genuineness and absolute

FIGS. 269, 270.

want of artificiality. My candid and patient reader is kindly requested not to call this "a new method." It is neither a new nor an old method, nor is it a method at all. It is nothing but a very skillful device for stimulating the pupil's creative activity, but, as such, very valuable.

9. THE BEST-EQUIPPED SCHOOL.

The Sixth Bürger School in Leipsic is, as far as my knowledge of schools goes, the best equipped in the world.

I do not mean the best manned, but best equipped with means of instruction. Wherever in Leipsic I inquired what school would yield the largest crop of valuable observations, I was told to go to the Sixth Bürger School. I will say nothing of its organization. It differs materially from that of our common schools, but all the differences I noticed are sequences of peculiar German social distinctions which we do not care to adopt. This school shows a wealth of equipment with means of instruction that might make Pestalozzi turn green with envy in his grave.

While in Paris I was much delighted when I saw the magnificent and generous equipment of the primary schools there, but this school far surpasses them all. No apparatus ever invented to illustrate instruction in physics is wanting here. Many of these devices and machines are made by the

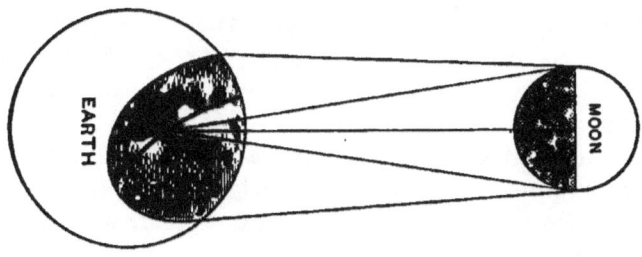

FIG. 271.

rector, Mr. Schmidt. Natural history is here represented by innumerable stuffed birds and animals, mineral specimens, prepared sea-animals and fishes, and, finally mounted dried plants in portfolios. This natural history cabinet vies with that of the pedagogical museum in Paris.

Astronomy, which appears to be the hobby of this gentleman, is well represented by devices which are nearly all patented. Every total or partial eclipse that occurs during the year is carefully sketched and represented in movable pasteboard devices, showing the courses the shadow takes over the surface of the earth. (See Fig. 271, a sketch of the last total eclipse of the sun, which was observed by the pupils after a lesson which prepared them suitably for the phenomenon.)

In the corridor hangs a device showing the relative size of the sun, earth, and moon. (See Fig. 272.) The mean distance of the moon from the earth, as represented in the simple device, is made the one-thousandth part of the length of the corridor. Large planetariums and tellurions of his own make were exhibited in great number by Prof. Schmidt.

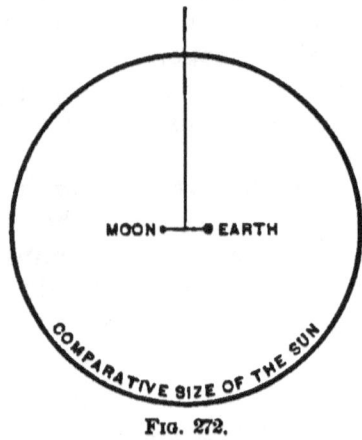

Fig. 272.

Preparations for illustrating instruction in physiology filled an entire room. There were such of plaster, of *papier-maché*, of pasteboard, even of marble. Geographical maps, relief and plane-surface maps, were here collected and so nicely arranged that a mere glance sufficed to find the desired one. Perfect order reigned supreme, for the professor allows no one to handle his treasures in the cabinet. All requisitions are filled by himself.

In regard to inventing devices for illustrative teaching he is a genius. I select one of the numerous articles to prove the originality of the man. It is a device illustrating "borrowing" in subtraction. The thing is made of paste-board, has three compartments, each covered with glass, under which are seen ten round apertures. If a strap at the side is pulled,

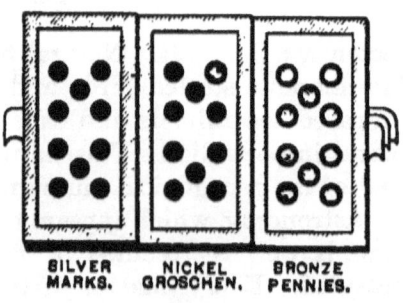

SILVER MARKS. NICKEL GROSCHEN. BRONZE PENNIES.

Fig. 273.

there appear ten silver marks in the holes of the first compartment ; if another is pulled, nine of them disappear, one is left ; this one is borrowed and changed to nickel groschen, which is done by pulling a second strap. The device itself is perhaps of less methodical value, as the inventor may think ; still, with especially dull pupils, it may be of service.

Another thing worthy of imitation is a pictorial presentation of the changes that have been going on in the city. The history of the city is illustrated by three water-color charts of very large size. The first represents Leipsic at the time of Luther. The " Grimma Gate," the " Pleissenburg," and the old fortifications, are there in exact copy of old pictures preserved in the city museums and archives. The second picture represents the same places at the time of Napoleon I, with all the changes that had been made since the time of Luther. It is the scene of that memorable day, the 18th day of October, 1813, when the Prussian Landwehr stormed the Grimma Gate. The third, and naturally most handsome of the three pictures, represents the city as it is now. The view is taken from the same standpoint from which the others are taken. What notable changes this picture shows! It is a speaking proof of the marvelous industry of our century, such as no description and no column of numbers could give. These large pictures are mounted on muslin, provided with light frames, and used frequently in teaching home history and geography. Other pictures, scenes from the history of civilization and culture, were there, but the above mentioned interested me most.

A geological map of the earth's crust on which Leipsic is situated deserves to be described. Think of a glass-covered case, in which the different strata of the earth, so far as known, are made of real minerals. From the granite upward to alluvial and diluvial layers, each layer is represented in approximate thickness. There were " grauwacke," brown coal, ocean gravel, erratic blocks, loam, etc. I thought

I might suggest to our high-school teachers to prepare such a map *in natura*, for their own city, so far as the crust is known to them. I would illustrate the condition of the crust on which their pupils live, and the treasures under foot, better than a description. Or, still better, they may suggest to their pupils to make one.

In each class-room of this superb school a wind-rose is painted on the ceiling such as in Fig. 274. Care is taken to have the cardinal points exactly right by the compass, thus indicating the position of the school-house. It will hardly do, though, to leave the execution to the tender mercies of some ignorant painter, lest he may consider his convenience. This reminds me of a good joke:

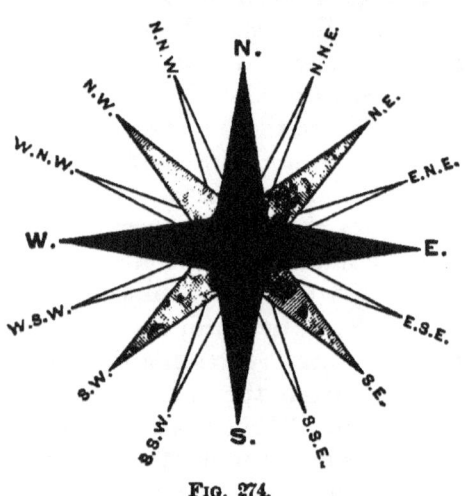

Fig. 274.

A man in a village of Holland was seen one day painting a heavy black line on the gable-end of his house and attaching to it a date, say November 18, 1882. Asked what he was about, he said: "I am moving my high-water mark up to where the boys can't scratch it out again. I am sick of their pranks."

The most imposing thing to me in this Sixth Bürger School was the sight revealed in the laboratory. Think of a fully equipped laboratory in an elementary school—not a high-school, a fact which I wish to emphasize. Here were amphitheatrically arranged seats, a well-stocked counter, and several large glass cases full of chemicals. What a wealth was collected there may be judged from the fact that the costly platinum wire and sundry expensive chemicals were there used extensively without regard to cost.

The lesson in chemistry I heard here proved that the professor, Rector Schmidt, was not only a man who could invent mechanical contrivances for illustrative teaching, but was also a master in teaching. One is apt to think (at least I have heard the charge made) that much illustrative or objective teaching prevents self-activity on the part of the pupils. This may be true, if the teacher thinks that by explaining a fact in appealing to the senses he has done all that is necessary. But to see this man use the direct appeal to the senses merely as a starting-point, and then drive the boys by hard questioning into corners from which only their own exertion in thinking could rescue them, was a memorable sight. He was a Pestalozzian in principles and practice, and possessed all the qualities that were wanting in Pestalozzi. Had that reformer had Schmidt's talent not only for awakening thought but for exercising it, had he possessed his excellent executive power, Pestalozzi would not have been the great failure in teaching and managing that he was. I say this with due reverence for his undying philosophy.

All the teachers I saw at work in this school (see article "Notes from the Schools of Leipsic") were true assistants of the principal. I saw lessons in the primary and middle grades, and was soon convinced of the fact that the citizens of Leipsic have just cause to be proud of this school. It is a grand temple of popular education, this Sixth Bürger School in Leipsic! When I left it I could not avoid comparing it with others I had seen in two worlds, and in all my recollections I found nothing equal to it.

10. Notes from the Schools of Leipsic.

It is generally admitted that the best methodicians are not found in the higher schools of Germany. The teachers there are college and university graduates, who have a great deal of knowledge but little skill in applying it. If one wishes to see good teaching one must visit so-called people's schools. But there are exceptions of rare merit. Some of these may be seen in Halle. Another I found in Leipsic. His name is Dr. Böttcher, and he is every inch a genius in the school-room and outside of it.

The subject of his lesson was measuring circular planes. The class was Lower Prima (the thirteenth school year). What a rapidity in questioning and answering; what a fertility in application; what a versatility in referring to other fields of knowledge not intimately related to the subject of the day, but well adapted to furnish means for comparison and contrast; and what a breathless attention on the part of these young men who in other lessons perhaps made sport of their teachers! Even literature was drawn in and had to serve to enliven the lesson.

When a boy mistook the square of a radius with the double of the radius and arrived at entirely wrong conclusions, the professor led the pupil *ad absurdum* and then sagely remarked, "It is the curse of an evil deed that continuously it must beget evil" (Schiller). The pupil saw the fun in his case and started over again. When the bell announced the close of the lesson, I saw several of the pupils consult their watches, as though they could not believe that an hour had passed. I do not wonder that all candidates for positions in the high-schools of Leipsic are sent to Dr. Böttcher to listen to his instructions.

In the school described in a previous chapter, called the "best-equipped school," I heard two lessons in the primary grades which gave unimpeachable evidence of the fact that objective teaching, and much of it at that, does not prevent the important function of the teacher, "exercise." For in a third grade I found the little boys multiplying orally with ease and rapidity such examples as 7×19, 18×25, 17×16. The first example was solved thus: Twenty times seven less seven. The second was solved first by saying, "Twenty times eighteen, plus five times ten, plus five times eight." Then it was solved by adding two naughts to eighteen and dividing this number by four. Examples in adding and subtracting, such as 1625+1335 and 1987−1598, were solved with equal celerity. Fractions were also handled easily, such as $\frac{16}{2}$ how many whole ones? 7½ weeks how many days? $4\frac{2}{3}+5\frac{2}{3}=$? etc.

An object-lesson in the lowest primary grade that I heard in the same school consisted of a review of what the children had observed in the woods during an excursion. Although the review gave evidence of a remarkably well-developed sense of observation, it recommended itself to me more by the wonderful skill in linguistic expression on the part of the pupils. I note this fact as a proof of my former statement, that objective instruction as a means is not faulty; it only becomes so when it is considered an aim in itself.

CHAPTER XI.

DRESDEN IN SAXONY AND MUNICH IN BAVARIA.

1. EXAMINATIONS IN DRESDEN.

On my trip through Thuringia, Saxony, Austria, and Switzerland, I arrived in Dresden at an unfavorable time. It was during examination week. Teachers who can not imagine an annual examination except by picturing before their inner eye a class of pupils sitting bent over their foolscap paper answering a set of ten questions, may follow me into a school in Dresden to see that a totally different sight presented itself to me.

The entire building was in holiday attire. On the lower floors several class-rooms were opened for visitors. There were collections of written work, not done for the occasion, but each pupil's daily work from Easter, 1887, till Easter, 1888—every copy-book, every composition-book, every book of problems, every language-book, every note-book, every spelling blank book used during the year, neatly labeled with name, class, age, and address of the pupil. It was a bewildering sight. All these rooms were visited for five hours a day all through the week by parents and friends of the pupils, who inspected the work closely.

I turned away ashamed after looking over several stacks, thinking of the slovenly appearance of the books in my own schools and comparing them with this exquisite beauty of penmanship and this immaculate cleanliness. Other rooms were filled with drawings in portfolios and mounted drawings. The desks had been removed, and the walls were covered with drawings. There had been no "natural selection," no "survival of the fittest," but every scrap, every drawing furnished during the year in that entire school (the Seventh Bürger School, on Ammon Street) was there, good, bad, and indifferent.

After having feasted my eyes with the beautiful colored ornamental drawings furnished by the girls, studied the results of manual work of the boys in form of pasteboard and wood-work, after having inspected the industrial work of the girls (knitting, crocheting, embroidering, patching, darning, sewing, etc.), I was conducted up-stairs to the session-room of the school. This room was very handsomely decorated, and arranged as indicated in Fig. 275. Section A was a raised platform for the magistrate, the councilor of education, the inspectors, the rector of the school, the committee on public examination, and other persons of importance, who sat at a large official looking table and made notes. Section B was partitioned off for the class under examination. The pupils faced the teacher, and in a long row at the banister sat the faculty of the school. Section C was reserved for the public, who attended the examination very numerously.

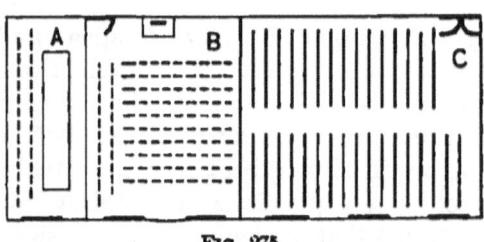

Fig. 275.

A commission determines a few days previously in what three branches the class is to be examined publicly. This examination is oral. The class under trial was a class of girls of eleven to twelve years of age. The branches in which they were examined were biblical history, physics, and languages. Fifty minutes were given to each branch, and each child was called upon, and rarely failed to respond. It was not possible to determine how much of this "performance" was show and how much honest work; but, taking into consideration that the teacher went over very much ground, I concluded that there was very little, if any, prepared show.

What I heard was apparently a review lesson pure and simple. The subjects had been determined upon and announced two days previous, so that an elaborate deception was out of the question. If we further consider that this public examination does not decide the promotion of pupils, but is held chiefly to show the effectiveness of the school and to establish a closer connection between home and school, we may find many redeeming features in this kind of examining.

In several other cities, chiefly in southern Germany, I noticed another kind of annual examination which commended itself to me. The school, teachers, and pupils, were all in holiday attire. Each class sat in its own accustomed room. The entire daily programme was carried out as it is done during the year, and the visitors, parents, and friends of the pupils, the city and school authorities, representatives of the learned professions, teachers from other schools, and other people interested in public education, came to the class-rooms and listened to the reviews going on. This was called *review or visiting week.*

The lessons were so arranged (where it could be done without much disturbance) as to give each teacher of that particular school a chance to hear his colleagues also. This "visiting week," as it was called even in hotels, drew a great number of visitors to the school, people who would perhaps never have come if it had not been for this occasion. The card which usually hangs on the outside of each class-room door and which reads, "Persons not connected with this school must not enter this room without permission of the authorities"—this card is removed and everybody is welcome, provided he causes no disturbance.

It happened in my presence that a lady, chagrined at the apparent ignorance of her "dear little sonnie," broke the rule and asked the teacher to give him a better chance to show off. The teacher, a good-natured, charitably inclined man, instead of ordering her off the premises, complied with her angry request, and pelted the sleepy youngster with questions, every one of which seemed to be very fair and appropriate; but the youngster stared at him and failed to respond. So the teacher lowered the standard of his questions, asking easier ones, and still the boy failed. At last the woman broke the painful silence, crying, "Wait till I get you home, Bob!"

This occurrence, though exceptional as it certainly was, and several circumstances attending the examinations in Dresden, made me doubt the advisability of such public examinations; and if I consider that we have reason to object strongly to the customary American written examinations also, I admit that the proper and best form of examination has not yet been found, that despite all suggestions and discussion the question as to the best mode of conducting examinations in school is still an open one. The problem should be solved solely with regard to the educational influence of examinations.

2. Notes from the Schools of Dresden.

In Dresden it was that I witnessed public examinations. I had no opportunities for seeing or hearing lessons. Being well acquainted with Prof. Kleinert, the editor of the foremost German educational journal, I procured from him printed reports and courses of study which are very interesting reading-matter. They go here less deeply into statistical details than we are accustomed in America, but what they publish is of more lasting value. I cull a few interesting facts from the annual report of 1888, and present them in English garb. The numbers given may not be very imposing, but the facts are. I think them well worth presenting to American readers.

Vacation colonies for sickly school-children were established in the country, and three hundred and fifty-three pupils were benefited thereby. With renewed strength and vigor these children returned after a sojourn of six weeks. On the outskirts of the city so-called city-vacation colonies were established last summer, which benefited four hundred and thirty pupils, who went out in the morning in six troops with their teachers, and returned home in the evening. For many weeks, they were fed well and spent their time in playing and making excursions into the woods and fields on foot. The results of this enterprise also were very gratifying. Children who, at the beginning of the season, could hardly walk two miles without great fatigue, could at the close of the season walk five and six miles on a stretch.

Play-Grounds.—The "Society for the Common Weal" secured the right to use some conveniently situated groves in the immediate vicinity of the city for play-grounds. Many children made use of them; four hundred and fifty-eight boys in twelve groups and four hundred girls in forty-eight groups played here daily, under the inspection of the teachers of gymnastics, male and female. It is the intention to secure for each school-house a public shady play-ground outside of the city. This prevents intercourse with morally bad elements and contamination of vice in back alleys. The teachers are paid an extra salary for the time they devote to these play-grounds.

Manual Training.—The manual training school supported by the same society was attended by two hundred and forty-six pupils in fifteen classes. More is said of a similar school elsewhere. (See pages 262-270.)

Free Dinners.—The "Society for the Suppression and

Prevention of Beggary" contributed twenty-five hundred marks toward furnishing warm dinners to needy schoolchildren. The school authorities were enabled, with this and other sums of money, to furnish 58,424 plates of soup and other warm dishes. More than one thousand children enjoyed the luxury of a warm dinner who otherwise would have gone without any dinner, or, at best, with a cold lunch.

Boy-Asylums.—The "Society for the Establishment of Boy-Asylums" maintain four such institutions (see page 312) for boys, and one for girls. The city school authorities gave the desirable rooms, and suitable teachers were engaged who acted as leaders and supervisors. The children are here fed and kept after school hours, if they have no home to go to, both parents being out working, or the mother being worried by numerous little ones. Manual training is one of the chief occupations on winter evenings.

Baths and Gardens.—The city government in summer offered free bathing to children of needy parents. Other children paid a nominal price for admission. The bathing-places are in the Elbe River, and under constant supervision of swimming-masters. Ice-ponds for skating were kept clean at the expense of the city, and reserved for the use of schoolchildren. The zoölogical garden is always open to schoolchildren, one's card for free admission being confiscated in the event of misconduct. The botanical garden furnished the teachers of the city schools with seventy different plants, each of which in hundreds and thousands of specimens, for the use of pupils studying botany.

What a difference between now and times gone by ; and yet people talk of "this materialistic age," "want of charity," and the like! The world has become better, and associated charities extend their blessings to thousands of needy creatures whose like used to die in fence-corners and squalid garrets for want of sympathy and actual assistance. There is less sentimental twaddle and immensely much more charity than in former days !

3. Manual Training in Germany.

Since the year 1880 more than two hundred manual training schools have been opened in Germany. Several of these, notably those in Halle, Leipsic, Dresden, Vienna (though this city is not now in Germany, it is essentially a German city), Munich, Mülhausen, I visited and reported upon the work done in them. When I arrived in Vienna I found the idea had made better headway than could have been expected in conservative Austria. Messrs. Petzel and Herbe, two Vienna teachers, the former of whom I have mentioned elsewhere in this book, had recently made a journey through Germany for the sole purpose of inspecting the manual training-schools. Their report is very interesting. I translate a few passages from it, selecting those which point out the essential differences in these schools.

In *Schandau, Saxony*, they found three distinct classes of schools: 1. A school for wood-carving in which patterns of geometrical forms are practiced, until the pupils' skill is developed enough to begin the ornamentation of articles of use, such as picture-frames, visiting-card plates, stools, easels, arm-chairs, tables, etc. These things are made of nut or cherry wood, are then stained or polished, and sell well. There are more than a dozen of these schools in the kingdom of Saxony. 2. An industrial school. Here baskets are woven—baskets of all sizes and patterns, from the stout market-basket to the fine flower-basket; peeled willow switches, split cane, and even straw, are used. All articles made in this school find a ready sale. There are six such schools in Saxony. 3. A braiding-school, in which straw is used as material. Door-mats and other things, such as bottle-packing, etc., are made here. These braiding and industrial schools sold goods for 5,372 marks in one year. There are seventeen such schools in Saxony.

In *Dresden, Saxony*, a manual training school purely for educational purposes is established. It was opened in 1881 with forty-seven pupils, and had in 1887 as many as one hundred and seventy-five, of which fifty-six were between six and eight years of age. Only cartoon or pasteboard work and work in wood is done here. The latter consists of joiner-work and carving. As in all other German manual training schools, the children learn to use tools by making articles, not merely doing exercises, as is done in Paris. It is quite amusing to see the boys find the necessity of leaving nothing plain, but carve furniture as neatly and handsomely as artisans. In a number of boy-asylums (see article "Knabenhort") in Dresden manual occupations are also introduced.

Strange as it may seem, modeling is introduced and very successfully taught in the *blind asylums* in Saxony. Groups of twenty children and more are taught in one class, and with almost incredible dexterity these children model in clay and wax, led only by their sense of touch. They are thus initiated into the world of forms, and seem to enjoy life better in consequence of it. One must have seen these blind children at work to believe it possible.

The school visited had three classes. In Class I, only geometrical forms are made, but with an accuracy that might put to shame many a seeing child. In Class II, forms of life are made—leaves, plants, animal heads, and entire animal forms. An elephant, not larger than a man's fist, yet every part of which was in exact proportion and as well built as the "much-lamented Jumbo," is still vividly impressed in the visitor's memory. It was made by a boy totally blind ! In Class III, wax-flowers are made. These are so astonishingly true to nature, that no one can believe it unless he has seen it done. Fuchsias, rose-buds, and other flowers were imitated in wax incredibly true in number of leaves, thickness and size of leaves, petals, and stamens, except in color—that the teacher had to add. What a world of forms is opened to such children, who thus effectually learn to see with their finger-tips! One blind boy in this institution found a radish in the garden. He picked it up, carried it to his own bedroom, and there imitated it in clay or wax. When he brought his work to his teacher, the latter was much pleased to see that his instruction had made the boy self-active.

In *Stolberg, Saxony*, the visitors found a school in which pasteboard-work, book-binding, and joining is done. No boy over fourteen years of age is here admitted. Instruction is offered after school hours. (Course like that in Dresden.)

In *Aue, Saxony*, on the slope of the Erz Mountains, a most remarkable school is established. It is a tinsmith-school, and therefore ought to be classed among the special or industrial schools. It offers instruction to tin and zinc workers only. It is mentioned here simply because it has pupils of school-going age.

In *Markneukirchen, Saxony*, near the Bohemian line, a single man, an enthusiast in manual training, has established a school, and teaches scroll-sawing and wood-carving. It is not a money-making affair, but a purely educational enterprise.

In *Adorf, Saxony*, a fine and well-attended manual training-school is maintained by the city authorities, in which joiners', turners', and carvers' work is taught. The Royal Saxon Ministry of Instruction aids this school with the stipend of eight hundred marks per annum. The greatest attention is paid to wood-carving.

In *Zwickau, Saxony*, a school of this kind was opened in 1882 ; it has now over one hundred and fifty pupils. Cartoon or pasteboard work is here the favorite occupation. The course is well conceived, and innumerable objects of practical value are made here. It would need two pages of close print to mention them all. A wonderful taste in selecting paper and colors to make the articles pretty is exhibited, and all the articles have a ready sale. The first task in wood-work is to hollow out a square piece of birch-wood for a pencil-box. This makes the boys learn the use of the chisel, then a spoon is carved out ; after that and similar tasks, ornamental carving begins. Every object made has a practical use, and in ornamentation every line, every curve, every spiral applied is in harmony with the form of the object, or its use.

Very few schools will be able to surpass the results of this one. There are tools enough in this school to supply each pupil with an entire set, and he is held responsible for their condition. The aim of this school is purely educational, and the teachers hope that "it will accustom the boys to work ; train their hands to acquire skill ; direct their will-power upon the useful and beautiful ; give them an insight into industrial pursuits, as well as a comprehension of the forms of art-industry, and thus prepare not only a greater number of skilled artisans and thinking men, but also create a desire for more and more artistic work in the purchasers—that is, get people to appreciate the beautiful, recognize beauty in designs, and discriminate between genuine artistic work and shoddy imitation."

In *Leipsic, Saxony*, the manual training school gave the visitors much food for reflection, especially the normal school for manual training recently opened. I have reported upon this at length (see page 265).

In *Halle, Prussia*, in the great experimental station of education in Germany, the "Francke-Stiftungen," maintain a flourishing manual training school. There are also four "Knabenhorte" (boys-asylums) in which manual work is taught. Outside of the "Francke-Stiftungen" there is a manual training school in the city, which is reserved for the pupils of the high-schools. The sons of the most influential and wealthy families attend it, and the number of pupils increases with every term.

In *Berlin, Prussia*, the manual training schools are under the protection of her Majesty the Empress and Queen Victoria. One of these schools is situated in the Falk-Gymnasium, another in the Lessing-Gymnasium. Other schools have been opened since 1887. Also a normal school for manual training teachers is established, and all efforts are made to come up to the standard of Leipsic and Vienna.

In *Bremen* and other towns of northern Germany, schools of this kind are in a flourishing condition, but the report referred to says nothing about them.

In *Görlitz, Prussia*, these schools are the best in Prussia, as those in Leipsic are the best in Saxony. The teachers in Görlitz avoid all money-making efforts, and base their instruction strictly upon educational principles—that is to say, they are not moved by such considerations as, In what way may this or that occupation benefit the town ; but how may it benefit the pupil in developing his latent talents ?

In *Wüste-Giersdorf, Prussia*, the school has a more worldly object, namely, to draw the children away from the unwholesome trade of weaving, which has for centuries been the leading trade of the town, and has shortened more lives than can be told.

Dörnhau, Oberwaldau, Gottesberg, and *Rudolfswald*, villages in the Prussian province of Silesia, have similar schools, all of which do good work.

The gentlemen who reported their observations made on a journey through Saxony and Prussia, say, "It is the unanimous opinion of all concerned that the boys who have gone through a course of manual training, and then chosen a trade, are climbing the ladder of promotion faster than other apprentices." A well-informed gentleman in Görlitz, maintains that the tradesmen and owners of factories select the pupils of the training schools in preference to unskilled hands, and give them the best testimonials, saying they are accustomed to work, and therefore are more diligent as well as more skilled.

The following two pages of drawings, representing many useful things, are inserted here to give the reader an idea of the variety of articles made of wood in various schools of Germany. They are reproductions of the Swedish *slöjd system*. *Slöjd* (pronounce sloid) is a Swedish word, and may be rendered in English by the word *skill*, having in its modern application particular reference to manual skill. The drawings are not by far as handsome as those from

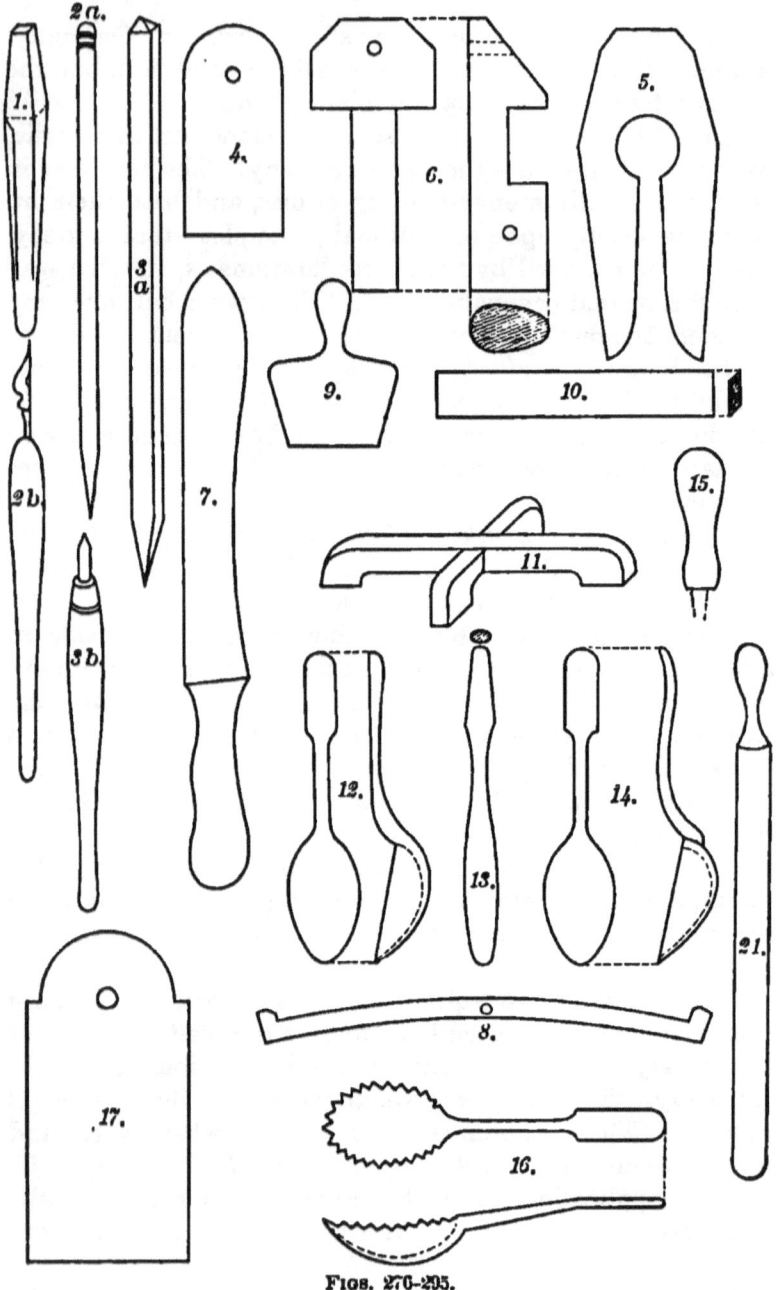

Figs. 276-295.

MANUAL TRAINING IN GERMANY. 301

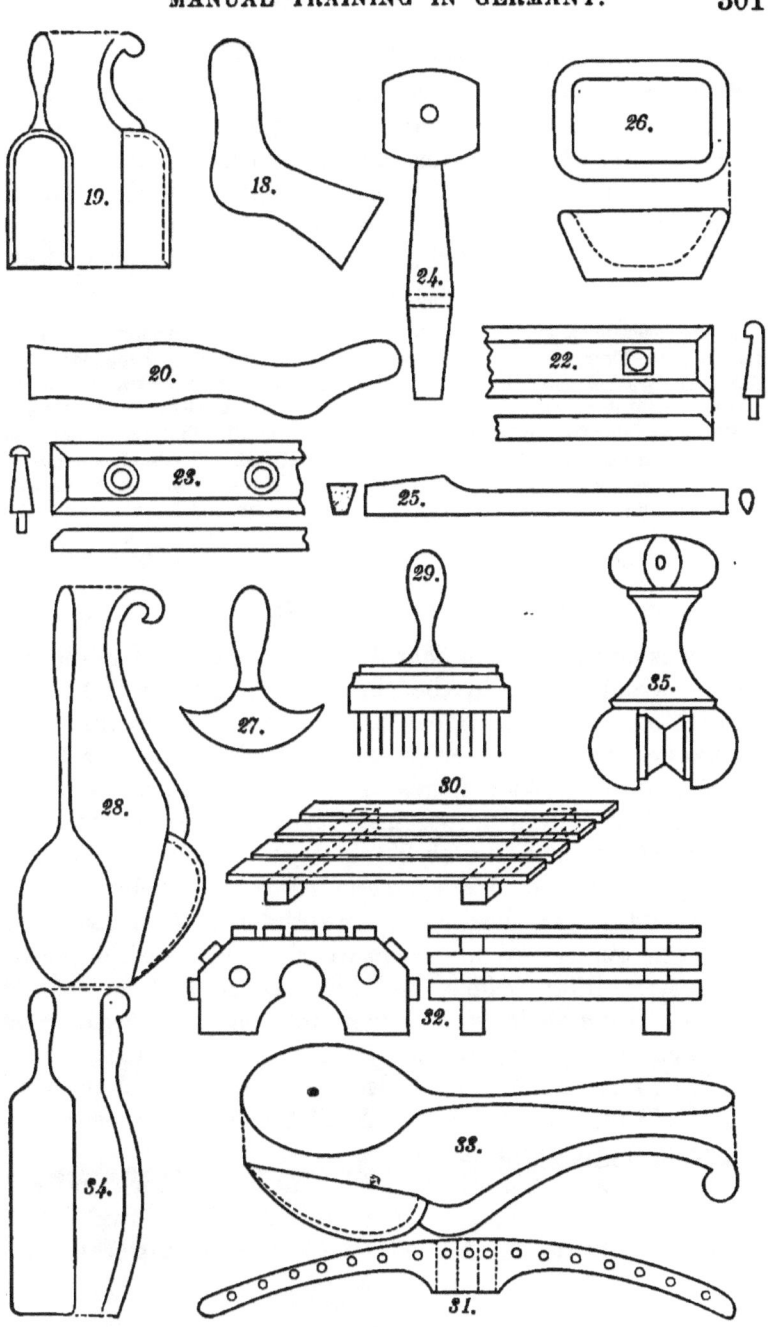

Figs. 296-313.

Paris, but they are eminently fit to illustrate the one vital difference between the French and German or Swedish schools, to wit: In France the pupils learn the use of tools by doing exercises; in Germany they produce useful articles, and thereby learn the use of tools indirectly; or, in France the boys learn the grammar of manual work, in Germany the work itself, which carries the grammar with it.

FIGS. 276–313.

1. Peg used in calculating-machine. 2a. Net-weaving needle. 2b. Pen-holder. 3a. Flower-prop. 3b. Pencil-holder. 4. Slat for writing names of plants. 5. Wash-clamp. 6. Plug. 7. Paper-knife. 8. Loom-bow. 9. Butter-spattle. 10. Ruler. 11. Stand. 12. Spoon. 13. Hammer-handle. 14. Spoon. 15. Chisel-handle. 16. Butter-spoon. 17. Kitchen-board. 18. Stocking-stretcher. 19. Sugar-shovel. 20. Large stocking-stretcher. 21. Sickle-sharpener. 22, 23. Clothes-hooks. 24. Gardener's plug. 25. Axe-handle. 26. Soap-dish. 27, Hack knife. 28. Grocer's shovel. 29. Bread-comb. 30. Flower-stand. 31. Bow used in calculating-machine. 32. Foot-stool. 33. Large spoon. 34. Wash-beater. 35. Loom-roll.

5. WHAT I SAW IN MUNICH.

It was on the 16th of March that I reached Munich, the day on which in Berlin the Emperor William was buried. Munich looked like a widow in her weeds. From the massive towers of the "Frauenkirche" and other churches hung broad and long black flags. All business houses and innumerable dwelling-houses had German or Bavarian flags out draped with crape, or black flags. Not a single store was open. The people promenaded in dark-colored Sunday attire through the streets. Hundreds and thousands of ladies and gentlemen were seen wearing crape on the sleeve, and every military officer had his epaulets and his helmet craped. Not a variegated ribbon, not a bright-colored dress was seen anywhere on the streets; not a peal of joyous laughter, but all the signs of deep-felt sorrow, as though all belonged to the personal friends of the dead emperor, and were walking behind his hearse.

From 10 A. M. till 4 P. M. no business was done; no restaurant, no cigar-stand was open. At places the slowly marching multitude stopped to view some tastefully arranged funeral decoration in a shop-window, the emperor's bust veiled with crape amid a beautiful and bountiful decoration of flowers and leafy plants. The day was warm, sunny, and the air balmy. The churches were full to their utmost capacity, and when the dinner-hour arrived the multitude decreased perceptibly, only to turn out again after one o'clock in full force to take up its slow march through the streets. "What a change!" I thought. Twenty-two years ago William fought these people and conquered them, and to-day they consider him one of their own.

Of course there was no chance for visiting schools that day; but on the following days I spent some very profitable hours in the schools of the city. I do not, as a rule, admire German school architecture, but here I gave way to a burst of enthusiasm, when I saw a public school-house, and a primary or people's school at that, provided with electric bells, clocks, and light, with sumptuous gymnasiums, wide corridors, and spacious school-yards and gardens. But the most novel feature of this school was that it had a regular bathing establishment, with numerous bath-tubs that could be filled with warm and cold water. I was assured that they were used quite frequently. It had been found desirable to provide the new school-houses of the city with bath-tubs because the poorer classes did not possess this commodity in their own houses.

"If," said the rector, "harmonious education is to be our aim—that is to say, the development of a strong intellect and a good heart—then the strong, vigorous body must be included, and the latter is gained by good food, plenty of exercise in form of manual work and gymnastics, and cleanliness. We simply offer the means for cleanliness as a necessary requisite of an education."

The idea is unquestionably correct. The more home education and parental care recedes in these latter days, the more must schools provide for them by suitable substitutes. These provisions for cleanliness in Bavaria can be defended with precisely the same argument with which warm dinners in Paris are defended, or vigorous gymnastic exercises in Prussia, or free clothes and text-books for indigent pupils in America. They belong to the sum total of common-school education. It is the business of the state to do the greatest possible good to the greatest possible number, provided it is for the benefit of the state as such. I can not see how we can refuse to have bath-tubs in school, like the Bavarians, hot dinners like the Parisians, manual work and gymnastic halls like the Saxons and Prussians.

It is but natural that a school system which has at its head a leader like Dr. Rohmeder is in the foremost ranks of educational progress. Here in Munich I found flourishing manual training schools, Kindergärten, admirable primary schools, well-reputed high-schools, an industrial art-school, sundry special schools, such as an art academy, conservatory of music, and a university.

In a second-year grade I witnessed a lesson in orthography, the results of which were very fine. The results of an object and language lesson were dictated, and all the new and difficult words viewed on the board. When the work was afterward examined, the teacher and I found that among forty-four pupils twenty-one had made no mistake whatever; twenty had made one mistake in a word the orthography of which is still a mooted question; two had made two or three mistakes; and one only had made fifteen mistakes. This last one was a sickly child who suffered from epilepsy. The piece dictated was by no means easy, and might have offered difficulties to many an older child.

From a lesson in arithmetic which followed I gathered the following examples. The reader will please notice that this was the second year:

$43 + 9 + 7 = ?$ $6 \times 8 - 36 = ?$
$32 + 27 = ?$ $45 \div 7 = ?$
$28 + ? = 53.$ $\frac{1}{2}$ of $42 = ?$
29 how many halves? $65 - 8 - 7 = ?$
$64 - 19 = ?$ $63 - ? = 37.$
$56 = ? \times 6.$ $8 = \frac{1}{4}$ of what number?

Divide 51 into 3 equal numbers.

How many whole ones are 56 quarters?

It was a pleasure to see the little urchins get up and say: "Five sixths of 42? One sixth of 42 is seven, then five sixths must be five times that, which is 35." No slate or pencil was used. I selected the above examples promiscuously from a great number given out in quick succession, and solved orally more rapidly than I could write them down.

In a third-year grade I heard a lesson in home geography which reminded me vividly of Prof. Schmidt's historical pictures of the city of Leipsic (see p. 285). The teacher had sketched a city plan on the board and proceeded to widen the children's horizon by starting from known points. The history of Munich greatly assisted him, for the city has been widened three times, and the ancient fortifications can still be traced; even the names of the streets betray their former designations. I enjoyed the teacher's circumspection and the tact with which he drew into use what of geographical knowledge was already established.

In other classes I heard lessons which resembled the best I had heard elsewhere. Altogether I was well pleased with the results of the primary schools.

6. An Ideal of a Course of Study.

This was found in Munich. Though in many cities in Germany I had noticed well-arranged courses, this one struck me as remarkable, inasmuch as it did not contain the matter of instruction chopped into bits, but left the teacher of each grade free to divide the matter according to the needs of his class. Of course, this presupposes a corps of teachers who are prepared professionally. With us such a course of study would hardly suffice, since too many of our teachers have no professional training; but I wish to bear testimony to the fact that teachers of large experience and much methodical and didactic skill might be left more free to select the matter of instruction than is done in many graded school systems. A little freedom in this direction bears good fruit. The best feature of the course referred to, though, seemed to me that each branch of study was introduced by a set of principles of method, according to which instruction was to be given. These "preambles" contain much good sense, as may be seen from the following English rendition of a few leading sets:

A. *Reading. Aim.*—Instruction in reading shall enable the pupils: 1. To read fluently, with proper pronunciation and emphasis; and, 2. To enable them to make the contents of the reading-matter their own so that they may obtain a perfect comprehension of the pieces under consideration, and a taste for good literature.

(*a.*) In every grade of the course attention is to be paid to the so-called *mechanical, logical,* and *æsthetic* reading.

(*b.*) Since reading is nothing else than a correct repetition of the thoughts of others, a complete comprehension of these thoughts must go hand in hand with the reading. This makes it necessary: 1. To give the pupils a good model in reading; 2. To awaken a comprehension of the subject-matter by skillful questioning; 3. To make the pupils tell in their own words what they read; 4. To call for the meaning of an entire passage before each sentence is treated separately; 5. To call attention to the forms of expression after the underlying thought is understood; 6. To call for written reproduction of the reading-matter as often as time and circumstances allow. In discussing the reading-matter, the unity of thought is to be preserved by not introducing irrelevant matter; but, for the sake of thorough understanding, it is essential to refer to matter previously treated so that by means of comparison and contrast new cognitions shall be properly founded upon others.

(*c.*) Oral expression is to be practiced: 1. By accustoming the children to speak in complete, well-rounded sentences; 2. By oral repetition of the contents of a reading piece after they have been understood ; 3. By oral prose rendition of poetry ; 4. By memorizing and declaiming six to twelve easy model pieces from the reader. Proper emphasis is invariably the result of perfect comprehension of the matter.

(*d.*) Both substance and form of the reading-matter is to be utilized in lessons in orthography, grammar, and composition.

(*e.*) For history, geography, physics, chemistry, botany, zoölogy, etc., the reader contains many valuable contributions which should be used.

B. *Language. Aim.*—Instruction in language is to enable the pupil to apply the laws of "New High German," so far as they are necessary to the pupil to comprehend, speak, and write the language within the limited course of the people's school; instruction in grammar is therefore to be restricted to that which is absolutely necessary in practice.

(*a.*) In the lower grades the pupils learn to speak and write correctly, *ex usu*—that is to say, they are practiced in the correct use of word and construction forms orally and in writing, until that habit is gained which results in a correct feeling or instinct for language. This, for the time, guides the pupil, and in higher grades assists materially in learning grammar. A pupil who has that sensitive ear for language which tells him whether an expression is right or not, will easily learn the laws of the language (grammar), because he recognizes them in his own speech and in that of others; while a pupil who has failed to acquire skill in the correct use of the language will only with difficulty acquire the grammar, it having to be learned by memory alone.

(*b.*) All forms and rules should be deduced from models taken from the reading-matter; proverbs and examples from classic literature are preferable to any other examples. A rule which has been discovered by comparison should first be framed by the pupils themselves, then it may be rendered more comprehensive by the teacher, and brought into definite form. It is not advisable to let more than one rule be searched for in a paragraph. One difficulty at a time is sufficient. And a form or a rule, once recognized, should be practiced till it becomes the inalienable property of the learner. So, then, there are three steps : 1. Finding the rule by comparison of similar examples ; 2. Looking for proofs of the rule in literature ; 3. Incessant practice in applying the rule by tasks suitable to the age and grade of the pupils.

(c.) In framing models for comparison, repetitions are to be avoided. New thoughts should be offered, so that, by enriching the treasures of the pupils' language, their stores of thought shall be increased as well. Physics, natural history, geography, history, and such branches as are thought-bearing, should be made to yield a plentiful crop of models for language-work, so that the entire course of study becomes a homogeneous whole.

(d.) Etymology should always be based on syntax, in order to enable the pupil to recognize the word as part of the sentence which determines its form.

C. *Orthography. Aim.*—Instruction in spelling should aim at correct writing of simple documents, according to the spelling in vogue, including punctuation-marks.

(a.) The means to that end should be to let the words to be written be seen and heard clearly first. Afterward words may be grouped and practiced according to similarity and dissimilarity, to awaken consciousness of underlying rules. All rules which suffer from too numerous exceptions are to be omitted.

(b.) The exercises in orthography should consist in oral and written reproduction of words in the form of sentences : 1. In copying ; 2. In dictation ; 3. In writing memorized stanzas and prose paragraphs; 4. In writing the pupil's own thoughts.

(c.) Material for orthographic exercises is found in the reading-matter, and in every branch of study on the curriculum. New words (technical) that occur in any lesson should be noted on the blackboard at once, and left there for some time.

(d.) Incorrect writing is to be prevented, so as to avoid the formation of incorrect word-pictures in the memory.

Words which may give occasion for making mistakes should be presented in writing, and if possible in print, before they are dictated. It is, at any stage of the course, better to avoid mistakes than to correct them.

Other branches of study are introduced similarly, but it would go beyond the object of this volume to translate them all.

7. Cause and Effect in Geography.

It was a spirited lesson in geography that I heard in Munich, and I think it worth sketching. The children were of the same age as our pupils in the highest grade of the grammar-school course—thirteen or fourteen years, I should think. Maps were there in abundance, and a handsome large globe was brought in.

The teacher first stated the fact that the heat equator is not synonymous with the mathematical equator ; that it is an irregular line lying on an average of ten degrees north of the actual equator. Now he led the pupils to find causes for this apparently singular fact. Did not the sun strike the earth with equal force north and south of the equator ? With the aid of a large globe, on which the prevalence of water on the southern hemisphere could be seen distinctly by all the pupils of the class, the fact was soon established that this prevalence of water caused more evaporation than on the northern hemisphere. Evaporation, however, they knew from the little study of physics they had had, caused absorption of heat, while land would radiate the heat it received and thus cause a higher degree of temperature in the atmosphere.

Now proofs of this fact were searched for, and it was interesting to see how quickly the pupils reasoned backward from effect to cause. In the Deserts of Sahara and Gobi they thought that they found the effect of great heat on large bodies of land. In the indented coast-line of Europe they found the cause of a temperate climate and an absence of dreary wastes of deserts.

Then the climate of the different continents was discussed and the general rule established, (a) that great bodies of land have hot summers and fierce winters. Proofs: Inner North America, inner Asia, inner Australia, even Russia in Europe; (b) much water was the cause of cool summers and mild winters. Proofs: Western Europe, South America, Southern Africa, and the Asiatic isles and peninsulas. Water tempers the climate.

I was very sorry not to possess skill in writing shorthand, because the further part of this lesson was truly admirable. I can only give its bare results, and must abstain from even an attempt at outlining it.

The latitude, it was easily inferred, caused the climate. But the latter was greatly modified—that is, made milder or fiercer—by the situation or elevation of the country. A plateau would naturally be cooler than a low plain under the same latitude. Quito in Ecuador, and Pará in Brazil, both almost under the equator, were yet very different in their climates, the former being situated ten thousand feet above the level of the sea, the latter almost on a level with it.

Mountain-chains like the Andes, the Rockies, the Himalayas, the Alps, etc., are also causes of great differences in climate, as they may protect the land from certain atmospheric currents and other influences. This was proved by the great fertility of the eastern slope and the rainless western slope of the Andes, also by the two slopes of the Rockies.

These different considerations were summed up in this: Latitude, formation, and elevation of a country condition its climate.

But climate alone does not make a country a desirable place to dwell in. Other things are needed to make it fertile, otherwise Australia ought to be overcrowded, whereas it is but thinly populated. Irrigation is an important condition. Look at Western and Central Europe, at the United States: these countries are admirably irrigated—i. e., watered and drained. The teacher dwelt on this by showing that the United States have in their Mississippi Valley the granary of the world, a most ideally irrigated, fertile region. Fertility was traced to irrigation in France, Germany, Italy, Turkey, and Spain.

The latter country served as an example to prove that climate, elevation, and irrigation will not suffice to maintain life if the soil is not favorable. In Spain the forests that used to crown the lovely mountains, and constantly feed the picturesque and navigable rivers meandering through the valleys, have been uprooted. Ruthless extermination of the forests had made the hills bare, the rain had washed the fertile soil from the unprotected mountain-sides, and the rivers now dry up in summer and threaten death and destruction in spring when the melting of the snow fills the river-beds and causes inundations.

So, then, proper soil is another condition of life, and we have the principle that climate is caused by latitude, formation, and elevation of the country; that proper climate, favorable irrigation, and good soil condition an exuberant vegetation. Vegetation, of course, is a condition necessary for the animal kingdom. But, while the latter depends for subsistence upon vegetation, the former is in no small degree dependent upon animal matter for subsistence. So, again, we have cause and effect. And the chain lengthens: latitude and elevation cause climate; climate and irrigation condition vegetation. All these are necessary to support the animal kindom.

Where all these conditions are favorable, human existence is assured ; and the human population of a country stands in exact proportion to the presence or absence of these conditions. This was conclusively demonstrated by the population of North America. The United States, situated in the temperate zone, traversed by lofty mountain-ranges which afford admirable irrigation, possessing on the whole a very fertile soil, had all the conditions of an exuberant vegetation and support of animal and human beings. Consequently, we find them populated by about sixty millions, while north and south of them, in Canada and Mexico, the population is comparatively sparse.

The pupils were almost breathless with attention, and, when called upon, gave geographical facts in support of the teacher's assertions quite readily. I was told that this was a review lesson, which, while offering new vistas into the science of geography, caused the pupils to brush up their knowledge of geographical facts.

The task given out for the next lesson was: "Find proofs for the truths we have discovered to-day."

"Will they be able," I asked, "to find more proofs?"

"I should think so!" was the reply of the teacher. "They worry their fathers, mothers, uncles, and aunts for further proofs; they consult the libraries, they ransack every source of information, until they find proofs. A truth thus discovered, as we did in this lesson, acts like leaven, it grows and induces the learner to proceed in his investigations. And it will scarcely be necessary to recapitulate these facts, for indigenous thoughts are like words engraved with steel into granite, while borrowed thoughts, such as are learned by heart from the printed page, are words written with a reed on dry sand; the next rain will wash them out."

8. "KNABENHORT" (ASYLUM FOR BOYS).

In Germany and Austria it has been repeatedly remarked in Parliament and teachers' meetings that a degeneration in the manners and morals of youth is noticeable in late years. It is claimed, not in Europe alone, but with us too, that the male youth grows rough and unmanageable by being allowed to run wild. Short-sighted people have laid the cause of this fact—if fact it be—at the door of the common school. Speculations are rife as to proper remedies, and I am glad to notice here that a most effective one has been found which deserves to be imitated in the United States.

Mr. R. Petzel, a teacher in Vienna, whom I took occasion to mention elsewhere, has addressed the Austrian Government in regard to this matter. I take pleasure in presenting an abstract of his essay. If we admit, for the sake of the argument, that the morals and manners of our boys *are* less commendable than in former years, we must in justice also admit a very vital change in the social condition of the families whence these boys come. Only about a generation ago, the cities were crowded with thousands of tradesmen and artisans who had their own workshops, in which the boys were apt to be found at work after school hours. To-day machine-work has absorbed the many little shops, and huge factories with tall chimney-stacks and steam-engines perform the work which formerly diligent workmen did at home. The men are in the factories from 6 A. M. till 6 P. M., and often later here in Europe. Thousands, yea, hundreds of thousands of women have found occupation within the gloomy and sooty atmosphere of these factories. The great battle for subsistence deprives parents of time and inclination to look after their children. And the public schools have not increased their educational activity in the same ratio in which home education has receded. School is what it was, a school for instruction, not so much an asylum of education. Though it has increased its usefulness immensely, the prevailing social misery overpowers its influence. Where formerly it was an adjunct to home education, it is now expected to be both school and home at the same time.

The author referred to says: "It would lead us too far to refute the claim that faulty treatment in school causes this degeneration, for schools can not correct the manners and morals of children while they are not within its pale of influence. But it seems desirable to call attention to a remedy the good effect of which we have noticed in many places. It is the establishment of boys' homes or boys' asylums.

"The great majority of children in cities come from very poor families. The parents, in this age of machine and factory labor, are compelled to leave their children unattended during the greater part of the day, and many boys take advantage of this to run wild in the streets. It is an ancient truth that unemployed hands work mischief. Such unemployed children are apt to suffer from neglect. In the larger cities of Germany societies have been formed whose aim it is to collect children of school-going age who, for want of proper home influence, are in danger of being lost in the paths of vice. These children are gathered in rooms called "Childrens' Homes, or Boys' Asylums," after school hours, and are there supervised by suitable persons, chiefly teachers of the common schools, and employed pleasantly in such a manner that their entire education is assisted and supplemented.

"These asylums are not schools; they are intended to restore (or act as substitutes for) the missing home-training. The boys here learn circumspection and discretion; are trained to order, obedience, regular activity, and good manners. They are here kept from the degrading influence of the street and back-alley companions. Only teachers who have the reputation of being philanthropists, and who govern by the Christian spirit of love, are employed. That the efforts of these societies are not in vain can be observed in the "Knabenhorte" of Munich, Leipsic, Dresden, Halle, Cologne, Frankfort, and other cities. To show how these institutions work, we will go into a more minute statement of their programme.

"Soon after dinner on days when there is no school, and on school days after four o'clock P. M., the boys come to the 'Hort,' and remain till seven, at some places till eight, in the evening. There they receive a lunch of milk and bread at four o'clock; then they do their home-tasks for school, aided, if need be, by the supervisor. After that an hour is spent in social games out-doors. On rainy days, lotto, checkers, dominos, and other indoor games are indulged in. Some who like to read are furnished with books—good books, the best that can be found. After that an hour or two is spent in manual work. This consists of folding paper, making pasteboard articles, modeling, carving in plaster, chiseling, joiner-work, scroll-sawing, and such like work. Every boy finds some favorite occupation and is kept at it.

"These hours are full of gayety and frolic, and pure happiness seems to dwell here where idleness is considered the

"KNABENHORT" (ASYLUM FOR BOYS). 315

blackest of vices. From time to time cheerful songs are sung in chorus while the work goes on. At times the supervisor tells thrilling stories of adventure, or some musically

Fig. 314.

inclined member of the happy family plays a piece on a musical instrument, be it only a Jew's harp. Every innocent enjoyment is welcome. The manual training in these asylums has not the purpose of making special artisans, but of training the boys in the use of tools, and giving them occupation during their leisure hours. They make kites when the season of kites comes, make tops, carve and rig boats—in short, they make their own playthings. With the training of the hand goes the training of the eye, a pleasant stimulation of the intellect, and all this will result in making better men as well as better artisans of them.

"In summer, the boys play much out-doors, and the supervisor is one of their own number. He has no privileged position in the social games, save that which his greater fertility for suggesting and arranging games gives him. He is the boys' leader pure and simple, a true pedagogue (boy-leader). Excursions into parks and out into the commons are frequent. Baths are taken in a shallow pond or streamlet. In winter skates are furnished, and the whole band goes out skating or coasting. At every one of these excursions the supervisor is among the boys, and always 'in the thick of it.'

"In order to secure good supervisors the society pays a good price—say four marks per evening. This is a handsome addition to the teacher's salary. In Leipsic these men get a fixed addition of seven hundred and fifty marks to their salary as common-school teachers; in Halle, six hundred marks. In order that it may not appear as though these asylums are purely benevolent institutions, a tuition-fee of ten German pennies (two and a half cents) per week is asked. At Christmas a grand festival is held, for which every boy must do something. Deserving boys are clothed on this occasion; school-books are distributed, and even savings-bank books, with a handsome credit 'to begin with.' A real home with all its love-tokens and various interests is created, and it is no wonder that the boys love the 'Hort,' as children love their home when their parents are well situated and inclined to make home happy.

"These Knabenhorte have had results which far surpass all expectation, and they are now established in every large city of the German Empire. A few have just been opened in Switzerland also. Strict order and discipline are kept, but not that death-like stillness so frequently noticed in school. All rudeness, indoors or outdoors, is punished by an exclusion from a favorite occupation, while innocent enjoyment is encouraged. Many a boy who was going down an inclined plane has been brought back to the level path of duty by the wholesome influence of the Knabenhort, and thousands have been prevented from ever leaving it.

"No better testimonial can be given to these institutions than that in many cities the number of applications for admission is fourfold greater than the number of pupils that can be accommodated. It has become a great privilege to be admitted."

The establishment of "Knabenhorte" in America may be only a palliative remedy for the correction of social evils that exist in an alarming degree, but, still, it is the most effective known as yet. A Knabenhort may prove to be that ounce of prevention which saves the pound of legislative cure. There is no reason whatever why the girls might not be benefited likewise.

CHAPTER XII.

PARIS.

1. INDUSTRIAL EDUCATION OF BOYS IN PARIS.

An Argument.—There can be no doubt whatever that the Americans and Germans have solved the "manual training question"—the sensible resolution of American school-men not to make artisans, but aim at a many-sided training of the hand by employing it in no definite trade, but in occupations that are common to many if not all trades. It is just so with arithmetic. If we should follow the dictates of the merchant, he would drive us into business rules at the expense of other arithmetical work necessary for thorough training of the mind. If we were to follow the artists, they would propel us in another direction quite as foreign to the purposes of the common school. If we were to follow the ideas of certain short-sighted "practical" people, we should have to make tinsmiths', carpenters', cobblers' shops, etc., of our manual training halls. The very nature and character of the American school are opposed to that ; though it has often to bow before the dictates of a senseless spirit of utilitarianism, it always, after a time, returns to its true object, to wit, to offer the multitude what is of common use, or to do the greatest good to the greatest number.

In the following pages I intend to state accurately what the Frenchmen do in the way of manual training. I trust that my readers will without prejudice read this report. My words may at times sound enthusiastic, because the work is really very fine ; but from the start I must emphatically assert that the whole course of manual training in Paris, as I saw it in operation in more than a dozen schools, starts with an entirely erroneous intention. It is this: "We want to give our boys skill in some trades, so that they may be able to abridge the time of apprenticeship, and get to earn a living at an early age." Not, that I saw this in print or heard it from the teachers, but it can be read clearly and unmistakably from all they do. One more word by way of explanation : The schools I shall speak of are not private schools, nor special schools, but purely and simply common schools, and elementary schools at that, not high-schools.

Of the one hundred and seventy-four boys' schools in Paris,* maintained from state and communal funds, there are ninety-nine (according to a report of 1887) which, having room enough, have arranged a workshop. Others will follow soon, as I understood from Monsieur Grandpierre, the

---

* There are one hundred and seventy-five communal girls' schools in Paris.

inspector of "travaux manuel" (manual work). All the school-buildings I saw which were specially built for school purposes had a large hall on the first floor. This hall is used for three purposes: (a) for recreation at recess and on rainy days ; (b) for gymnastic and military drill ; (c) as a dining-hall at noon. Part of this large hall, extending over the entire floor, is partitioned off for a workshop. All the shops I saw contained from twelve to twenty joiners' work-benches; six to ten lathes ; one or two forges; a great number of vises, tool-boxes, many models, and much material, such as wood, rod-iron, stones, and imitation marble blocks.

On the walls are exhibited models to be reproduced and copied. These in themselves are the course prescribed. There is no printed course—at least not to my knowledge—and I searched sufficiently for it to know that there is none. The models are of four kinds: 1. Of wood, being joiner's and carpenter's work; 2. Of wood and horn, being turner's work; 3. Of iron, being smith's work; 4. Of stone and plaster, being builder's work. The fourth kind does not really belong to the course, being extra work of that one particular school in which I saw it. In short, joiner's, turner's, and smith's work is learned. Now, pause a moment, dear reader, and think of the consequences. Here are ninety-nine schools of about five hundred pupils each. All these boys learn the trades of joining, turning, and forging. If not perfectly, they certainly get start enough in these three directions to feel inclined to' make a living in these trades.

What will these boys do in a few years when these three or four professions are well provided with artisans ? Will not the supply be greater than the demand ? And what will the superfluous number of young joiners, carpenters, turners, and smiths do, after having been systematically trained in these industries and in no others ? Besides, what moral right has any government to thus predestine the future of thousands and tens of thousands of boys ? It seems a most short-sighted policy. But, then, it is argued that Paris needs just these apprentices, that in these branches of industry Paris is particularly interested, etc. Well, I am not sufficiently acquainted with the population of Paris and its needs to prove the contrary, but I strongly suspect that to train joiners, turners, and smiths is a most unwise procedure, and that the time will come when there will be an overproduction.

What, then ? Ah! well, it is claimed, school is not an immovable fixture in all its departments. It will adjust itself to changed circumstances and teach other trades when others are desired. This is so decidedly a French argument that I need not continue to combat it. It is unmindful of the sound principles on which rests the entire practice of the American as well as German common school.

I. *Results.*—And now I will proceed to state what I saw done in the workshops. My objection against the work is aimed at the course and not at the method of teaching. The latter is admirable. So systematic and careful is the teaching that its results far surpass every expectation I had entertained. In Rue Titon, eleventh arrondissement, I saw a class of twenty-four boys at work at their joiners' tables and turning-lathes. The teacher, a skilled artisan, went over the entire course, carefully showing me all the steps, and I sketched some of the models, knowing that "Augenschein gilt für Beweis." Others which I failed to copy on the spot I copy from a book of models. Though the collection I offer is not one twentieth of the entire number, it is a typical one.

A plain rough board of hard wood a foot in length is given to the pupil to plane smooth, sand-paper, and polish. It may take the boy a number of weeks to accomplish this; but, if it should take him a year, he is not permitted to proceed to the next piece of work till that board is found in every way correct as per order, namely, smooth and with parallel corners and sides. (See Fig. 305.)

Next a square post is to be reduced to an octagonal column. Same conditions as in task No. 1. (See Fig. 306.)

Then saw and chisel come into requisition and are used

INDUSTRIAL EDUCATION OF BOYS IN PARIS. 321

in practicing "dovetailing," and very accurate work is required. (See Fig. 307.)

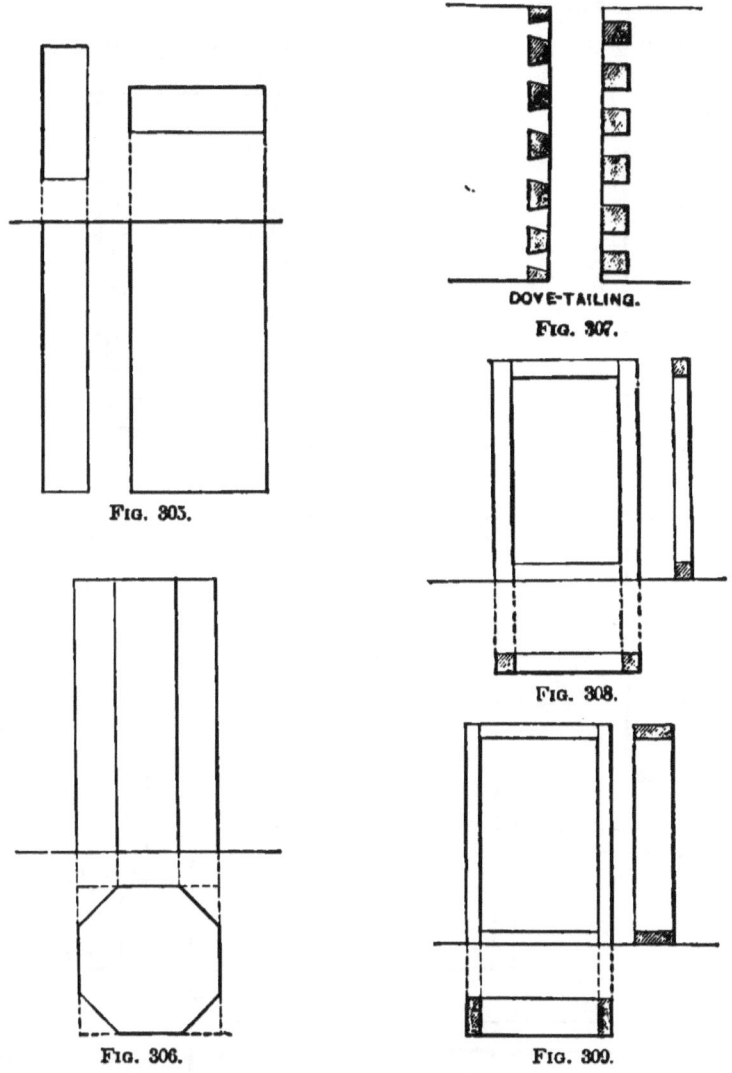

Fig. 305.

Fig. 306.

DOVE-TAILING.
Fig. 307.

Fig. 308.

Fig. 309.

After thus learning to use plane, saw, chisel, etc., the first joint is made. The simplest kind of a frame is produced. (See Fig. 308.) The same practice is had with a box, the joints of which are made by some pupils with dovetailing. (See Fig. 309).

Among the models furnished by the pupils, few of which

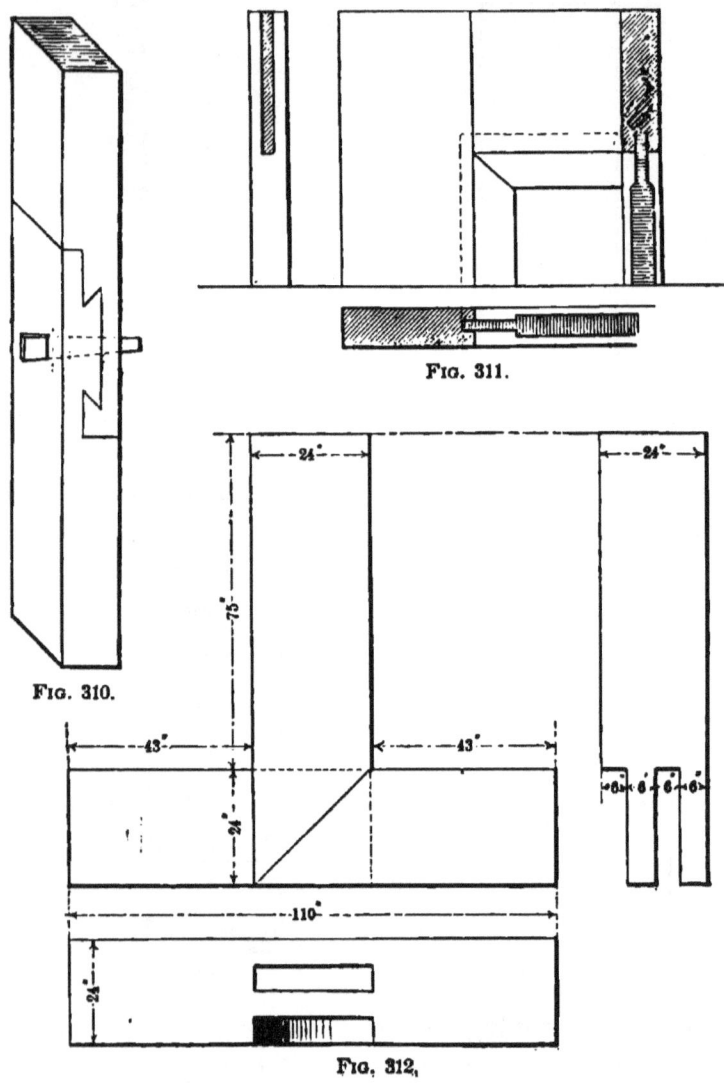

Fig. 311.

Fig. 310.

Fig. 312.

I venture to copy, I found also a joint (see Fig. 310) which was made of two different kinds of wood which fitted exactly. It was a very intricate combination, and evidently a fine piece of work, of which teacher and pupils were proud.

Figs. 311 and 312 show not only how a frame-joint is made, but how it is drawn first. Of course, there are many steps omitted between this and the other models; but I had not the time to copy them, nor can it be my object to furnish a manual for this kind of work. Indeed, I should have to restrict myself entirely to reporting upon what is done in the manual training department, if I should give more than a bare outline in these pages. The few sketches I offer are gathered here and there in different schools. They enable the reader to see what is being done in the carpenter class. Thus the drawings are made, and well made, as I know, from ocular inspection; but these sketches do not adequately show the real manual work or its results. In order to illustrate this, I procured the work of Messrs. Laubier and Bougueret, which exhibits in lithotype the models made by the pupils of a school in the Rue Tournefort. They show the methodical steps in acquiring a skill in the use of the saw and chisel, and I offer the models here in the hope that they may better state what is done in the Parisian schools than a whole volume of description. Appended to these models will be found some samples of joiner's work. All the models are rough as yet, and prove unmistakably that this is boys' work, but it also proves the methodical skill of the teachers. (See Figs. 313–329, and also Figs. 330–339.)

II. Partitioned off from the joiners' and turners' hall is the forge, and here the work of locksmiths and toolsmiths is done. Strong steel vises and anvils are found here, though somewhat smaller than adults would want them. They are well placed, and the boys here work with much zeal, and the teacher acts with great circumspection to avoid accidents from fire or dangerous use of metals. I am very sorry I am unable to offer in *sketch* illustrations what is done in this department. Suffice it to say that the instruction is fully

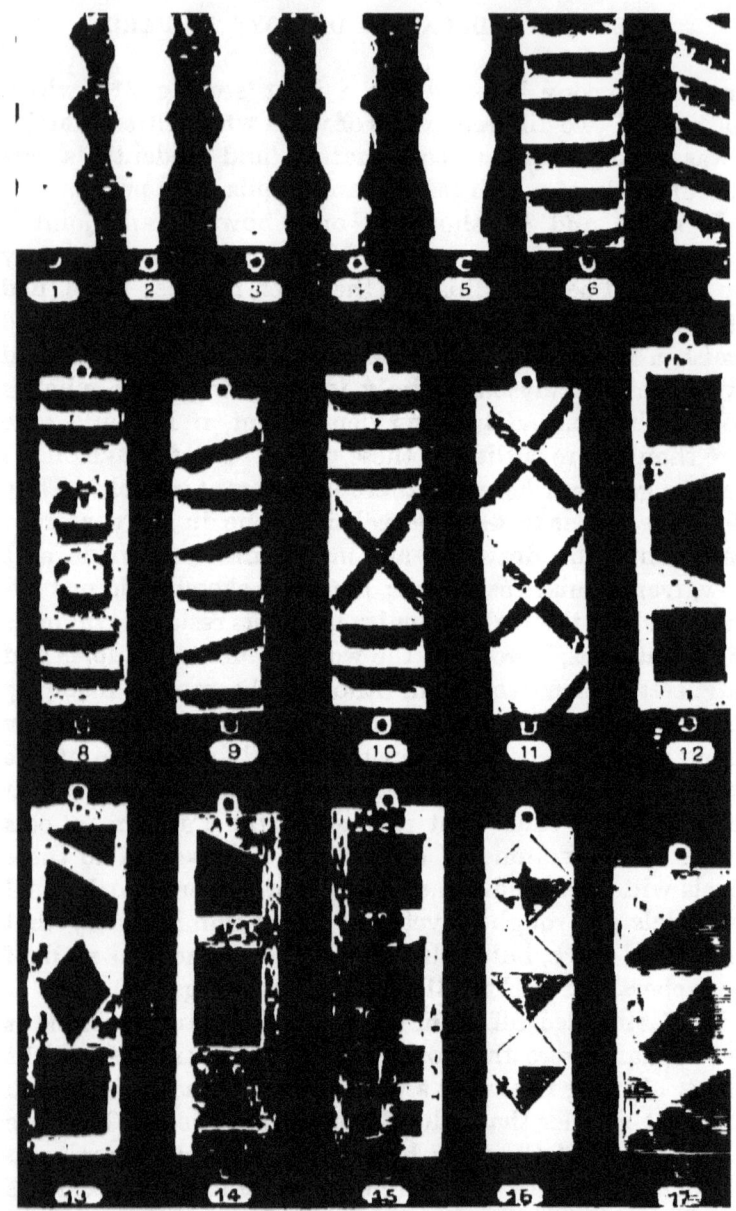

FIGS. 313-329.—PUPILS' WORK. LEARNING TO USE SAW AND CHISEL.

INDUSTRIAL EDUCATION OF BOYS IN PARIS. 325

as comprehensive as that in the joiners' department. The copies of models I offer in Figs. 340–348 are fair samples.

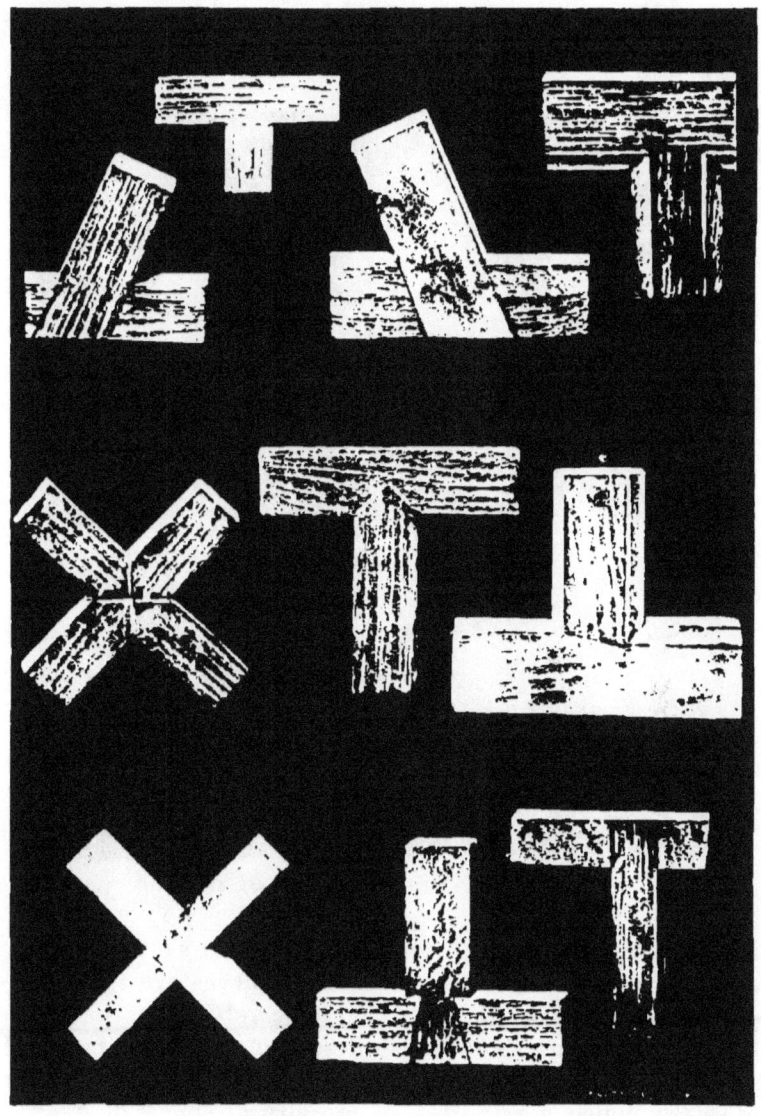

FIGS. 330–339.—PUPILS' WORK IN JOINING.

326 PARIS.

III. *Turners' Work.*—Side by side with the work in carpentering and joining goes a course in turning. Not every boy of the class takes up both occupations, but most of them confine themselves to one only. I am unable to sketch any of the great number of drawings exhibited and used in mak-

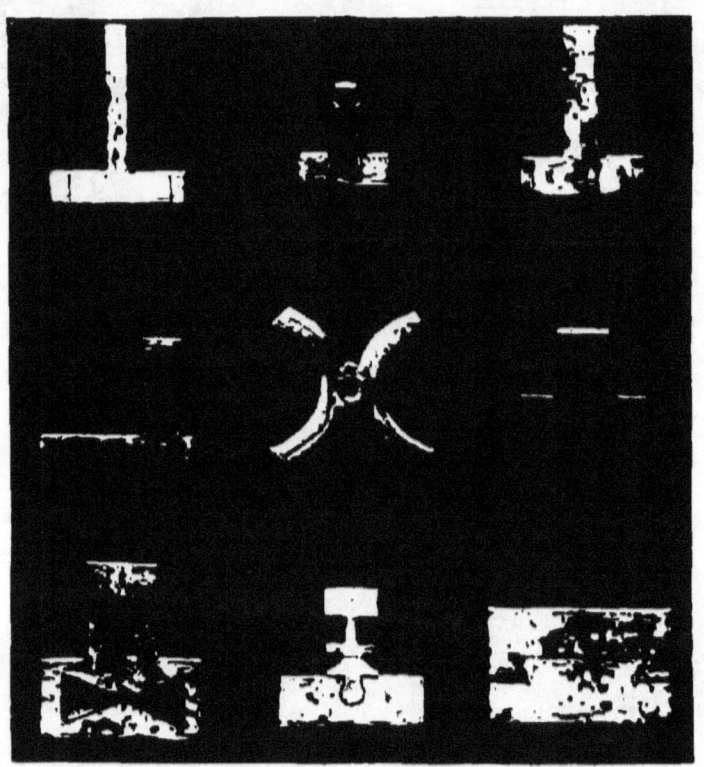

FIGS. 340-348.—PUPILS' WORK IN BRASS AND IRON.

ing the models—partly because I failed to sketch rapidly enough, and partly because circular curves are rather beyond my capacity. I must therefore rely upon the lithotypes referred to above and offered on the next page. I select only a few sets, because the models show, as a matter of self-evidence, a great deal of similarity. The sets I offer

INDUSTRIAL EDUCATION OF BOYS IN PARIS. 327

are Nos. 1 to 6, and 12 to 17. They show some varieties of edged and circular curves.

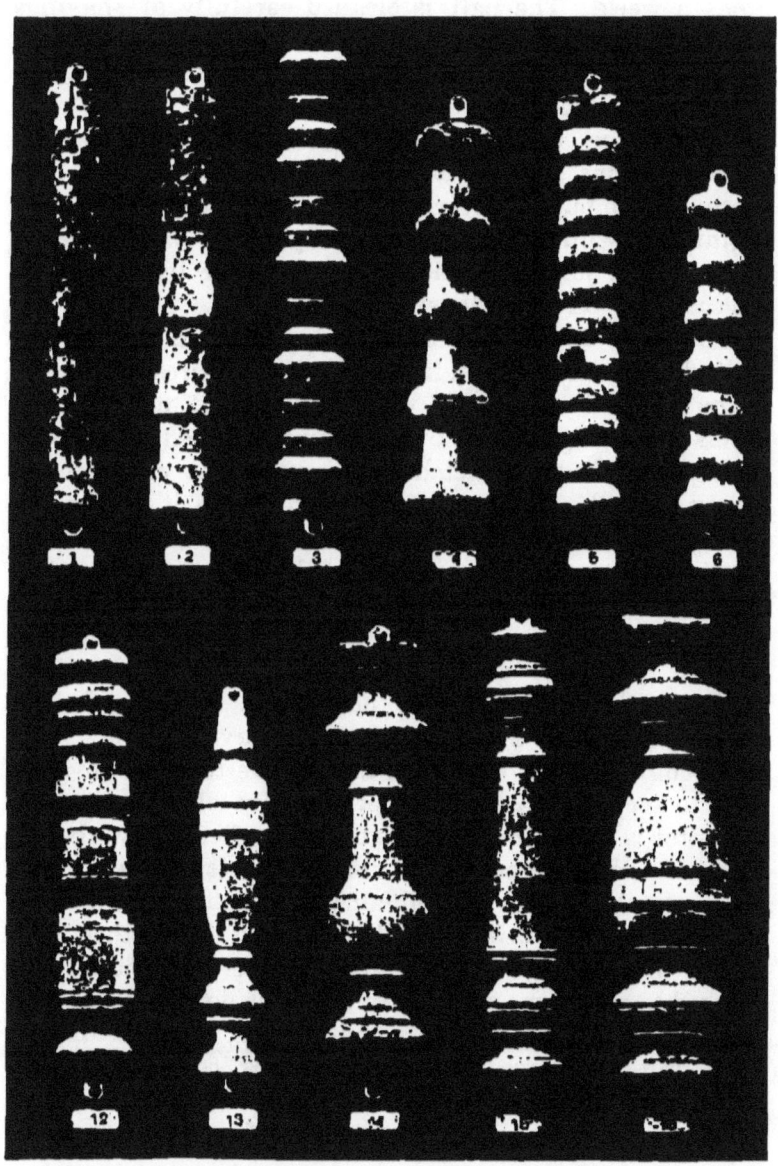

FIGS. 349-359.—PUPILS' WORK IN TURNING.

The boys who do this kind of work are from twelve to fourteen years old. They have a lesson of an hour three times a week. The hall is cleaned carefully of shavings and dust after each lesson, and all the tools are placed away, or hung up in rows, so that the next class will find everything "ship-shape."

Though the boys have only three lessons a week in manual occupations, they get a great deal of instruction in four years. Some pupils never go beyond the most elementary beginnings, while others learn rapidly and actually turn out to be skilled joiners, turners, locksmiths, or toolsmiths, as the case may be, when leaving school.

The *secret of this success* is partly found in the natural aptitude of some children in that particular direction, partly in the fact that no piece of work is furnished, no task is set unless a drawing is made of it, such as I furnish in the preceding and following sketches. Any one who can conceive a form in such a manner that he can sketch it on the flat surface can produce that form also *in natura*, provided he has the necessary skill in the use of the tools. And it is this happy combination of drawing and executing the drawing which causes the success of the French manual occupation schools. Not one of these halls in Paris and elsewhere in France is without ample blackboard space; and it is frequently used, as I had occasion to observe.

Though it is the evident desire of the teachers in these halls to keep the classes together and give class-instruction, the latter is found impossible, and soon after a new class is admitted the pupils proceed at different paces and drift apart. So the teacher has to individualize and confine the attention of a class to a few things which they must do together.

IV. *Wood-Carving and Inlaid Work.*—And now I will proceed to give some sketches of the work done in ornamenting. The work consists of wood-carving, scroll-sawing, of "inlaying" and veneering. The sketches 360 to 367 are executed in wood after drawings designed by the class; in a few instances plaster is used. I copied these few drawings partly

INDUSTRIAL EDUCATION OF BOYS IN PARIS. 329

from the class-work, partly from a hand-book I found in use, partly from models on exhibition in the "Musée Pedagogique." Though these schools may not be our ideal manual

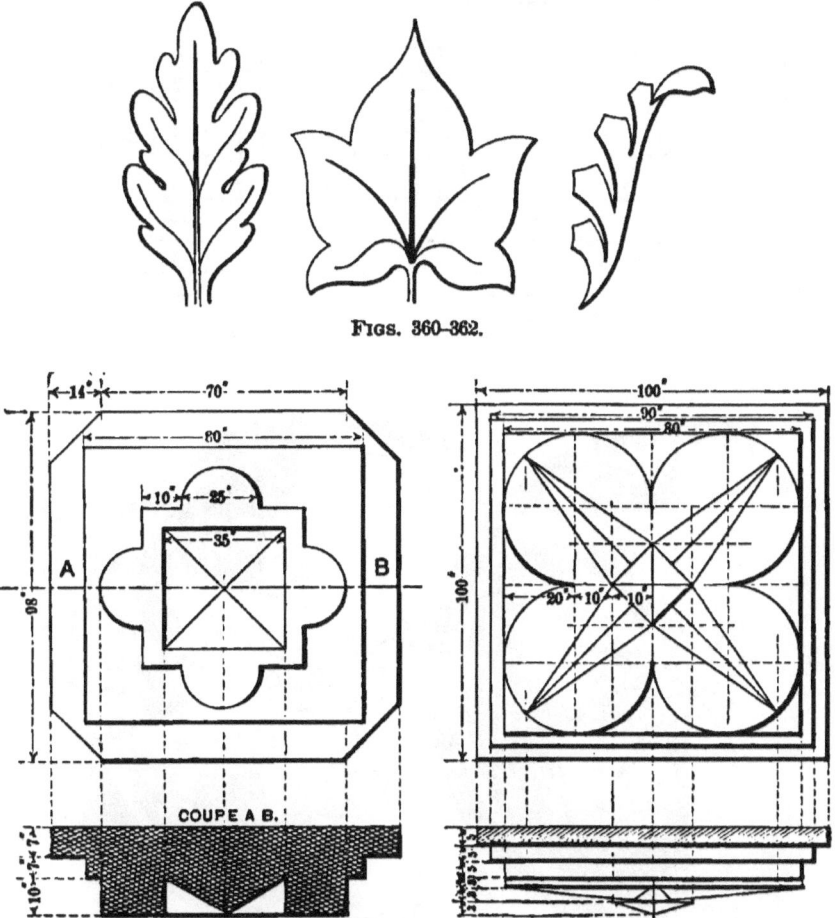

FIGS. 360–362.

FIG. 363.   FIG. 364.

occupation schools, it is evident from these drawings that excellent work is performed in them.

Figs. 363, 364, and 365 will be found on subsequent pages among the models in lithotype. These models begin with

330 PARIS.

easy work and end with remarkably artistic work, all done by boys below fourteen years of age. Scroll-sawing is not practiced as much as in German schools. It is chiefly used where inlaid work is made.

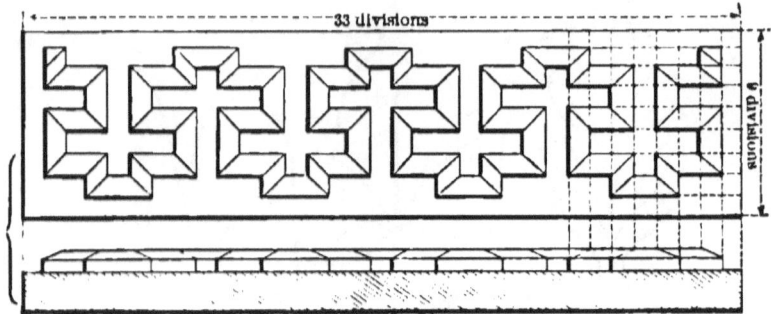

FIG. 365.

FIGS. 366, 367.

The lithotype copies of models are less pretentious than some work I saw in the pedagogical museum, but, as in preceding collections of models, they show the methodical treatment better than a printed course could do it. It would need the space of a volume alone for a description of all the numerous designs executed in wood and plaster. My selections, however, I think, are ample.

FIGS. 368, 369.—PUPILS' WORK IN INLAYING.

He who has not had occasion to observe a person engaged in wood-carving will not likely see much in these models or patterns. All who have some knowledge of it will notice that in the samples offered distinct stages of the course are noticeable, from the simplest outlining and stamping to deep carving. The same designs are used in inlaid work.

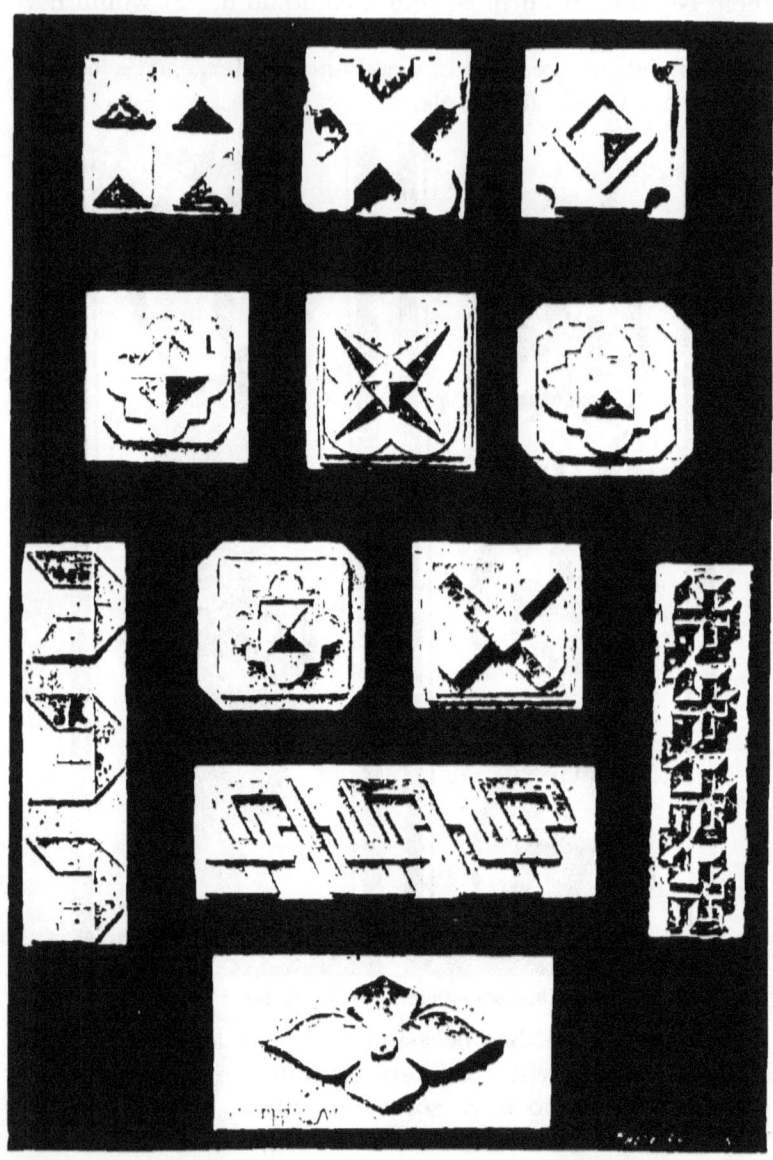

FIGS. 370-381. PUPILS' WORK IN WOOD-CARVING.

Figs. 366 and 367 represent deeper carving and the beginning of inlaying. I saw such charming work, among the specimens on exhibition in the museum referred to above, that I lingered in contemplation of these treasures. I was assured, by the director of the institution, that every piece of work of the entire collection had been furnished by pupils of French schools, not merely from schools in Paris. From the paper-folding done in the Kindergarten (here called maternal schools) to the close of the course of elementary schools at the age of fourteen, and even from the work of higher schools, samples are here collected. Some of these things might do honor to skilled artisans. I offer a few designs executed by higher-grade pupils in Figs. 368 and 369.

V. In *modeling in clay* the manual training schools in Paris go too far, it seems to me. Though I saw most excellent articles ready for exhibition, and many boys at work on similar figures, I can not suppress a lurking doubt as to the genuineness of some pieces found in the museum. I miss also the strict methodical treatment found in all the other departments of manual occupation. I select a few samples which show so bold a conception of form despite the traces of unskilled labor, that I suspect the teacher lent a helping hand. Still, it is claimed that the boys use no measures, except the eye, and that frequently they depart from given models and produce new forms.

My own want of skill in modeling, I will frankly admit, may lead me to suspect that the boys "plowed with Samson's heifers," and experts tell me there is less difficulty in forming and constructing in clay than there is in wood-carving While I grant that the boys in Paris do better work in carving and joiner work than those in Germany, vastly better, I think the work in modeling, as I found it in Vienna and Leipsic is better suited to the capacity of young pupils, it being more in line with elementary instruction. In German manual schools modeling of geometrical bodies is the first step, then follow simple leaf-forms which are conventionalized in ornaments afterward.

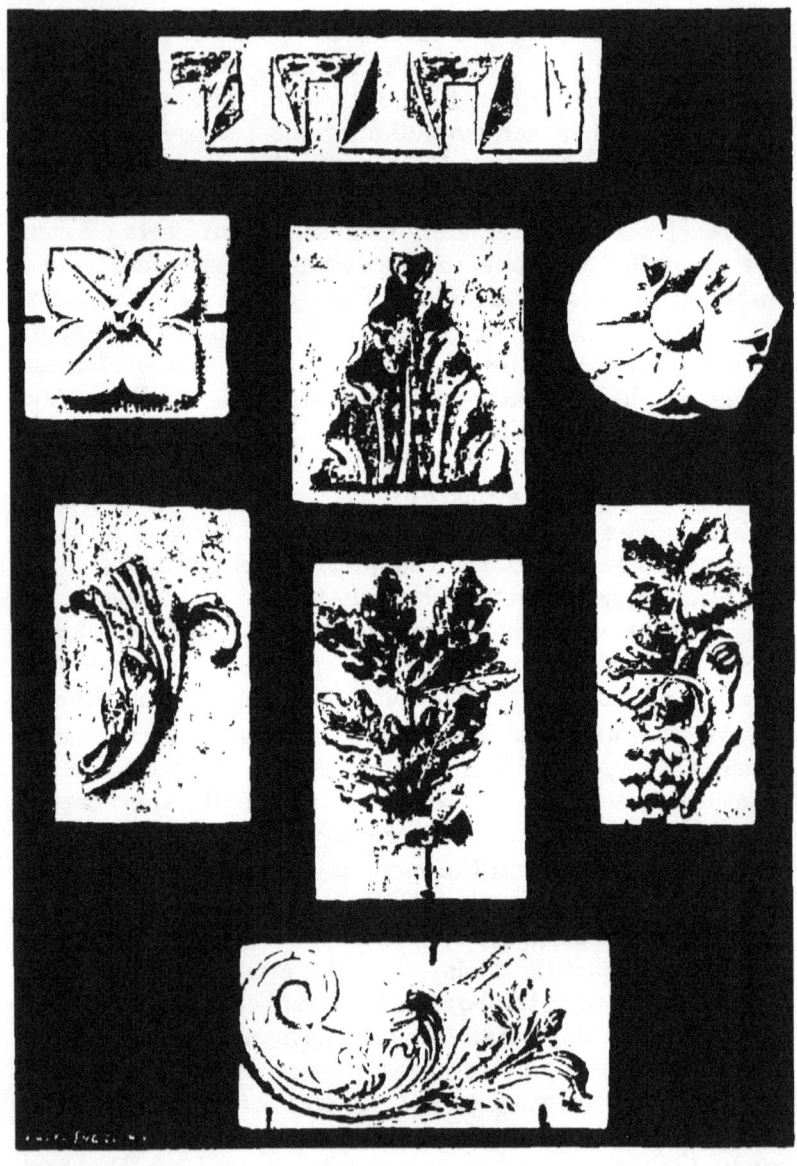

FIGS. 382-389. PUPILS' WORK. MODELING IN CLAY.

INDUSTRIAL EDUCATION OF BOYS IN PARIS. 335

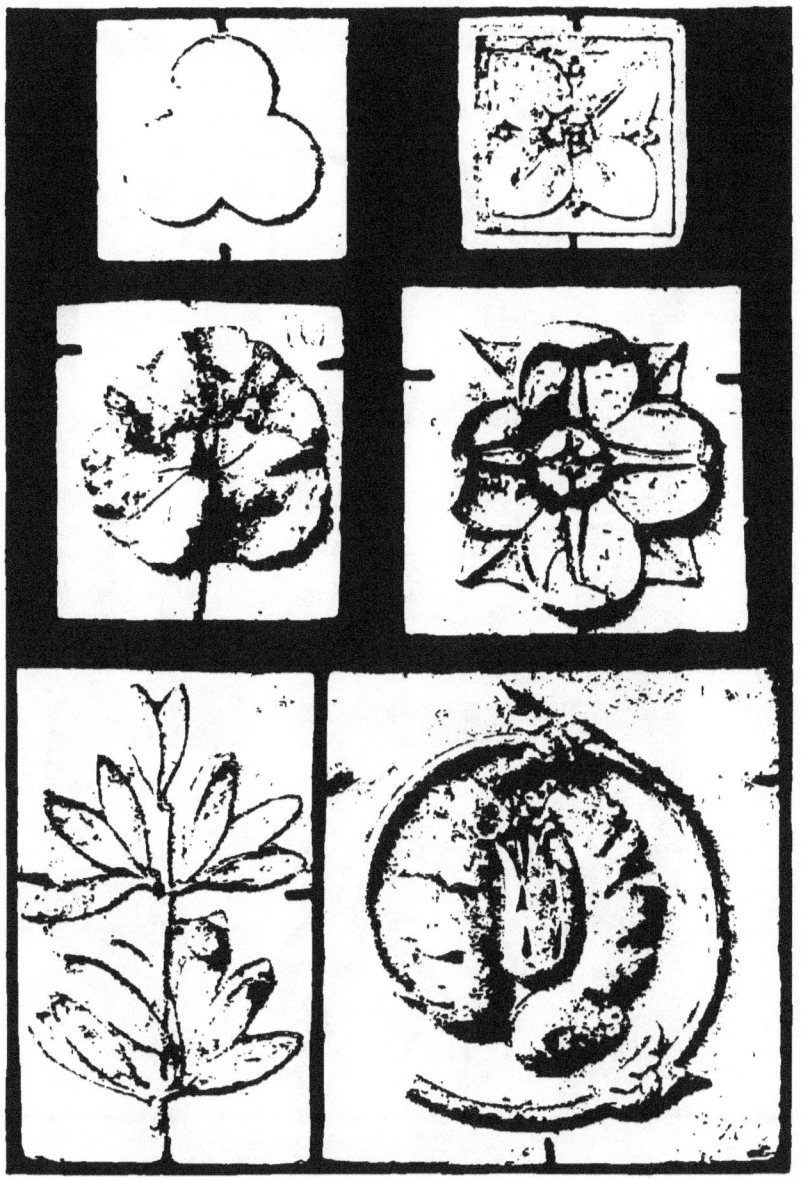

FIGS. 390-395.—MODELING IN CLAY.

FIGS. 396-399.—MODELING IN CLAY.

INDUSTRIAL EDUCATION OF BOYS IN PARIS.

The fact that in Paris artisans and artists, that is, specialists who are not professional teachers, conduct the manual occupations, is noticeable in every department, but in none more than in modeling; while in Germany none but *bona fide* teachers who have passed through a regular course of training in a manual training normal school are seen in the industrial halls or workshops. This explains why in France much is done for effect, while in Germany the idea of harmonious education is carried out strictly.

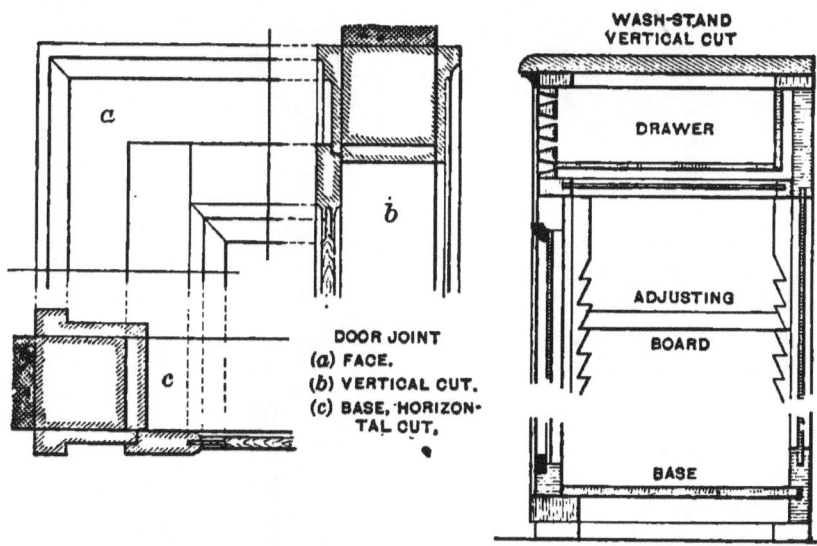

DOOR JOINT
(a) FACE.
(b) VERTICAL CUT.
(c) BASE, HORIZONTAL CUT.

WASH-STAND VERTICAL CUT

FIGS. 400, 401.

Manual Training in Evening Schools.—In some French and Swiss schools the course of industrial education is extended beyond the common-school age. Evening schools are arranged. In these post-graduate courses the joiner's and carpenter's trades are taught and very creditable work is done. Some sketches may show the extent of the course. Fig. 400 shows a door-joint and the setting in of panels. Fig. 401 is a more complicated affair, which is made by several boys, each being charged with one or two items, each

338   PARIS.

of which must be made according to measure. The entire work is done by following the drawing made previously.

VI. *Pupils' Work in Building.*—In the post-graduate course *building* is a branch of study. The material used here is to some extent cut to size so as to fit given models. These models are put together in the way in which our toy

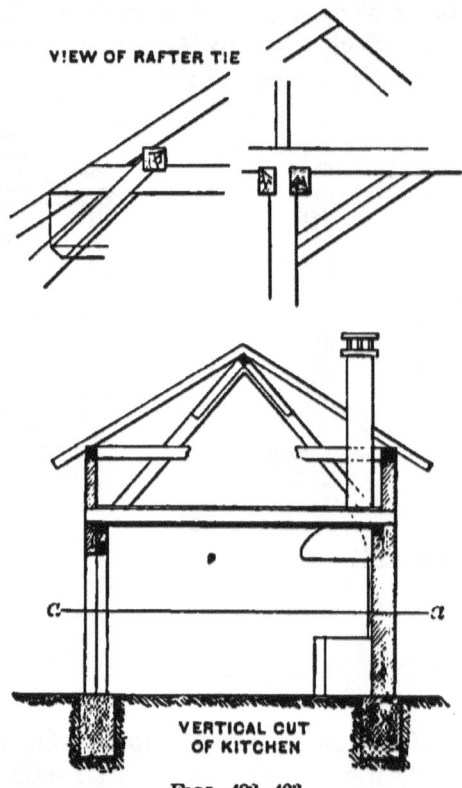

FIGS. 402, 403.

building-blocks in the nursery are used, only with this difference, that every structure must comply strictly with a drawing, perspective and isometric.

First, a structure is made with the miniature blocks (imitations of pressed clay), say, a self-supporting arch, then it is drawn. Another lesson is to draw the object according to

INDUSTRIAL EDUCATION OF BOYS IN PARIS. 339

certain given measures, and then to build it with the material prescribed accurately according to the drawing.

In order to give an idea of what difficult structures are expected from the working lads, I will mention that among the beautiful models of imitation stone (pressed clay) I saw in a school on the Boulevard de Belleville, in Paris, was the difficult "Œil de Bœuf arch"; an arch with plain center, a "vouter d'arte" (a vault); an "arc descente biaise" (an inclined arch); an "arc platebande" (with border). I counted about sixty different structures, all of which were erected

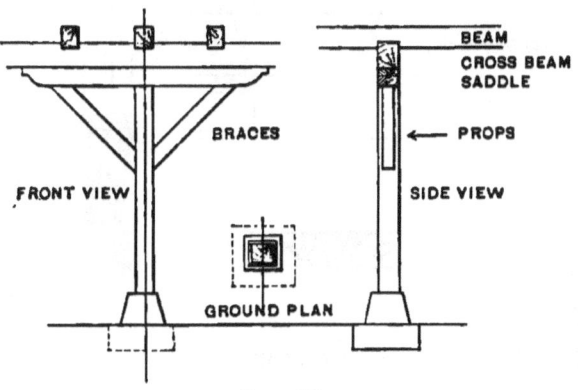

FIG. 404.

without mortar. They were simple self-supporting structures. The drawings accompanying these models were stupendously intricate. The sketches I submit here (Figs. 402–410) are very simple, taken from a hand-book of a Swiss teacher. They will in a measure indicate how thorough the instruction is. Though being but an infinitesimal part of the work, they may show better what kind of problems are solved than a number of pages of text.

In discussing this subject I feel that I have not done justice to the manual-training department as it deserves; but my inability to give more than mere suggestions must excuse me.

Figs. 405–410 show the details of a window such as is

340 PARIS.

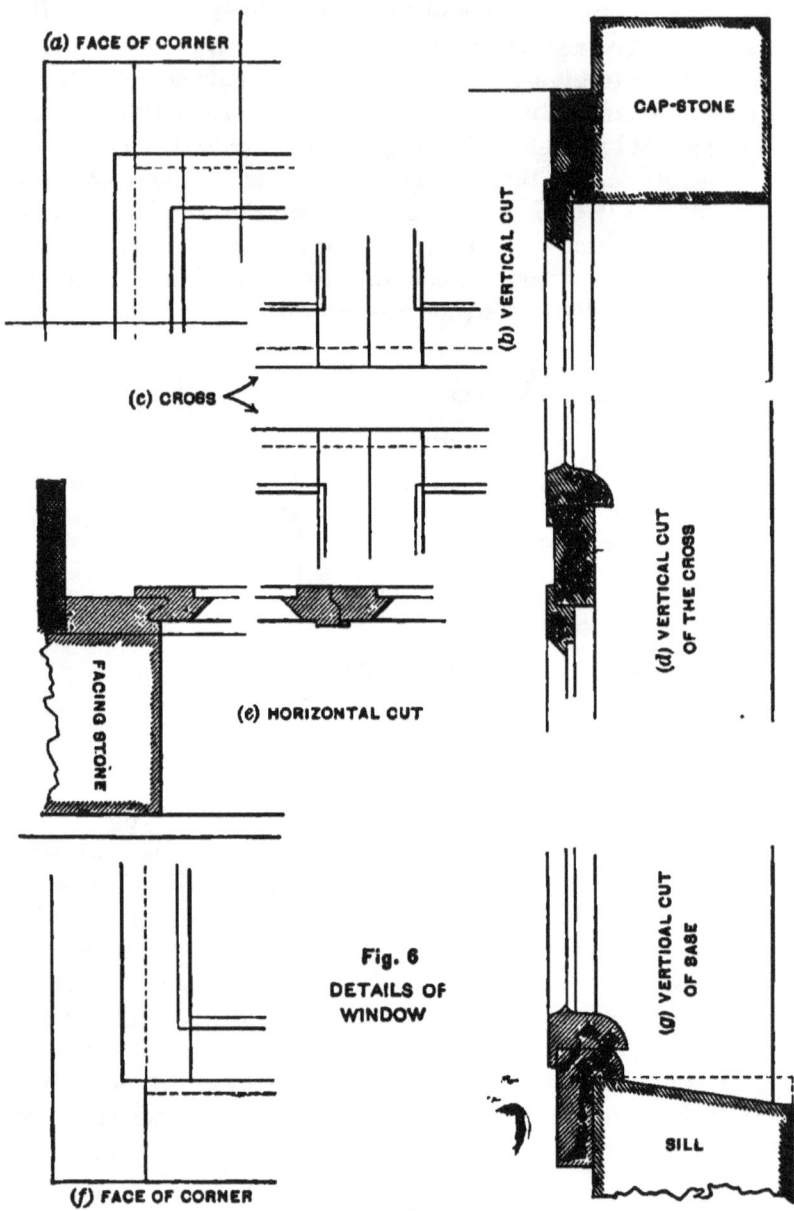

Fig. 6
DETAILS OF WINDOW

FIGS. 405–410.

used on the Continent in Europe. There are a great number of highly interesting and knotty problems connected with this task, all of which are solved.

2. INDUSTRIAL EDUCATION OF GIRLS IN PARIS.

This topic, though of equal interest with that discussed in the preceding chapter, can be treated but briefly. A woman may be able to discuss it with more skill than I. All I can do is to furnish some facts. Of that I believe myself fully competent. Of necessity the facts must be but few.

The girls' schools are "manned" with women teachers exclusively. No man, not even a special teacher, is allowed to teach girls in Paris. The only men who enter a girls' school here are the inspector, the maire, and doctor of the arrondissement (ward of the city). The principals of these schools are splendid women, highly refined in manner and address, and well trained in disciplining. Since they are not engaged in teaching they have not that proverbial look of care on their countenances seen among women teachers here as well as at home.

No knitting and crocheting is taught in these schools, for it is argued that that kind of work can be had ready made by machines; but sewing is taught to perfection. All kinds of sewing, plain and complicated (for it is argued that that is a necessity in every household), and darning and patching, are raised to a fine art in these schools. The results are brilliant. The reader is referred to what is said of the industrial education of girls in Cologne. He will find there much that holds good for Paris. Each pupil has a bag of strong canvas like the sketch in the margin, which holds the sewing utensils, the patterns, and the work under hand. It is a very convenient bag. Home tasks are given in sewing, and the bag is to be carried home.

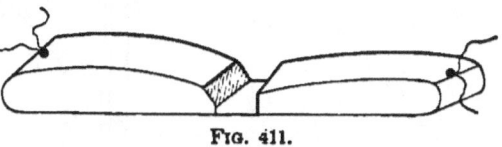

FIG. 411.

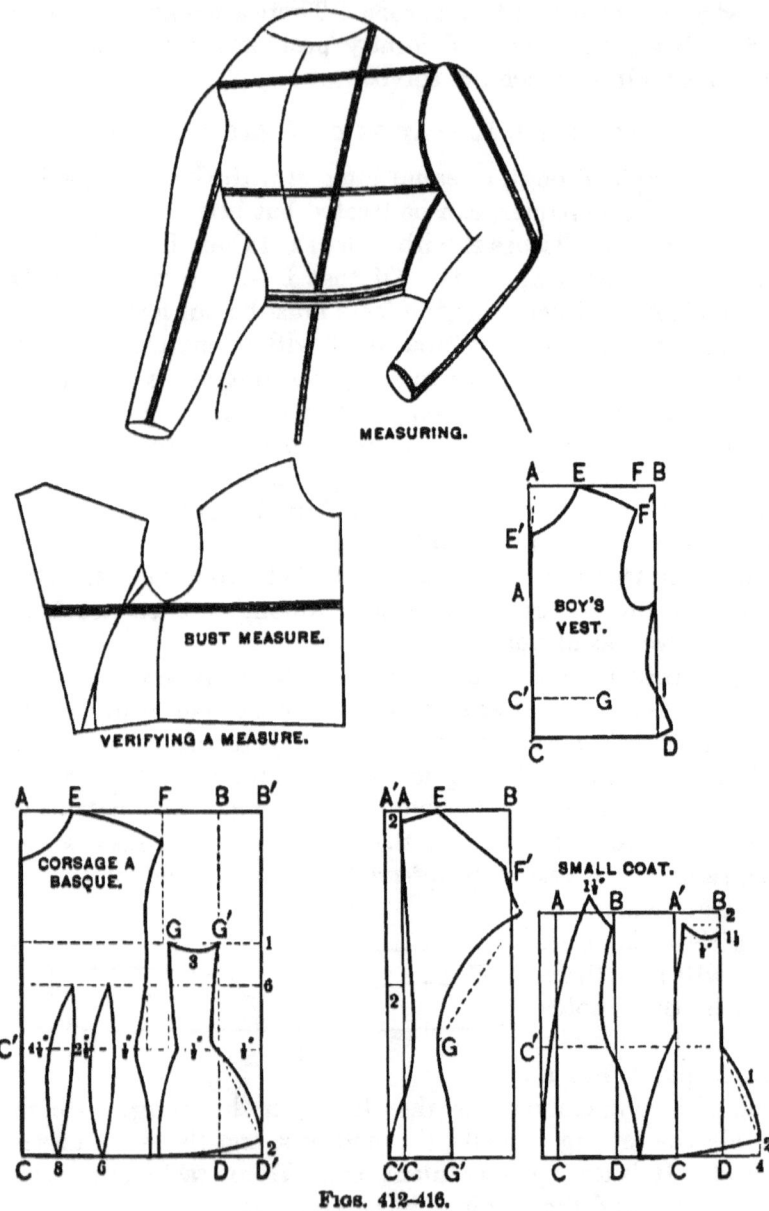

Figs. 412–416.

INDUSTRIAL EDUCATION OF GIRLS IN PARIS. 343

In one thing the girls' schools in Paris far surpassed anything I had seen before: I mean in cutting out and fitting garments, not only undergarments, as is done in Cologne and elsewhere, but dresses, cloaks, hoods, bonnets—that is, all the garments for children and adults. They are made in miniature form by fitting them to dolls first. Drawings are made, the patterns are then cut out of manila paper. After these are found correct (see Fig. 413, "Verifying a Measure") the stuff (commonly calico or merino) is cut according to the patterns, and the garment is basted. Then again it is fitted; at last finished. It is laborious work; but the great variety of garments, from a boy's vest to a woman's cloak, adds interest to the work.

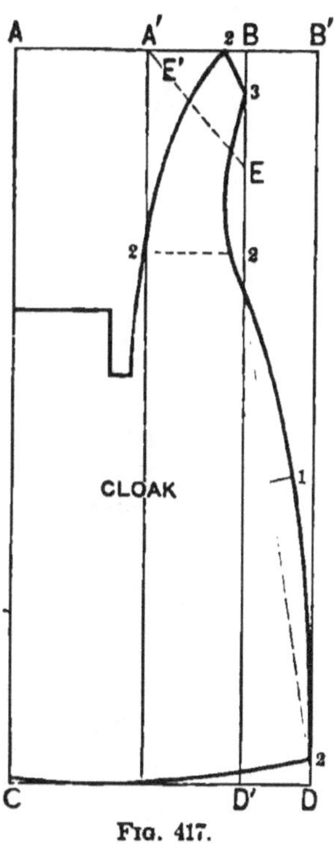

The upper grades have a textbook for this study (costing twenty cents), entitled "*Coupe et Confection de Vêtements de Femmes et d'Enfants.*" I can in no better way illustrate the work going on than by copying some of the patterns I saw cut out. They must speak for themselves. The figures and letters attached agree with the ones given in a short description furnished by the children.

Whether this course of instruction is a wise one; whether underneath it is not the same vital error found in the boys' manual training, I must leave unanswered, or refer to the more competent judgment of my female readers. I merely state facts. In the higher classes, I understand, other occupations, the so-called genteel occupations, are added to the course, painting on china, etc. I saw specimens of that which were very

Fig. 417.

fine. This, however, seemed to me so foreign to the course of study in common schools that I felt no desire to further inquire into it.

That there is a strong desire to prepare the girls in Paris for housewifery may be seen also from the fact that a reader

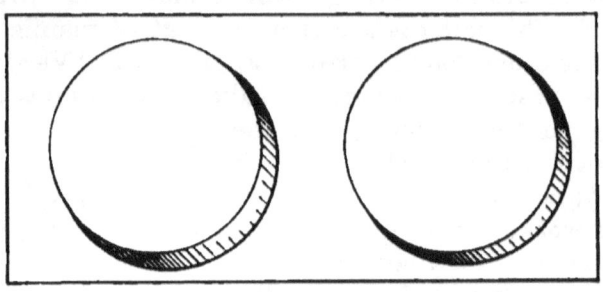

Figs. 418, 419.

is used in the upper classes of the common schools for girls entitled "*Le Menage: Causeries d'Aurore avec ses Nièces sur l'Economie Domestique*" ("The Household: Aurora's Talks with her Nieces about Domestic Economy").

From the composition-books I inspected, I copied a few headings on account of their significance. They characterize the Parisian female education :
1. "The History of a Bird that had lost its Liberty."
2. "Review the Events of the Year 1887 that concern you."
3. "What Wishes have you formed for yourself and your Family at the Beginning of the New Year ?"
4. "What will most enhance the Comfort and Welfare of a Family, and why ?"
5. "Domesticity, the Noble Virtue of Woman."

That drawing is not neglected in the girls' schools in Paris may be seen from the two specimens (Figs. 418, 419) of work done from plaster casts, by girls ten and eleven years old. I insert them, and think the artist has reproduced them accurately (see page 344).

3. DINNERS FOR SCHOOL-CHILDREN IN PARIS.

The problem how to obtain regular afternoon attendance, yet give the school-children the much-desired recreation, avoid cold lunches, and not worry the mothers at noon, who are almost all hard-working women, this very complex problem is satisfactorily solved in Paris. About eighty-two per cent of the pupils stay in school during the noon-recess, and are fed from the school-kitchen. The large hall found in every communal school in Paris, and which I mentioned elsewhere, is used as a dining-hall. Long tables and benches, that can be folded together and removed when military and gymnastic drill is to be had, are set up by the *concierge* (janitress) shortly before noon, and the children march down from their class-rooms in slow procession.

On a counter at a window of the kitchen are placed some three hundred to four hundred tin plates and an equal number of tin bowls. Each child, as it passes the window, gets a bowl of delicious soup and a plate with meat and some vegetables. Then he marches to his seat. The whole process of dealing out does not last longer than a quarter of an hour.

Each child brings with him a chunk of bread and a small flask of wine. Do not get disgusted dear reader ! It is wine, red wine, very inoffensive, drinkable wine ; though you might drink a gallon of it, it would not cause intoxication. Still, I grant that water would be better. But such is France. Wine belongs as much to a dinner in Paris as water does with us, and I did not feel over-anxious to play the *rôle* of temperance apostle while in France for reasons too obvious to mention.

The food thus furnished is of excellent quality, and it is furnished free to all indigent pupils. All who can pay do it. From the teachers I understood that few parents send their children without the necessary obolus. The price of a dinner (*déjeuner*) is ten centimes in some schools, fifteen centimes in others, or, in our money, two or three cents. Think of it ! Good, nutritious soup, a plateful of well-cooked meat and vegetables (potatoes, beans, peas, lentils, as the case may be), and gravy—all for two or three cents. I could scarcely believe my ears when I heard " A meal for two (or three) *sous*," yet it is a fact, and I saw the boys pay cheerfully.

Children who live in the immediate neighborhood of the school-house go home to get their dinner, but the majority remain in the hall or yard, and are under the supervision of a teacher till the afternoon session begins. It can not be emphasized too much that cold lunches—particularly if they consist of pastry—are abominations, and we Americans might learn something from these Frenchmen in feeding multitudes, except in partaking of alcoholic drinks, for, alas! we know that only too well.

Now, of course, my female readers will want to know something of the bill of fare. I copied the one prescribed for February in a school on Rue de Recluse St. Martin, M. Z. Bertrand director. The bill is changed every month, so as to afford changes as the season dictates them. There is no school on Thursday ; that day is as firmly established a school holiday in Paris as Saturday is with us.

Menu for February.

First and Third Week of the Month.

Monday : Soup with haricot-beans, mutton-stew, and beans.
Tuesday : Soup with boiled beef, brown cabbage.
Wednesday : Onion-soup, veal-roast, fried potatoes.
Friday : Soup with boiled beef, macaroni.
Saturday : Soup with sorrel and greens, mutton, lentils.

Second and Fourth Week of the Month.

Monday : Potato-soup, mutton-stew, peas.
Tuesday : Soup with boiled beef, haricot-beans.
Wednesday : Soup with rice and greens, veal-stew.
Friday : Soup with boiled beef, fried potatoes.
Saturday : Soup with lentils, mutton with peas.

This is a two-cent institution ; the fare for three cents is more sumptuous. "*Bon appetit.*"

4. GYMNASTIC AND MILITARY DRILL IN PARIS.

In my former reports I have said nothing of the excellent gymnastic exercises in German schools, though I was strongly tempted to do so; but it would have involved the necessity of sketching the human body, and that is beyond my capacity as an artist. Any presentation of gymnastic exercises in print without sketch or outline illustrations would be stale reading-matter, and therefore a senseless undertaking. Here in Paris the "study" of gymnastics has a few peculiar features not found anywhere else, and I will therefore mention them:

1. Fencing is taught, not with foils and swords, but with hazel-sticks of considerable length. It was a novel sight for me to see the boys go through a regular course of fencing exercises in which the strokes fell heavy and thick but were parried skillfully except once, when an unemployed hand stuck out too far, and that was the teacher's hand.

2. Each boys' school has a rifle company, consisting of

the upper grade of pupils and called "bataillon scholaire." They are furnished with Chassepôt rifles (breech-loaders) somewhat reduced in size, very light, and *blind*. The boys can not shoot with them, but use them in their disciplinary drills. Knapsacks containing the necessary utensils for cleaning the gun and clothes when on a march complete the outfit. Every company has a drum and fife corps. I believe that, when the present generation of French boys is grown up to manhood, France will have a better army than at present, for what I saw of French soldiers much reminded me of our militiamen in peace. The French soldiers' marching was slouching and anything but inspiring.

The discipline in the lower boys' school in Paris is rigid to a fault in the class-room, corridors, and yard. I really believe what one teacher told me: "We used to be very lenient to the pupils; but the wonderful discipline of the German soldiers and the fact that they have to begin that discipline in school at an early age, induced us to change our tactics. I think we are beginning to see an improvement in our pupils, and hope to see the young men of our country cope with the Germans in strength, order, and obedience in a generation or two from now. It is slow, up-hill work; but the people of France are determined to proceed upward, not downward." The man was no braggart; but, having observed during many months the influence of a century of public-school and army discipline in Germany in both boys and men, I doubt sincerely that the Frenchmen will ever be able to "catch up" with the Germans in that respect.

5. Equipment of School-rooms in Paris.

The scholars' desks and seats here are much better than in Germany, much more convenient, but not near so well adapted as our American single desks and seats. Rarely are more than fifty pupils seated in a room. On the nicely tinted and scrupulously clean walls (in a few schools I saw them covered with fresco ornaments) hang so many means of objective instruction that an American teacher who still believes in the saving grace of the printed page would shake his head. I will enumerate: A handsome engraving of the "Bill of Rights" (a document as important in French history as is our "Declaration of Independence") and a fine bust with the inscription "R. F." (République Française) are seen over the teacher's desk. Then there is a case with a glass door containing different scales with weights—liquid and long measures—according to the metric system. These are used frequently in arithmetic. Casts of plaster and *papier-maché* are suspended at various places on the walls, acting as ornaments and being used as models for drawing.

Then there are seen in rows a number of charts for object-lessons, illustrating natural history, the trades and industries, history, and geography. One set of charts was a novelty to me. A description of one of them must suffice. In the upper part was printed, under the name "flax" and the proper botanical heading, a statement of where flax is raised and how it is used. Then a bundle of flax-stems with leaves and blossoms in a good state of preservation is fastened with strings to the chart. Under that the different stages through which the fibers have to go till they can be spun are shown. Then follow samples of coarse and fine linen thread. Finally, samples of linen are shown; all this *in natura*, not in pictures. The educational value of such a chart is indisputable.

The same objective presentation is offered to illustrate the manufacture of cotton, wool, and silk stuffs. Then follows the leather industry, and so on. Every essential industry is thus treated. On the chart headed "wheat," little bottles filled with grains, flour, bran, alcohol, etc., are fastened with wire. Different kinds of wool, wood, leather, etc., are attached to charts; all the more important minerals (ores and metals) likewise. Then follows a set of charts showing the leaves, blossoms, and fruit of plants *in natura*, not merely in chromo-lithographic print. Each leaf is well varnished to protect it from moisture.

Each class-room in which primary geography is taught is provided with a heavy cast of a relief-map of Paris and vicinity. In the corner of the room of the two highest grades stands a neat cupboard of white wood filled with apparatus such as is used in the studies of physics and physiology. The lower shelves are filled with globes, telluriums, and stuffed animals and birds. It is a museum of no mean importance for successful teaching. The treasures of the museums were usually in very good order. Now and then I noticed a chaotic disorder, and I inferred that the teacher who suffered his apparatus to get into such disorder could not be very orderly and systematic in his discipline and teaching. Where I subjected the matter to a test I found my idea verified. Verily, human nature is the same at home and abroad.

In a few school-rooms I found one wall entirely reserved for meritorious pupils' work. There I found, tacked to strips of wood, hundreds of excellent geographical maps colored and drawn well. Being requested to pick out a few from this great number to take with me, I selected some that seemed to me to represent the average. My hesitation to accept the gift was cut short by the pupils, who said without reserve that I was welcome to them, and the teacher remarked that they had an *embarras de richesse* and would not miss any. I shall treasure these maps as a pleasant memento of my visit.

In most primary classes I admired a set of chromo-lithographed geographical charts representing "primary ideas" of geography, such as valley, canal, glacier, cape, isthmus, etc. These appeared to me of special value in schools in Paris, where the pupils grow up between high houses and rarely see anything else than streets. As to geographical maps I shall mention them under the head of geography, and therefore beg to refer the reader to the next chapters.

The school-rooms in Paris have more blackboard space than similar schools in Germany. One board is provided with lines for music; one is used for drawing; it has an apparatus for holding plaster casts; another is used for daily work, such as arithmetic and writing. Every communal school of Paris has a store-room in which the more valuable casts, busts, and physiological apparatus are kept. Each object is labeled and numbered. I counted as many as one hundred and eighty objects, some of very large size, in one school. What a wealth and lavish expenditure, and what a wise policy!

These schools are by far better ventilated than the schools in Germany. Except one which had been changed from a mirror-factory to a school-house, all the schools I visited in Paris were comparatively well ventilated (I beg to refer to the fact that I saw them between February 2d and 25th) and had much light falling over the left shoulder of the pupils.

It is evident that the city and state school authorities in France do not grudge the schools what can serve to increase their efficiency, as far as equipment with means for objective instruction goes. To a complete equipment belongs also a set of merit medals on silk ribbons. These medals are of silver, neatly engraved, having the form of the star of the French Legion of Honor. The "star pupils" wear the medal during school hours, and when school closes they return them to the teacher's desk, where they are locked up. Pupils of higher grades are permitted to wear them on the streets and at home, and I venture to assert that many a student wears his medal with more just pride than some owners of the star of the Legion of Honor. The medals change owners once a month. The one who gains the greatest number of simple merits is entitled to wear the silver badge. That this is a bad and very objectionable custom it is scarcely necessary to state; but the custom is so interwoven with French ideas that it can not easily be changed. It is very difficult for some people, even in our country, to see that competition may be a natural tendency, but that it is not a moral law, and that it should not be fostered in school.

In perfect accordance with the French character was the incident I witnessed in a school on the Rue des Recluses St.

Martin. The teacher had drawn on the board with colored crayon an ancient feudal castle, with battlements and waving banner, standing on the top of a mountain. Below it at the foot of the mountain on the bank of a river was pictured a rude hut where a poor fisherman lived. Under the picture stood an inscription which read, "Before 1789." I inquired for the object, and heard that the teacher taught history, and that this illustrated the cause of the great French Revolution, the centennial of which would be celebrated in 1889.

Nearly all the school-rooms I saw in Paris are provided with gas-fixtures, the weather being rather gloomy in winter, and dark early in the afternoon. The immensely high houses increase the darkness. Five, six, and seven seem to be the usual number of stories the houses in Paris have. Houses with two or three stories are rare.

6. Drawing in the Communal Schools in Paris.

On former occasions much was said of drawing as it is taught in the schools of Germany. Had I seen Paris sooner, I might, perhaps, have said less in praise of what is done in drawing in Germany, for what I saw here far outshines any thing I saw across the Rhine. I must urgently request my readers not to express their incredulity (they will be sorely tempted, though), for I brought the proofs with me, stamped and signed by the rectors of the schools where I obtained them. I offer them for inspection to teachers who, being accustomed to seeing inferior results, may be disposed to doubt the statements in this chapter.

First and foremost of all it may be said: There is actually *no copying done from the flat-surfaced copy* in the schools of Paris. In the third year of school where instruction in drawing begins, solids are drawn at once. I should have to repeat my former statements, if I intended to sketch the course in the lower grades. Even before the third year, a kind of drawing solids is found; a simple object is outlined in a network of lines as the following sketch shows. The work is extremely interesting to the little ones. In regard to the course the reader is kindly referred to previous chapters, in which the method employed is suggested.

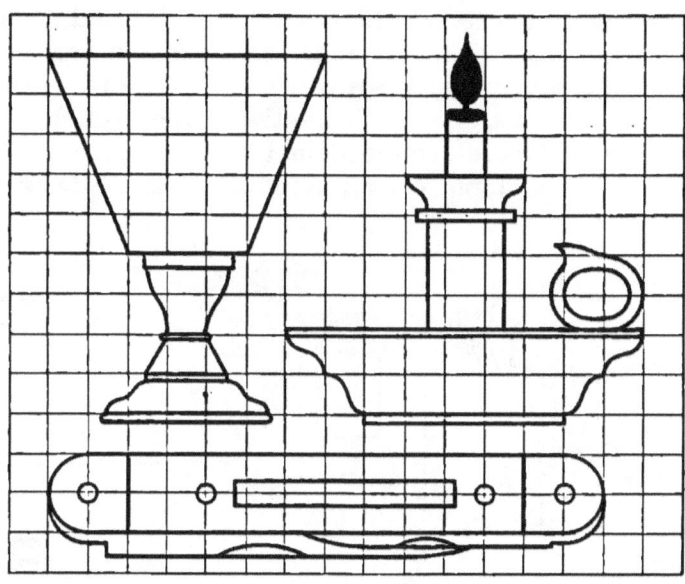

Fig. 420.

When a grade similar to our C Grammar (twelfth year of age) is reached, the drawing is taught in a hall specially arranged for the purpose, having north light. Here the drawing tables and seats are arranged amphitheatrically, so that the plaster cast, or other object to be drawn, can be seen by all pupils equally well. In order to facilitate the seeing of the object, a blackboard is placed behind it, and drapery is used for increasing the shadow. The tables and seats are adjustable, as the sketch in the margin shows.

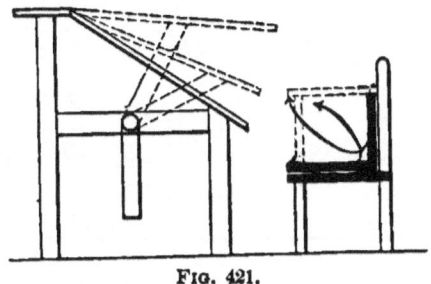

Fig. 421.

The hall looks more like an artist's studio than a schoolroom.

If I were asked, What do these pupils draw? I should feel embarrassed for an answer to the question. If I said, geometrical bodies, plaster casts of relief ornaments, plaster busts, casts of human limbs, torsos of statues, furniture—in fine, anything that is set before them—the answer would be too indefinite, yet more definite than I ought to give it. For my answer would not convey an idea of the masterly me-

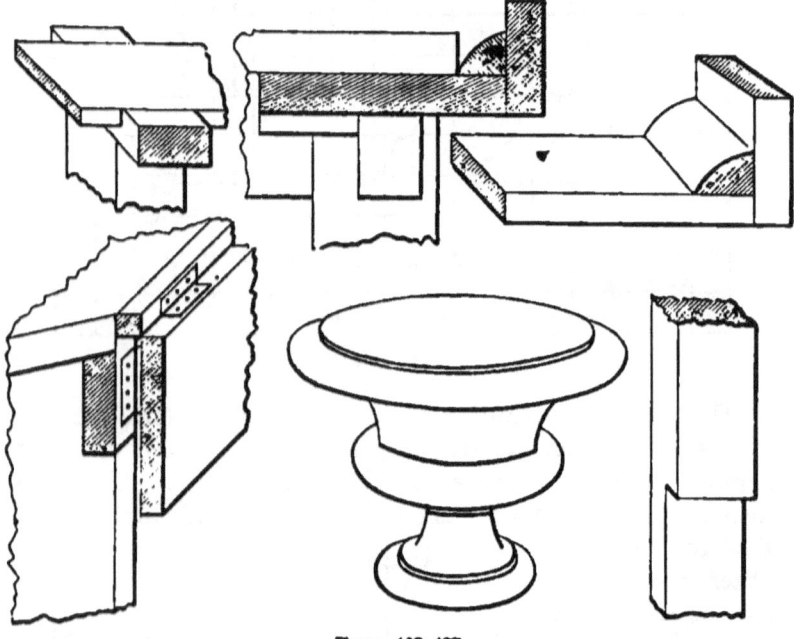

Figs. 422-427.

thodical treatment and infinite systematic care bestowed upon the course of instruction. I came away from several schools loaded with drawings which teachers and pupils presented to me, and these, I trust, will bear me out. The aim of this instruction is what the true aim of drawing in the schools ought to be, and which can be reached by drawing from the solids alone, not by imitating flat-surfaced copies. It is: to make the pupils observe objects correctly, present them in outlines first in tolerably exact perspective view, then shade them artistically. The specimens seen under the hand (not merely those on exhibition) were more perfect than one, used to seeing the pupils copy, could have expected. I certainly had not expected to see what I did see.

Side by side with the course of free-hand drawing from solids goes a most rigid course of geometrical drawing which enables the pupils to use the ruler and compasses, etc., and gives them most accurate knowledge of isometric and industrial drawing. This course, as well as that of free-hand-drawing, assists the industrial instruction in the shop spoken of elsewhere. The preceding sketches (Figs. 422–427) are only very incomplete indications of the work, but as suggestions they may prove of value to my American colleagues who are endeavoring at present to find "the true inwardness" of manual training.

7. Sketching.

The skill of French boys in sketching leaves everything behind that I ever saw in other countries. At my request the principals of different schools made me a present of some copy-books *used daily*, in order to prove my assertion of the superior teaching in the schools of Paris. The request was cheerfully granted after the pupils had expressed their willingness to part with the books. I have these books now, and hold them ready for inspection. In them can be seen geographical maps drawn hastily, but very accurately, sketches of animals, plants, physical apparatus, etc., serving as illustrations to the text. Each lesson or exercise is dated, and a comparison of these dates enables one to prove how much more work these pupils are expected to perform daily than our American pupils.

The sketches I insert below are cut out of these books, and I am happy to say that the artist has reproduced them with all their errors and short-comings, so that a true repre-

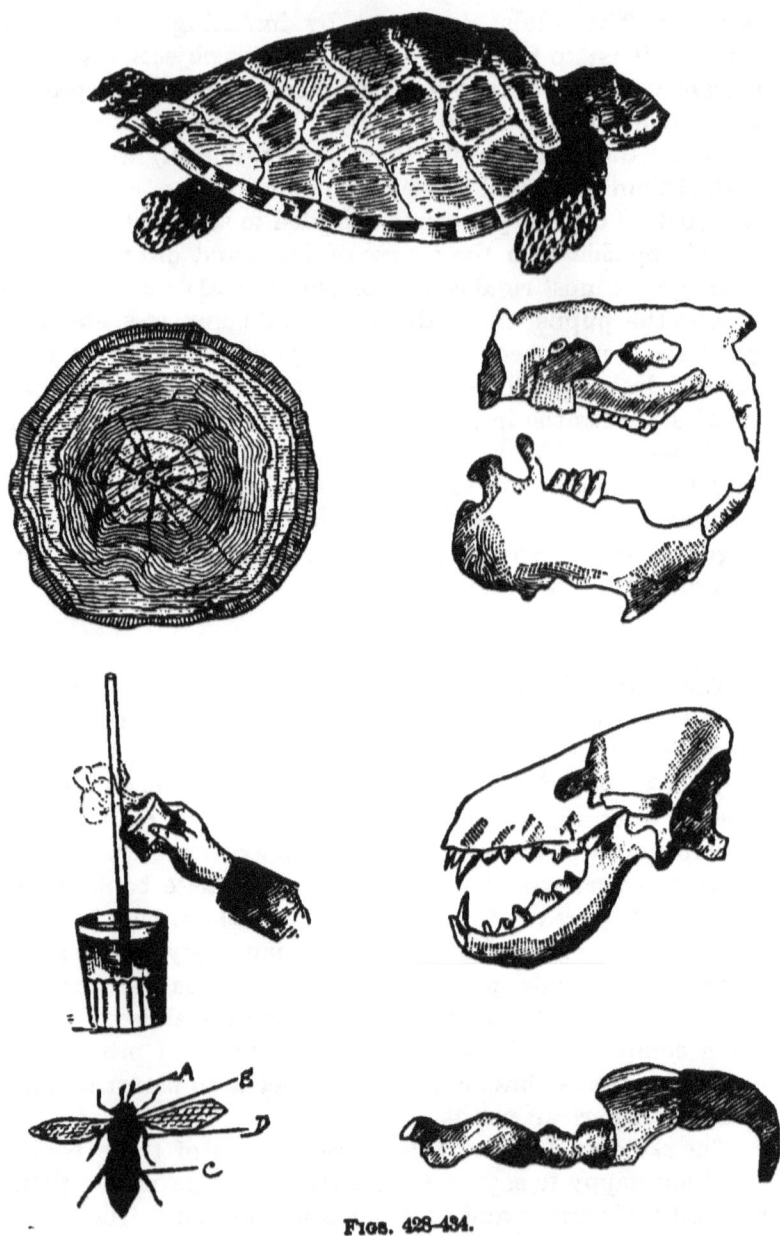

Figs. 428-434.

sentation of the work can be offered. They are by no means exceptionally fine specimens. The books contain many more and better ones than these, which are selected for insertion on account of their convenient size. I trust they will speak for themselves. See Figs. 428–434.

It would be manifestly unjust to speak of the drawings on exhibition in the "Musée Pedagogique," for they are selected from thousands and tens of thousands. They represent the best work performed. I do not mean to fall into the mistake of presenting what I recognize as exceptions, but the average of work done. As such I wish to have the work regarded. If it were not attended with too great an outlay, I should have those fine drawings of marble and plaster busts which I carried away from these schools photographed and inserted in my report; but it is impossible. If there should still be any of my colleagues who persist in doubting the results of drawing from objects to be superior to copying from the flat surface, I can only say, Go to Paris, and convince yourselves.

One word more: *Slates are not used* after the first half-year in the schools of Paris. At the close of the first year, or at most at the beginning of the second year of the course, the daily work in arithmetic and writing is done with lead-pencil or pen and ink. This gives the young pupils a dexterity in the use of pen, paper, and ink which can not be acquired where work on paper is the exception, and slate-work the rule, as it is with us.

8. How Geography is taught in Paris.

Time was when the average Frenchman believed Germany to be situated somewhere near the north pole, that her inhabitants were barbarians, and that wolves, bears, and foxes swarmed in the impenetrable forests of the wild country. Well, the war of 1870 and 1871 awakened them rudely, and the French Government has since then made heroic efforts to raise the average degree of intellectual culture of the people. A fortnight of careful inspection in the schools of Paris has convinced me of the thoroughness of French common-school education and of the wonderful start upward which the people have taken since 1871. Side by side with the communal schools there is a system of parochial schools kept by Catholic brethren and sisters which is doomed to extinction, since a governmental decree has fixed the date of closing these schools for good on the 1st of January, 1889. I did not see any of these parochial schools; all my observations were made in communal schools. It is here where I saw very good teaching in geography.

In the lower primary grades geography consists of object-lessons on home, schools, and their environs. These close during the third year and geography proper begins. They have here a very useful map resembling my silhouette practice maps. It is called a mute map. It consists of a black slated canvas, on which are printed with oil-paint the outlines of France, the main rivers, the boundaries of every department, with no name or lettering whatever. These maps are very costly, and are treated with much care. They are used, like my silhouette practice maps, as geographical blackboards for inserting geographical data as they are learned. The work thus added can be erased, and the maps are ready for another lesson. Such a mute map may be found in every school-room from the third to the eighth school year. A set of regular wall-maps as we have them is used also.

There are other means for illustrating geography such as our American schools have not. On the wall of every school-room (from the third grade upward) is found a large relief-map of Paris and vicinity suspended in a heavy frame. This map is made of plaster and artistically colored. It affords an opportunity for illustrating all the essential topographical ideas, since the vicinity of Paris, even the city itself, is diversified by elevations and depressions, shows an island (in the Seine), rivers, canals, harbors, woods, railroads, etc. The map is a neat piece of work, and it must have cost the school authorities much money to furnish each class-

HOW GEOGRAPHY IS TAUGHT IN PARIS. 359

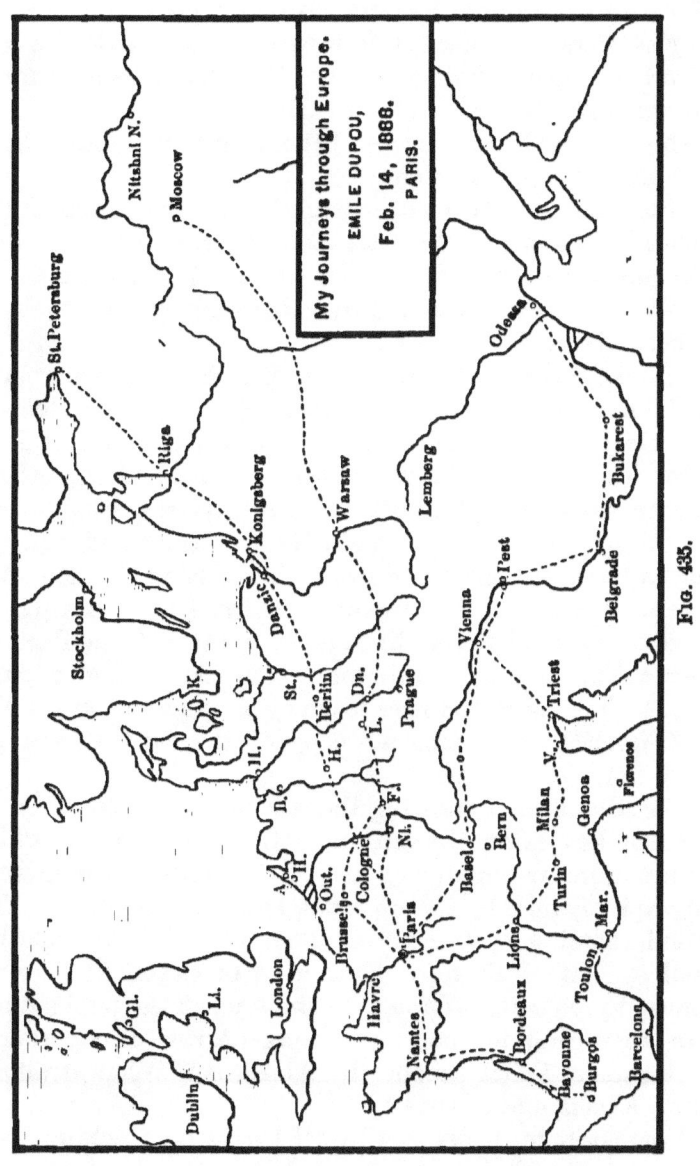

Fig. 435.

room with a copy. On this map may be seen the new girdle of forts drawn around the city. It really looks as though as many soldiers were needed to invest and blockade the city as there are people living inside. This double belt of fortifications looks formidable.

The geographical chromo-lithographs used have been mentioned in a previous chapter.

From all these means of instruction at the disposal of the teacher it may be inferred that the instruction does not rely upon rote learning and memory cram. I had occasion to listen to an oral examination in geography conducted by a teacher. Thus he proceeded:

"Louis, describe a journey from Suez to Yokohama"; and Louis would go ahead and start "by proxy" in a steamer from Suez, travel through the Red Sea, the Strait of Bab-el-Mandeb (the Gate of Tears of the Arabians), etc., mentioning seas, bays, capes, harbors, countries, rivers, islands, etc. Thus he would recite, and, while he did so, he drew on the board a hasty but pretty accurate sketch of the route. Another pupil was called to travel by railroad from Burgos, in Spain, to St. Petersburg, in Russia; another from Paris to Moscow, etc. I copy a little map from the book of a pupil to show that the pupils here learn by seeing and doing. The cut (Fig. 435) is an accurate copy of the work except the inscription, which I translate.

The second map, showing the tour by water from Calais to Marseilles, is an illustration both of the way in which examinations are conducted and of the fact that commercial geography comes in for no little share of attention. This second sketch map (a copy of a pupil's work) exhibits the canal system of France. This kind of examination work seemed to me better adapted to show what the pupils know than answering ten such questions, narrow as a razor, as, for instance, What seaport in Alabama? What strait between Alaska and Siberia?

I am sorry to report that in all this good teaching there was a bit of genuine humbug. When the teachers heard

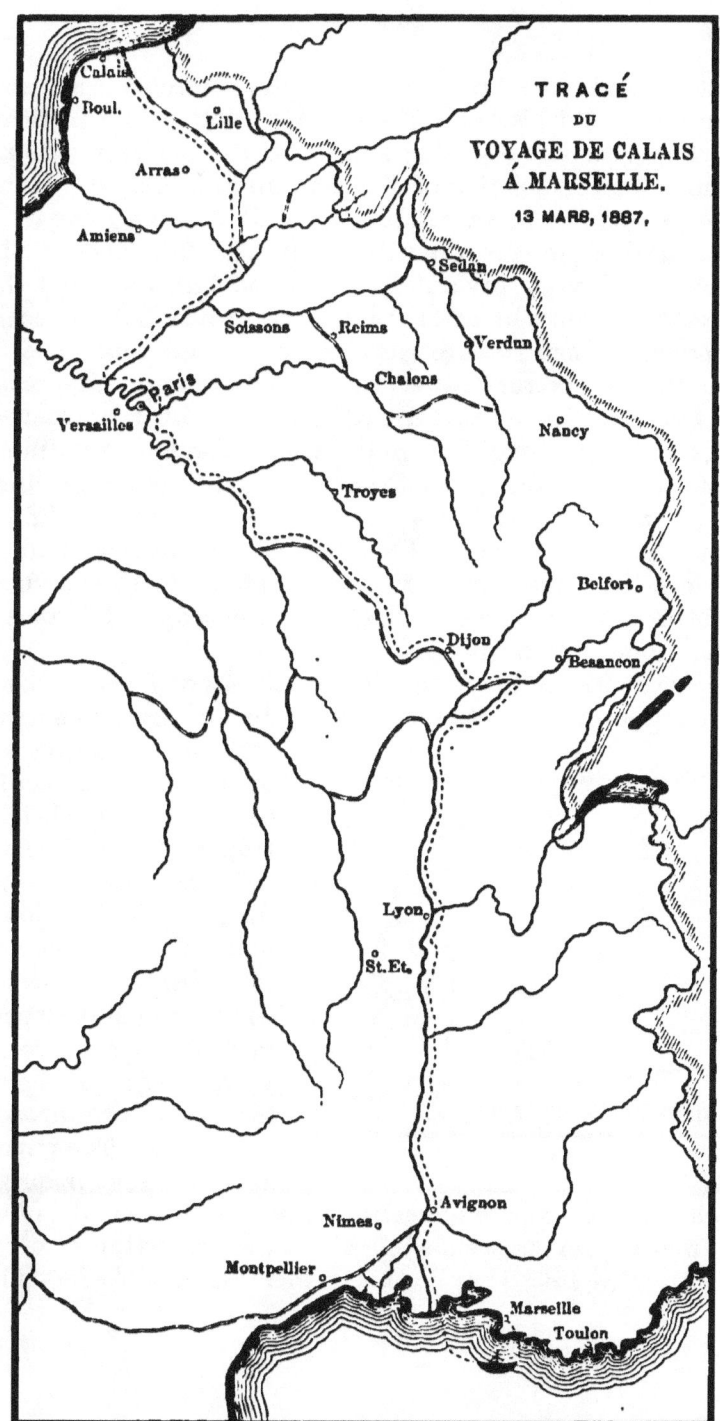

Fig. 436.

that I hailed from America, they wedged in some American geography and history. Their pronunciation of American cities was barbarous—I "reckon" as barbarous as a genuine Yankee's pronunciation of French names would be. However, I was fire-proof against that. It did not generate a great deal of pleasure when the fourth or fifth question in American history invariably concerned Lafayette and the excellent services he had rendered the United States in their infancy. When you are reminded of a kind deed done to you, the remembrance of it ceases to be pleasant. My readers may imagine my surprise when in one school the teacher, after duly extolling Lafayette, said: "Though the United States may owe thanks to France, we must not forget that we owe thanks to America also. The citizens of the United States first among the civilized nations demonstrated that in modern times the democratic form of government is as possible as in ancient times. They gave the people of France a great impulse to try it too."

Due consideration is paid in the schools of Paris to commercial geography. The railroad system of France and Europe is a subject of much study, as could be seen from sketch-maps on the blackboard and from work done by the pupils in their journals. The little map in the margin is an exact copy of a home task performed by a girl twelve years of age. It shows the important railroads of France. The pupils draw different maps of each country—topographical, climatic, railroad, canal, political maps—also maps showing where the grape-vine or olive is cultivated, etc. They do this in their blank-books for daily

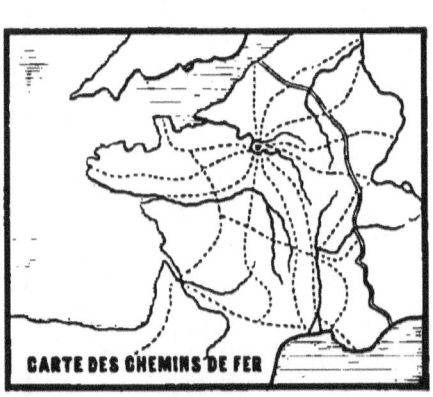

Fig. 437.

work and not on special drawing-paper. The maps, a copy of which is inserted in this chapter, are reproduced in the same size in which they were furnished by the pupils.

In one of the journals (pupils' blank-books filled with daily work) I brought with me I noticed a remarkable task. It is this: A statistical table of the most noted countries of the world, headed "Tableau Comparatif." This table contains the comparative figures of their area, population, density of population, armies and navies, their productions, value of exports and imports, tonnage of merchant marine, and sundry other items. I inquired whether this had been learned by heart. "No," was the reply; "this table is to cause an impression, nothing else. We dictate it and compare the figures, to make our pupils see where France stands. The figures themselves have no abiding value, being subject to frequent changes; but we can not know ourselves unless we compare ourselves with others." A golden truth—a truth which will do a great deal toward redeeming France.

9. FRENCH TEXT-BOOKS.

The text-books I picked up and examined in French schools all have the same essential fault found in American text-books—they contain too much. The arithmetics are very bulky and objectionable on account of the multiplicity of "cases" offered in the different chapters. The geographies are burdened with text, as ludicrously incongruent with the children's degree of comprehension as ours are; but these French books contain admirable maps, much better than many of ours. These maps, however, are also to be objected to, because they are too minute, and offer a multiplicity of detail which must bewilder the pupils. The readers have much stale conversational matter, and do not come up in usefulness to the readers used in German schools. Except the primers, which are more carefully prepared, the French readers are wretched, and the teachers help themselves by introducing other suitable reading-matter wherever they find it.

I noticed a few books of great usefulness, called readers, to wit, a domestic economy for girls, a science reader for boys, and a number of special readers, such as geographical, botanical, zoölogical, and historical readers, which seem to me to meet a long-felt want. They are not used as text-books, but as supplementary sources of information, since no special text-books for the sciences, such as physiology and natural history, are used in the *écoles primaire* (elementary communal schools).

Perhaps the best text-book I found in use was the one used in the study of history. It was well illustrated, and presented history in biographies and topical essays. If we consider that France has a history of more than a thousand years, it will readily be seen that the most scrupulous economy is needed to present that which is of essential importance. Paul Bert's book is also applied in natural science and history, but its use is not obligatory.

All text-books and stationery are furnished free of cost to the pupils. The city pays for the "means of instruction," and the consequence is, that competition is killed. The books are badly printed, the paper is flimsy, and the binding shabby. The blank-books furnished are miserable, their paper is poorly calendered, and the flimsy cover easily torn. American school stationery is by far too costly, French school stationery by far too wretched. The two countries represent the two extremes, while Germany seems to have struck a happy medium.

10. How Reading and Spelling are taught in Paris.

In discussing this topic, interesting to American primary teachers, I regret that it is difficult to fix sounds by signs. This difficulty may give rise to misunderstandings, but that can not be avoided. I hope to be able to offer a few suggestions to young teachers who are using the phonic method. Those who insist upon spelling, and do not comprehend that letters and sounds are not identical, may omit this chapter; I have nothing new to offer them:

QUATRIÈME LEÇON

Plu**me**s

m *m*

mi, mu, mu ni

mi, mu, mu ni

SIXIÈME LEÇON

r  *r*

Voitu**re**

ri, ru, ro, mu ri,

ri, ru, ro, mu ri,

or, ur, ir, mu ni

Figs. 438, 439.

I. *Reading.* — 1. The simple vowels *a, e, i, o, u, y,* are taught alone in the schools of Paris, simply by memory. Such aids as "*i* is a little boy throwing up his cap," etc., are used, but not the word-method. The vowels are shown in script and print, and pronounced.

2. Simple consonants are taught, as the accompanying two lessons show. It is plain that no word is used, but simple combinations of one vowel and one consonant. This may seem mechanical, and I do not hesitate to pronounce it so, but there is consistency in the method.

Frequent reviews (the little primer has one on every third page) prevent forgetting sounds previously learned. It will be noticed, in the above and following illustrations, that each consonant appears with the silent *e* attached to it. This refers to a peculiarity in the French language which can not be explained in print. The pictures used are very simple, and serve to bring out the particular sound to be learned, and no others.

Figs. 440-443.

The first reader from which these illustrations are taken contains no word with greater difficulty than simple combinations of one vowel and one consonant, as is seen from these words: *Fa ri ne, fi de li té, re ga li a, qua li té, a ma zo ne, ma xi me, ex po sé, ca ma ra de.* (As a sign of the deep-felt desire among Frenchmen to regain Alsace

HOW READING AND SPELLING ARE TAUGHT. 367

and Lorraine from Germany may be regarded the fact that in this first primer a small map of those provinces is printed to illustrate the word "Al sa ce." The thing looks childish and strangely incongruous, but it is bitter earnest with the Frenchmen of to-day.)

From the most difficult and last review lesson of this first book I quote: *Il pa-ti-ne-ra sur le ca-nal; u-ne mo-de de ri-di-cule; le to-tal de la fac-tu-re.* This little book has forty pages, and the pupils complete it in about six weeks; it never takes more than three months.

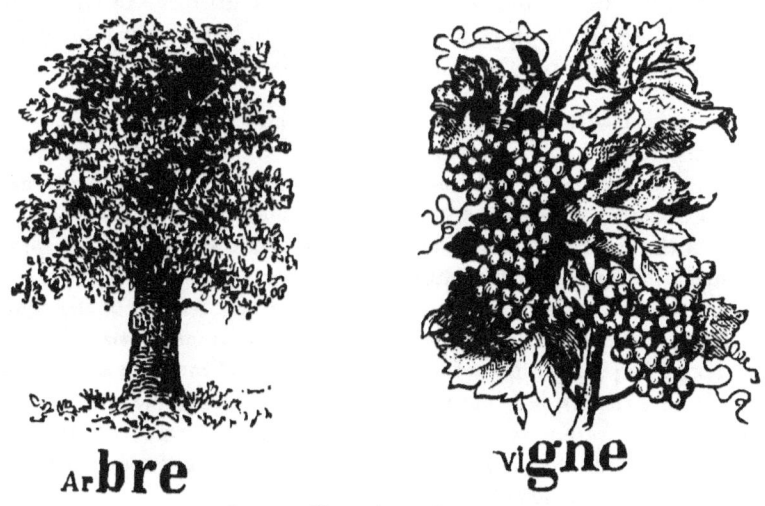

Figs. 444, 445.

3. The second primer (the reader will pardon the expression, but it is used advisedly; for the first book, commonly called primer with us, is here divided into two; the one containing the simple sounds and their combinations, the second the more complex combinations) is finished also in less than three months, so that at the close of six months at most the mechanical difficulties of reading are overcome. This second book of sixty-four pages contains such vowels as *ou, oi, eu, oeu, au, eau, ei, ai, ie,* and such consonants as *ch, gn,*

ph, qu, gl, fr, st, sp. The method of this book is best illustrated by copying a few lessons:

gn-i, gn-o, gn-a, gn-é,
gn-e, gn-u, gn-è;
gni, gno, gna, gné, gne,
gnu, gnè.
vigne, signe, bagne, gagné.
ligne, digne, regne, rogné.
ignoré, chigné, signal.
Here follow sentences for practice.

br-i, br-o, br-u, br-a, br-e,
br-é, brè.
bri, bro, bru, bra, bre,
bré, brè.
sobre, bride, abri, brigade.
brodé, abricot, brutal.
brume, arbre, brave.

At the foot of each lesson are given a number of notes to the teacher in "eye-powder print," which tell him how to proceed. I add one here for illustration's sake:

Procedure.—Object-lesson on the grape-vine, its culture, fruit, and products. How many syllables in the word vigne? Two, *vi* and *gne.* Take the second only. Drop or cover the last letter, it is a silent one. Now sound *gn.* Connect it with *a, e, i, o, u,* thus, gn——a, gn——i, etc. Prevent the separation of the sounds till the pupils acquire skill in pronouncing the entire syllable without first analyzing it. Exercises on the blackboard: Reading of the word written in script; reading of the copy in different forms and sizes; reading of the copy from the slates. Use the board frequently. Do not let the chalk go out of your hands. Watch over it, that the lesson is not learned by heart. Change the order of the words on the board; let them be read in the book backward, forward, upward, downward. See to it that the new sound *gn* is articulated well in all the words of the lesson.

To give an adequate idea of the great difficulties in reading surmounted in this second book, I will copy the last lesson found in it. It is characteristic, inasmuch as it proves that the French teachers employ the same abominable tone of sentimental preaching that characterizes the reading-matter in some of our first readers:

Chers enfants: Aimez vos parents et gardez-vous de leur jamais désobeir. Aimez votre maître qui se donne beaucoup de peine pour vous; écoutez ses leçons, suivez ses conseils. Aimez votre école; venez-y tous les jours avec plaisir et n'y arrivez jamais en retard. Aimez le travail, aimez la lecture. Ayez de l'ordre; ayez soin de vos vêtements, de vos livres, de vos cahiers, et de tous les objets à votre usage. Les livres coûtent cher; il faut aussi beaucoup d'argent pour acheter des vêtements, des chaussures et tout ce qu'il faut pour votre nourriture. Et l'argent coûte beaucoup de peine, beaucoup de mal à votre père pour le gagner. L'ordre mene à l'économie, l'économie mène à l'aisance, souvent à la richesse. Soyez bons pour vos frères, pour vos sœurs et pour vos camarades; ayez le mensonge en horreur. Ne maltraitez jamais les animaux. Ayez pitié de pauvres, des malheureux, de tous ceux qui souffrent et qui sont dans la peine. Respectez les vieillards. Aimez la France, notre Patrie, si grande et si belle. De retour de l'école, rendez à votre mère les petits services que nous pouvez lui rendre, pour alléger son travail et ses peines. C'est ainsi que vous vous ferez aimer, et que vous grandirez en vous préparant à devenir des hommes de bien.

It is to be regretted that our American printing-offices are not supplied with the types in which the above lesson is set in France, for the silent letters are marked in a most ingenious way. This kind of matter is read at the close of the sixth month! Words like *vieillards, animaux, chaussures, travail!* When I first "struck" a first-year's class busy with a reading-lesson, and was told how quickly the pupils learned to read, I thought this an exception, owing to the excellence of the teacher—as any one would have done. But an examination in more than a dozen schools in different parts of the city convinced me that the case met first was no exception, but a fair average sample.

Now I beg my American colleagues to consider—1. That the French children *do not spell* words and syllables for the purpose of learning to read, but "*sound*" exclusively. 2. That they learn to read with great fluency almost anything in French print or legible script that is put into their hands, after the first year of school—and then let the reader draw the conclusion himself.

The subsequent readers need not be described. Suffice it to say that they have the same faults which our American readers have, and none of their virtues and excellent qualities. They are miserably printed and bound, and the cuts do not come up to our standard.

II. *Orthography.*—How is orthography taught? By avoiding spelling (splitting), and by copying much of the reading-matter. The French teachers have found the secret of orthographical teaching, to wit: The secret of vivid knowing is vivid seeing. Dictation-lessons are given daily. Not detached words but sentences are dictated, and the work is corrected according to the text of the book from which the lesson is taken, be that the reader, geography, arithmetic, or history. I was presented with dozens of blank-books filled by the pupils with their daily work; misspelled words are met in them but rarely. I preserve these books for inspection. They bear the official stamp of the rectors of the schools; and the date, in the upper right corner of every page, tells how much more practice in writing the boys and girls in Paris have than ours, whose work on the objectionable slate is all a fleeting show. The only class in which a slate is used in the schools of Paris is the first grade or primer class, and there only during the first half-year; and even there it is not a slate, but a thin board without a frame. The lines are red, and one side is covered with a network of lines for drawing purposes.

The penmanship found everywhere in the common schools of Paris is not "Spencerian," but remarkably excellent. The books I brought with me exhibit truly admirable penmanship. The headings are written in a bold, round hand, and the arrangement of arithmetical work very fine. Of course, there is indifferent work here as elsewhere, but the average is very high.

11. The "Musée Pédagogique" in Paris.

The last day of my stay in Paris I devoted to the Museum of Instruction. It took me some time to find it. It had shifted its abode several times, but is now in permanent quarters in the Rue Gay-Lussac, No. 41, a street situated between the Panthéon and the Palais de Luxembourg. The building used to be a convent; it has many quaint corners, passages, courts, and cool, shady rooms and corridors. The institution is maintained by the state, and M. Martel, a gentleman well known in America, used to be its director, but, since he has been promoted, M. Beurrier is the director. When I presented my *passe-partout*, and a special card of introduction from our Bureau of Education in Washington, I was very hospitably received. I stated that I was laboring under a want of familiarity with French, though I could understand all that was said, and could speak it slowly; and the director called one of his chief clerks, who spoke a commendable English, with that delightful French pronunciation which is and always will be a subject of study to me.

Well, we started out to see the educational treasures here collected from all parts of the globe. First of all, the library; four large rooms full of books, scientific and practical, chiefly pedagogical books, graced the walls. Ah, what would I have given to be the owner of such treasures as were here collected ! The catalogue contained the titles of French, German, English, American, etc., books on education. Among the latter I noticed Horace Mann's "Importance of Education in a Republic." The books were well arranged in cases according to subjects. One feature of the library was so characteristic that I must mention it. The chief countries had each one separate case in which were collected samples of their best school-books (I say "best," because I was so informed). In the case reserved for American school-books I found many well-reputed books, as, for instance, Hepburn's Rhetoric, Colburn's Arithmetic, Appletons' Readers, and many others. It was with a feeling of some pride that I discovered one of my own children among the number, and another in which I had done a good share of the work. The American school-books were distinguished from those of other countries by their excellent binding, strong paper, and clear print.

Then I was taken into a room which looked like a bookseller's packing-room. All the thousands of books here had a uniform black cloth binding. Clerks were engaged here in packing books in little boxes of about a cubic foot in size. The boxes had been in the hands of the postal authorities many a time which was seen from the mail labels pasted on them. This, I was told, was the circulating library, where books were selected and sent to candidates for examination in the provinces. "All state examinations for professorships in normal schools, rectorships in common schools, superintendency and for positions in higher schools, have to be passed in this building, and, to regulate and facilitate the studies and preparation of the candidates, we lend them the books necessary. The books are returned by mail free of postage (this being a state institution) before the examinee presents himself."

"But is not this a rather questionable procedure, my dear sir?" I asked. "Why should you think so?" "Well, I should judge that this would prevent teachers from buying books themselves; does not this circulating library make them rely on state aid?" "Ah! I see," said the director; "you are from America, where 'help yourself' is the favorite motto. No, we can not expect that here. From time immemorial the Frenchman expects aid from his Government, and it would seriously diminish the number of candidates for higher positions if we were to cease lending books to them. This circulating library is one of the strongest ties that hold the entire French teachers' profession together. Besides, it increases the usefulness of this museum, for all the candidates for promotion and examination, when they come here, spend days and weeks in studying our educational treasures, which we will now proceed to show you."

And now the gentleman took me from room to room. There was one room entirely filled with objects for illustrative instruction in natural history. All kinds of fruit imitated in wax were seen here. Charts and pictures for object-lessons were seen in such numbers that a choice would have been a difficult task. A room full of pupils' work followed: penmanship, drawing, arithmetic, composition, map-drawing, etc., in great stacks, French, American, German, English, Japanese, etc.—a wealth which it must have taken much ingenuity and diligence to arrange systematically.

Then there was a glorious art-hall, containing marble and plaster casts used for drawing; a hall filled with relief and other maps as well as pictorial means of instruction in geography; telluriums, globes, etc., and hundreds of other things, old and new. There were samples of school furniture in miniature and iu actual size, all imaginable blackboards, reading-charts, music-charts. I was bewildered, and, though I tried to hold on to my *nil admirari*, I soon forgot that and myself, lost in contemplation of the ingenuity of the schoolmaster. Here were collected all the school devices invented in all the civilized countries, and those of Japan and China besides.

I had seen several museums of this kind in Cologne and Berlin and in southern Germany, but this one surpassed them all in every respect, owing to the centralized efforts of the Government. In an octagonal room, formerly a vestibule, were selected models in miniature of school-houses and plans of similar buildings. I was pleasantly surprised to find a model of a Massachusetts normal school, and of a schoolhouse in Milwaukee, Wis. The gentleman who took me through this room expressed his disgust at *such* school architecture, saying: "They look like barracks. We want to see large portals, inner courts, and lofty, airy structures, not brick piles."

Up-stairs I saw the hall in which the state examinations are conducted. In alcoves are found the collections of school-work prepared for world expositions—Paris, Antwerp, Philadelphia, and New Orleans; drawing in portfolios, penmanship and compositions in bound volumes, pupils' work from Japan, Belgium, America—an immense exhibition. One room is reserved for a chemical laboratory, another for a physical laboratory. These are used for lectures to the teachers who pass through a special course in the natural sciences. The apparatus here collected would rouse the envy of any teacher who is obliged to rely on home-made apparatus. In the basement, in small alcoves, and broad, light corridors are seen the results of manual training-schools.

Here are on exhibit collections of tools forged by pupils, specimens of joiner's work, carpenter's work, wood-carving, turner's work, inlaid work, scroll-sawing, and building. Here is also seen the entire course of industrial education for girls, beginning with paper-work done in the maternal schools (Kindergärten) and ending with complete garments. All departments are well arranged, systematically showing the courses of instruction and the methods employed. It is altogether a marvelous exhibition.

How all else sinks into insignificance when these treasures, made by little hands and comparing favorably with master-works of adults, are viewed by one who is interested in them! All the priceless treasures of the Louvre and the École des Beaux-Arts seem to lose their luster when compared with these beginnings of art. It may sound heretical, but I assure my readers that I had more genuine pleasure in this museum than in looking at the miles of painted canvas in the Louvre. My admiration and interest grew with every new room opened to me, and I soon gave up trying to prepare a detailed account of what I saw. Weeks of study would barely suffice for it.

A few items I picked up may close my report. How systematic the instruction in geography is in Paris, may be

FIG. 446.

seen from this fact: In a collection of work furnished by the pupils of the normal school in Paris I noticed an ideal relief-map on the margin of which were placed other reliefs such as seen in Fig. 446. The work led over from the idea *face* to *surface* of objects. The same school had also exhibited a number of fine specimens of china painting and embroidery.

A CALCULATING-MACHINE. 375

The many devices for illustrating number lessons were bewildering, and the director told me frankly he was unable to explain some of them. One department is filled with children's toys. Among the blackboards there seen, I sketch an adjustable one. It is easily made, works up and down, and can be turned. Fig. 447.

Had I known what treasures this quaint-looking, ancient building contained, I should have timed my stay in Paris so as to spend several days in the museum; but my departure was necessary, to fulfill an engagement for addressing an assembly of teachers in a city on the Rhine. I am grateful, though, for having lived to see the "Musée Pédagogique" in Paris. If any of my colleagues should chance to go to Paris, I advise them urgently not to neglect to ask for a permit to see it. This, I believe, can be readily obtained of Monsieur Buisson, at the ministry of Public Instruction, in the Rue de Grenelle, No. 110, third floor, door to the left.

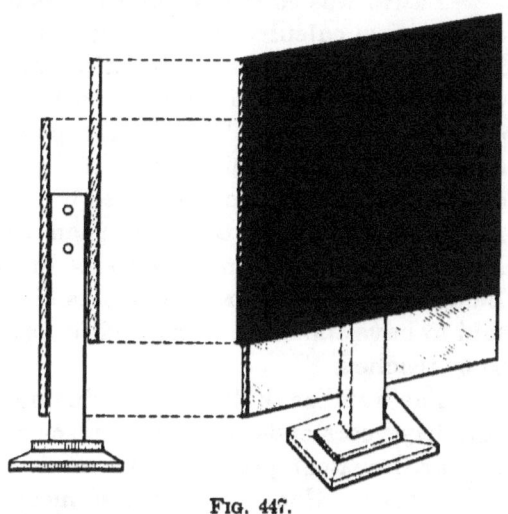
Fig. 447.

12. A Calculating-Machine.

The "arithmograph," an apparatus for absolutely correct arithmetical calculation, was on exhibition in the "Musée Pédagogique" in Paris. In an educational journal published in Paris, entitled "Le Progrès de l'Enseignement Primaire," I met with a description of the apparatus. The article contains some interesting facts concerning the history of inventions of arithmetical calculators. I translate a few passages for that reason. The author does not seem to know much of similar inventions in other countries:

"Pascal was convinced of the possibility of reducing all arithmetical calculations to mere mechanical manipulations. He invented the first arithmetical machine in 1642. Employing in his work all his extensive mathematical knowledge, he came to believe in the possibility of making an apparatus which would successfully replace thought and calculation. This conviction led him to expend large sums in the manufacture of more than fifty different devices. Nevertheless, he did not live to see his speculations realized. Being the first who undertook this kind of work, he may be said to have shown the way and to have pointed out the aim to be reached.

"The number of those who during nearly two hundred and fifty years endeavored to replace mental activity in solving arithmetical problems by mechanical contrivances is quite large. Some few of the most noted are *Leibnitz*, *D'Alembert*, *De Lepine*, and *Dr. Roth*, all of whom continued the labors of *Pascal*. *Napier* invented the calculation by logarithms; *Thomas de Colmar* the "arithmometre"; *Babbage*, aided by the English Government, spent (or shall we say squandered?) a half-million of francs and the best of his years upon a "universal calculator," which, like so many other similar inventions, remained incomplete.

"It may be said that, despite the astonishing amount of labor that has been employed in its solution, the question, like that of a manageable air-ship, has not yet been solved, though it would be presumptuous to say it will never be solved. Still, the work begun by Pascal has not been without tangible results. There are several indispensable qualities which a calculating-machine must have to make it practicable and applicable everywhere, and it has until recently been impossible to furnish a device which could boast of all these qualities. It must be inexpensive, must be easily transported and manipulated. It must be so arranged that every average intelligence is able to make use of it in all conditions of life and for all simple calculations. Simplicity, indeed, is its most necessary condition. So simple it must be in its workings that one would not care to expend brain-power in solving problems such as life offers every moment.

"The '*arithmograph*' of Monsieur Troucet offers all these advantages at the first glance; but it works only problems in the four fundamental rules—addition, subtraction, multiplication, and division. The apparatus is remarkably simple. It has no cylinders, no cranks, no wheels, no springs, no mechanical clock-work, subject to disturbance and disorder, but consists of a light white board on which are fastened a number of slats set in grooves. These slats work independently of each other, and are moved up and down by a peg.

"It can not be asserted that the 'arithmograph,' like many other inventions, is the result of a happy accident. On the contrary, the simpler an invention is, the more time, labor, and expense it takes to realize it. This invention is the result of six years' hard, incessant labor. The passion of the inventor is perhaps the most ethical of all human passions, since it is not destructive, but of benefit —if not to the inventor himself, it is so at least to the human race; but it is to be hoped that M. Troucet will find the remuneration he deserves before he dies. He seems to be a professional inventor, for he has secured a number of patents; but this one is destined to pay for them all."

When carefully examining the apparatus I asked myself, Will it not be of serious evil consequences for the intellectual culture of children to replace their mental activity by a machine? For this machine adds, subtracts, multiplies, and divides with absolute accuracy, provided one makes no mistakes in touching the correct digits. All the manipulator has to do is to put the peg into a little aperture corresponding with the digit beside it and pull the slat down or push it up as the operation demands, and the answer appears at another hole provided for it. Or rather, Is not all addition, subtraction, multiplication, and division a mechanical process depending upon the memory? To me it was and still is a perplexing question. Perhaps the apparatus will soon make its appearance in America. I leave my colleagues to decide upon its merits.

13. CRUMBS.—NOTES FROM THE SCHOOLS OF PARIS.

A French flag (the tricolor) hangs over the entrance of every communal school-house in Paris. These flags look rather shabby, being exposed to all kinds of weather.

I found a room filled with plaster casts, geometrical bodies, and other models for drawing purposes, in every school-house I visited in Paris.

The city maintains many evening schools for young men. In one of them I saw the students model human forms from life. Think of a nude person posing before a class of unripe boys under or little above twenty!

Drawing and mathematics are the chief subjects of study in the evening schools.

Most of the young boys and girls in the schools of Paris wear black blouses, not jackets and coats. When I asked whether that was a sort of uniform, my informant smiled and answered no; that was the usual style of children's outer garments in Paris.

When a guest or the principal enters a school-room in a boys' school, the pupils promptly jump up and salute him by raising the right hand to their head—that is, give the regular military salute. If the guest fails to answer in the same manner, they remain in that position until he does answer or leaves.

The pupils here are not dismissed by classes, but in groups according to the streets they live in. All the pupils of one street go together till they reach the boulevard, where a policeman pilots them safely through the maelstrom of cabs, wagons, and omnibuses.

Comparatively few children are seen in the streets of Paris, partly owing to the high houses, the upper stories of which they inhabit, partly because the French families have fewer children than the Germans, for instance.

The hissing sound sss! or sh-sh-sh! as an order for silence, is not heard in Parisian schools. Both male and female teachers here, in order to call for silence, make either that smacking sound which we employ in driving horses, or the sound of a kiss. It sounds odd if one is not accustomed to it.

In the corridor of each school in Paris is seen a very elaborate and beautiful "Table of Honor" in heavy gilt frame, containing the names of meritorious pupils.

In one of the girls' schools I noticed that canceling was resorted to in the study of arithmetic as early as the fourth year of school.

In another girls' school, in a class parallel to our D Grammar (fifth year of school), I found girls of ten and eleven years of age working problems in percentage and interest. This was the problem: "To find the interest on 52,100 francs for two years and a half at the rate of 3·75 per cent."

The schools in Paris do not teach singing as thoroughly as this is done in Germany and in the United States. Their songs are not melodious and harmonious, but dramatic like the "Marseillaise." The children's voices are weak, and the most difficult song I heard in Parisian schools was two-part music.

In regard to the manner of teaching seen in Paris, I am confident that altogether too much reciting in chorus is resorted to. To hear a class solve a problem in chorus has something like the aspect of a panic in a theatre—the strong ones reach the door, the weak ones are trampled under foot or are dragged along.

To see the happy crowds of French boys employed in sawing, planing, polishing, turning, carving, modeling, building, etc., is a sight never to be forgotten. They jabber, spit into their palms, and handle hammer, saw, and plane as though their lives depended upon the completion of the work under hand.

But to see the pale and yellow countenances of all these children, among whom the red, healthy, glowing cheeks of our Western school-children is rarely found, is also a sight worth remembering, and pondering.

The number of "écoles primaire" (elementary common schools) in Paris is four hundred and fifty-four, namely, one hundred and seventy-four boys' schools, one hundred and seventy-five girls' schools, and one hundred and five maternal schools. The latter have pupils below six years of age, and resemble the Kindergarten.

The faces of the children in Paris are not pretty, to put it mildly. Many very ugly visages are seen among them.

Teachers are not the same all the world over. I noticed a peculiar indefinable air of immaturity among them here in Paris which is not found among American teachers. Principals and inspectors are much more men of the world, since they come in contact with the world more frequently.

Among all the teachers I saw in Paris, the women principals make the best impression. They are very refined in manners. They are splendid-looking women, indeed, and the teachers look up to them with much reverence.

The principal of one of the schools I saw is an Alsatian. He had his school in very good trim, discipline and order were perfect, and the results exhibited were quite commendable. He spoke with great enthusiasm of the excellent results he had noticed in German schools lately. During the last summer he had employed his vacation in making a trip through southern Germany. When I spoke to him about the excitable nature of the French children and teachers, he said: "We know no better, and think this the normal state of being. When I was in Frankfort I wondered greatly about the (what seemed to me) listlessness of the pupils. They were very quiet and apparently stupid, and raised their hands only when questions were asked. It was a strange spectacle to me. I suspect, though, that this quiet, slow movement hides a great, robust, physical, and mental strength. France experienced something of that strength and discipline at her expense in the war of 1870-'71."

This principal regaled us with a taste of Alsatian wine which proved genuine "stocking-wine" (so sour that it draws the holes in the drinker's stockings together). Do not be shocked, kind reader; it was in his own dwelling that he offered us the wine. And please remember that it is not well to air your American predilections and principles when journeying through Europe. When in Rome, do as the Romans do; and when in Paris, drink wine. Shun the water as you would poison, for reasons too near at hand to mention them.

CHAPTER XIII.

FROM OTHER FRENCH CITIES.

1. MAKING BEAUTY CONTAGIOUS.

WHILE I greatly admired the beauty of the French display of school-work at the New Orleans Exposition, and the skill it betrayed, I harbored a lurking doubt as to its genuineness, and an apprehension of sham. At least I suspected that the splendid apparatus, contrivances, and devices for objective teaching, exhibited there, were the results of a few advanced schools only. so to speak ; of a few bright educational lights. The brighter the light, the darker the shadow. On my tour through northeastern France I was determined to set my mind at rest with regard to this.

Undoubtedly in Paris the schools are doing fine work, but Paris is not France. I am now prepared to say that my doubt was justified, and that the majority of schools in France are much inferior to the average of our city schools in America. Yet, at every place where I stopped, and in every school I visited, I found a strong onward movement. The heroic efforts of the lamented Minister of Education, M. Paul Bert, and those of his less famous but equally active successors, are beginning to be felt everywhere. The deadening influence of the monks and nuns in school has ceased, only lay-teachers being now allowed to teach.

It is only a few years since this new order has gone into effect, and one can not stamp and thereby raise an army of well-equipped teachers from the ground. But already one can see the beneficial influence of the act which separated church and school in France. Many are the indications which tend to prove the progressive spirit that has entered the French school, but I can not enumerate them here for want of space. One instance may suffice, one which will be found characteristically French.

Let me tell what I saw in a convent school that had been changed into a city school. The city authorities—either the council or the school authorities—when assuming control over the school, ordered the walls of the class-rooms to be decorated with fresco-paintings. That order was carried out regardless of cost. It is a charming sight to see these walls beautifully bedecked with exquisite workmanship, truly artistic allegorical figures in glorious, luminous colors ! It was said, when the matter came up for deliberation, that many pupils never have the opportunity of seeing beautiful rooms at home, living in squalid, filthy houses. They should therefore be surrounded by beauty in rooms where they were obliged to live six hours every day.

I mention this fact because it is freighted with the suggestion to imitate it. The American people, perhaps the richest nation on the face of the globe, can well afford to surround their children—the hope of the future—with things of beauty, which are "joys forever." Æsthetic education, however, is yet in its infancy in America. The children need to see beautiful things to learn to appreciate them. Much is done with us by beauty-loving women teachers, who succeed, with hardly any means at their disposal, in decorating their school-rooms with pictures, flowers, etc.; but it should be preached from the house-tops that the schools ought to be perfect treasuries of art and beauty. Money spent in that direction is never thrown away. We must accustom our children to beauty and make beauty infectious, just as Superintendent Howland, of Chicago, says that the good should be made contagious.

2. COMPOSITION-BOOKS IN FRENCH SCHOOLS.

It is well known that the French people have a trained eye for beauty. All the patterns of their machines and other contrivances, even the boxes in which they pack their goods, are ornamented elaborately and artistically. This highly developed sense of form and beauty I knew was due to the loving care which French teachers bestow upon drawing and sketching in school, and in no small degree to the many art-schools maintained by the state and by communities.

But I was struck with wonder when I went through a lyceum at R—— (a high-school). I was requested to look over the composition-books of the pupils. There I thought I had found the secret spring of French art—its fountain-head.

Each composition was headed by a pencil-sketch drawn either in rude outlines or beautifully shaded. Some of these illustrations were real masterpieces of drawing, representing landscape scenery; others were clumsy delineations, but all compositions contained at least some attempt at illustration. (Compare also page 356.)

Being desirous of showing my readers some specimens, I selected a few composition-books and asked for their loan with a view to copying some of the designs. After school a delegation of students called at the hotel and brought the books, asking whether they might assist me in copying. I could not well accept their services—though politely offered —and traced some sketches myself. Here is the result:

The subject of one of the compositions was "The Zones," and this was the sketch accompanying it. (Fig. 448.)

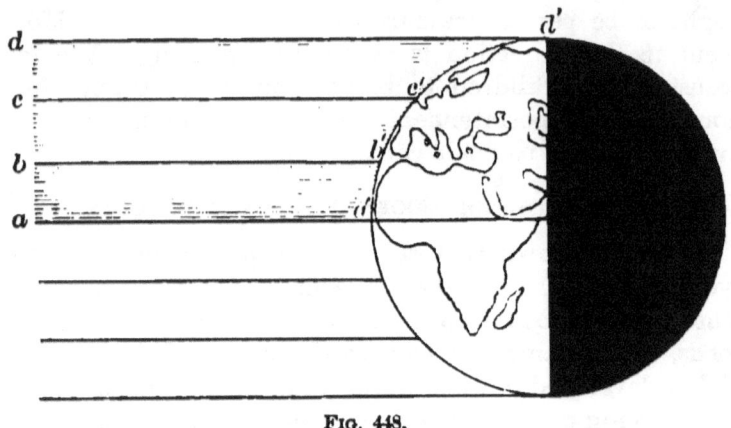

Fig. 448.

Another was "The Digestive Organs," and the liver, here minutely reproduced as I found it sketched, served the writer as one of his illustrations. (Fig. 449.)

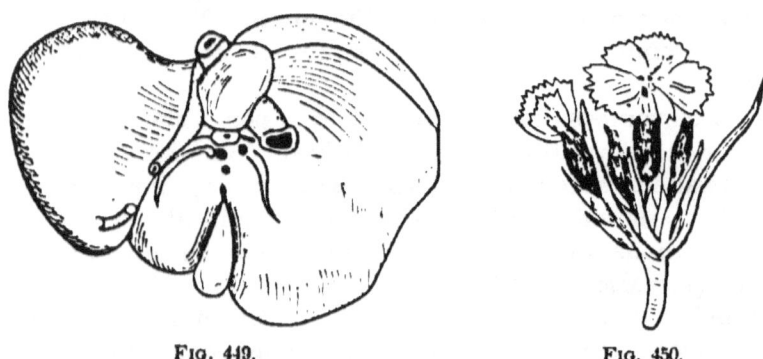

Fig. 449.   Fig. 450.

The third composition was profusely illustrated with sketches of flowers. I copied the simplest, to show the accuracy of representation. One glance shows what flower it is (Fig. 450.)

A fourth, again on a physiological subject, was illustrated with sketches of bones and muscles. This is one of them. (Fig. 451.)

A fifth treated of the human teeth, and these sketches may suffice to prove the artistic skill of the boy. (Fig. 452.)

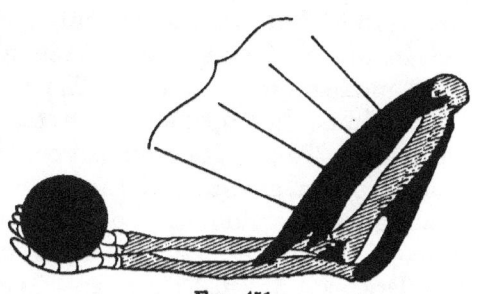

FIG. 451.

I will refrain from reflections which are crowding my mind with regard to this practice, but call attention to the fact that the subjects of all the compositions I examined were taken from the studies the pupils then pursued. A class studying astronomy would write compositions on astronomical subjects; a class in history would write on historical subjects, and sketch battle-fields and maps, chiefly exhibiting changes in boundaries and movements of armies, etc. And so on, *ad infinitum*.

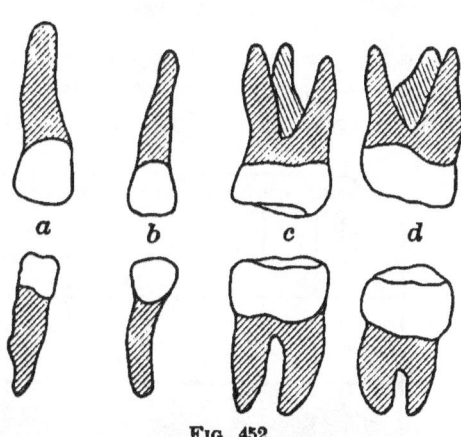

FIG. 452.

It is worthy of our notice that composition thus treated is the legitimate offspring of the day's studies. These pupils can not complain of having to write of something foreign to their comprehension or experience. The compositions they furnish are summaries of what they learn in a certain study, and such composition-work greatly assists the retention of matter in the memory.

I sincerely hope that my readers will give this a little

consideration. The practice of composing in pictures as well as in words seems eminently suggestive and worthy of imitation. Don't let us say, "What good can come from Nazareth?" but try the sketching, and see whether we can not, in ten or twenty years from now, beat the French in their models and patterns. The Centennial Exposition in Philadelphia has opened our eyes, as it did those of the Germans. To-day, our endeavors in art are vastly better and much in advance of those previous to 1876, but a systematic propagation of the art of sketching in our high-schools, academies, and other secondary schools, will do wonders, as it did in France and Germany.

3. More Devices, not Methods.

In the pretty, picturesque town of M——, in France, about twenty miles southeast of Sedan, I visited several schools with the view to mining them for treasures of methods of

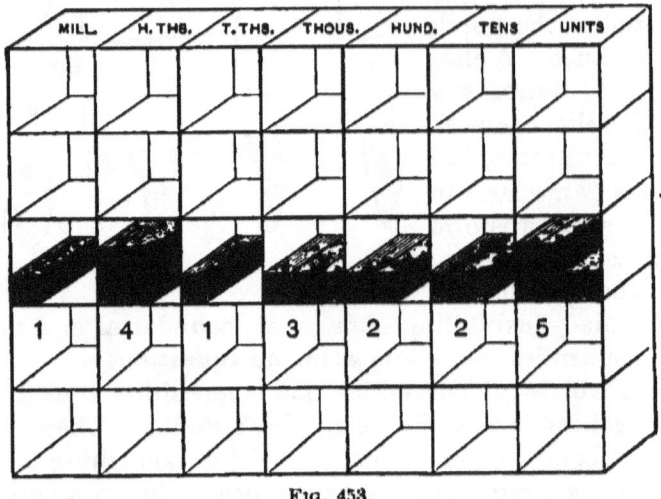

Fig. 453.

teaching such as I found in Germany and Holland; but I was very much disappointed until the rector who took me around was called away. Being left to myself, I began to search without help, and, chatting more at ease with the teachers, I unearthed a few things worthy of notice. The most practical thing was a set of pigeon-holes called a "numeration-box." Here is a sketch of it (Fig. 453).

Each compartment was large enough to hold nine little blocks of uniform size—only nine, not ten, as one would naturally suppose when speaking of numeration and notation. I inquired why not ten, and was told that just so soon as ten units were completed they were exchanged for a different-colored block which stood for one of the next higher order and was placed in the second compartment. Numeration, addition, and subtraction, multiplication and division, were practiced by means of this device, of course with rather limited numbers.

The same idea, illustrated by a similar home-made contrivance, I had met in the Female College of Dr. S. Lander,

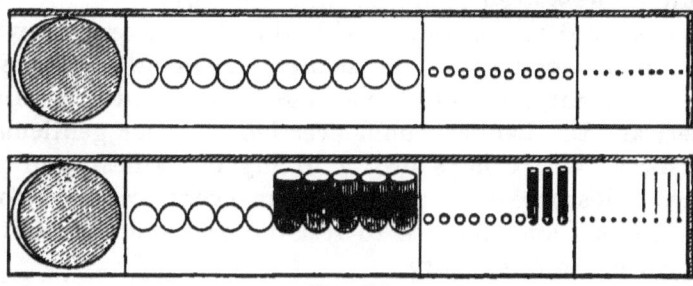

FIG. 454.

in Williamston, S. C. He had invented it, and you can imagine my astonishment when here in France I found it in general use. The idea of giving room for only nine units of each order in each compartment certainly is the same, whatever differences there may exist in the shape of the devices in France and South Carolina.

One would naturally suppose that room for ten units should be provided for as I did in my "numeration board," explained in "Chips from a Teacher's Workshop." (Fig. 454).

There will perhaps always be an honest difference of opinion as to whether nine or ten units of each order should be provided for. So much, however, is clear to my mind, that the fact of the blocks being of uniform size confuses the child, who can not see that the mere placing a block in the second compartment should raise its intrinsic value ; and if it is not to be thus understood, the whole device is valueless.

I understand that a digit being placed or moved to the left should change its value. A 6 in the second place is the same kind of a 6 used in the unit's place; but it will not do to make symbols of the *objects*. While on the numeration board ten pencils fastened together make a bundle of ten or one unit of the ten's column, the numeration-box does not permit the *fact* to be illustrated. It only *symbolizes the fact*, and that at the very moment when the fact itself should impress itself upon the child's mind.

I discussed this question with the French teacher, who grew quite eloquent on the matter—much more eloquent (and vehement, too) than the cool and level-headed genuine American, Dr. Lander, could ever be. Neither gentleman convinced me, perhaps owing to my obtuseness, and we agreed to disagree. By placing the two contrivances before my readers, I am prepared to rest the case and to submit it to the decision of the jury.

4. Also a Device, but oh!

Noticing a queer-looking, rubber, hose-like apparatus hanging in easy reach of a teacher in a French school, I inquired after its use, and was shocked to hear that this instrument was employed in flogging bad boys. "Why don't you use an old-fashioned switch or elastic cane?" I asked ; and with a cunning wink and a look of deep comprehension of all the bearings of the case, the teacher said, in subdued tone, "This stings better, clings to the body, and leaves no welts or discolored marks." Of course, this led us into a conversation on corporal punishment, which revealed the fact that we barbarians at home are better than these highly civilized people, who with all their varnish of artistic culture are ignorant of the true dignity of the human being which should be respected even in the child.

5. Ignorance and Chauvinism of French Teachers.

Several amusing incidents occurred during my visits in French schools. In N—— a teacher (a monk) asked me, when I was introduced to him as coming from Ohio, whether I had come overland or by way of Panama. Perhaps he mistook Oregon for Ohio. Another claimed that "the French language was the ruling language in Louisiana and other States (*sic*) which were originally settled by the French." That we in Ohio need not necessarily daily dread the loss of our scalps, being in such immediate neighborhood of the wild Indians (as they believe), is a thing impossible to make them see.

The worst case of "mistaken identity" I ever met with in a school-teacher I found in a French school, where the teacher taught a middle grade, something like the sixth school year, I should judge. It was a geography-lesson I heard, and America was the topic of the day. The teacher, without blushing—on the contrary, with the chest tone of conviction and the gestures of a stump-speaker—told his class that the United States were founded by men who were nurtured by the grand and lofty ideas of the French Revolution, which great event had actually changed not only the European modes of government, but those of America also. During the short recess which followed, my patriotism got the better of me, and I asked him for the date of the French Revolution, which he gave correctly, to wit, 1789. Then I asked him for the date of our national birthday, and his answer was a blank stare. I quietly told him it was 1776. I will do the man justice, though. He blushed like a girl of sixteen, remembering the vainglorious statement he had made to the class in my presence.

6. Molding Maps.

Interesting was a lesson in molding I saw in France in a class of young children studying geography. Nothing but putty and a small board of hard, polished wood was used. And thus the teacher proceeded:

"Children, spread out the putty evenly, as you see me do it. Now, when you see land level like this, without hills and valleys, we call it a plain. Do we live on a plain? No, we do not. Over yonder is a pretty big hill. Now, let us make a hill on the right side of the molding-board. 'Tis done. But, Charles, your hill is too steep; no person could climb it. Look through the window at the hill there. Is that as steep as your hill? Now suppose the hill was very high, so high that it reached into the clouds, what would we call it? A mountain, assuredly, a mountain. Just think, there is a mountain in *la belle* France, the top of which is always covered with ice and snow; it is more than 15,000 feet high." (The actor—pardon, the teacher—did not give the height in metres; perhaps he thought "15,000 feet" would make a deeper impression. Everything for effect!) "Now suppose that another hill is on the other side. Make one. Make it higher than your first hill. Very well, indeed! What is that low place between the hills called? Oh, yes; a valley. But if the hills were very near together, and the valley very steep, would you call it a valley? No? Quite right; we would call it a gully, or ravine."

Then he let the pupils see that water seeks its level by pouring water from the top of his hill of putty. It filled the ravine and formed a river. Now rivers, lakes, watersheds, and sundry topics were mentioned, cities were located, and soon the lesson was brought to a close. It was as good as going to the theatre to hear this excitable man talk and see his gestures. The pupils, of course, were like so many globules of mercury. *Moral.*—A sedate, calm, self-possessed teacher has quiet pupils; an excited teacher unruly pupils, and not only in France, but all the world over.

7. "Ad Oculos" Evidence.

As to the work done in French schools, it remains forever true that that depends entirely and exclusively upon the teacher. A good teacher is very conspicuous here, though, being a *rara avis*.

A little incident amused me greatly when attending a class which wrestled with the rudiments of geometry. A very active and demonstrative French teacher, and evidently a successful one, proved to his class that the sum of the three angles of any triangle is equal to two right angles. And he did it by first cutting a triangle out of a sheet of pasteboard; then drawing a straight line on the blackboard, he laid one side of the triangle on the line and drew the angle a. Then he placed angle b side by side with angle a, and of course angle c completed the space above the straight line. That there are two right angles on a straight line was known from the definition of right angles.

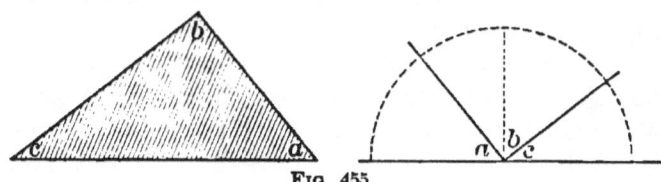

Fig. 455.

It was a demonstration *ad oculos*, though not new to me, having seen it used by Dr. R——, of New York. The amusing part of it was, that it was "performed" by a French teacher who was a born actor, and it afforded a rare sight, equaled, perhaps, only by Prof. Sauveur's inimitable movements when he intends to indicate a French word, but does not want to translate it into English. This same French teacher caused his pupils to make of pasteboard most of the geometrical bodies used in the class. The well-developed sense of form of the boys was proved by the faultless specimens exhibited. However, that feature of school-work I had seen so often in German schools that it did not interest me any longer.

CHAPTER XIV.

VIENNA.

1. A Successful and an Unsuccessful Lesson.

In a people's school in Vienna I chanced to hear a lesson on metals. Iron, lead, copper, silver, and gold were discussed, and numerous specimens handed around, rather to illustrate the lesson, as I thought, than to aid the comprehension of the subject-matter. The teacher lectured, only throwing in a question now and then, like, "Is it not so? Don't you think so too?" A handsome reference was made to a proverb and that was applied in a new way. A dim specimen of gold quartz gave occasion to quote the wise saw, "Not all is gold that glitters," and then amend it by adding, "Neither does everything glitter that is gold." One feature of the lesson struck me as worthy of mention. When the weight of different metals was spoken of, it was difficult to convince the pupils that gold is heavier than copper. But the teacher showed an Austrian copper kreutzer (worth one cent) and a German golden ten-mark piece (worth $2.50). Both coins are of the same size and thickness. He laid the two on the scale, and thus proved that gold outweighs copper. No better *ad oculos* proof could be brought.

When the methods of obtaining gold from mines were touched, the digging and washing were first mentioned, then the crushing of ore; and thus the teacher lectured: "The quartz is brought up from the mine" (a specimen was handed around); "it is laid under a heavy iron column which vibrates up and down, and with its tremendous weight crushes the ore, so that it becomes fine sand. The little gold leaves that adhered to the mineral are thus loosened. The column is worked up and down by cog-wheels, as this sketch shows." (Teacher drew the figure on the board.) "Now the question arises, How to separate the gold from the sand? It is done by giving the gold a friend that takes hold of it, namely, quicksilver." (Specimen is shown, and its affinity for gold proved.) "This unites with the gold and gathers up all the small particles loosened from the mineral.

"Now the gold is severed from the mineral, but the next question arises, How to separate the quicksilver from the gold? This is done by letting the quicksilver evaporate in a furnace. The gold remains in the bottom of the crucible. Thus the gold is set free from useless matter." The manner in which the teacher presented facts might have been very interesting to older pupils, and on the surface the lesson appeared a highly successful one. But, while I must admit that the pupils followed him in his "lecture" very attentively, I doubt whether their being left mere passive recipients of knowledge insured the success which he expected.

In another grade of a similar school I witnessed a lesson in physics which on the surface appeared a most unsuccessful one. Magnetism and electricity was the

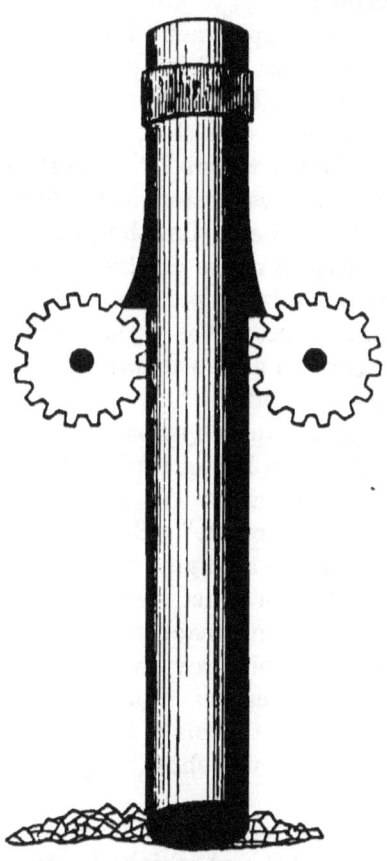

FIG. 456.

subject. The experiments performed miscarried in many instances, because the pupils who performed them did not employ that care and circumspection which is so necessary with apparatus for illustrating this subject. But the teacher made his pupils work out every problem, think out every conclusion, and be as self-active in the pursuit of knowledge as they could be. He never made a positive statement, never announced a result himself, but allowed and even begged the pupils to do that for him, "to help him a little," as he craftily termed it.

One experiment failed also under the skillful hands of the teacher, and, when he appeared much worried (not that he was so, but he wanted to appear so), he said: "I want to prove this and that, and my experiment has failed; what can be the reason?" Suggestions were made by the pupils, and each was tested, until some one's suggestion proved to be right, namely, that the glass rod had not been rubbed sufficiently to cause electricity which could be noticed. Thus, with laudable perseverance of both teacher and pupils, the desired effect was produced, and was the more gratifying, inasmuch as the cause of the failure had been discovered without aid.

The pupils' sympathy with the teacher's feigned discomfort, when his experiment failed, was touching to behold, and one said, "We believe your statement without seeing the experiment." But he replied: "No, children, though I heartily thank you for your confidence, I can not rest satisfied; you must see it to remember it." With rare circumspection the teacher kept order, looked after the language of his pupils, reviewed from time to time to keep the whole train of causes and effects vividly before the class; he animated the class to ever-new efforts, and, while seeming to be a "side-show," he really was a motive power of rare effect.

Is it necessary to state which of the two lessons was the successful and which the unsuccessful one?

2. An Object-Lesson in the Primary Grade.

It was in the practice-school of the classic "Paedagogium" in Vienna (Dr. Fr. Dittes was rector of the institution for many years), that I heard a lesson in arithmetic according to Grube. The children were just climbing from 10 to 20 in numbers, and solved such examples as $8+6$, $9+8$, $7+5$, etc. Every example was solved by doing (that is, performing it with match-sticks and other objects) and thinking. At the close of the lesson, all "helps" were laid aside, and examples were solved orally alone. The subject is too well known to sketch this beautiful lesson.

Then followed a language-lesson, which had for its subject "The Winter." A large picture (published by Eduard Hoelzel, in Vienna) was used. It is a magnificent winter landscape. In the background was seen a city, with smoke-stacks, church-steeples, etc. On the left, a road with a blacksmith's shop; on the right, a pond on which children skated; in the foreground, a coasting-slide and a group of children making a snow-man, were seen. The picture offered several other interesting scenes, such as cutting ice on the pond, sleighing, shoveling snow, etc. High up, in the gray, wintry air were seen crows. The hill-sides, roads, roofs, trees, and bushes were covered with snow. This picture is quite large and can be folded together. It belongs to a series of four pictures (mounted on muslin) representing the four seasons. I found these lovely pictures in many primary schools on the Continent of Europe, they are even more frequently provided in England than in Germany and France.

I can not sketch the entire lesson. Only one episode is vividly imprinted on my memory. I will endeavor to reproduce it, for it is a proof of how consistently little children of six years can "reason out things," and how well they talk when they have something to say:

Teacher. "What kind of a bird is this?"

Pupil. "A crow."

Teacher. "What do you notice on the snow around the bird?"

Pupil. "Many of the crow's footprints."

Teacher. "What do they tell you?"

Pupil. "That the bird must have hopped about there."

Teacher. "What may it want there?"

Pupil. "It is looking for food; it may be hungry."

Teacher. "Is the crow a shy bird, or as free and easy as a sparrow?"

Pupil. "I think it is a very shy bird."

Teacher. "Where does it build its nest?"

Pupil. "High up in the trees of the woods, far away from houses."

Teacher. "What, then, may be the reason of its coming so near to the blacksmith's shop, where boys are playing and dogs are kept?"

Pupil. "Because it is likely to find food near a shop like that."

Teacher. "Yes, but, if it is so shy a bird as you say it is, I should think it would not dare to come so near men and their houses?"

Pupil. "Well, I think it wouldn't if it could find any food in the fields. But don't you see the fields are covered with deep snow! how will a poor crow get food there? So it comes near the blacksmith's shop. It is very hungry, and I think those crows high up in the air have sent this one down to see whether there is any food to be found. If they get a chance, they will come, too, and get some."

Teacher. "Yes, dear, that's very well said. I think that must be it."

The language of the school-children in Vienna is very good. The absence of those detestable dialects found near the Rhine, in Berlin, in Bavaria, and especially in Switzerland, makes teaching in Vienna delightful. Aside from the word "halt," used perhaps too frequently, the German of the people in Vienna is very good.

3. A Lesson in Grammar.

A very instructive lesson, illustrating the "constructive method" in grammar, was given in my presence in Vienna. The subject of the lesson was the use of prepositions requiring the "genitive case." The so-called adverbial prepositions *instead of, for the sake of, without* or *outside, within* or *inside, in virtue of, according to, in spite of, on account of, for the sake of, notwithstanding, in consequence of, in behalf of, in presence of, in the midst of,* and numerous others, were placed on the board, and it was required to introduce or apply them in sentences all of which stood in connection and formed a composition. Since the children of Vienna, as a rule, speak the German language singularly free from grammatical errors, the cases dependent upon prepositions make little difficulty. While children in other parts of Germany avoid a noun in the genitive case and substitute the nominative or the preposition *of (von)* the children in Vienna say correctly, for instance, " *Des Wetters wegen,*" " *In Gegenwart des Lehrers,*" " *Diesseits des Flusses,*" etc.

The work I saw was class-work, and all the pupils worked to make a readable composition. The above-mentioned prepositional phrases, together with simpler prepositions, such as *above, below, along,* were used, and the result was a very pretty description of the city of Gratz. When this was finished, the prepositions were underscored, and the nouns dependent upon them marked. It was a most interesting lesson, which proved that grammar may be learned by doing better than by learning it by heart *verbatim et literatim*. But the best part of the lesson followed when the teacher suggested to the pupils that they might make similar compositions. The result of this work was very gratifying. One of the compositions was a description of "A Pretty Spot," somewhat like the one in my "German by Practice," which is reproduced here.

The reader who has not studied German grammar will perhaps object to the use of the term "prepositional phrases" as used above; but it is really the most convenient name for such expressions. I reproduce also a little narrative which was used to illustrate the use of prepositions governing both the dative and accusative case. It is reasonable to suppose that children find more pleasure in thus practically learning grammar than in first learning rules by heart and then applying them.

"*A Pretty Spot.*—*Not far from* our house stands a pretty grove. People from the city often come to have a picnic in it *during* the hot season. *Above* a mighty rock *in the middle* of the grove a spring bubbles forth. Its water flows along *within* a narrow bed between flowery banks. *This side of* the brooklet a foot-path leads toward the mill-dam. *Below* the latter stands an old mill leaning against the rocks. A narrow bridge without a railing leads across the brook, and *on the other side of* it a shady arbor invites the weary wanderer to take a rest. *Inside of* the old building the mill clatters lively, and *outside of* it the great mill-wheel turns slowly. *Despite* its slow course, it sets the whole machinery in motion. The splashing water and the shade-trees cause a pleasant coolness, even *during* the hottest season. I like to sit here with my books *on account of* the beautiful scenery before me."

"*The Light of the Faithful Sister.*—Many years ago there lived a girl in a lonely fisherman's hut on the coast of the North Sea. Father and mother were dead, and her brother was far out on the sea. With a longing heart she remembered the dead, and waited patiently for the return of the absent brother. When the brother went to sea, she had promised him that she would place a light in the window every night. The light would shine far over the sea, and it was to tell him that his sister Elke was still alive, and waiting for him. She faithfully kept her promise. Every evening she placed her lamp near the window, and many an hour in the daytime was spent by her in looking out on the waves and passing vessels. Whenever a ship hove in sight, she hoped it would bring her dearly beloved brother back to her. Months passed, years passed, but the brother did not return. Perhaps he was shipwrecked. Elke grew old and gray, but, still faithful to her pledge, she often sat near the window of her lonely hut, gazing out upon the sea, and not an evening passed on which she did not place on the window-sill a lamp well provided with oil. Thus she waited and waited; she waited fifty years. One night the light went out; her window remained dark. The neighbors saw it from afar and cried, "Ah, at last, Elke's brother has come!" They hurried to her hut to welcome him home. When they opened the door they found old Elke dead and stiff, still leaning toward the window, as though still gazing out on the troubled waves. Beside her stood the lamp, the light of which had gone out."

4. MANUAL TRAINING-SCHOOLS IN VIENNA.

Introduction.—It is difficult to decide which of the two cities—Vienna or Leipsic—accomplishes most in manual training. In Leipsic the efforts are more concentrated; in Vienna they are spread over the different parts of the city, and I believe in due course of time this wise policy will result in popularizing the work sufficiently to call for its introduction into the common schools. At present (March, 1888) manual training is not a part of the curriculum of the common schools, though all the manual training-schools are held in public-school houses. The work is done after school hours; but the popularity which manual occupation has obtained among pupils, teachers, and school authorities in Vienna bids fair to predict an early introduction of manual training into the daily programme.

The manual training normal school in Vienna is rapidly increasing the number of instructors who can teach the occupations rationally and methodically, and teachers who have a professional preparation are considered the *conditio sine qua non* in Austria as well as in Germany. I am aware of the stubborn fact that the average American school official argues differently. Professional training is not so much in demand here as in Europe. The question whether a normal-school graduate or a college graduate is the better prepared teacher is still a mooted question with us. We are very apt to shirk responsibility by introducing new methods without the wherewithal to maintain them. Singing, drawing, objective teaching, Kindergarten occupations, and other things, were introduced without much, if any, preparation on the part of the teachers. The result has been, as Dr. Hailmann has so convincingly shown, that they were seized by "the machine." I am very much afraid that manual training will have a similar fate, because not a sufficient number of instructors can be had in America to teach the work to justify so broad and general an introduction as recently took place in New York. Still, I shall be happy to find that I have been mistaken; and, if this book contributes its mite toward helping manual training along, it will find in that its best reward.

Mr. Alois Bruhns, the rector of one of the manual training-schools, has published a hand-book which is used exclusively in Vienna. The sketches of pupils' work on the following pages are selected from this hand-book; but before I selected them I convinced myself that they were copies of pupils' efforts. I found the boys at work at them, and what they accomplished agreed exactly with the drawings I here submit.

They are typical selections, and are here inserted to show:

1. That the occupations of the boys are more like those in Leipsic than those in Paris. The boys produce articles of utility, and not merely exercises for the purpose of learning the use of hands and tools.

2. That, like the work in Leipsic, that in Vienna, is methodically arranged and well graded.

3. That in wood-carving and modeling they accomplish more than in Leipsic, though less than in Paris.

4. That they confine themselves in Vienna to pasteboard work, joiner's and carpenter's work, wood-carving, and modeling, and that they have not introduced metal-work as yet.

My observations in the Vienna manual training-schools lead me to say that their educational influence upon the boys is far greater than that of "travail manuel" schools in Paris, because the teachers are specially prepared for this kind of work and are public-school teachers, while the instructors of the "travail manuel" schools in Paris are artisans who pay more attention to the technical results than to the educational influence which the work may have upon the pupils. Nowhere in Germany and in Vienna did I find any non-professional teachers at work in manual training-schools except in one instance. This case is worth mentioning. In Leipsic I met a master-joiner as instructor in the common school who sneered at American tools, saying that the waving handles of our axes and other "so-called" improvements (*sic*) were useless; that for effectiveness he wanted straight-handled German tools, etc. In justice to the institution I must say that he stood alone in his opinion; all others present—instructors and students—agreed that American tools far surpass the German in durability and usefulness.

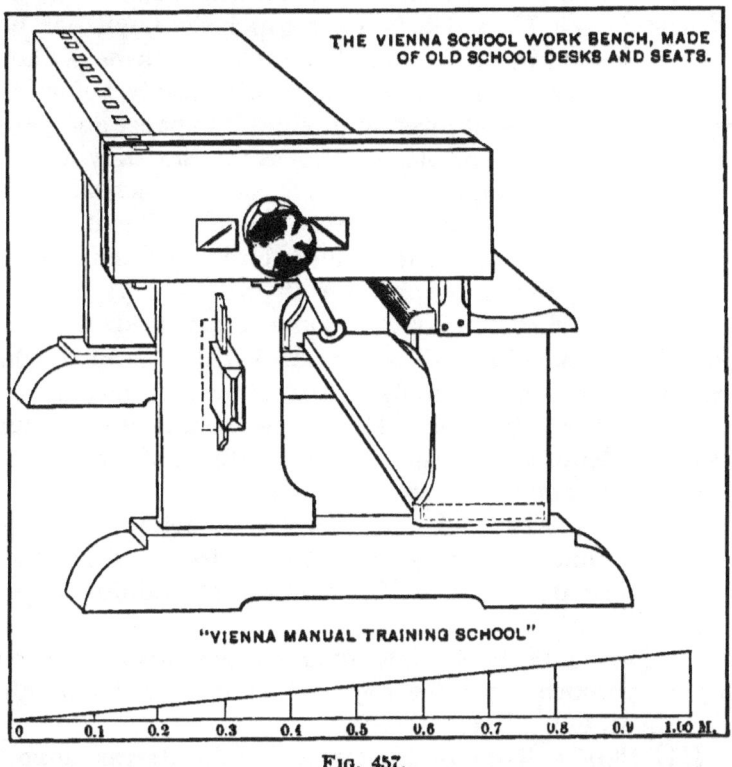

Fig. 457.

National pride is a virtue, but it becomes a vice as soon as it is blind to the excellent progress other nations are making, and effectually prevents the individual from improving himself. It matters not whether we find it in an Austrian workman, or in an American teacher who objects to "German methods" on the plea that this is America, etc. We all know the song; and we know the author, too.

A Work-bench.—The reader will find in the following illustrations some attempts at "doing exercises," but they are not by far as numerous here as in Paris, and the articles made are, indeed, very elaborate affairs, as will be seen by comparing them with the work done in Paris. Like all other schools of this kind, those in Vienna insist upon drawing and sketching. No article is made which the pupil has not first represented in lines on the flat surface with or without shading. Only when the object stands clearly before his inner eye will he be allowed to produce it in paper and pasteboard, in wood, clay, or plaster, etc., as the case may be.

In Vienna I found a novel and rather practical work-bench made of old-fashioned school-desks and seats. This bench enables the teacher to do more class-work than he can do where single work-benches are in use. I copy a sketch of this bench, since it may give some of my readers an impetus to do likewise with old, discarded double desks that drag out their existence, under a load of dust, in the garret or cellar of the school-house. Making use of this old furniture may considerably decrease the cost of a first outfit for a manual training-school or class (Fig. 457).

I. *Pupils' Work.*—A few samples of articles made of pasteboard and paper may show the variety and exactness of the work done in the Vienna manual training-schools (Figs. 458–465).

II. *Pupils' Work.*—A few samples of joiner's work, showing the practical bent the boys get in the Vienna manual training-schools (Figs. 466–476).

III. *Pupils' Work* in joinery and carpentering done in the Vienna manual training-schools (Figs. 477–491).

IV. *Pupils' Work.*—The work in turning is not by far as tedious here in Vienna as I found it in Paris. The desire to apply the skill gained by making articles of use is well illustrated by the few typical specimens I here offer (Figs. 492–510).

MANUAL TRAINING-SCHOOLS IN VIENNA. 403

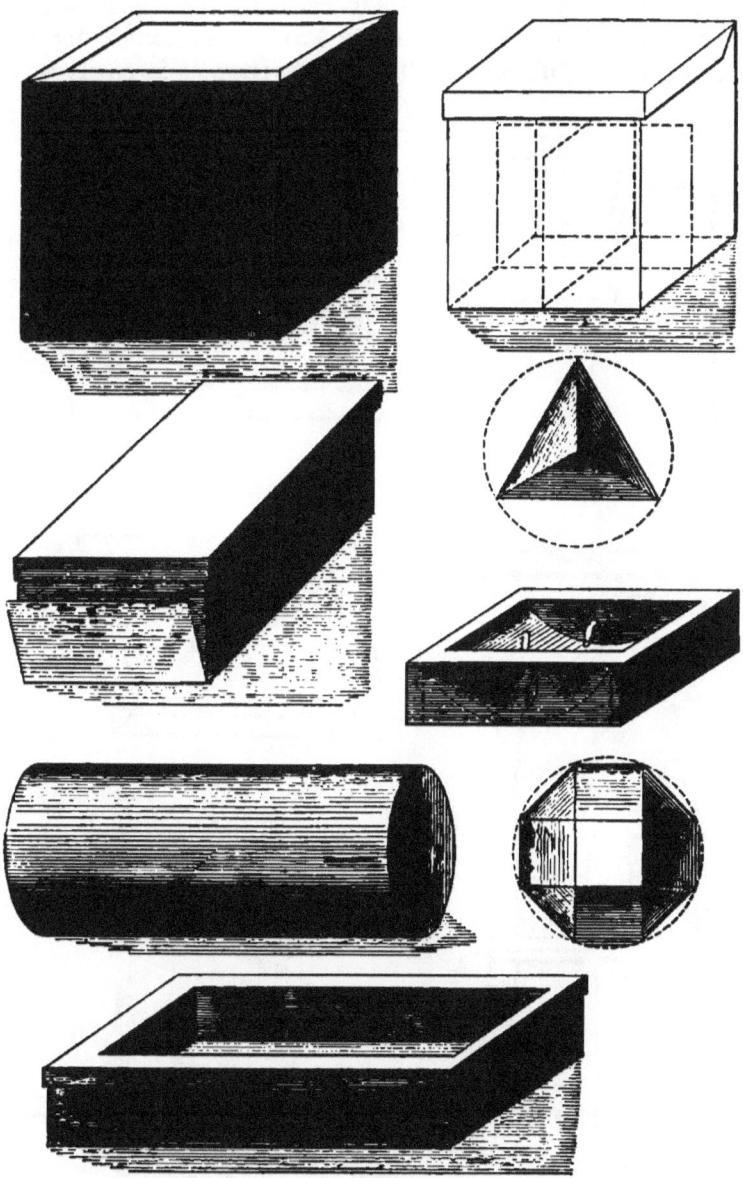

FIGS. 458–465.

404   VIENNA.

V. *Pupils' Work.*—In wood-carving the work is also more practical in Vienna than in Paris. Although decoration is the chief object of all wood-carving, it is easily seen

Figs. 466–476.

MANUAL TRAINING-SCHOOLS IN VIENNA.

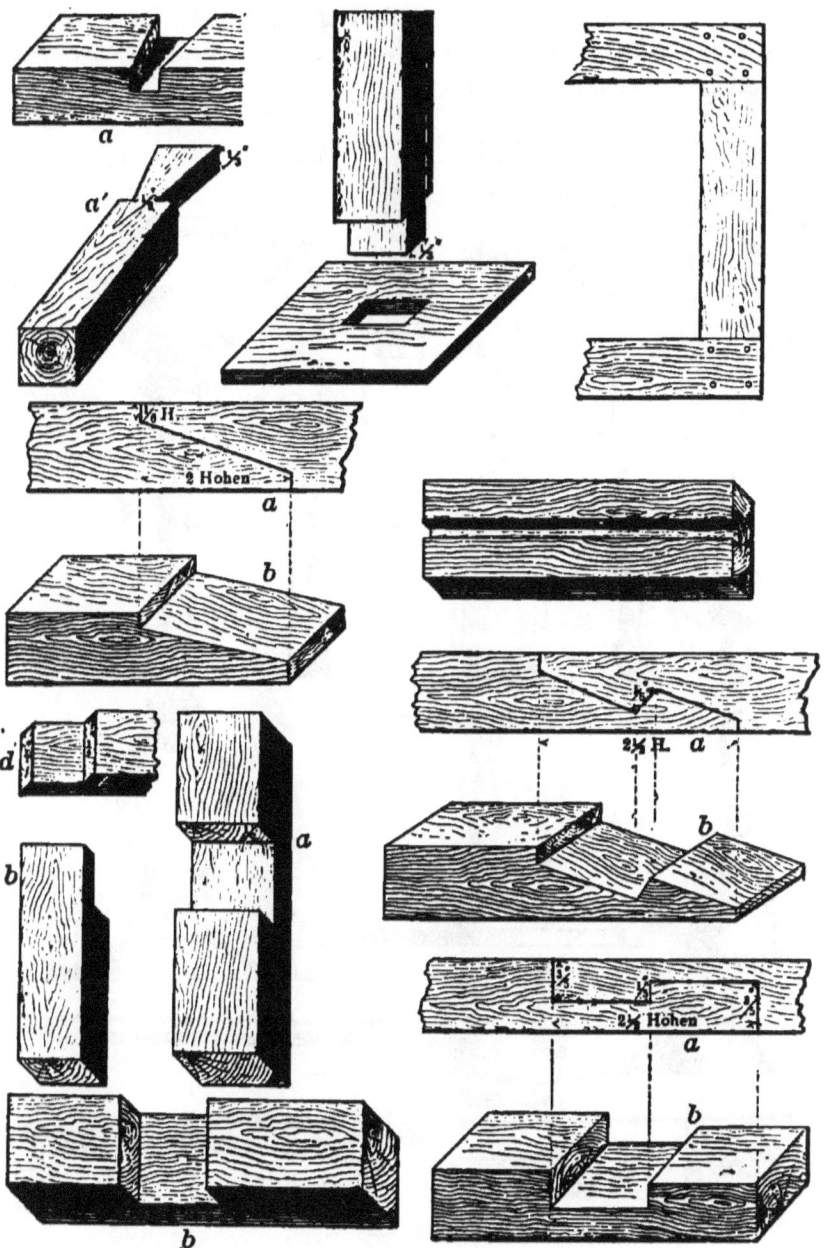

Figs. 477-491.

406   VIENNA.

from the following specimens that the boys will labor with more pleasure at this kind of work than at doing exercises exclusively (Figs. 511–518).

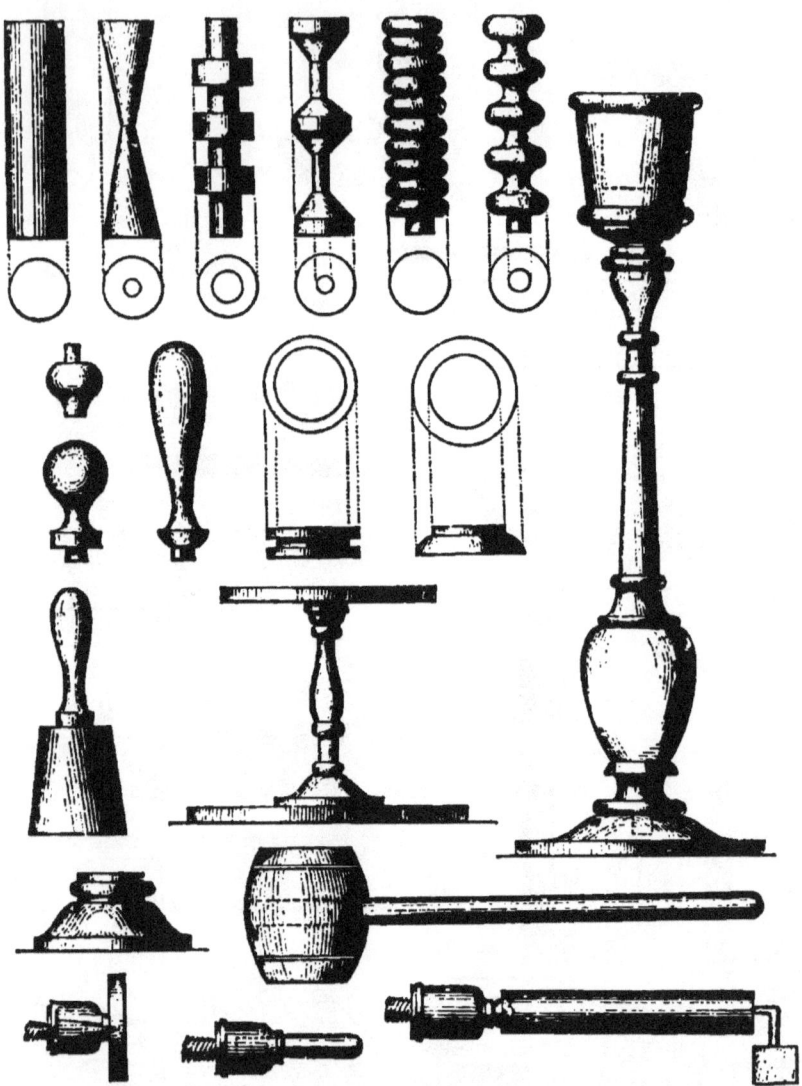

FIGS. 492–510.

MANUAL TRAINING-SCHOOLS IN VIENNA. 407

VI. *Pupils' Work.*—Though all the work done in the manual training-schools in Vienna is commendable and even praiseworthy, the best is that in *modeling in clay and casting in plaster.* Instead of many specimens, I will offer

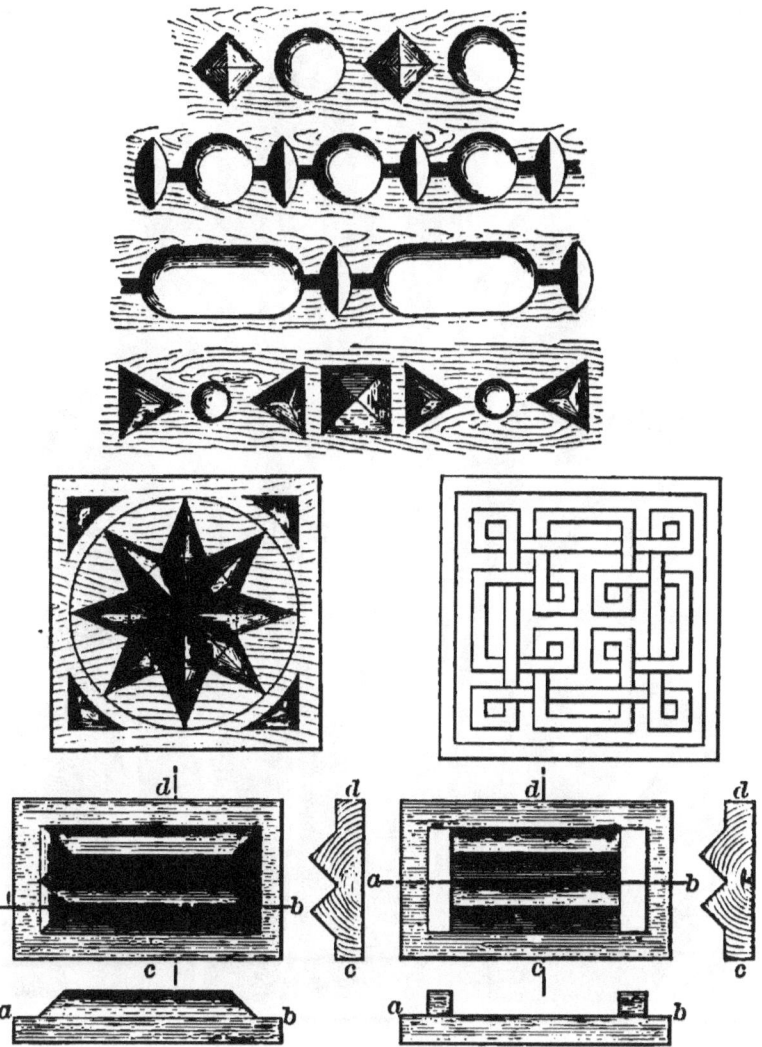

FIGS. 511-518.

408 VIENNA.

only one of the handsomest figures I found in the collection. It will speak more eloquently than I can do it of the development of the form, sense, and skill of the hand secured by modeling. I had frequently seen drawings made by pupils

Fig. 519.

shaded beautifully; but here I saw the drawing executed in clay and plaster by boys about fourteen years of age. Needless to say that I admired them, and, I am afraid, showed it too plainly (Fig. 519).

CHAPTER XV.

SWITZERLAND AND ALSACE.

1. SIMPLICITY IN THE WRONG PLACE.

SIMPLICITY in manners and customs is a proverbial virtue in the citizen of a republic ever since the time of Lycurgus; and Cincinnatus and Curius, Fabricius and Fabius are noted examples of ancient Rome of that simplicity and civil virtue which seem to vanish before the conquering progress of culture. Without being conscious of it, we connect in our mind simplicity with honesty, and, though luxuriously inclined ourselves, we can not but do homage to a true example of simplicity when we meet it. I went to Switzerland, and there found what I never expected to see—a sample of simplicity in the wrong place, a misdirected simplicity, coupled with a miserly economy and a brutal honesty—mark the words!

The Germans, and in these latter days the French also, consider the best barely good enough for their children. They are therefore always on the alert to catch what improvements are offered in common-school education. I will not speak of material things, such as books, etc., but will confine myself to the world of ideas. There is no new idea in the realm of education that they do not instantly welcome; no device whose usefulness they will not test without delay; no method that they will not at once apply in some experimental station; no principle which they will not quickly seize to serve them as a subject for discussion; no branch of study which they will not give a place in the curriculum of some school.

It is an undeniable fact that the German school lives in the most unrivaled luxury with regard to ideas, branches of study, text-books, and other material things. Whether the fact that it is equally well supplied with teaching forces is the natural consequence of the undying aspiration and remarkable activity of the German school, or whether the latter is the result of the fact that the schools are manned with professional teachers, is a question of no importance here; for Switzerland, where I found a deplorable absence of that luxury referred to, has also a profession of teaching.

Having spent nearly nine months in France, Germany, Austria, and other countries of Europe, I came to Switzerland fully prepared to witness in the land of Pestalozzi a progress in the schools of the people such as would take my breath away; but never was I more disappointed than when I did see schools in Switzerland. The poverty, or let me say the simplicity, of these schools in aims, in methods, and in equipment fairly disgusted me. I confined my observations to "people's schools"—that is, the primary schools, which in many places have a four years' course. Spending some time in many classes of various schools, and comparing the courses of study and the methods applied, I gathered a fair picture of the *status quo* of the Swiss public school for the lower strata of society, which does not satisfy me.

In order to be able to defend this sweeping assertion in case it should be attacked, I provided myself with the printed courses of instruction, the manuals used by the teachers, and some samples of pupils' work which were offered me by the teachers as excellent specimens. Judging from these proofs in black and white and from ocular evidence, I concluded that the proverbial republican simplicity is here found in the wrong place. Since education in Switzerland is, as with us, not a matter of legislation of the Confederation, but of each separate canton, it is reasonable to suppose that my experiences are exceptional ones, and I am perfectly willing to offer the benefit of the doubt to any one who feels unjustly treated by my criticism.

Let me proceed to state in what way I met with the "simplicity" referred to. I purposely avoid mentioning the names of the cities I visited. The results in drawing are very poor. There is a manual for instruction in drawing, in use in one of the larger cities, showing the work to be done in four years. This course is primitive to a fault. It can not be alleged to be an antiquated document, for it bears the date January, 1887. At the beginning of the fourth year, after three years' practice on slate and paper, the pupil's sense of form is still fed with "forms" like these:

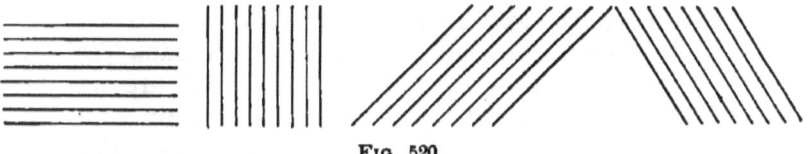

Fig. 520.

In arithmetic there is equally little progress made. In the primer grade only addition and subtraction within the compass of 1 and 15 are practiced. In the second grade the children learn to count up to 100 by two's, three's, etc., and begin multiplication; at the close of the second year, easy examples in division, such as $15 \div 3 = 5$. In the third year the compass is widened to 1,000, but each of the four fundamental rules is treated separately. No Grube method, or indeed any approach to it here. Grade four works long and short division examples in abstract numbers and is introduced into the world of denominate numbers. No fractions! And when by rare chance an expression, such as "⅓ of 16," escapes the lips of the teacher, he intends it to mean, "Divide 16 by 3 and tell the remainder." I inquired very anxiously after fractions, and was told that there was no attempt made at teaching fractions till the pupils entered the intermediate grades. Compare with this mental poverty what I observed in other schools. See, for instance, page 152, "The Augusta School in Berlin."

I awaited a lesson in geography anxiously, to see whether

in that branch also the same "conservatism" was exhibited. To be sure it was! The geographical horizon of the pupils in the fourth year did not extend beyond the little landscape surrounding the city, and the maps made by the pupils of this home geography were the rudest possible. I was requested to look them over. The pride of the teacher over this work was so evident that I asked him to let me have a few to show my friends in America. The request flattered him, and he selected a few of the best, which I am ready to exhibit as proofs of my statement. From these best ones one may judge of the worst.

In language the results seemed anything but satisfactory, the teachers having to contend with an abominable dialect. How narrow the teachers of these Swiss schools are may be seen from the fact that they actually make a difference in pronunciation of ei and ai, two diphthongs for which the German language has but one sound: Rhein and Rain, mein and Main, are indistinguishable by the ear. Exercises in orthography are painfully monotonous, and the school-tone in reading and reciting found here is so abominable that it resembled a sing-song such as can be surpassed only by the old-fashioned oral spelling of the American school of times gone by: "C-o-n, Con, s-t-a-n, stan, Constan, t-i, ti, Constanti, n-o, no, p-l-e, ple, Constantinople."

In singing, too, the results were unsatisfactory. No two-part music in the fourth school year, nothing but the simple melodies of popular and sacred airs, did I hear. Since it is reasonable to suppose that teachers and pupils put their best foot foremost when a visitor is present, I take it for granted that they regaled me with the best they could set before me. My visit occurred during the last month of the school year, and it can therefore not be urged as an excuse that the course of each school year had only just begun. The school year in Europe generally closes at Easter.

A hand-book for teachers, entitled "Principles of Instruction in the Primary Schools," which I procured, is full of narrow views and antiquated methods. No wonder the teachers looked like sleepy horses in a treadmill! Nowhere here did I find that fire of enthusiasm, that personal magnetism, so often observed in other European and in American schools. Oh, what a disappointment that was for me, who had come to Switzerland with eager expectation to find ideas and practices worthy of being transplanted to the fertile soil of the New World! Three cities I visited in Switzerland, and much money I spent in traveling and in costly hotels, and found nothing worthy of note. I left the country sorry that I was poorer by a cherished illusion.

Still, I must not close this chapter without doing justice in some manner to the fact that reports of others are not in harmony with mine. Whether these people applied a different standard of measurement, or I happened to strike the wrong places, I can not say. I read glowing accounts of some special Swiss schools, regular mines of information regarding theory and practice, and the professional journals published in that country also are, as a rule, not so conservative and backward as one would think, judging from what I saw in the schools I visited; but my sense of justice will not permit me to gloss over what seemed to me faulty *in toto*.

In one place in Switzerland I found a school for dullards (such as I described on pages 77-91), the influence of which was noticeable in the other schools, since it raised their standard considerably. I also found manual training-schools, but nowhere so finely an organized one nor such brilliant results as in Prussia, Saxony, Austria, and France.

2. Industrial Education for Girls.

In Mülhausen (in Alsace) the schools have undergone great changes since Germany has regained it. Under the firm but wise management of Inspector Hipp, one improvement after another has been introduced, so that to-day the schools of this busy town rank among the best known in Alsace. The French rulers grievously sinned against the best interests of the province by neglecting school education. The buildings are still wretched, for the increase of pupils makes too great a demand upon the city treasury. Old factory-buildings are changed to school-houses, and it needs no fertile imagination to picture to one's self the inconveniences arising therefrom.

I found a "unicum" of a school here such as I hope never again to see—a school containing no less than sixty-two class-rooms, several offices, and the rector's dwelling, all in a conglomerate of buildings rickety and shabby. The pupils on the third floor must wait till the other floors are empty before they can be dismissed. The whole building is one great dangerous man-trap. In case of a fire, thousands of children's lives would be in danger. This school is a blot upon the fair reputation of the city of Mülhausen.

But what excellent work is done in this old building! Here is found an industrial school for boys, having four workshops. Here is also a most successful industrial school for girls. Compare these figures: Within the year 1887 the girls worked articles, such as stockings, shirts, tidies, etc., which were sold for 5,534·23 marks, the material having been furnished by the city authorities, and had cost 3,218·81 marks, so that the busy hands of the little girls had produced a value of 2,315·42 marks. This entire gain is used to furnish the schools of the city with means of instruction—charts, apparatus, musical instruments, tools, etc.

How practical the women are who teach in this department is seen from the fact that there is no waste. The bands or straps knitted by the six-year-old girls, on which they learn the different kinds of knitting, are sewed together to make pretty little petticoats. The pieces of muslin left over from cutting out aprons are sewed together for quilts, and thus all waste is prevented. The exhibition of girls' needlework was fully as interesting as that in Cologne.

That the work in this industrial school is no mere mechanical humdrum is seen from the care with which each article is drawn and cut according to given measurements. I append a few sketches which will illustrate this.

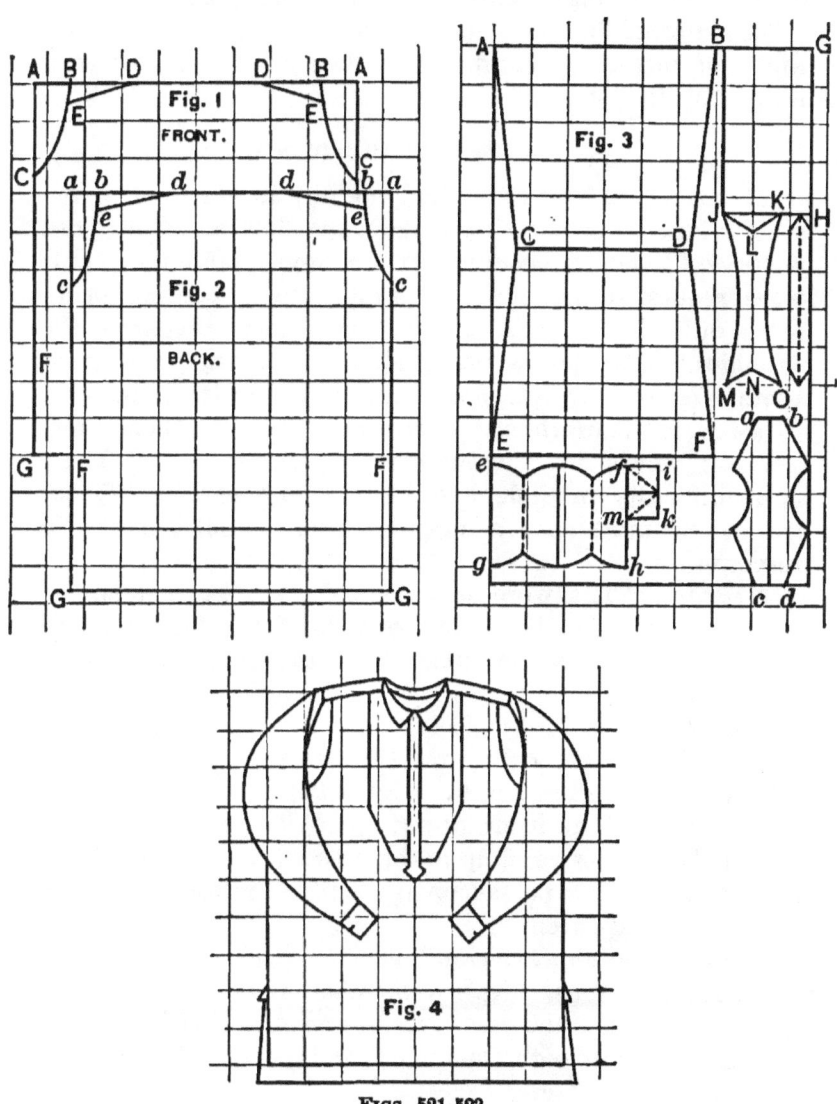

FIGS. 521-523.

The different benevolent societies of the city buy the articles made by the little school-girls. Thus, for instance, I find the following societies mentioned—"The Benevolent Society," "The Lying-in Hospital," "The Sisters of the Poor," "The Maternal Society"—as purchasers. Darning and other kinds of mending are important branches of needlework here in Mülhausen.

3. A Lesson in Philology.

It was a rare treat that I had one day in a school of Alsace, where I listened to a language-lesson. The word "*Kleinod*" (jewel) occurred in a sentence, and the pupils were requested to define or paraphrase it. There being some difficulty in this, the teacher asked, "Separate the syllables." The pupils hesitated, not knowing whether to write *Klein-od* or *Klei-nod;* but they finally determined to separate them thus, "*Klein-od.*" "Well, then, there are two words in one, namely, *Klein* and *od*. There is no difficulty in understanding the first part (*little*), but the second must have a meaning also. What is it?" No response.

Teacher. "The word is quite old. We have to search for its meaning in the oldest records of the German language. Who was the greatest of the gods in German mythology?"

Pupil. "*Odin.*"

Teacher. "Yes; Odin was the greatest of gods. And what did the word god mean originally?"

Pupil. "I think it meant *gut* (good)."

Teacher. "Yes; and up to the present day the word *gut* is used to signify a possession (goods). Mention a word in which this is apparent."

Pupil. "*Landgut* (farm)."

Teacher. "True. Now remember that *gut* (good or goods) and *od* are the same words, and mean as in ancient time so even now both *Gott* (God) and *gut* (good or goods). Now, what does *Kleinod* mean?"

Pupil. "It must mean a little possession, or perhaps a little treasure."

Teacher. "Exactly—some valuable goods, as precious stones, small, yet whose intrinsic value is greater than that of many bulky possessions. A synonym of *Kleinod* is *jewel*. Now, think of the opposite meaning of *Kleinod*."

Instantly the reply came, "It must be *Allod*."

Teacher. "Yes; state its meaning."

Pupil. "Possessions in land belonging to an ancient aristocratic family."

Teacher. "Correct; the allodial possessions could not be divided, but remained forever inalienable in a family. Such allods are still found in England, where only the eldest sons of aristocratic families inherit the lands and titles. From the explanation of such words as *Kleinod* and *Allod* you may judge how consistent the German language is in word-building."

The conversation did not last many minutes. But what an amount of thought-bearing information was given! What openings into other realms of thought were offered! What an interest was awakened among the pupils who thus "made the acquaintance of words"! This short episode of the lesson reminded me of that inscription over the gate of an Arabian school, "Here is a place where children are taught the beginning of words"; and again it reminded me of the fact that English and American children often use words thoughtlessly which might be to them as transparent as crystal if the dictionary were diligently used. Such a word as *atonement*, Latin as it looks and sounds, is yet an easy word to understand if built over again from at-one-ment. Children who are taught to apply to the dictionary acquire a remarkable command over the queen's English, while without it they forever remain as ignorant as my servant who "spelled" through a newspaper in his leisure hours, and thought "the constitutionality of a measure" meant the size of a bushel or yard-stick!

4. CRUMBS.—NOTES FROM THE SCHOOLS OF MÜLHAUSEN.

A good deal of sketching is done here, such as I described in other chapters of this book. The children talk with chalk as readily as they express their thoughts orally and in writing. Thus, I saw a boy go to the board and illustrate his recitation of the bees by sketching rapidly and very accurately the wings, head, and feet of a bee. Another, speaking of birds, sketched the characteristic forms of wings and beaks. This sketching is an enviable skill, and possible only where the practice of sketching is made a daily occurrence.

When I inquired for the causes of the almost faultless orthography I noticed in the composition books, I was told that they had a rule in these schools which made mistakes almost impossible—to wit, "Do not correct but avoid mistakes." Every word dictated is looked at and dissected before it is written. If, perchance, a pupil does err, he is made to erase it and insert the correct form so carefully that the productions or reproductions are absolutely faultless.

While the recitations here are generally individual where the pupils' own thoughts play an important *rôle*, a novel thing to me was the perfection in class recitation. I heard classes speak in chorus as though it was but one voice. Poems were thus recited faultless in emphasis and accent. In no other school in all my wanderings through Europe did I meet a similar perfection in concert recitation.

Each teacher here keeps a "diarium," a day-book, in which the subject of each lesson is noted down. When the inspector, whose desire is to keep the different classes of the same grade on a level, enters a school-room, he never fails to inspect this book, and he frequently takes occasion to enter a note of commendation or reproof. The teachers are nearly all of Prussian descent, not natives of Alsace, and the use of the French language is consistently discouraged.

The citizens of Alsace and Lorraine are still somewhat obstinate against the German rule, but they are unanimous in praising the common schools with which they have been blessed. During the French rule their schools were kept by superannuated men, who "did much in patriotism" but little in real teaching. I gathered these facts from men of the people, with whom I took occasion to speak of the schools while traveling through Alsace.

THE END.

INTERNATIONAL EDUCATION SERIES.

Edited by WILLIAM T. HARRIS, LL. D.

A library for teachers and school-managers, and text-books for normal classes—including works on *Historical, Critical, Theoretical,* and *Practical Education.*

VOLUMES NOW READY:

Vol. I.—**The Philosophy of Education.** By JOHANN KARL FRIEDRICH ROSENKRANZ, Doctor of Theology and Professor of Philosophy at the University of Königsberg. Translated from the German by ANNA C. BRACKETT. Price, $1.50.

Vol. II.—**A History of Education.** By Professor F. V. N. PAINTER, of Roanoke College, Virginia. Price, $1.50.

Vol. III.—**The Rise and Early Constitution of Universities.** WITH A SURVEY OF MEDIÆVAL EDUCATION. By S. S. LAURIE, LL. D., Professor of the Institutes and History of Education in the University of Edinburgh. Price, $1.50.

Vol. IV.—**The Ventilation and Warming of School Buildings.** By GILBERT B. MORRISON, Teacher of Physics and Chemistry in Kansas City High-School. Price, 75 cents.

Vol. V.—**The Education of Man.** By FRIEDRICH FROEBEL. Translated from the German by W. N. HAILMAN, Ph. D., Superintendent of Public Schools at La Porte, Indiana. Price, $1.50.

Vol. VI.—**Elementary Psychology and Education.** By Dr. J. BALDWIN, author of "Art of School Management," etc. Price, $1.50.

Vol. VII.—**The Senses and the Will.** By W. PREYER, Professor of Physiology in Jena. Translated from the original German by H. W. BROWN, Teacher in the State Normal School at Worcester, Mass. Part I of THE MIND OF THE CHILD. Price, $1.50.

Vol. VIII.—**Memory.** By DAVID KAY, F. R. G. S. Price, $1.50.

Vol. IX.—**The Development of the Intellect.** By W. PREYER, Professor of Physiology in Jena. Part II of THE MIND OF THE CHILD. Price, $1.50.

Vol. X.—**How to Study Geography.** By FRANCIS W. PARKER, Principal of the Cook Co. (Ill.) Normal School. Price, $1.50.

Vol. XI.—**Education in the United States: A History from the Earliest Settlements.** By RICHARD A. BOONE, Professor of Pedagogy, Indiana University.

D. APPLETON & CO., Publishers,
New York, Boston, Chicago, Atlanta, San Francisco.

EDUCATION IN RELATION TO MANUAL INDUSTRY.

By Arthur MacArthur, LL. D.   12mo.   Cloth, $1.50.

"Mr. MacArthur's able treatise is designed to adapt to the usual methods of instruction a system of rudimental science and manual art. He describes the progress of industrial education in France, Belgium, Russia, Germany, and Great Britain, and the establishment of their professional schools. The technical schools of the United States are next reviewed. Mr. MacArthur is anxious that the State governments should take up the subject, and enable every girl and boy to receive a practical education which would fit them for use in this world. This valuable book should be carefully read and meditated upon. The discussion is of high importance."—*Philadelphia Public Ledger.*

"The importance of this book can not be too greatly urged. It gives a statistical account of the industries of various countries, the number of workmen and workwomen, and the degree of perfection attained. America is behind in native production, and, when we read of the importation of foreign workmen in simple manufacture such as glass, it is a stimulus for young men to train themselves early as is done in foreign countries. The necessity of training-schools and the value and dignity of trades are made evident in this work. It is particularly helpful to women, as it mentions the variety of employments which they can practice, and gives the success already reached by them. It serves as a history and encyclopædia of facts relating to industries, and is very well written."—*Boston Globe.*

"The advocates of industrial education in schools will find a very complete manual of the whole subject in Mr. MacArthur's book."—*Springfield Republican.*

"A sensible and much-needed plea for the establishment of schools for industry by the state, supported by the practical illustration of what has been accomplished for the good of the state by such schools in foreign countries. Great Britain has never regretted the step she took when, recognizing at the Crystal Palace Exhibition her inferiority in industrial art-work, she at once established the South Kensington Museum, with its annexed art-schools, at a cost of six million dollars."—*The Critic.*

"The aim of the book is succinctly stated, as it ought to be, in the preface: 'What is industrial education? What are its merits and objects, and, above all, what power does it possess of ministering to some useful purpose in the practical arts of life?' These are questions about which we are deeply concerned in this country, and the author has essayed to answer them, not by an abstract discussion of technical instruction, but by giving a full and accurate account of the experiments in industrial training which have been actually and successfully carried out in Europe."—*New York Sun.*

"A most interesting and suggestive work on a matter of immediate and universal importance."—*New York Daily Graphic.*

"An admirable book on a much-neglected subject. Those countries have made the most rapid advance in the line of new industries which have paid the most attention to the methods here recommended of primary instruction. The land that neglects them will sooner or later cease to be in the front ranks of applied science and the useful arts."—*New York Journal of Commerce.*

For sale by all booksellers; or sent by mail, post-paid, on receipt of price.

New York: D. APPLETON & CO., 1, 3, & 5 Bond Street.

BOOKS FOR TEACHERS.

Spencer's Education:
INTELLECTUAL, MORAL, AND PHYSICAL. Divided into four chapters: What Knowledge is of most Worth?—Intellectual Education—Moral Education—Physical Education. Price, $1.25.

Bain's Education as a Science.
The author views the "teaching art" from a scientific point of view, and tests ordinary experiences by bringing them to the criterion of psychological law. Price, $1.75.

Bain's On Teaching English,
WITH DETAILED EXAMPLES, AND AN INQUIRY INTO THE DEFINITION OF POETRY. Price, $1.25.

Johonnot's Principles and Practice of Teaching.
This is a practical book by an experienced teacher. The subject of education is treated in a systematic and comprehensive manner, and shows how rational processes may be substituted for school-room routine. Price, $1.50.

Baldwin's Art of School Management.
This is a very helpful hand-book for the teacher. He will find it full of practical suggestions in regard to all the details of school-room work, and how to manage it to best advantage. Price, $1.50.

Greenwood's Principles of Education Practically Applied.
The object of this work throughout is to impress this important question upon the mind of the teacher: "*How shall I teach so as to have my pupils become self-reliant, independent, manly men and womanly women?*" Price, $1.00.

Sully's Outlines of Psychology,
WITH SPECIAL REFERENCE TO THE THEORY OF EDUCATION. Price, $3.00.

Sully's Hand-Book of Psychology,
ON THE BASIS OF OUTLINES OF PSYCHOLOGY. A practical exposition of the elements of Mental Science, with special applications to the Art of Teaching, designed for the use of Schools, Teachers, Reading Circles, and Students generally. Price, $1.50.

Bain's Moral Science.
A COMPENDIUM OF ETHICS. Divided into two divisions. The first—the Theory of Ethics—treats at length of the two great questions, the ethical standard and the moral faculty; the second division—on the Ethical Systems—is a full detail of all the systems, ancient and modern, by conjoined abstract and summary. Price, $1.50.

McArthur's Education,
IN ITS RELATION TO MANUAL INDUSTRY. The important subject of manual education is thoroughly and clearly treated. Price, $1.50.

Hodgson's Errors in the Use of English.
A work for the teacher's table, and invaluable for classes in grammar and literature. Price, $1.50.

Descriptive Catalogue sent free on application. *Special prices will be made on class supplies.*

D. APPLETON & CO., Publishers,
New York, Boston, Chicago, Atlanta, San Francisco.

APPLETONS' MATHEMATICAL SERIES.

FOUR VOLUMES.

THE OBJECTIVE METHOD PRACTICALLY APPLIED.

I.—**NUMBERS ILLUSTRATED**, in Language, Drawing, and Reading Lessons. An Arithmetic for Primary Schools. By ANDREW J. RICKOFF and E. C. DAVIS.

Introduction price, 36 cents.

It is the design of this book, in the first place, to familiarize the child with numbers and their combinations, not by means of repeating such formulæ as 4 and 3 are 7, but by provoking observation to lead him to the adoption of the formula as a statement of his own experience.

Beautiful illustrations by the best artists afford pleasing subjects for language-lessons, in which the immediate design is to excite thought and cultivate expression, and at the same time suggest counting, comparison of numbers, etc., up to ten. By means of these illustrations the imagination is called into active play, and the child is led to give independent and original expression to the ideas gained from the pictures.

II.—**NUMBERS APPLIED.** A Complete Arithmetic for all Grades. By ANDREW J. RICKOFF, LL. D.

Introduction price, 75 cents.

III.—**NUMBERS SYMBOLIZED.** An Elementary Algebra. By D. M. SENSENIG, M. S.

Introduction price, $1.08.

IV.—**NUMBERS UNIVERSALIZED.** An Advanced Algebra. By DAVID M. SENSENIG, M. S.

Send for full descriptive Circulars.

D. APPLETON & CO., Publishers,
New York, Boston, Chicago, Atlanta, San Francisco.

APPLETONS' INSTRUCTIVE READING-BOOKS.

By JAMES JOHONNOT,
Author of " Principles and Practice of Teaching," "Geographical Reader," " How we Live," etc.

THE NATURAL HISTORY SERIES.

No. 1. **Book of Cats and Dogs, and other Friends.** 17 cents.

No. 2. **Friends in Feathers and Fur and other Neighbors.** 30 cents.

No. 3. { **Neighbors with Wings and Fins and some others.** 40 cents.
Some Curious Flyers, Creepers, and Swimmers. 40 cents.

No. 4. **Neighbors with Claws and Hoofs and their Kin.** 54 cents.

No. 5. **Glimpses of the Animate World: Science and Literature of Natural History.** $1.00.

THE HISTORICAL SERIES.

Book I. **Grandfather's Stories.**

Book II. **Stories of Heroic Deeds.** 30 cents.

Book III, Part I. **Stories of Our Country.** 40 cents.
Part II. **Stories of Other Lands.** 40 cents.

Book IV, Part I. **Stories of the Olden Time.** 54 cents.

Part II. **Ten Great Events in History.** 54 cents.

Book V. **How Nations Grow and Decay.**

Unexcelled for Supplementary Reading.

Specimen copies mailed to teachers at the introduction prices, as quoted above. Send for full descriptive circulars.

D. APPLETON & CO., PUBLISHERS,
New York, Boston, Chicago,   Atlanta, San Francisco.

A HISTORY OF THE UNITED STATES AND ITS PEOPLE.

FOR THE USE OF SCHOOLS.

BY EDWARD EGGLESTON.

Dr. Eggleston's new History of the United States is one of the most interesting and attractive school-books ever published. The author has used his art as a story-teller, and his experience as a writer, to make American history something living, human, and real, and therefore delightful. The illustrations have been secured from original sources, and the artists engaged upon the work include some of the most noted and expert in this country.

CHICAGO TRIBUNE, Sept. 22, 1888.

"Dr. Eggleston has prepared not only a new American text-book, but he has prepared it on a plan combining so many advantages that Americans many years out of school will find it delightful reading, although primarily designed for school use. There is compacted in it a narrative of our development from the earliest times to the present. . . . Adorning and enlivening it are maps which keep pace with the story and make familiar by colors and drawings, specially contrived for episodes and epochs, all the surroundings which fasten not merely events but their full significance on the mind. These maps are to be cordially commended. . . . The literary style of the book is worthy of its scholastic character. Edward Eggleston has long loved the function of the teacher. He has long practiced the art of writing good English. Combining that spirit and this art, he offers what will probably not be challenged as the most pleasing, the most convenient, and the most fascinating popular text yet produced upon the subject that ought to be dearest to American youth."

Introduction price, $1.05.

Copies for examination mailed to teachers at the introduction price Send for specimen pages.

D. APPLETON & CO., PUBLISHERS,

New York, Boston, Chicago,   Atlanta, San Francisco.

APPLETONS'
STANDARD GEOGRAPHIES.

Comprehensive, Attractive, up to Date.

THE SERIES:

Appletons' Elementary Geography.

This book treats the subject objectively, makes knowledge precede definitions, and presents facts in their logical connections, taking gradual steps from the known to the unknown. The work is designed to be **elementary**, not only in name and size, but also in the style and quality of its matter and development of the subject. The illustrations have been selected with great care, and the maps are distinct, unencumbered with names, accurate, and attractive.

Introduction price, 55 cents.

Appletons' Higher Geography.

This volume is not a repetition of the Elementary, either in its matter or mode of developing the subject. In it the earth is viewed as a whole, and the great facts of political as depending on the physical geography are fully explained. Great prominence is given to commerce and leading industries as the result of physical conditions. The maps challenge comparison in point of correctness, distinctness, and artistic finish. Special State editions, with large, beautiful maps and descriptive matter, supplied without additional expense.

Introduction price, $1.25.

Appletons' Physical Geography.

The new Physical Geography stands unrivaled among text-books on the subject. Its list of authors includes such eminent scientific specialists as Quackenbos, Newberry, Hitchcock, Stevens, Gannett, Dall, Merriam, Britton, Lieutenant Stoney, George F. Kunz, and others, presenting an array of talent never before united in the making of a single text-book.

Introduction price, $1.60.

Specimen copies, for examination, will be sent, post-paid, to teachers and school-officers, on receipt of the introduction prices.
Liberal terms made to schools for introduction and exchange.

D. APPLETON & CO., PUBLISHERS,

New York, Boston, Chicago,   Atlanta, San Francisco.

STANDARD TEXT-BOOKS.

Appletons' Readers.

SIX BOOKS. Perfectly graded, beautifully illustrated. These books have held a foremost place among school readers from the first day of their publication to the present time, and they will continue for many years to delight the hearts of thousands of children, who will ever find new pleasure in their freshness and novelty.

"Always new." "Always interesting."

Appletons' Standard Geographies.

ELEMENTARY, HIGHER, PHYSICAL. Unequaled in point, attractiveness, and completeness. Thoroughly up to date in all departments. **The new Physical Geography** was prepared by a corps of scientific specialists, presenting an array of talent never before united in the making of a single text-book. It stands unrivaled among works on the subject.

Appletons' Mathematical Series.

NUMBERS ILLUSTRATED. By A. J. Rickoff and E. C. Davis.
NUMBERS APPLIED. By A. J. Rickoff.
NUMBERS SYMBOLIZED. By D. M. Sensenig.
NUMBERS UNIVERSALIZED. By D. M. Sensenig.

The "objective method" successfully applied. A distinct advance on any mathematical works heretofore published.

Appletons' Standard System of Penmanship.

Perfectly adapted for all grades. The only books in which **graded columns** are used to develop movement.

Krusi's System of Drawing.

FREE-HAND, INVENTIVE, INDUSTRIAL. For all grades. Strictly progressive. Thoroughly educational.

Introductory Course. *Supplementary Course.*
Graded Course. *Industrial Courses.*

Send for full descriptive circulars, terms for introduction, etc.

D. APPLETON & CO., Publishers,
New York, Boston, Chicago, Atlanta, San Francisco.

KRÜSI'S FREE-HAND, INVENTIVE, AND INDUSTRIAL DRAWING.

Adapted to the Requirements of all Grades of Schools. By HERMANN KRÜSI, A. M., Instructor in the Philosophy of Education at the Normal and Training School, Oswego, N. Y.; and formerly Teacher of Drawing in the Home and Colonial Training School, London.

EASY DRAWING LESSONS, for Kindergarten and Primary Schools. Three Series, Twelve Cards each, with Instructions.

GRADED COURSE. New revised edition.

> **Part I. Synthetic Series.** (Primary.) Four Drawing-Books and a Manual for Teachers.
>
> **Part II. Analytic Series.** (Intermediate.) Four Books and Manual.
>
> **Part III. Perspective Series.** (Grammar and High School.) Four Books and Manual.

Krüsi's New System of Drawing is pre-eminently adapted to meet the wants of our public-school instruction in this branch.

It is strictly progressive, and adapted to every grade, from the primary classes to the higher departments of the high-school.

It has for its basis a knowledge of the actual forms in Nature, leading the mind to accurate observation, as well as training the hand to skillful and artistic representation.

It acknowledges the fact that children have a great deal of ingenuity and power of combination, and like to wander in the regions of fancy. It therefore supplies an *Inventive Course*, restricted only by the laws of taste and order.

It applies art to all the wants and requirements of industry.

In short, it is the only system which has fully, philosophically, and practically, developed the subject for public instruction in our common schools.

SUPPLEMENTARY SERIES. No. 1. Elementary Leaves and Flowers. No. 2. Animals in Outline. No. 3. Studies of the Human Form. No. 4. Exercises in Shading, Foliage, and Trees. No. 5. Landscapes. No. 6. Flowers.

THE ORIGINAL-DRAWING BOOK. By EDWARD L. CHICHESTER.

Designed as a Supplementary Drawing-Book, and especially adapted to Krüsi's Synthetic Drawing Series. The author tells the story of "Tim's Journey," and the pupil illustrates it by drawing the objects described, in blank spaces left for the purpose. It is arranged for twenty-nine large illustrations.

New York: D. APPLETON & CO., 1, 3, & 5 Bond Street.

KRÜSI'S INDUSTRIAL DRAWING.

ELEMENTARY MECHANICAL DRAWING. By FRANK B. MORSE, Instructor in the Massachusetts Institute of Technology. Six Books.

This course gives a knowledge of the uses of different drawing instruments, with practical exercises, line and brush shading, and the conventional methods of representing different materials used in construction, as earth, stone, wood, and metals. It then presents and explains all the useful problems in geometrical drawing, with their practical applications.

ELEMENTARY ARCHITECTURE. By CHARLES BABCOCK, Professor of Architecture, Cornell University. Nine Books.

The series includes the course pursued by the students in the architectural department of the University, and contains the practice necessary for every student in architecture. It is eminently practical, and the work furnishes that training of the muscles and knowledge of the use of instruments which practical life demands.

OUTLINE AND RELIEF DESIGNS, representing Architectural and Sculptural Ornaments, and their Historical Development. By E. C. CLEAVES, Professor of Drawing and Designing, Cornell University. Six Books.

This series is a companion to that upon the Elements of Architecture, and, while serving its purpose of furnishing valuable drawing-lessons, and instruction in the decorative art, it will also be found of great value as illustrating the successive steps in æsthetic attainment, and the effect of natural environment in determining the taste of a people.

TEXTILE DESIGNS, for Calico and other Print Goods, Carpets, Wall-Paper, Silks, Laces, Cashmeres, and the like. By CHARLES KASTNER, Lowell Professor of Design, Massachusetts Institute of Technology. Six Books.

The series upon Textile Designs is intended to show the application of the general principles of drawing to designing; to give practical instruction in the technical preparation of designs for the various fabrics; and to cultivate the taste, so that a higher art may result.

KRÜSI'S DRAWING TABLETS, for Elementary Exercises in Drawing. Prepared especially to accompany the Easy Drawing Lessons and the Synthetic Course. Oblong 16mo. 36 sheets, ruled on one side in quarter-inch spaces.

PRIMARY DRAWING CARDS. For Slate and Blackboard Exercises. In two Parts of twelve Cards and thirty-six Exercises each. Accompanied by instructions for drawing, and a test ruler. By M. J. GREEN.

New York: D. APPLETON & CO., 1, 3, & 5 Bond Street.

www.ingramcontent.com/pod-product-compliance
Lightning Source LLC
Chambersburg PA
CBHW022141300426
44115CB00006B/289